Educating Pupils with Special Needs in the Ordinary School

Seamus Hegarty and Keith Pocklington
with Dorothy Lucas

NFER-Nelson

Published by The NFER-Nelson Publishing Company
Darville House, 2 Oxford Road East,
Windsor, Berks. SL4 1DF.

First Published 1981
© NFER, 1981
ISBN 0-85633-234-8
Code 8085 02 1

Photoset by The Yale Press Limited
Printed in Great Britain.

Distributed in the USA by Humanities Press Inc.
Atlantic Highlands, New Jersey 07716, USA

Printed in Great Britain by
Biddles Ltd, Guildford, Surrey

Contents

Educating Pupils with Special Needs in the Ordinary School

LIB/LEND/002

UNIVERSITY OF
WOLVERHAMPTON
KNOWLEDGE · INNOVATION · ENTERPRISE

Walsall Learning Centre
University of Wolverhampton
Gorway Road
Walsall WS1 3BD
Telephone: 0845 408 1631
Online Renewals:
www.wlv.ac.uk/lib/myaccount

Acknowledgements

The team would like to express their gratitude to the many people who have made this study possible. In particular, we wish to thank the Department of Education and Science who funded the research; the LEAs and schools who gave us access; the many staff from the education and health services who gave so generously of their time; the parents and pupils who agreed to talk to us; and the Steering Committee which was an unfailing source of wisdom and constructive criticism.

It is with regret that we cannot name the school staff who gave us such generous access. Their professionalism and dedication inspired us, and their willingness to allow us as outsiders to examine their practice and subject it to criticism was far more than we could have asked for. We thank and commend them for that. We thank them also for the companionship they shared with us. We feel sure that they like us will remember the monks of Spode House with particular affection.

The individuals to whom we are indebted are too numerous to acknowledge by name, even if we were not bound in many cases to maintain their anonymity. Some must be mentioned however: Ron Gulliford who chaired our Steering Committee and helped us in many other ways; Glenys Jones who carried out valuable observations on our behalf; Edward Britton and Joyce Baird, both members of the NFER Board of Management, and our colleagues Ray Sumner and Dick Weindling, who commented in detail on the final manuscript; George Cooke and Peter Mittler who contributed to our seminar groups and assisted in many other ways; John Fish, HMI; Keith Cawdron and Philip Edwards, DES; and Jane Pagett our colleague and secretary who contributed in many ways to the successful outcome of the project.

Foreword

The special school has been the usual way of providing special education for pupils with marked learning difficulties and for those with physical and sensory disabilities. Special education has been regarded as virtually synonymous with special schooling. However, even in the immediate post war years when a period of expansion in special school provision began, the first signs of alternative forms of provision were appearing: the first units for partially hearing pupils were being set up in ordinary schools from 1947; a few local education authorities as a matter of policy organised special classes in ordinary schools for educationally subnormal pupils and later for others.

One is tempted to wonder why these examples of new practice were not more frequently followed in the development of special educational provision. One explanation may be found in the many other preoccupations of an education service responding to changes in society, the reorganisation of schooling, raising the school leaving age, developing new curricula and examinations. Moreover there was no serious challenge to the view that the special school was the best way of ensuring that handicapped children received the specialist teaching and care that they needed – a view reinforced by the manifest shortage of teachers and others with specialist training and experience. It was the growing recognition in psychology and education of the environmental and social influences on pupils' educational and personal development together with the stimulus of sociological concepts which provoked questioning of the practice of separate education. Other trends of thought in society which stressed the rights of individuals for normal experiences and opportunities were an additional factor.

In the subsequent integration debate, views often appeared to polarise though probably the majority of educationalists took up a middle position. The report of the Warnock Committee reconciled apparently opposed views by offering a definition of special education in terms of its essential functions without reference to where it took place and by delineating a range of alternative forms of organisation which included several types and degrees of special educational help in ordinary schools. Many of the Report's other recommendations flow from the view that the majority of children with special needs are provided for in ordinary schools.

The framework proposed by the Warnock Committee has received wide support. What is needed now is a process of well-considered experiment together with evaluation of practice since relatively little research has been undertaken into schemes for integrated education in this country, the studies of Elizabeth Anderson being a notable exception. It is important to know whether children with special needs, particularly those with the most specialised requirements, make good progress in ordinary schools and how far they do in fact benefit from the wider social and educational opportunities. Equally important, we need to know the problems which arise in organising integrated education and by study of good practice how these may be avoided. Many issues need to be explored: requirements for the physical environment of schools; the attitudes of staff, parents and pupils; the means of providing specialist teaching and therapies to pupils as well as advice and support to staff. There are implications for the organisation of schools and for curricula, resources and of course for costs.

This book is based upon a three year study of a variety of schemes whereby children with special needs are being educated in ordinary schools. Most of the schemes were in an early stage of development and we must be grateful to all those involved who have readily shared their experiences with the project team and have thus made it possible to identify and discuss matters which will be important for others planning similar developments. It should prove not only a guide to practice but a basis from which other evaluations of schemes might be planned.

RONALD GULLIFORD
Professor of Special Education, University of Birmingham

Introduction

This book is the outcome of a three year research project carried out at the National Foundation for Educational Research under sponsorship from the Department of Education and Science. It examines a wide range of issues bearing on the education of pupils with special needs. The discussion is based on the detailed study of a number of integration programmes. Some fourteen of these are described in detail in an accompanying volume *Integration in Action*.

Integration has become a central focus of concern in special education in recent years. Despite the widespread advocacy of it, many educationists view the trend toward integration with some unease. Special school staff fear that the systems of support they have built up will be dismantled and pupils' special needs may go unmet, while many teachers working in ordinary schools feel that they lack the competence to educate these pupils. Debate on the matter has been bedeviled by lack of clarity. Integration is not simply a new form of provision, another option as it were. It is a process rather whereby the education offered by ordinary schools becomes more differentiated and geared to meeting a wider range of pupil needs. This process can take many forms and in any case is a dynamic one both at local level and more generally. Its effects are pervasive within the school and throughout the education system.

So the first task for Part One is to examine the concept of

integration and untangle the conceptual ambiguities surrounding it. Further clarification comes from looking at the extent of integrated provision in practice. Arrangements in other countries, especially where total integration is claimed to be the practice, are noted briefly. The situation in England and Wales is examined in detail in order to identify any changes in integrated provision that took place over the '70s. A further introductory chapter looks at the research that has been done into the topic and sets the scene for the present study. Much of this research has been done in America and takes the form of efficacy studies comparing segregated and integrated arrangements.

Part Two elucidates the concept of integration in practical terms by outlining a model of educational provision whereby the different ways of meeting special educational needs can be described. Integration can take many forms organisationally as well as conceptually. As a means of coming to grips with this diversity, the integration programmes being studied here are grouped into three categories: links between a special school and one or more ordinary schools; special classes or centres in ordinary schools; and individual integration arrangements.

One of the earliest decisions to make in setting up integrated provision is to select a model. There are distinctive advantages and opportunities associated with each but potential drawbacks as well. As well as exploring the process by which LEAs opted for integrated provision and the reasons for choosing particular forms of provision, we examine the practical preparation carried out when a programme was being set up – selecting and approaching a suitable school, and preparing staff and pupils already at the school.

Staff constitute the major resource available to an integration programme, as for any form of educational provision. In Part Three we turn to the personnel involved in meeting special educational needs – teachers, classroom ancillaries and professionals from outside the school. Chapters five and six focus on those teachers and ancillaries who have a major responsibility for pupils with special needs, documenting staffing levels and sample characteristics and discussing the roles carried out that bear on integration. All school staff are affected by integration programmes, and chapter seven looks at the involvement of teachers who do not have a major responsibility for pupils with special needs and the implications for their professional roles. Chapter eight turns to professionals outside the school – advisory staff, educational psychologists, speech therapists, physiotherapists and doctors – who have important contributions to make. The services they offer and the context within which they offer them are discussed, along with some of the issues involved in inter-disciplinary working. Finally in this part, training is considered, particularly from the perspective of what can be done at local level.

Part Four turns to the practicalities of integration. It may be necessary to make alterations to school buildings or to manage the space available in new ways. Questions of cost are implicit here and indeed run throughout the effecting of educational change. Chapter eleven draws attention to the cost implications of educating pupils with special needs in the ordinary school and outlines a simple structure for looking at the monetary costs of integration programmes. This structure is used in chapter twelve to examine the cost-incurring factors in the integration programmes studied.

Part Five deals with the curriculum. Whatever other functions they serve, integration programmes must meet pupil's *educational* needs if they are to be justified. In chapter thirteen we give some examples of the curricula offered by special centres or otherwise available to pupils with special needs. Some of these are little different from special school practice, while others draw on the opportunities of the ordinary school to provide a distinctive curriculum and programmes of work. The curricular aspects of preparing young people for adult life are considered in chapter fourteen. Chapters fifteen and sixteen turn to the implementing of the curriculum, discussing various pedagogical aspects of integration and the critical question of systematic monitoring and recording of pupils' progress.

The social aspects of integration are taken up in Part Six. Successive chapters discuss the opportunities for interaction between pupils with special needs and their peers and how interaction can be promoted, the social and emotional development of pupils with special needs in integrated contexts, and how they were perceived by teachers and other pupils in the school. There is a good deal of overlap between these chapters since the opportunities for interaction influence relationships, attitudes are affected by the amount and nature of contact, and individuals' social development depends on their contact with peers and the attitudes they encounter.

Part Seven examines parents attitudes toward integration and the contact they had with the school, and considers ways of promoting parental involvement. The final Part summarises the main findings and notes implications for policy and practice.

A few general points about the nature of the book may be made. First, extensive use is made of examples. This is partly because of the intrinsic interest of the examples – many features of integrated provision are relatively novel and illustrations help to bring them to life – and partly because the detail is essential to abstracting guidelines for informing practice elsewhere. The findings presented here are not intended to be statistically representative. The aim is to sensitise readers to the key aspects of integrated provision. A given integration programme will be embedded in a particular context which will shape the programme to a greater or lesser extent. By documenting and analysing situations in detail, readers should be able to identify those factors arising out of the particular situations and abstract from them whatever applies to their own context. Secondly, in addition to examples, there is much use of quoted material. The convention followed in presenting this is that single quotation marks signify extracts from written material, double quotation marks extracts from spoken material.

Finally, the scope of the book and the multiplicity of audiences in mind may be noted since both have added considerably to its total length. In order to treat the wide range of topics addressed in an accessible way the book is broken down into numerous headings, with some overlapping discussion if judged necessary. The intended readership includes not only the many practitioners and parents involved with integration programmes but all those who are concerned to change the education system so that ordinary schools can deal effectively with a wider range of pupil needs. Readers will naturally use the book selectively and concentrate on those sections of particular interest to them. This means that certain topics recur at different points, in apparent repetition, since it is not being assumed that readers will work straight through the book.

PART ONE

Integration and the Problem for Research

Chapter One
Integration: Theory and Practice

Educators devised segregated classes and schools that were to be the respositories for all the varied kinds of children that could not fit into the regular class without creating problems for the system . . . Mainstreaming seeks heterogeneity in the classroom in order for children to perceive, understand and tolerate diversity within their midst (Sarason and Doris, 1979, writing on the history of special education in America)

This is a book about educating a certain group of pupils in ordinary schools. The pupils in question are those known traditionally – and somewhat misleadingly since their difficulties do not reside exclusively within the pupils themselves – as the handicapped. It seeks to examine what is at stake in providing education for these pupils in ordinary schools: by drawing attention to the significant factors in such provision; by documenting the experience of practitioners, and noting the lessons to be learnt; and by offering guidance to inform practice.

The book does not set out to make a case for integration, unless demonstrating possibility and attending to optimum practice are to make such a case. Indeed, in an important sense it is not about integration. That may seem a perverse way of introducing a report on what has become known as the NFER integration project. This is no mere verbal quibbling however; there are important distinctions to be made. 'Integration' has been something of a slogan word and a good deal of advocacy has gone on without the benefit of clear thinking or good reasons.

In this first chapter we outline the development of special education in Britain and note how, in the words of the Warnock Report, integration has become 'the central contemporary issue in special education'. This leads to an analysis of the concept of integration, concluding that there are major limitations to it. We argue for a broader concept in its place. This broader concept has implications for the kind of study into school practice carried out by the project team and reported here. Before developing these and outlining the study, we look at the extent to which pupils with special needs are in fact educated in ordinary schools in other countries as well as in Britain.

Integration in Context

The development of special education

Special education for pupils with special needs is a relatively recent development in Great Britain, as elsewhere. Much of this development has centred on special schools separate from the mainstream. Indeed special education has tended for many years to be seen almost by definition as the preserve of special schools.

Throughout the nineteenth century various special schools were established, first for pupils with sensory handicaps, and then as universal elementary education spread, for those with learning difficulties. Early developments were sporadic, arising as they did from particular local initiatives rather than from legislation. In the first instance the concern was as much to relieve distress and perhaps provide gainful employment as it was to educate. As time went by, educational legislation gradually changed from permitting special provision to requiring it. Where school boards had been merely allowed to raise funds and make provision for certain categories of handicapped pupils, the early years of the twentieth century saw such provision charged as a duty on the local education authorities which succeeded the school boards in 1902. The prevailing means for discharging this duty was to provide special schools, and this led to the further development of a separate system. (The reader interested in the historical perspective is referred to Pritchard (1963) or chapter 2 of the Warnock Report.)

It should be noted that separate provision was in accord with the prevailing understanding of handicap. The notion of defect was paramount. The effects of physical and sensory impairment were seen in a deterministic way, while learning difficulties were conceived in terms of mental deficiency. A child's handicap was seen as an unalterable characteristic of the child – and indeed one that might well keep him in juvenile status even when advanced in years. Given this, and the conviction that the handicapped were different in kind from the rest of children, it made sense to develop separate educational systems.

There were some early moves away from total separation but they had limited impact. The Wood Committee reporting on feeble-mindedness in 1929 called for a single system for dealing with the feeble-minded and the retarded. This had integration implications since the feeble-minded were intended to be placed in special schools, though not all were, while the backward were those who were failing in the ordinary schools. The Committee also argued that special schools should be brought closer into line with ordinary schools – legally, administratively and in common perception – and indeed should be seen 'as a helpful variation of the ordinary school'.

The 1944 Education Act, and more especially the regulations and detailed guidance that followed it, opened up the possibility of integration. It was couched in terms of special schools as the prime source of special educational treatment, but it did allow that ordinary schools might also play a part in this. LEAs should ensure that 'provision is made for pupils who suffer from any disability of mind or body by providing, in special schools or otherwise, special educational treatment' (section 8(2)). They 'shall so far as is practicable, provide for the education of pupils in whose case the disability is serious in special schools appropriate to that category, but where that is impracticable, or where the disability is not serious, the arrangements may provide for the giving of such education in any school . . .' (section 33 (2)). This was hardly an integrationist's charter but it represented a development from the Education Act 1921 which had provided for handicapped pupils to be educated only in special schools or special classes.

The limited legislative space created in this way was however barely used, with the notable exception of provision for partially hearing pupils. The ordinary school system was struggling in the immediate post-war years with inferior accommodation and insufficient trained teachers. Providing special educational treatment could not be accorded high priority when resources were strained to provide a basic education for the majority. Moreover, as the Warnock Report notes, local education authorities were able to purchase large town houses and country mansions relatively cheaply, and this furthered the development of separate special schools, many of them sited in splendid rural isolation.

For a number of years then segregation prevailed. There were in fact two separate systems, running in parallel and commonly on different levels. Special schools catered for the more seriously handicapped pupils, while ordinary schools provided for the 'non-handicapped'. Ordinary schools had their problem pupils of course and, if they could not offload them to the experts in special schools, provided for them as best they could. This was not always good enough however, either because they lacked the expertise or the possibility of giving individual attention or they did not have the commitment to special educational treatment. That after all was the domain of the special school, which had the requisite staffing and expertise. Special schools meanwhile were suffering from their isolation. Many professionals, parents and young people who passed through these schools, felt they were too removed from the mainstream of education, and were not preparing pupils adequately for adult life. (This was not, nor could it be, a universal criticism: many special schools continue to equip young people for independent adult living in a wholly commendable way.)

It became clear that pupils' needs were not being met as well as they might be under the prevailing arrangements. Special education went through a period of upheaval and self-examination. One of the major features of this was a reaction against segregation and a corresponding movement toward integration. (The statistical evidence for this trend, in terms of school placements, is examined below.) The impetus for this came from many sources: new concepts of handicap were emerging, which saw handicap less in terms of individual characteristics and generated at least in part by the environment; associated with this was a reaction against categories and labelling and the segregative mechanisms associated with them; there was a gradual moving away from the statutory framework of the 1944 Act with its emphasis on formal ascertainment, as assessment procedures improved and enabled greater differentiation, and the need for more flexible provision became clear; school reorganisation and the comprehensive school debate furthered the process as the concept of the ordinary school changed and it became legitimate to have wider expectations of it; growing concern for human rights and the status of minorities led to calls – and campaigns by active pressure groups – to provide the handicapped with as normal an environment as possible; reports on practice in other countries, especially the US, Denmark and Sweden, though sometimes exaggerated or based on misperceptions, added to the pressure for changes here; finally, the experience of innovators in this country, who pioneered a wide range of developments within ordinary schools, generated a momentum which as much as anything else has led to the present position where integration is a prime focus of special education debates.

The concept of integration

'Integration' in its widest usage entails a process of making whole, of combining different elements into a unity. As used in special education, it refers to the education of pupils with special needs in ordinary schools. Integration provides a 'natural' environment where these pupils are alongside their peers and are freed from the isolation that is characteristic of much special school placement.

There are many reasons for the movement of opinion in favour of integration, and these have just been outlined. As one might expect from the diversity of forces in operation, the concept is a complex and dynamic one. It has evolved from a simple opposition to placement in a special school to encompassing a variety of arrangements in ordinary schools. This diversity is commonly described in two ways: first, in terms of the nature of the association between the 'special' group and the ordinary school; and secondly, in terms of organisational structure.

Warnock distinguishes three main forms of integration in terms of association: locational; social; and functional. Locational integration exists where special units or classes are set up in ordinary schools or where a special school and ordinary school share the same site. Social integration is 'where children attending a special class or unit eat, play and consort with other children, and possibly share organised out-of-classroom activities with them'. Functional integration is the fullest form of integration and is achieved when locational and social integration lead to 'joint participation in educational activities . . . where children with special needs join, part-time or full-time, the regular classes of the school, and make a full contribution to the activity of the school' (pp 100-1).

A more elaborate, though similar structure is offered by Soder (1980). Summarising a good deal of Swedish thinking he offers the following schema:

PHYSICAL INTEGRATION	FUNCTIONAL INTEGRATION			SOCIAL INTEGR-ATION	SOCIETAL INTEGR-ATION
	Co-utilisation	Simultaneous Utilisation	Co-operation		
Facility integration	Administrative integration		Activity Integration Subject integration		
Organisational integration Formal integration Structural integration					

Adapted from Soder (1980)

This outlines the different concepts used in relation to four different forms of integration: physical, functional, social and societal. The key notion is that of reducing the distance between two groups. Thus, physical integration (corresponding to Warnock's locational integration) means 'the physical distance between the mentally retarded and the non-mentally retarded being reduced', functional distance means the functional distance between the two groups is reduced, and so on (op.cit., p10). The main elaboration is with respect to functional integration, seen as reducing functional distance by joint utilisation of resources: on separate occasions; on the same occasion but separately; and on a fully co-operative basis. It is clear that this encompasses very great differences ranging from negligible contact to Warnock's joint participation in educational activities.

These three – physical, functional and social – are geared to describing different forms of integration associated with special school/ordinary school links and can be readily applied to other forms of school integration. They must be distinguished from societal integration which has to do with taking a place in society comparable to that of peers. School integration is related to societal integration and may be instrumental in achieving it – though the latter must not be taken for granted – but is quite distinct from it. Integration in school can be viewed both as an end in itself and as a means toward the achievement of societal integration.

A second way of elaborating the concept of integration is to describe the different organisational arrangements it encompasses. One of the most popular follows Deno's (1970) cascade model.

Following this, various writers and official reports in this country, e.g. Anderson (1973), Cope and Anderson (1977), Snowdon Report, Warnock Report, have sought to describe the organisational arrangements in terms of a continuum between placement in an ordinary class without support and in a residential special school. These vary slightly but the essential patterns is something as follows:

  i. ordinary class with support in classroom
  ii. ordinary class with withdrawal
  iii. special class part-time, ordinary class part-time
  iv. special class in ordinary school full-time
  v. special school with contact with ordinary school

Strictly speaking, this does not necessarily entail a continuum, since a pupil in a special school but having some lessons in an ordinary school may well be more 'integrated' than one who is full-time in a special class and has little contact with the rest of the school. Likewise, intensive support provided within the classroom could be more segregative than short periods of withdrawal. These various arrangements are discussed in more detail in chapter 3 where we describe the different models in practice whereby ordinary schools seek to provide for pupils with special needs.

Difficulties with integration

Notwithstanding the fact that integration has come to feature so prominently in educational debates, there are serious difficulties with the concept that call its usefulness into question. These have to do with the way that 'integration' is used and, more substantively, with the understanding of special educational treatment that tends to be associated with it. The difficulties can be summarised as follows:

  i. Integration has become a catchword, laden with unanalysed assumptions.
  ii. Integration is used to mean different things, sometimes in a confusing way.
  iii. The understanding of special educational treatment associated with prevailing concepts of integration is misconceived in important ways.

i. Integration as a catchword

Integration has made great strides as a desirable educational goal in recent years. It is not simply a neutral description of provision but rather the connotation of a state of affairs we should all be striving toward. There are strong emotive overtones. Like motherhood and democracy, integration is a good thing and no right thinking person who cares for children could be against it.

This is nonsense of course. Integration is a means, not an end in itself. Pupils with special needs do not need integration. What they need is education. Integrated placement may well turn out to be important in achieving educational goals or in facilitating certain aspects of development, and to that extent becomes important. The primary concern however must be with individual development, and other considerations such as where the education takes place have relevance only in relation to it. This is not to say that integration must wait on supporting evidence or even that one cannot have a presumption in favour of integration in the absence of such evidence. What it does say is that the case needs to be made. Integration is not a self-evident goal and must be justified in a rational way. Whether this is done purely by reference to value judgements or empirical evidence is adduced as well, the essential criterion must be the development and well-being of pupils.

When this is overlooked and integration is seen as a goal in its own right, all sorts of unfortunate consequences are possible. Pupils with special needs are automatically assumed to be better off in ordinary schools than in special schools. The imperfections of integration arrangements in the latter are seen as passing and incidental – if they are not totally ignored – even when the reality is one of disastrous educational provision. This produces a reaction that can be just as unreflective. People see that pupils' needs are going unmet in the ordinary school, attribute the blame to integration, and refuse to countenance any form of integration as a consequence. To do this is as incorrect as to take integration as one's goal.

ii.   Different senses of integration

A second difficulty with the use of integration is that it tends to mean rather different things. In its original usage integration means a process of making whole, of uniting different parts in a totality. This sense occurs widely in common parlance, in phrases such as integrated circuit, and in personality theory in psychology. The meaning begins to shift in usages like 'the integration of ethnic minorities'. Here the focus is on a part, ie the minority group, not the whole. When integration does not have purely negative connotations (ie departure from isolation or segregation), it tends to concentrate on the minority group and what is entailed in its assimilation into the mainstream. The most positive sense of integration here is when the minority becomes an integral part of the majority group. In other words, integration is at root a problem for the minority group. This is a significant change, since the original sense of a synthesising process involving all parts in a mutually adaptive interaction is lost.

There is a similar confusion in special education usage. In theory integration should mean a process whereby an ordinary school and a special group interact to form a new educational whole. Sometimes that is what is meant, but more often the sense is narrowed. First, there is the tendency to talk of the integration of the handicapped, implying that it is something done to or by the handicapped. Integration is *their* problem, and success is when they are assimilated into an ordinary school. Secondly and even narrower, integration is widely used to mean simply association or the existence of links. This impoverished sense of integration is implicit in the locational/social/functional distinctions. Using a phrase like 'locational integration' only makes sense if one takes integration to mean the making of contact or the sharing of experiences. These imply that there are successive levels of integration, each representing an overlay as it were on the preceding level. This is an unfortunate usage in some ways. One does not doubt the existence of the realities in question, but they are not well-described in terms of the basic sense of the word 'integration'. Apart from the confusion it generates, it is not compatible with the richer sense of the creation of a new entity through the fusion of separate parts.

iii.   Views of special educational treatment

The prevailing concept of integration is associated with a number of misconceptions about special educational treatment. Four interconnected strands can be picked out. First, integration is geared to the two per cent of pupils with serious problems and not to the much larger number whose problems may be less but are still of concern. Secondly, it is based on a dichotomous notion of special educational treatment. Thirdly, it is equated with a particular type of placement. Fourthly, it is insufficiently critical of 'ordinary' reality and its suitedness to those with special needs.

It is estimated that at any given time about one pupil in six needs special educational provision. Of these only a small proportion (currently less than two per cent of the total schoolgoing population) are in formal receipt of special education, either through special schools or special classes. It is this group that is usually in mind when integration is at issue. The 15 per cent or so of pupils with less serious needs are not eligible for integration since they have never been separated! In a similar vein teachers may say, 'Of course we've been integrating for years' – meaning that the school has had a seriously handicapped pupil or pupils, not that it runs a remedial department or other provision for slow learners.

If pupils were ascertained for special education in a uniform way and schools were catering adequately for the 15 per cent, this distinction might make sense. Integration would be a matter of extending what the ordinary school is already doing so that the more seriously handicapped could be provided for as well. Neither supposition is true however. While some schools serve all their pupils very well, it would be rash to claim that all do so. As for ascertainment, the extent to which pupils are deemed in need of special education varies widely from authority to authority. DES figures show a range from 1.2 per cent to over 3 per cent, with well under half of LEAs falling withing 10 per cent of the mean (1.83) (cf Warnock Report, p38). Unless one is to make the implausible assumption that the incidence of serious special needs is grossly uneven, the conclusion is forced that what is recognised as a serious need depends in part on local provision.

It is an excellent thing that the education of the two per cent with serious needs is being scrutinised and the effort is being made to bring it closer into line with the mainstream. The intermediate group of those with less serious needs must however be taken into account in an integral way. Otherwise their needs will continue to be ignored or met inadequately. This is all the more likely to happen if integration is conceived just in terms of the two per cent.

A second difficulty with integration is that it is based on a dichotomous view of education. Most pupils go to ordinary schools and receive an 'ordinary' education there, while the handicapped go to special schools and receive special education, so the task for integration is to bring them together. This may be a little unfair, but it certainly is the case that much integration thinking is predicated on a simple distinction between ordinary education and special education – a distinction moreover that frequently is not articulated or analysed. There are of course clear differences in the educational treatment one provides for different groups, but it would be as educationally unsound as it would be an inaccurate reflection of current practice to reduce these differences to a simple dichotomy or to see them as fundamentally different. We recall that as far back as 1929 the Wood Committee urged a view of special schools as no more than 'a helpful variation of the ordinary school'.

Educating pupils with special needs in the ordinary school is not simply a question of importing special education to the ordinary school. Some specialist techniques that will be new to the school may be required depending on pupils' needs. Using radio microphones or adapting material for braille users may attract a lot of attention but they are peripheral to the problem or at least incidental to it. What is required is that the school adapt its educational provision so as to be able to cater for a wider variety of pupils. This means a highly flexible range of provision, planned as a whole – since the school is a single entity – but incorporating a multitude of possibilities and not just a simple choice between ordinary and special tracks.

A third consequence of concentrating on the more seriously handicapped two per cent is that integration tends to be seen in terms of placement. If one is focusing on a group that at the moment attend special school for the most part, then a first step will of course be to change the location. This entails tackling ascertainment procedures, the category system and the various factors that lead to segregated placement. This can only be a first step however, regardless of the difficulty of achieving it. The danger is that, precisely because of the difficulty that can surround it, it becomes a prime objective whose achievement blunts the concern for further objectives.

The location of education is of course important but only in the sense in which the infrastructure is important. What matters is what happens within the infrastructure. Accommodation, resources and so on may have implications for what can be achieved but they do not determine it. The quality of educational provision is what must be of concern, not its location. To the extent that integration diverts attention from the former to the latter it is unhelpful.

Viewing integration primarily in placement terms leads to the fourth difficulty, viz the tendency to be insufficiently critical of ordinary reality, what Soder (op.cit.) calls 'the romanticisation of the normal'. The eagerness to place pupils with special needs in 'normal' environments can be so great as to deflect attention from the unsuitedness of these environments. If a primary reason for removing pupils from ordinary schools in the first place is that their needs are not being met, it does not make sense to return them without the closest examination of what goes on within the ordinary school.

This argument, it should be pointed out, does not depend on the existence of bad schools of the 'ordinary kids shouldn't go there so why should the handicapped' type. One does not doubt that there are such schools. They are irrelevant to the argument however, despite their frequent citing by those who would oppose integration – just as the existence of bad doctors is not relevant to an assessment of medicine. (The argument might be stronger if a very great number of such schools existed, but even then one could only point to untimeliness and not to difficulties in principle.) One does not want any pupil to go to such a school and to refrain from sending a pupil with special needs is hardly to be anti-integrationist. Indeed, one may simply be exercising a positive option which one regrets not having for all pupils in the catchment area of such a school!

If the argument does not depend on the existence of bad schools, where does its force lie? The answer is in the very nature of the ordinary school and the segregative mechanisms inherent in it. Schools have not by and large been charged with the education of the more seriously handicapped and so they are not geared to their needs. This is obvious in the case of buildings that do not give access to the physically handicapped. That is only the tip of the segregating iceberg however. Other factors such as the curriculum and timetabling arrangements, socialisation patterns, the ethos of the school, can be far more potent barriers – and considerably more difficult to circumvent. The everyday reality of the ordinary school is not necessarily one that is conducive to the education of pupils with special needs, and it behoves those who advocate integration to remember this. Once again, the conclusion that emerges is not that pupils should be transferred from special schools to ordinary schools, but that ordinary schools should be re-modelled so that they can provide for a wider range of pupils.

Meeting special needs in the ordinary school

The drift of the above is that there are considerable difficulties associated with the concept of integration. This is not to condemn its usage. Integration has been useful in conceptualising alternatives to segregated special schooling. It has provided a simple and direct objective with a great deal of intuitive appeal. It will doubtless continue in use as a convenient shorthand way of referring to meeting special educational needs in the ordinary school. Given the difficulties however – the sloganising uses, conflicting senses of the word, restricted concept of special educational provision associated with it, focus on placement rather than nature of provision and the implications for the ordinary school – it is clear that there is need of an alternative description. We propose to speak in terms of 'educating pupils with special needs in the ordinary school'. This may lack conciseness but it is a less misleading description of the area of concern and one that takes account of the difficulties discussed above.

The education of pupils with special needs must be seen in terms of the educational system as a whole. Separate provision developed at least in part because of system difficulties: ordinary schools were not sufficiently differentiated and could not cope with the wide range of needs they faced, so it seemed that the most effective procedure was to set up alternative institutions free of the constraints of ordinary school. (This was in accord with the prevailing ideology of segregation and institutionalising differences.) If it is now accepted that the ordinary school system should cater for these pupils wherever possible, the ordinary school system must change. It must become more differentiated and take on a range of functions that it had previously rejected or that were not assigned to it.

This follows in any case from the fact that the school is an organic system and changes cannot be made in one part of it without affecting other parts and the school as a whole. If the changes are such as to affect staffing, the curriculum, patterns of socialisation – as will setting up a special class or making other specialist provision – the implications for the school will be far-reaching. What is at stake here is an extension of the comprehensive ideal. The initial inspiration of the comprehensive movement was to provide a rich and highly differentiated learning environment that would cater for pupils of widely differing abilities. Many pupils were still excluded however on the grounds that they would be better provided for elsewhere. If these are now to be catered for in the ordinary school, then a further extension of the notion of comprehensive education is required.

Integration in Practice

So much for the theory of integration. What of its practice? Are there clear trends to be discerned? What relevant changes have there been in the educational options open to children and young people with special needs? In this section we look briefly at the enormous diversity of practice in different countries. Cutting across this diversity are the moves away from segregated provision and toward educating as many pupils as possible in ordinary schools. The criteria by which children are excluded from ordinary schools can throw a clear light on issues central to integration. Accordingly, two programmes – one in America, one in Italy – are described which operate to a philosophy of total integration and claim not to exclude any pupil from the ordinary school system. Finally, we look at the extent of integration in England and Wales and examine the paradoxical situation whereby the number of special schools and pupils in them increased throughout the 70's when integration was supposedly on the increase.

An international perspective

Educating pupils with special needs in ordinary schools is a concern of education systems throughout the world. As in other human activities where common problems have to be solved in different settings, there is much to be learned from sharing experience and examining how others have tackled the problems. One must be aware of too-ready comparisons however. Any educational innovation has to be seen in the context of a particular school system and prevailing socio-cultural and economic factors. In special education moreover there are considerable conceptual/linguistic problems. Not only are special needs categorised and described quite differently in different countries, but the forms of provision by which they are met relate to very different education systems. The possibility for confusion is compounded by the fact that similar terms are used to describe forms of provision which in reality are quite unlike each other. Thus, 'special unit', 'resource room', 'opportunity class' as well as the more general terms like 'integration' and 'mainstreaming' are used in different ways in different education systems.

It is well to be aware of the enormous diversity of provision that exists in practice. Thus, in the European context Jorgensen (1980) reports on developments and trends within the European Community – which, relatively speaking, is fairly homogenous. Though there are common trends, the differences are considerable and wide-ranging – terminology, organisation of special education, legal basis, administration and finance, placement procedures and teacher training. For a concrete example of diversity we can look at data on the placement of hearing impaired pupils reported by Martin and Moore (1979).

Type of school attended by representative samples of hearing impaired pupils in Europe 1977-78							
	Belg.	Den.	Ger.	Ire.	Italy	Neth.	UK
			(All figures are percentages)				
Special schools for the deaf	83	49	98	60	39	92	45
Ordinary schools	11	44	0	35	50	4	52
Inapplicable/ missing data	6	7	2	5	11	4	3

There are marked differences between countries in the type of school attended. The proportion of hearing impaired pupils attending special instead of ordinary schools varied from 39 per cent (Italy) to 98 per cent (Germany). Incidentally, the proportion attending ordinary schools is higher for the UK (at 52 per cent) than for any other country listed.

A similar picture of diversity emerges from the CERI project on the Education of the Handicapped Adolescent. This has been conducted in OECD countries since 1978. The two principal foci of the project have been the integration of handicapped young people in ordinary schools and the transition from school to working life. The first phase is now complete and has assembled a great deal of information on integration and the associated policy and social changes in OECD countries. A summary of the findings is given in CERI (1979). This notes the diversity in conception and practice of integration – legal measures, administrative and funding arrangements, forms of service delivery, teaching approaches, use of multi-disciplinary teams and in-service teacher training. (Further publications on this project are in hand.)

It should be realised that these considerations apply only to the industrialised West, and only to parts of that. If we broaden the perspective to take in the Soviet bloc and developing countries, a picture of far greater diversity emerges. Thus, Magne (1976) noted that East European countries have predominantly segregated education, though still with a goal of ultimate societal integration. This contrasts strongly with the prevailing zeitgeist in the West. In Third World countries there is often intense pressure on the school system to provide a basic education for the majority of young people. Special education cannot have a high priority in this situation. Large classes and limited resources preclude individual attention for pupils with special needs. Typically, there is limited special school provision – often run privately or by religious bodies – for a small number of pupils. To those pupils fortunate enough to have access to special schools where specific help and individual attention are available integration offers a very poor alternative.

One of the markers of the trend toward integration is legislation. Recent years have seen the enactment of legislation in many countries – Norway, Sweden, US, Italy, UK, Denmark, France – that seeks to further the integration of pupils with special needs. (This legislation is often associated with moves to ensure that all children and young people no matter how great or complex their needs receive education or receive it under the auspices of education rather than health or social welfare agencies.) In Britain this has taken the form of an amendment to the 1944 Education Act (Section 10 of the Education Act 1976, discussed in the following chapter) and the impending legislation. (A White Paper 'Special needs in education' was presented to Parliament in August 1980, and it is anticipated that this will issue in legislation in the course of 1981.)

If we turn to the United States we find a very different situation.

Legislation there has had far reaching effects on every aspect of special education, especially with regard to integration. The Education for All Handicapped Children Act (PL94-142) was enacted in 1975, with its provisions coming into force over a period of years beginning in 1977. This is a major piece of legislation which mandates a national commitment to educating all children and young people with special needs, no matter how great or complex their needs. State education agencies must provide a 'free appropriate public education' for all handicapped children and young people between 3-18 (later 3-21). It has numerous stipulations re identification, service delivery, nature of provision, evaluation and funding. Of particular interest here is the requirement that handicapped children be placed in the 'least restrictive environment'. The least-restriction principle is spelled out in the *Federal Register* Rules and Regulations as follows:

1. That to the maximum extent appropriate, handicapped children, including children in public or private institutions or other care facilities, are educated with children who are not handicapped, and

2. That special classes, separate schooling or other removal of handicapped children from the regular educational environment occurs only when the nature or severity of the handicap is such that education in regular classes with the use of supplementary aids and services cannot be achieved satisfactorily. (Quoted in Turnbull *et al.*, 1981)

One must be clear that PL94-142 does not require all pupils to be educated in ordinary schools. Educational provision must be *appropriate* as well as being non-restrictive. If placing a pupil in ordinary school were to result in harmful effects or to reduce the quality of education received this would not accord with the legislation, and a segregated placement might be required.

While other countries have legislated for integration PL94-142 is of especial interest since it is such a comprehensive piece of legislation and has attracted so much attention. Two points may be noted briefly. First, legislation cannot make sweeping changes overnight. Special education is the concern of numerous overlapping systems and changes in it require changes in teacher training, patterns of professional working, the nature and structure of all schools, and so on. The requisite system changes to accommodate radically new approaches cannot be expected to occur all at once, nor indeed at the same speed. Secondly, while these various pieces of national legislation generally provide an impetus for integration, their intention is not to bring about the wholesale integration of pupils with special needs. The burden of national legislation has been to extend education to all children and young people with special needs, and to do so in association with the ordinary school system as much as possible, not – with the possible exception of Italy – to place all pupils in ordinary schools.

It is clear then that even in education systems committed to integration many pupils are still segregated since in general terms legislation cannot abolish segregation nor does it seek to. This is not to say that the progress of integration is adequate. There are enormous variations in provision and undoubtedly many pupils are segregated who could be educated in ordinary schools. Comparative figures are difficult to obtain however, and even more difficult to interpret.

Rather than detailing practice in other countries, we propose to look at some situations where complete integration *is* the target. This issue crops up regularly in integration debates and is often seen as posing critical questions. What becomes of the most severely handicapped under such arrangements? Can the needs really be met in ordinary schools? The nature of the provision to be made for pupils with extreme or highly complex needs – those with severe learning difficulties, deaf-blind pupils and those displaying severe emotional and/or aggressive behaviour – raises taxing problems. Is integration feasible for these pupils too? Does it mean that they must join ordinary classes? If not, are they to be confined to small enclaves of unstimulating and minimally-achieving peers?

These are difficult questions but they bring the limits and the meaning of integration into sharp focus. There is general agreement that more pupils than at present could be educated in ordinary schools. The lack of agreement is over which pupils and how many, where the line should be drawn as it were. But what if the line is not drawn? What if there were only one education system and all pupils, regardless of their needs, were educated within it? We look here at two contrasting examples where precisely this is happening: one in an American city; the other in a rural district in Italy. Apart from the intrinsic interest of these examples, they are valuable in forcing attention on the reasons for segregating pupils. It is all too easy to take it for granted that because certain categories of pupils have always attended special schools that is the place for them. Whether or not one accepts the claims that all pupils can be educated within the ordinary school system, it is salutary to have the burden of proof shifted to those who would retain special schools and to have to articulate reasons why certain pupils cannot be educated alongside their peers.

Madison is a small city in Wisconsin, USA. Details on its special education arrangements are provided by Gruenewald and Schroeder (1979). The district has a total population of 170 000 and serves 26 000 pupils – and so is smaller than most education authorities in Britain. Some 1 900 of these (just over 7 per cent) receive specialised educational services, 'ranging from minor modifications in the regular educational classroom to placement in a self-contained classroom for the total instructional day'. Within this group some 150 are considered to be 'severely handicapped'.

The school district 'serves all students – regardless of the severity of the handicapping condition – within the regular educational campus'. (This does not involve the expedient of ex-district placement; the district in fact receives 150 pupils from neighbouring districts with less comprehensive provision.) How was this achieved, and what does it entail in practice? There has been segregated provision in fact and the present situation has entailed shutting down a special school and decentralising provision. Pupils with severe learning difficulties were admitted to education in 1963. Initially they were provided for in units attached to ordinary schools but a separate special school catering for 'severely/profoundly/multiply handicapped students' was soon established. This school was closed down in 1977 and replaced by decentralised services within ordinary school buildings. This development 'did not occur as a result of strong parental or advocacy pressure', being motivated rather

'by a strong departmental commitment to the principles of normalisation, to a system-wide belief that interaction between handicapped and non-handicapped students is beneficial to both groups, and to strong superintendent support for a search for alternatives'.

The details were worked out by a task force set up to consider the implications of legislation. A comprehensive plan for locating special educational programmes was developed. Seventeen schools were designated 'to provide a barrier-free environment for handicapped students'. These were selected according to criteria of location, accessibility, availability of services and receptivity of teaching staff. Physical modifications were made to the schools where necessary and support systems established.

There are four forms of service delivery:

1. Resource programme. Any instructional setting to which the student comes for a specified period of time.
2. Consulting teacher/programme support teacher. Any instructional setting in the regular classroom where the support teacher and class teachers work together to solve students' learning or behavioural problems.
3. Self-contained integrated programmes. An instructional setting outside the regular classroom to which pupils come for the major part of their school programme, the remainder being supplied within mainstream arrangements.
4. Self-contained special programme. An instructional setting to which students come for all of their school programme, designed for 'those students who are so severely handicapped that they cannot operate in any ongoing part of the regular school day'.

Some 700 students, rather more than one third of those receiving specialised educational services, follow self-contained programmes (levels 3 or 4). For many of these students, including all at level 4, integration does not mean joint classroom activities for any period of the day. It means rather attending the same school as age peers, joining in common extra-curricular activities and having the opportunity for social interaction. This interaction is seen as particularly important for those with severe learning difficulties since it makes it possible 'to better prepare the students for community/vocational and domestic environments'.

The Severely, Profound/Multiply Handicapped programme in one school is described as follows:

'The Program currently utilizes six classrooms. The chronological ages of these children range from 5 to 14. Cognitively, the students are functioning at the sensori-motor and early pre-operational stages of cognitive development. Many of these students have physical and emotional disabilities as well as severe or profound retardation. Some of the complications that interfere with assessment and programming are hearing impairments, seizure disorders, physical handicaps, and recurring health problems. All these children are in self-contained classes but are integrated with regular education students for various activities that can include socialization and play activities with kindergarten children and early childhood to art, music and leisure time activities with the fourth and fifth graders. For example, fourth and fifth graders work on specific instructional and/or self-help activities within the special classroom for severely retarded under the supervision of the teacher. Another example is the interaction and participation with nonhandicapped peers in the lunch room, school cultural affairs and the community (field trips).'

The hearing impaired programme offers a different example with greater flexibility which progresses from limited association at pre-school level through segregation at infant stage to gradually increasing and carefully planned social and academic interaction as pupils move through the school system. Thus we read:

'At present there are 7 youngsters in the kindergarten program (ages 5-6). The children are totally self-contained for most of the day. This teacher has the responsibility of programming and assessing the progress of these children on an ongoing basis. Very often by second semester there may be 3 or more youngsters who are ready to have some type of socialization activities with either the Early Childhood unit or with a kindergarten class. The teacher of hearing impaired children plans with the kindergarten teacher as well as with one of the early childhood teachers. In order to plan most effectively these three teachers have developed the following procedures:

1. Each teacher observes in one another's instructional environment in order to learn the expectations of one another's classrooms.
2. The teachers then decide who will be responsible for specific instruction of the students and make plans based on the children's needs.
3. The teachers implement the actual plan, whereby children are integrated in one another's classrooms; again this gives teachers an opportunity to observe, interact, and possibly review if needed, any of the mainstreaming or integration process.

Grades 1-2 (in a combination classroom) comprise the next level of the hearing impaired program. A regular education teacher with 20 first and second graders teams on a daily basis with a teacher of the hearing impaired with 6 hearing impaired children. After assessing the students, the teachers form instructional groups based on the students' skills and needs. For instance the teacher of hearing impaired children may work with a reading group of 5 children, 3 of whom may be hearing impaired and 2 non-hearing impaired. At the same time, on the other side of the room the regular education teacher may work with a reading group of 7 children; 6 non-hearing impaired and 1 hearing impaired.'

What this example makes clear is that a commitment to educating all pupils in ordinary schools does not have to entail indiscriminate integration. Indeed it shows that a desegregated system such as this embodies a good deal of totally separate provision (within the ordinary school) and that careful planning and high levels of support are necessary in some cases to achieve even partial integration. What the example lacks perhaps is a demonstration of its relevance or feasibility in situations with more limited resources. Specialised educational services in Madison are well funded and enjoy high levels of administrative, professional and ancillary staffing. The high degree of integration achieved depends at least in part on the strong support available in this way, and it is a moot question whether anything similar could be achieved with the more limited resources that are the norm elsewhere.

A radically different approach to total integration is provided by the Italian situation. (Details are taken from Pasternak, 1979 and Vislie, 1980.) Legislation strongly supports integration. Act 118 in 1971 marked a clear departure from segregation with its requirement that education must take place in *regular* classes in ordinary schools 'except where the subject suffers from severe intellectual deficiency or from physical handicaps so great as to impede or render very difficult the learning processes in the regular classroom'. Any similarities with section 10 of the 1976 Act in Britain need not detain one however as this was succeeded by Act 227 in 1975 which removed the possibility of exclusion on the grounds of severity of handicap: 'the severity of the disablement (mental or physical) cannot be a limitation to integration in the regular class as long as admission is positive and possible for the handicapped child'. This established integration as no longer the problem of the individual pupil or the special education sector but of the ordinary school. This national legislation was supported by the requisite regional legislative and administrative frameworks. While there is considerable variation and some regions have espoused integration less effectively and wholeheartedly than others, there are numerous examples of total or near-total integration.

Pasternak (op.cit.) describes some of these. Thus, in Parma (population 180 000) 'all children, including the most severely handicapped, have access to education within the ordinary classes of the pre-school and state system'. Traditionally, physically and mentally handicapped children attended residential institutions or special schools. Parents' groups started to press for change in the late sixties. This gained political and professional support and gathered momentum in the context of the anti-psychiatry movement. Integrated educational programmes were gradually set up and children discharged from the segregated institutions. (The only pupils still segregated are those older ones who had grown up in the segregated system and whose parents felt they would be at risk in ordinary classes.)

The practice is to place children in ordinary classes in their neighbourhood schools. Special classes are purposely avoided. Pupils are dispersed in all classes and schools and overloading does not occur. There is great emphasis on the earliest possible intervention: infant schools are for children up to the age of three and every effort is made to absorb handicapped children in these. Support to teachers takes the form of resource teachers who are available to class teachers as required and outside specialists who assist with assessment, educational programming and general support. Particular mention is made of the close links with parents or grandparents and their active participation.

By contrast with Parma which is in the industrial north, Cutrofiano is a small city (population 91 000) in a rural and economically deprived part of southern Italy. Here too the practice is total integration. With the exception of a very few profoundly multi-handicapped children 'all the rest, whether incontinent, with epileptic seizures, psychotic or with difficult behaviour, are in regular classes'. Support is available to teachers in the form of increased staffing, resource teachers, and guidance and instruction from a specialist centre which formerly catered for some 300 handicapped pupils and now devotes itself to promoting integration. The amount of support, especially from trained support teachers, is limited however.

These examples present a considerable challenge to special educators. Integration has been achieved for virtually all pupils with apparently a limited expenditure of resources. This is moreover a radical form of integration that eschews special classes, which are seen as a form of segregated provision, and places all pupils in regular classes. Vislie (op.cit.) finds that 'the policy of integration in Italy represents a new and on the whole a totally different approach to the education of the handicapped'. Integration is not as in other countries an alternative way of organising special education. It is the *only* way – to which the handicapped have a legal right.

There is the question of evaluation of course. Are the pupils' needs being met as well as they might be under other arrangements? What are the implications for the education system generally? The literature available leaves these questions open, though it does testify to widespread enthusiasm and commitment on the part of many professionals and parents – a consideration of some significance. It must be recognised that evaluating a development of this nature with such broad social and political as well as educational implications cannot be tackled on a narrow canvas. Isolated measures would be quite inappropriate. Having said that, one must be clear that evaluation is necessary. In its absence doubts must remain about the quality of educational provision being offered. A change of this order has many demonstrable implications and outcomes – nature and extent of support necessary and provided, identification of pupils' needs, pupil achievement, teacher training, relationships with peers, and much more. These must be addressed systematically if the model is to be of use. It is to be hoped that forthcoming CERI publications will provide more detail on this major national innovation in special education.

Extent of integration in Britain

The present study was carried out within the British context, and in this section we examine in some detail relevant figures and trends for this country. (Because of the nature of the figures available much of the discussion refers to England and Wales only.) It is difficult to make precise statements because of the problems in defining special needs and the associated limitations in official statistics, and because much provision is made on a local flexible basis or is not formally recorded. It is possible however to form an impression of the scale of the problem and identify likely trends by adopting pragmatic definitions and drawing on available statistics.

Epidemiological studies have used various means to assess the incidence of special needs. The Isle of Wight study (Rutter *et al.*, 1970) drew on psychometric information, defining intellectual retardation as an IQ of 70 or less and educational retardation as a reading age at least two years four months below chronological age. The National Child Development Study (Pringle *et al.*, 1966) reported for a national cohort the number of pupils at different ages who attended special schools, special classes in ordinary schools, or were judged likely by their teachers to benefit from such help. Webb (1967) examined the number of infant school leavers who were judged to need extra help or consideration on account of learning, behaviour or emotional problems. These and other studies though operating to different criteria lead to broadly comparable estimates of the extent of special needs – between 15 and 20 per cent of pupils can be expected to present particular educational problems. The Warnock Report summarises the findings with its recommended assumption for planning purposes 'that about one in six children at any time and up to one in five children at some time during their school career will require some form of special educational provision' (3.17).

This figure is widely quoted and crops up regularly in integration debates. One must be clear however that it is a summary figure and it would be unfortunate if its casual use were to add to the looseness of these debates. Quite apart from its tentative nature, being based as it is on pragmatic definitions and incomplete statistics, it is a global figure and does not discriminate between pupils who have very different special needs. Many speak of a continuum of handicap, and ideally it may be possible if not particularly useful to demonstrate a continuous line from gifted to severely retarded. There are qualitative differences in practice however and these can be far more important in determining provision. For example, a teacher can educate some pupils with special needs in an ordinary class with minimal support but cannot provide for others at all or only if given a great deal of support. As far as meeting special educational needs is concerned, the reality is one of a very large number of pupils requiring special education of different kinds.

In outline terms, how is this special education provided? In chapter 3 we discuss the continuum of special education provision from segregated special schools to support in an ordinary class and propose a detailed categorisation of provision. Official statistics do not take account of such detailed distinctions and we have to be satisfied with a relatively crude account here. Four broad categories can be outlined: special schools and related provision; designated special classes attached to ordinary schools; other special classes set up on the initiative of individual schools; and normal classes in ordinary schools.

In considering the allocation of pupils to these categories we have to distinguish between those formally ascertained as requiring special educational treatment and the others whose problems will generally be less severe. The latter of course are the far larger group, making up approximately 15 per cent of the school age population. They will generally be attending their local school where their needs may or may not be met. One may note that it is vacuous to speak of integration in their regard since they are already in ordinary schools and there is no question of their not being part of them. The question to be asked is: To what extent are their needs recognised and met? Those pupils formally ascertained as requiring special educational treatment will for the most part be in special schools or designated special classes, though increasingly some are found in other special classes or in ordinary classes – a development that is not noted in official statistics. The number of pupils formally ascertained (ie identified by LEAs as requiring special educational treatment) in England and Wales in January 1980 was 172 101; this represents 1.85 per cent of the total school age population.

The distribution of pupils between the different categories of provision (England and Wales) is as follows:

1. Special schools and related provision. This includes maintained and non-maintained special schools and independent schools, both boarding and day; tuition in hospitals, by means of hospital special schools, units or

otherwise; and tuition at home. In January 1980 there were 144 122 (1.55 per cent) pupils being educated in this way. (The great majority of those formally ascertained are accounted for in this way; the others are either in designated special classes or awaiting admission to special provision.)

2. Designated special classes attached to ordinary schools. These account for a further 21 659 pupils (0.23 per cent), mainly on a full-time basis. They cater principally for pupils in the ESN, partially hearing and maladjusted categories.

3. Other special classes. These are classes or resource bases, often set up on the initiative of individual schools and not formally designated as special education provision. Statistics are not compiled on these classes and, with the exception of 1976 when a one-off survey was conducted (HMSO, 1976), national data are not available. In 1976 there were classes of this kind in 10 845 maintained schools (nearly 40 per cent), catering for 494 248 (5.2 per cent) pupils. This was usually on a part-time basis with the vast majority spending less than half of their time in these special classes. Most of them were described as having difficulties in learning or problems of an emotional or behavioural nature.

4. Normal classes. Pupils with special needs attending ordinary classes on an individual basis constitute a group of unknown size. No figures are available apart from Wales where in recent years approximately one per cent of handicapped children are estimated as being educated in ordinary classes in maintained schools (0.96 per cent in 1977/8, 1.06 per cent in 1978/9, 1.20 per cent in 1979/80).[1]

These figures refer to single points in time. In order to examine the extent of any increase in integration we have to look at trends over a number of years. There are two ways of tackling the question: Is integration on the increase in Britain? The first is to refer to one's own experience of special education and changes within it, the second to analyse official statistics where they are available. Unfortunately, these two tactics seem to lead to rather different conclusions. The common assumption is that 'integration is on the march', that special schools are becoming depopulated and even

---

[1] The figures in this section are based on *Statistics of Education* (England and Wales), 1972-77; *Statistics of Education* (England), 1978; *Statistics of Education in Wales* 1978-79; and unpublished figures from the Department of Education and Science and the Welsh Office.

closing down, and that pupils who would traditionally have been placed in special schools are increasingly being placed in ordinary schools. Our own experience would verify that this is happening in some places. In the course of the study which forms the basis of this report we encountered numerous examples of pupils moving from special schools to special classes or ordinary classes and pupils who would once have been candidates for a special school receiving their entire education in ordinary schools. We are aware of many other situations where pupils who would once have attended special schools are now being educated in ordinary schools with support from school staff or a peripatetic service.

Why then do we suggest that the official statistics paint a different picture? The figures available allow one to identify trends for the first two categories only, special schools and designated special classes. Here however a number of pointers emerge. Special schools are not closing down, or at least the total number is not on the wane. On the contrary, throughout the 70's they have grown in number (from 1 501 in 1972 to 1 672 in 1980) and have provided for a steadily increasing proportion of pupils (from 1.35 per cent to 1.44 per cent over the same period). As for designated special classes, their enrolment has been increasing but at a modest rate, and this is still a relatively minor form of provision in terms of the number of pupils provided for. This goes counter to many received notions on the progress of integration and on the face of it suggests that there is very little transfer of pupils to more integrated placements. In order to get a clear view on the matter it is necessary to scrutinise the figures very closely.

Table 1 gives the number of special schools in England and Wales, along with the number of pupils catered for, for 1971-1980. It covers all maintained and non-maintained special schools but not independent schools. It will be seen that, with the exception of 1972 when there was a dramatic jump of nearly 50 per cent, there was a steady growth in the number of special schools each year up to 1979. The rate of increase was slowing down however and in 1980 the total was down by one on the previous year. The number of pupils attending special schools also increased throughout the period. This was not a steady increase and there appeared to be a noticeable drop towards the end. Computing percentages however demonstrates an increase in the *relative* number throughout the period. The number of pupils attending special schools as a proportion of the total school population increased or held constant, with the exception of 1974 when there was a large increase in the total school age population. The increase in 1972 was of course a consequence of the Education (Handicapped Children) Act 1970 whereby LEAs assumed responsibility for all handicapped pupils from April 1 1971.

Table I:		Special schools and pupils in attendance		1971/80
	Special schools	*Pupils*	*Percentage of all pupils*	*All pupils*
1971	1 019	90 361	1.03	8 800 843
1972	1 501	122 283	1.35	9 032 999
1973	1 537	127 804	1.39	9 190 030
1974	1 575	130 677	1.37	9 560 015
1975	1 603	131 940	1.37	9 617 474
1976	1 619	133 609	1.38	9 669 239
1977	1 653	135 261	1.40	9 663 978
1978	1 665	137 234	1.43	9 563 062
1979	1 673	135 610	1.43	9 454 101
1980	1 672	133 557	1.44	9 280 250

Table II: Number of handicapped pupils attending independent schools (under LEA arrangements)	
1972	5 520
1973	5 916
1974	6 133
1975	6 589
1976	6 769
1977	7 237
1978	7 417
1979	7 727
1980	7 659

Attendances at independent schools showed a similar trend over the same period. As Table II shows, the number of handicapped pupils attending independent schools under arrangements made by authorities went up from 5 520 in 1972 to 7 659 in 1980. There was a steady increase each year up to 1979, with a slight drop from 1979 to 1980. This makes it plain that the increase in public sector special school numbers cannot be explained through any decrease in authorities' use of independent schools. In fact, the percentage increase in independent school enrolment (39 per cent) was over four times greater than the comparable figures for maintained and non-maintained special schools (nine per cent) over the period in question – though the actual numbers are of course very much smaller.

Attendance at designated special classes is detailed in Table III. Full-time placements have increased from 11 027 in 1973 to 19 772 in 1980 – a large percentage increase but still catering for a relatively small number of pupils. Figures for part-time attendance at such classes are available only from 1975; there seems to be an upward movement but the trend is not clear. (It should be noted that since 1978 the returns from Wales do not distinguish part-time pupils from full-time pupils, all pupils being entered as full-time; the effect of this is a slight inflation of the full-time figures at the expense of the part-time ones in the three years from 1978.)

Table III:	Pupils attending designated special classes.		1973/80
	Full-time	*Part-time*	*Total*
1973	11 027		
1974	14 332		
1975	16 459	1 448	17 907
1976	18 667	2 003	20 670
1977	18 911	2 763	21 674
1978	18 978	1 986	20 964
1979	19 983	2 017	22 000
1980	19 772	1 884	21 659

Before concluding simply that these data show an increase in segregated provision and give no joy to those who would advocate integration, there are several points to be made which complicate interpretation and suggest that a straightforward reading of the figures is likely to prove erroneous. First, the official statistics contain inaccuracies that lead to an underestimate of the extent of integration. Secondly, looking at the statistics in global terms as above overlooks important sources of variation and can be misleading in several respects. Thirdly, there have been changes in the roles taken on by special schools, some obvious, some not easily quantifiable, which make comparison over time difficult. Fourthly, various inertial factors conspire to slow down the rate of change and keep trends from emerging clearly until they are well established.

i. The major inaccuracy in official statistics for present purposes is that pupils are designated incorrectly as far as placement is concerned. There is reason to believe that this is happening in such a way as systematically to underestimate the real extent of integration. Pupils attending ordinary schools are entered on official returns as attending a special school. This arises in two ways: special schools establishing links with ordinary schools; and special schools assigned responsibility for certain pupils attending ordinary schools. Thus when integration takes the form of a special school/ordinary school link, pupils attached to the special school may spend most of their time in the ordinary school without transferring to its roll. In some cases they are retained on the special school roll even when they attend the ordinary school full-time. Likewise, children with a clear-cut handicapping condition such as sensory impairment sometimes commence schooling in an ordinary school but under the aegis of a special school and nominally on its roll.

In the absence of national figures it is impossible to be precise about the number of pupils involved here but it is not negligible. Cope and Anderson's (1977) survey of provision for physically handicapped pupils revealed that in 1975 11 LEAs had special schools on the same campus as ordinary schools and sharing pupils with them. A further six LEAs were planning such arrangements, and others have been instituted since. (This is to be seen in the context of 102 special schools for the physically handicapped, and 108 for the delicate and associated categories – 1980 figures.) Schools for the hearing impaired have likewise developed a good deal of integration that is not reflected in the official figures. Of 51 special schools catering for the hearing impaired some seven to our knowledge – and possibly many more – are sending pupils on their roll to nearby ordinary schools on a part-time or full-time basis. In one case the entire special school roll of 71 pupils has been dispersed to ordinary classes or special departments in other schools. A conservative estimate of the number of pupils categorised misleadingly in this way would be 200/300.

ii. Closer analysis of the figures leads to a re-interpretation of them or enables changes to be pinpointed more precisely. This will be examined in relation to ascertainment rates, regional variations and changes across categories of handicap.

Differential ascertainment rates are perhaps the major consideration. This is because from the mid-70's onward ascertainment rates have been highest in the largest age groups. Thus, if we compare primary and secondary pupils, proportionately more of the latter are placed in special schools. (In 1979 the percentages of pupils in special schools at ages 6, 9, 12 and 15 respectively were 0.76, 1.34, 1.75 and 2.01. Similar patterns hold for other years.) But the number of pupils per year was greater at secondary level in the period in question since the population bulge reached secondary schools in the mid-70's. (Thus, the largest age group in 1976 was the 11-year-olds.) Hence, the number of pupils being ascertained would have been increased *even if ascertainment rates remained static.* Conversely, an increase in the number of pupils placed in special schools does not necessarily imply increased ascertainment rates or greater segregation.

When the interaction between ascertainment rate and number in year group is eliminated by computing the percentage of pupils ascertained for each age group, some interesting differences emerge. (Details in Appendix A1.) In point of fact, the increases that took place were all at the younger (5, 6 and, to a lesser extent, 7 year olds) and older ages (14 and 15 year olds). The percentage being ascertained in the middle years either stayed the same or fell slightly. These can be explained on the one hand by the greater appreciation in recent years of the importance of early diagnosis and consequently the care taken over the ascertainment of young children and on the other hand by the growing tendency for LEAs to deal with disruptive adolescents by designating them maladjusted and sending them to special schools.

A second consideration obscured when the figures are taken globally is that there are significant local and regional differences in provision. It is not possible on the basis of available figures to analyse such regional variations in detail, but it is clear that they have important effect. This is not simply because there is greater commitment to integration in some areas than in others, but rather because baseline provision can vary so much. Some areas have been slower than others in developing special educational provision. In such areas the commitment to educating pupils with special needs may result in building up special schools, *even though* the commitment to integration is not less than in areas with a longer history of provision. As an example, one authority which had unit provision only for physically handicapped pupils built a new special school so that it could phase out residential education in favour of day placements.

Thirdly, the changes occurring have not fallen equally across the different categories of handicap. There has been a considerable increase in segregated provision for the maladjusted for instance but a decrease for some other groups such as the partially hearing. It is difficult to draw precise comparisons because of the nature of the figures available. There are two possible bases for making comparisons: the number of special schools by category of major handicap provided for; and the number of full-time pupils in special schools by category of major handicap. The former allows of a direct albeit crude comparison; the latter permits a more detailed account but has to be seen in the context of ascertainment practices, demographic patterns and the other factors bearing on interpretation being noted here.

Table IV gives the number of special schools by category in 1972 and 1980. It is of interest to note where the changes have taken place. The net increase of 171 schools includes both gains and losses. The main increases are in the ESN and Maladjusted categories. The former is the bigger increase in absolute terms (86 schools) but the increase in provision for the maladjusted (66 schools – nearly 50 per cent) dwarfs it in percentage terms. There is an increase of 25 schools for physically handicapped pupils, though this must be offset in part by the decrease of 17 schools in the Delicate and associated categories. The increase in provision for the Multiply Handicapped (12 schools) may be noted, alongside the reduction by 14 in the number of hospital schools.

There is also the new provision (10 schools) for Autistic pupils. This picture is corroborated in part by the corresponding pupil figures. These are detailed in Appendix A2. The sharp rise in the Maladjusted category, along with the increase in the Physically Handicapped and the decrease in the Delicate categories, may be noted. There is also a considerable drop in the number of partially hearing pupils attending special schools. What is not corroborated at first glance is the ESN increase. The very modest increase in ESN pupil numbers shown in A2 does not correspond to the increase in schools designated for ESN pupils shown in Table IV. This reflects the fact that these schools are catering for a wider range of pupil

Table IV:	Number of special schools, by category.		1972 and 1980
	1972	*1980*	*Change*
Blind	17	16	−1
Partially sighted	19	17	−2
Blind & partially sighted	2	2	0
Deaf	20	24	4
Partially hearing	6	6	0
Deaf and partially hearing	22	21	−1
Deaf and partially sighted	1	1	0
Physically handicapped	77	102	25
Delicate	56	48	−8
Delicate & physically handicapped	71	60	−11
Delicate & maladjusted	4	6	2
Maladjusted	142	208	66
ESN	897	983	86
Epileptic	6	6	0
Speech defect	3	6	3
Autistic	0	10	10
Multiple handicaps	3	15	12
Hospital	155	141	−14
	1 501	1 672	171

needs than before, and also that LEAs were gradually improving their provision; improved pupil/teacher ratios and smaller teaching groups led to a larger number of *smaller* special schools. (Details on the growth in the number of schools for ESN pupils are given in A3.)

iii.   The nature of special schools and the roles assigned them have changed, and their target clients are not the same now as they were say ten years ago. This limits the comparisons that can be drawn. There are three facets to consider: wider age-range being served; changes in incidence rates; and improvements in provision.

First, special schools have come to cater for more young people aged over 15 and more pre-school children. The raising of the school leaving age in 1972 generated more older clients, and this was accompanied by greater efforts on the part of some special schools to cater for students in the 16-19 age range. Table V shows that the number of pupils aged 16 or more doubled between 1972 and 1979. There was a corresponding though smaller increase at pre-school level arising out of the trend toward early identification and intervention. When these two groups are removed from the special school total and a percentage (of total school population) computed for the 5-15 group, as in Table VI, there is no significant increase between 1972 and 1979. This should be contrasted with the apparent percentage increase in Table I.

Table V:	Special school pupils outside the age of compulsory schooling, 1972/80		
	Aged 4 or less	Aged 16 or more	Total
1972	3 032	4 575	7 607
1973	3 301	5 477	8 778
1974	3 457	6 507	9 964
1975	3 695	6 836	10 531
1976	3 959	7 023	10 982
1977	4 074	7 852	11 926
1978	4 027	8 543	12 570
1979	3 819	9 607	13 426
1980	4 749		

Table VI:	Special school pupils aged between 5 and 15 as a percentage of total school population, 1972/79
1972	1.27
1973	1.29
1974	1.27
1975	1.26
1976	1.27
1977	1.28
1978	1.30
1979	1.29

Secondly, the incidence of special needs cannot be assumed to be static. Precise estimates of variation are not available, but if there was an increase this would explain some of the growth in special school numbers. This can of course only offer a hypothetical explanation in view of uncertainty over incidence rates. Even with physical handicap where one might expect a clear-cut situation it is extremely difficult to establish precise figures. There have been dramatic changes over the past 30 years with on the one hand the virtual elimination of tuberculosis and polio and on the other the emergence into prominence of other handicapping conditions such as cerebral palsy. Decreases in infant mortality (and the consequent survival of weak and possibly brain-damaged infants) and new surgical procedures that ensure the survival of infants with spina bifida are factors at work here. As against these there are other factors such as improved perinatal care, the rubella vaccination programme, greater availability of amniocentesis and termination of pregnancy, that would reduce the figures. Although the overall position is far from clear, it may be noted that there has been in recent years a greater preponderance of physically handicapped pupils with associated neurological impairments. Anderson (1973) and others have shown that these present more complex educational problems and indeed that it is more difficult to educate them in ordinary schools.

If we turn to other categories such as Maladjusted or ESN, where the greatest increases have occurred, problems of definition intrude and make it very difficult to establish whether the increases are due to increased incidence or to other factors. Leaving aside the probability that pupils' need of special assistance is recognised more clearly, is the expansion in segregated provision due to greater incidence of maladjustment and educational failure or to diminished tolerance and capacity to cope on the part of the ordinary school? In any case, are these different possibilities that could be separated in practice? The definition of maladjustment or educational subnormality in practical terms must take account of the school's capacity to cope with deviance or educational failure. So while 'the growing tide of disorder' in schools could if proven account for an increase in segregation that was not anti-integrationist, the difficulty in isolating maladjustment or educational failure from the contexts in which they arise means that explanations of this nature must remain speculative.

Thirdly, it is likely that a greater awareness of special needs and a policy of improving provision will lead to some segregation, at least initially, regardless of commitment to integration. The obvious example is the admission of severely handicapped pupils to education in 1971; the network of special schools that resulted could hardly be taken as an anti-integration move. This example is perhaps so obvious as to be trivial for our purposes here. There are other examples however that crop up in daily practice. A partially-hearing pupil with additional learning difficulties might after protracted failure in a unit be considered to stand a better chance in a special school; a child with a communication disorder might be transferred from an ordinary class to a special class or from a day ESN school to a residential language school; a developmentally delayed child might be withdrawn to a totally controlled setting, or an unhappy child to a secure environment, for a period of time. These and similar examples increase segregated provision but they commonly arise out of a desire to meet pupils' needs better and in a context where integration/ segregation is irrelevant. One might disagree with the tactics adopted and regret the segregation that results, but it is important to realise that this has to do with the expansion of the role of the special school and not with any opposition to the principle of integration.

iv.   A final consideration that complicates interpretation is the effect of inertial factors. Official statistics cannot match the pace of events. This is particularly so where capital expenditure projects are concerned. Building a new school for instance is not a process that can be initiated, or halted, overnight. The time lag can be as much as five years or even longer.

Other factors that come into play here include the force of tradition and established routine, professional resistance to new ways of working and bureaucratic delay. These factors can impose an inertia that belies the real state of affairs and masks the degree of commitment to integration. It can mean too that current trends may not be evident in up-to-date statistics.

In this context it is of interest to note, from Table I, that the number of special schools peaked in 1979 and started to drop thereafter. (Precisely the same phenomenon is evident in the numbers of handicapped pupils attending independent schools; Table II shows a peak in 1979 followed by a slight drop in 1980.) If the downward trend continues, this could be evidence of a far greater movement away from segregation than appears at first sight. Thus, the growth up to 1979 could reflect the tardiness in closing redundant special schools and the long lead-in time to opening new schools (so that the decision on a school opened in 1978 might have been taken in 1974) rather than any commitment to segregated special education. This suggestion gains support from an examination of the average size of special school rolls throughout the seventies. Table VII gives the average number of pupils per special school from 1972 through to 1980 and shows a decrease from approximately 83 to 80 pupils. This was gradual until 1979 when a sharp decrease occurred.

Table VII:	Average number of pupils per special school
1972	81.5
1973	83.2
1974	83.0
1975	82.3
1976	82.5
1977	81.8
1978	82.4
1979	81.1
1980	79.9

What can be said in summary about the state of integration in Britain? Certainly, many common assumptions and much official rhetoric are without foundation. There is a great deal of segregated provision, and in some respects this is growing. Paradoxically, this does not mean that integration is not increasing as well. The growth in segregated provision is specific to certain localities and handicapping conditions. Also, some of this growth reflects a desire to meet special educational needs more effectively rather than any orientation toward either integration or segregation. In integrationist terms, this might be considered a failure to realise the potential of ordinary school placement but cannot fairly be taken as a commitment to segregation. Having said that, one must acknowledge that there are little grounds for complacency. The growth in integration is too little and too unevenly spread. Some pupils attend special schools, special classes or ordinary classes depending simply on where they live. What is common practice in some places does not seem even to have been entertained as a possibility elsewhere. Some of the growth in segregated provision on the other hand reflects expediency and a failure to restructure the ordinary school. It is hoped that this book will help both to extend integration and reduce segregation by drawing attention to the possibilities for educating pupils with special needs in ordinary schools and by analysing the problems and opportunities presented.

Chapter Two
The Contribution of Research

Given the centrality of integration in special education debates and its ramifications for ordinary schools, given also the numerous questions and conflicts associated with it, one is not surprised to find that the topic has generated a good deal of research. Traditionally, much of this was carried out in America. With a few exceptions, most of the studies were small scale and local in character. As the commitment to normalising the experiences of those with special needs and to educating as many pupils as possible in ordinary schools grew, the importance of integration as a matter for enquiry as well as action was increasingly recognised. A number of large scale studies have been carried out, some at national and even cross-national level.

It is not our intention to review these studies here. Cave and Madison (1978) in their review of special education research included integration as a major topic and covered the published studies up to the mid-70s. Later in this chapter we refer to the main British studies that have appeared since. Our intention here is to discuss briefly the contribution that research can make to clarifying the questions thrown up by integration, note the major recent studies and describe our own study on which this book is based.

The role of research

It is important to be clear on what the researcher can and cannot do. It is not for him to answer the big questions: Integrate or segregate? Integration for all or only some? He may observe that these questions are often loosely phrased and based on conceptual muddles, and that much of the attendant discussion is in consequence confused. There are many difficulties associated with the concept of integration. In the previous chapter we pointed out that integration is all too readily seen simply in placement terms and argued that the integration/segregation dichotomy is a misleading one and does not correspond to the practice of special education. Sound decisions depend of course on clarifying these conceptual difficulties so that inter-related issues can be disentangled clearly from each other and specific questions formulated. The researcher can assist, even play a key part, in this process but his contribution is an ancillary one. He may elucidate the terms of reference and provide relevant evidence but in the end it is not for him to say whether or not integration should prevail.

This can be clarified by looking at the two sorts of questions that can be asked. One has to do with finding reasons or explanations and identifying likely consequences, while the other is directed toward action. Examples of the former would be: What are the factors that determine attitude to disability? Given the resources that are likely to be available, what are the educational and other implications of educating pupils with special needs in ordinary schools – for the special pupils themselves? For other pupils? For the school as a whole? Given some such set of questions, one can ask in the light of answers to them further questions of the form: *Should* pupils with special needs be educated in ordinary schools? Is the educational experience likely to be acceptable and appropriate? The researcher can be expected to provide answers to the former set of questions but he has no special brief in respect of the latter. These are to be resolved in terms of political decisions, public value judgements and the wishes of those involved.

While the researcher should be able to clarify the issues at stake, indicate the likely outcomes of different courses of action and generally inform the decisions to be made, it is not for him to say whether or not a given form of educational arrangement should prevail. For example, a researcher may observe that physically handicapped pupils attending ordinary schools tend to receive less physiotherapy than pupils with comparable disabilities attending special schools. He may even document the implications for their physical and motor development as well as their general educational development. It is not for him however to rule on which form of placement is preferable. Even when the researcher can affirm that a form of placement is superior or deficient on a given dimension, there are still numerous other dimensions to consider; apart from the possibility that these others are more important anyway, some of them may be related to the success or failure on this dimension. Thus, to take the example above, intensive physiotherapy may encroach on academic time while attending the neighbourhood school can confer social benefits and enable a young person to maintain contact with his or her community. There are many facets to a young person's schooling. These are affected in different ways by different arrangements, and it is likely that any given arrangement will entail a combination of advantages and disadvantages. Decisions about an arrangement must rest on a comprehensive evaluation that weighs up the different factors in relation to each other. The researcher can assist with this by ensuring that the component judgements are firmly based on evidence, but he has no special competence as researcher to say how the different factors should be weighted against each other, what compromises are acceptable and so on.

This may be seen in clearer perspective by looking at the kinds of research that have been carried out. Research into integration falls within educational research in general and the same broad classifications could be used. By the nature of the topic however certain emphases have predominated. Five research approaches can be noted: basic; descriptive; comparative; qualitative; and action research.

1. Basic research

There is a great deal of research unconnected with integration that turns out to illuminate the process in important ways. This can be theoretical work in the social sciences: research on attitude formation or the nature of stigmas can help to clarify the processes of adjustment and assimilation that take place when pupils with special needs attend ordinary schools; studies of deviance and outgroup/majority group relationships can be helpful in understanding their status; more generally, the dynamics of organisational change can assist in explaining what happens when a sizeable special centre is set up in a school. Curriculum development or pedagogical enquiry into implementing the curriculum can be drawn upon: research into pedagogical innovations such as precision teaching is as relevant to integrated situations as it is to special education generally; outcomes from research and development in other areas that impinge on the practice of integrated teaching include developments in microelectronics, the establishment of common conceptual frameworks to facilitate inter-disciplinary and inter-professional working, and the pedagogical application of behaviourist principles. Research can also focus on policy issues: the development of integrated provision can depend on how policy is formulated and implemented at both local and national level; the nature of any such provision will reflect the relationship between Education and Health Authorities; in particular, the mechanisms by which resources are allocated play a crucial part in shaping integrated provision.

2. Descriptive studies

Descriptive surveys have played a major part in the development of educational research. While it is currently fashionable to disparage survey methodology, properly conducted surveys provide a useful knowledge base that indicates the size of problems and assists in planning services. As far as integration is concerned, a number of surveys have been conducted into the extent of provision for special pupils in ordinary schools. These have tended to be confined to single categories of handicap. They include DES surveys into units for partially hearing children (1967), blind and partially sighted children (1968) and special classes for pupils with various handicapping conditions (1972); provision for the physically handicapped (Cope and Anderson, 1977) and the maladjusted (ACE, 1980); language classes (Lancaster, 1981); and provision for pupils with various special needs in the Greater London area (Parfit, 1975). *Statistics of Education* Vol I (HMSO) also provides relevant information, especially the 1976 volume which contains a study of special class provision; the various interpretation problems referred to in the previous chapter should be noted however.

Another level of description arises in accounts of practice as often found in students' dissertations and journals dedicated to practice. Garnett (1976), McIver (1977) and Sinclair Taylor (1980) constitute examples of the former. There are numerous examples of the latter. Thus, recent issues of *Special Education: Forward Trends* feature descriptive articles on particular local initiatives: integrated provision for physically handicapped pupils (Sturges,

1980 and Spencer, 1980); social integration in a language unit (Hurford and Hart, 1979); secondary department for pupils with learning difficulties (Roberts and Williams, 1980); individual integration of hearing impaired pupils (Dale, 1979).

3. Comparative studies

Because of the polarisation that has developed around the topic of integration there have been numerous comparative studies contrasting integrated with segregated provision. These follow a definite pattern: two groups are selected for study, one integrated, the other segregated; the curricular and socialising opportunities that distinguish the two groups are identified; differences in outcome (eg, attainments, adjustment, self-confidence) are measured; and these differences are related to the status of the groups, thus 'Integrating pupils have higher or lower reading ages, are more or less well adjusted, and so on'. This pattern of research is popular also because it fits neatly into empirical research method and allows the use of sophisticated and powerful tools of data analysis.

The research effort expended in this direction has yielded a comparatively meagre payoff however. This is partly because it is misguided and based on a premise of limited relevance. Special education is not to be conceived in terms of a simple opposition between integration and segregation. There are major methodological considerations as well. First, the enterprise depends critically on adequate matching of the two groups. Unless this has been done any measured differences in outcome cannot be assumed to be due to the different educational programmes. In practice, matching is usually confined to age, sex and IQ – all readily available but hardly an exhaustive list of the factors that determine a young person's response to an educational programme.

A second set of considerations has to do with the practical interpretation of any results that might be obtained. Even if adequately matched samples have been achieved, a given study will usually only provide answers to specific questions. Thus, one may establish that a given teaching strategy or means of promoting social interaction is better than particular alternatives for a given group in a given situation. This can be valuable information but one must be clear that an integration programme comprises many strategies and means and in any case is more than the aggregate of them. Moreover, some of the most important variables – both individually and in interaction with others – are difficult to measure and so take into account. In consequence, the tendency has been to ignore factors such as the ethos of the school and the whole range of teacher variables.

4. Qualitative research

Qualitative research has gained rather more credence in recent years as the achievements of anthropology and, more recently, open-ended enquiries in sociology have been given greater attention. For present purposes a central feature is the emphasis on the individual entity – this can be a person (pupil, teacher, other professional), a process (classroom, integration programme) or an institution (school, peripatetic service) – and seeking to understand it from the inside. This is to eschew or at least to play down the role of preconceived frames of reference and to build up a picture in terms of the experience and ways of thinking of the participants.

Superficially an easy task, it is in fact one of the more elusive research styles. Anecdotal asides and longwinded transcripts of interviews do not constitute qualitative research any more than the columns of the popular press can be said to be contemporary history. A good example of this research style as applying to integration is provided by Jamieson *et al.*'s (1977) study of integrated provision for visually impaired pupils. This is described in more detail below.

5. Action research

Action research involves close working links between researcher and practitioner in a particular setting. There is a constant interaction between the two in monitoring practice closely, making changes in it and noting their effects. Instead of keeping research and practice separate the aim is deliberately to bring them together in a creative interplay. The study described below by Kiernan and Kavanagh (1977) has certain features of this research style.

Research in integration

Several reviews of research into integration have appeared in recent years. These include Cave and Madison (1978); Kaufman and

Alberto (1977); Corman and Gottlieb (1978); Watts *et al.* (1978); Meyers *et al.* (1980); and National Swedish Board of Education (1980). Numerous other publications have of course referred to or summarised research into integration. British examples include Cope and Anderson (1977), Galloway and Goodwin (1980) and Wedell and Roberts (in press). Cave and Madison is probably the oldest of these since the review was actually completed in 1976 and is the only one of the primary reviews to cover British research. Watts *et al.* offers an Australian perspective though it is strongly oriented to American research. National Swedish Board of Education covers the Scandinavian situation; it cites studies and introduces a perspective not readily available elsewhere. The other reviews are American in origin and virtually exclusively so in coverage.

Meyers *et al.* point out that the fundamental research question the public and most of the school people ask is whether the student who has a mental limitation is better educated in a segregated, self-contained class or in some mainstream integration programme with the regular class and its students. Allowing for the formulation in American terms, one recognises this as articulating a very general concern. It also explains the history of research into integration, which has comprised for the most part a series of comparative efficacy studies. The five categories of research referred to above have not all featured to the same degree. The widespread demand for answers to the comparative questions, allied to their congruence with prevailing methodology in educational research, has produced a spate of studies comparing pupils' academic and social development under different educational arrangements. This comparative approach has yielded place a little in very recent years as its limited achievements and the potential of other approaches have been more widely appreciated.

Most of the so-called efficacy studies have been conducted in America and seek to examine the relative efficacy of special and ordinary classes for mentally retarded pupils. (Only a few studies have compared pupils in special schools and ordinary schools, and they appear to be confined to Britain.) The great majority of these studies relate to pupils with mild mental retardation; many of them are culturally deprived and in this country would probably have attended ordinary school anyway. There is a broad consensus about these studies: in general, they are methodologically inadequate, and do not yield findings that consistently favour a given type of educational placement. Cave and Madison find that 'many, perhaps most, of the research studies are not only small-scale but methodologically weak' (p92). Kaufman and Alberto, in one of the most detailed of these reviews, analyse the experimental control of variables in efficacy studies along three key areas: random selection of sample; nature of classroom and instructional variables; and the appropriateness of measuring devices. They, and Meyers *et al.* subsequently, found the studies relied on biased or inadequate sampling procedures; did not take account of variations in classroom ethos, the programmes people followed and how they were taught; and used unsatisfactory or biased measures of academic and social development.

Given these methodological weaknesses, it is perhaps fortunate that the outcomes have been inconclusive. The latter is particularly the case where academic achievement is concerned. Neither special class nor ordinary class can claim consistent advantages. Moreover, as Corman and Gottlieb note, 'when positive effects have been reported for integrating pupils, it is difficult to determine which aspects of the mainstreamed treatment contributed to improvement' (p271). Findings on social adjustment of retarded pupils are also inconclusive though Meyers *et al.*'s reading of the studies is that social adjustment is generally poorer for pupils in ordinary classes, while there is general agreement that their social acceptance is less than that of peers.

In this context Bricker's (1978) rationale for the integration of pre-school children is of interest. She advances three sets of reasons: social-ethical, legal-legislative, and psychological-educational. Social-ethical reasons have to do with the possibility of altering societal attitudes and the damaging social/emotional effects of segregation, while legal-legislative reasons derive from legislative enactments and court decisions. These are important reasons but psychological-ethical reasons are central to the research context. Bricker acknowledges the common view that there is little empirical evidence to support or oppose particular educational or developmental groupings but goes on to erect a case for integration on the basis of relevant psychological theory. Two areas are selected – the developmental approach to early education and imitation learning – and theoretical and research evidence combined to demonstrate that integration is an effective educational alternative for handicapped pre-school children.

Studies of the integration of pupils with other handicapping conditions have been relatively sparse. Cave and Madison summarise studies on hearing impaired, emotionally disturbed and visually impaired pupils. These too are comparative in nature and as inconclusive as the studies referred to above. Fredericks *et al.* (1978) report a study on integrating severely handicapped children: when structured activities are provided improvement occurs in social interaction and some language skills.

The preponderance of comparative efficacy studies has been noted. Although it had long been clear that what was needed was an examination of what goes on *within* programmes, the emphasis on precise measurement of outcomes and drawing of comparisons continued. Some studies did of course eschew rigid quantification and sought instead to describe and analyse integration programmes, or did the latter in addition. An early example was Anderson (1973) who examined provision for physically handi-capped children in English primary schools. While this was in part an efficacy study, finding incidentally that ordinary schooling was academically and socially suitable for many physically handi-capped children, it also examined the components of the different forms of provision and how these related to the quality of education on offer. Birch (1974) described and analysed the mainstreaming programmes for mentally retarded pupils in six school districts in five states of America. The aim was to detail the unique qualities of each programme, documenting practical operation as well as theoretical principle, to show '*how* as well as *why* it works'.

A major recent study on mainstreaming has sought to build on the earlier efficacy studies by subjecting the programmes to detailed examination as well as comparing them. This is the PRIME project being carried out in Texas by Kaufman and associates. Reports on it have still to be published; Meyers *et al.* give an overview. Comparisons are sought between large samples of mainstreamed mentally retarded students, normal students and non-mainstreamed mentally retarded students. Outcome data refer to achievement measures and various social and personality indicators. A major part of the project however is to detail the characteristics of the programmes followed by the different students – in terms of amount of time integrated, size of groups, teaching given, other activities engaged in and so on – and relate these to both pupil characteristics and outcome data. This ambitious and complex project should provide information on how integration works in practice; if its findings lack the directness of earlier studies, this may be because they reflect the complexity of the real world.

Three British studies of significance have been published more recently and we would like to refer to them briefly. They are *Special Units in Ordinary Schools: an exploratory study of special provision for disabled children* (Cope and Anderson, 1977); *Toward Integration: a study of blind and partially sighted children in ordinary schools* (Jamieson *et al.* 1977); and *Nightingale Integration Project* (Kiernan and Kavanagh, 1977).

The first study was carried out by Christine Cope between 1973 and 1976 while based at the Thomas Coram Research Unit. The aims were to establish the extent of special provision for groups of phsyically handicapped pupils in ordinary schools and to evaluate such provision. The main effort was directed at primary level. An initial survey revealed that the number of special classes for physically handicapped pupils was extremely small. In order to evaluate these classes a comparison was made between the academic, social and behavioural functioning of 55 children attending them and a matched group of 55 children attending day special schools for the physically handicapped. Matching was done on the basis of sex; IQ; age; type of handicap; severity of handicap; and whether dependent on wheelchair or not. Outcome measures show that the attainments of the special class children were as good as (and in reading slightly better than) those of matched special school children. A great majority of children in both groups were by their own account happy at school. Special class children were found to have higher independence scores on tests of social competence. No significant differences emerged on behaviour scores.

Provision at secondary level was studied more briefly. Again, an initial survey sought information on the extent of provision in ordinary schools, in this case covering individual integration and campus sharing arrangements as well as special classes. An evaluation was made of the provision in 22 selected schools. This was not a comparative exercise but focused rather on the extent to which pupils were integrating and the adequacy of arrangements to meet their special needs.

The study is somewhat broader and more replete with insight than a bald description might suggest. The authors draw on their interview and observational material as well as the quantitative data to discuss the organisation of educational provision for physically handicapped pupils. Their concern is to relate this to the quality of educational provision in a direct data-based way. The burden of their evidence is that many more physically handicapped pupils could be educated in ordinary schools with no educational or social detriment – and in some cases with clear gains – and that special classes offer an alternative to special schools in many cases. They address the policy implications of this and offer a number of practical recommendations for setting up and running integration programmes.

The second of these studies (Jamieson *et al.* 1977) investigated provision for visually impaired pupils in ordinary schools. It was conducted at the National Foundation for Educational Research between 1974 and 1976. Coming in the wake of the Vernon Report (DES, 1972) which had comprehensively reviewed the education of the visually handicapped, the project team deliberately sought to be narrower and to concentrate on selected topics. Illuminative evaluation was espoused as the research approach. Indeed, the team saw the study as an opportunity to try out this approach on a larger scale than hitherto within education.

Just as the study did not have detailed goals at the outset but rather evolved them in response to clients' needs and emerging priorities, so the account that was written is not readily summarised. Within the general goal of contributing to the integration debate, five concerns were specified:

(i) to document developments in the integration of the visually impaired and the surrounding controversy; (ii) to investigate examples of integration programmes at work; (iii) to elucidate questions about classroom life when blind or partially sighted pupils are taught alongside those with normal vision; (iv) to explore the relationships between home and school; (v) to detail and examine a variety of policy concerns, and discuss a range of factual and philosophical issues associated with implementing integration.

This was done by drawing on a wide variety of interview and

some observational data. Case studies are presented documenting the educational experiences of four pupils. As well as giving a first hand account of the *experience* of integration, these demonstrate how numerous factors converge to shape an individual's schooling. The emphasis however is on combining descriptive with interpretive and critical comment. There is much detailed information about the practice of integration but an analytical thread runs through the whole. Assumptions underlying practice are clarified, different points of view juxtaposed and their implications for practice spelled out, and a wide range of issues raised by integration discussed.

The Nightingale Project (Kiernan and Kavanagh, 1977) was conducted in an outer London borough over a two year period from 1975-77. This was mainly concerned with developing and assessing language programmes for language handicapped children, with particular reference to generalisation from teaching sessions to other settings. It was also concerned with integrating such children into a normal school and devising ways of facilitating this.

A special class – Blue class – of six children was set up in a normal infant and junior school. All six had varying degrees of communication handicap, three of them coming from the local ESN(S) school. Their ages at the beginning of the project ranged from 4.4 to 6.11. The class was staffed by a teacher and full-time ancillary. Also, there was a researcher on site for four days a week.

In addition to the psychometric and observation data showing that the children made good progress in communication and other areas, detailed records were made via integration diaries of the nature and extent of contact between children from Blue class and other children in the school. There was a considerable amount of contact in fact. With one exception most of the children attended assembly regularly. They all joined their peers for play, though no details are reported. They took dinner as a group with one or two other children joining them. There were two forms of class time interaction: other children joining Blue class; and children going to other classes from Blue class. As regards the first of these, there were several arrangements: each morning two to four children joined Blue class for 1½ hours, doing language or craft work with the Blue class teacher while there; in the afternoon four children would join Blue class for PE, big toy play or going on an outing to the park; and a couple of older children came in to tidy up at the end of the day before Blue class children had left. Contact of this nature had been averaging nearly 9 hours a week during the study but settled down toward the end at about 6 hours. Blue class children also joined other classes, on a fairly minimal basis in four cases but for sizeable periods (3-8 hours a week and 9-16 hours a week) for the other two. One of the latter spent every morning in the reception class where he took part in all the normal infant activities; both of them joined the reception children for story at the end of the afternoon. When the others went along, once or twice a week each, it was in the company of staff from the Blue class.

The published report leaves many questions unanswered, but the experiment does show that even children with such complex needs as these can be educated and make good progress within an ordinary school. There was no effort at total integration, and the children received a great deal of individual attention within their own class, but they also spent much time with normal children.

The present study

The present study arose out of a commission from the Department of Education and Science to the National Foundation for Educational Research to carry out a study into the education of pupils with special needs in ordinary schools. Initial discussions had taken place in 1976 and a detailed research proposal was prepared in Spring 1977. Work commenced in Autumn 1977.

This fell between two significant landmarks in the special education scene in the 70's: the promulgation of Section 10 of the Education Act 1976 and the publication of the Warnock Report in 1978. Section 10 repealed Section 33(2) of the Education Act 1944: special educational treatment for those pupils requiring it should tend to be provided in ordinary schools rather than special schools. (Details in Appendix B.) Section 10 was never in fact implemented (and was superseded by subsequent legislation) and did no more than mark a change in emphasis since the 1944 Act allowed for special educational treatment to be provided in ordinary schools and the 1976 Act envisaged situations where the education of certain pupils in ordinary schools would be precluded on grounds of practicality, efficiency of instruction or expense.

Notwithstanding these considerations, Section 10 had a significant impact. It helped to focus the growing interest in the practice of integration. While this was welcomed by many, and especially parents, there was much concern about the possible effects on special schools and the capacity of ordinary schools to cope with large numbers of pupils with special needs. As a partial response to this concern it was felt that a study that documented and analysed existing integration programmes would be of use both in grounding the debate in the practice of integration and possibly allaying some anxieties thereby and in identifying the factors that make for successful integration.

The Warnock Report which was published while the study was in train had far-reaching effects on the whole practice of special education. Its comprehensive review of educational provision and resources for children and young people with special needs along with its detailed recommendations for practice has been a powerful stimulus for debate and action. It has moreover carried the debate about special educational needs into the education sector and indeed the public arena in an unprecedented way. A great deal of publicity attended its publication and teachers in ordinary schools, related professionals and the public at large have all become far more aware of the issues involved in special education. This new thinking and its widespread dissemination are relevant to a consideration of this study since the situation obtaining at the beginning had changed dramatically by the end.

The formal research brief was 'To examine in depth current provision for handicapped children in ordinary schools and to identify those factors which make for successful integration . . . The principal task of the project will be to carry out a detailed investigation of the various integration schemes set up by the co-operating LEAs'. It had been intended to carry out with the aid of teams set up by the LEAs taking part comprehensive monitoring and assessment of the development of pupils in these schemes. In the event, this did not prove feasible and it was decided to concentrate attention on structural and organisational factors, though some data relating to individual pupils were still collected.

In no sense then was this intended to be a comparative study. It has not sought to measure the efficacy of integration programmes in any precise way or establish the relative superiority of integration or segregation. In terms of the types of research outlined above, it is a mixture of descriptive and qualitative. It has documented a number of integration programmes in considerable detail and has analysed them along various dimensions relevant to practice. These dimensions derive in part from the data since a major concern has been to understand the provision in terms of the experience and ways of thinking of those directly involved in it, but theoretical considerations and established ways of looking at certain issues have not been ignored. Within this context, the effort has been to illuminate the process of educating pupils with special needs in ordinary schools and to make recommendations for practice. Close study of actual examples enables one to draw attention to the opportunities presented, clarify any constraints or problems that may arise, note extra inputs that may be necessary and discuss the implications for the schools as a whole.

To carry out this work 17 integration programmes in 14 LEAs were selected. The programmes varied enormously in terms of type of special needs catered for, age and number of pupils, organisation and number of schools involved. Special needs were categorised in terms of the statutory categories of handicap which prevailed at the time since this was how LEAs generally described provision. The main categories of handicap were represented, with the exception of Maladjusted (which was the subject of other studies at the time); the particular emphasis was on educationally subnormal and physically handicapped. Pupils' ages ranged from pre-school to 16+, with a slight preponderance in favour of the primary sector. The number of pupils involved in a programme ranged from eight or ten in a small special class to 100 or more in a large special centre or spread over several locations. The organis-ation of programmes involved links between special schools and ordinary schools, special arrangements made for a *group* of pupils with special needs in ordinary school, and the individual inte-gration of single pupils. Some programmes were confined entirely to a single school, though mostly drawing on a broader catchment area. Others involved a number of schools, sometimes covering an entire LEA.

Three programmes involved physically handicapped pupils: links between a comprehensive school and the secondary department of an all-age special school; a special department for some 40 physically handicapped pupils in a 13+ comprehensive;

and individual integration involving a large number of schools in an LEA, mostly at primary level but building up at secondary. Three programmes involved hearing impaired pupils: links between a comprehensive school and a school for the deaf (the special school was in the process of building up its secondary provision and the integration programme was in its infancy, so our study there was limited); a set of three special centres – infant, junior and secondary – catering for pupils with a range of hearing loss (about 60 in all); and the individual integration of 12 pupils, a mixture of partially hearing and severely or profoundly deaf at both primary and secondary stages. Six programmes involved ESN pupils: a special school for pupils with learning difficulties which timetabled some staff to work with primary school teachers so that they could better meet the needs of pupils in their classes; two large secondary departments – in separate authorities – catering for 60-70 pupils with moderate learning difficulties (and in one case a small number with severe learning difficulties) and also serving as the school's remedial department; a junior school with provision for pupils with moderate (7-11) and severe (pre-school to 11) learning difficulties; a set of five special classes catering for some 40 pre-school and infant age children with severe learning difficulties; and a set of large (80-120) secondary departments for pupils with moderate and mild learning difficulties (visits to these were limited). One programme involved visually impaired pupils: a resource area for 14 pupils in a primary school. Three programmes involved pupils with speech and language disorders, each comprising two or more special classes (6-10 pupils per class) at nursery/infant or junior stages. (Our study of one of these programmes had to be curtailed for reasons of time.) One programme involved infant age children suffering from developmental delay and frequently communication disorder as well; the special school which accepted these for short-term placement sought to place them in ordinary schools wherever possible.

The main research technique used was interviewing, initially loosely structured but becoming more focused as specific areas of concern and questions about them emerged. Initial visits to locations were essentially introductory and fact-finding at a comprehensive level. They entailed introducing the study and securing effective co-operation, obtaining an outline account of

The programmes can be represented in chart form as follows:

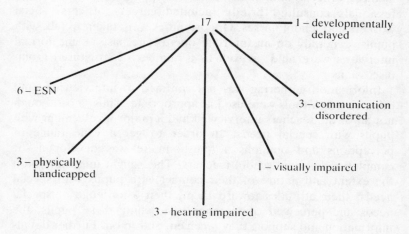

Category of pupil

17
1 – developmentally delayed
6 – ESN
3 – communication disordered
3 – physically handicapped
1 – visually impaired
3 – hearing impaired

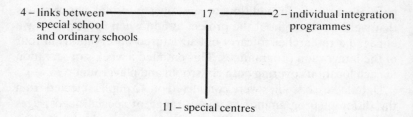

Type of programme

4 – links between special school and ordinary schools
17
2 – individual integration programmes
11 – special centres

the programme and the context within which it operated, identifying key individuals for subsequent interviewing and generally laying the groundwork for later fieldwork. Subsequent visits led to more specific questioning as a picture of the provision built up. Also, the emerging data from the different programmes interacted with and illuminated each other: issues raised in one location sometimes led to fruitful lines of enquiry in other locations that might not have arisen otherwise.

Interviews were held with teachers and ancillary staff in the schools, educational psychologists, advisers and education officers where they were involved, speech therapists, physiotherapists, medical officers and consultants, as appropriate. Other professionals consulted briefly included careers officers, social workers and school nurses. Opportunities were taken to talk with pupils, generally on an informal one-to-one basis; some formal interviews were held, as well as a number of structured group discussions.

Information gathering was not confined to interviewing, and other research tools were used as appropriate. Thus, most though not all of the teachers interviewed had a major involvement with pupils with special needs. In order to get a wide range of perceptions and opinions a questionnaire was developed for completion by main school teachers. This sought information on the extent and nature of their contact with pupils with special needs, their attitudes toward them, their knowledge of special needs and perceived competence in teaching these pupils, the information and support they received, and so on. Further details are given in Appendix C. A further questionnaire sent to integration programmes consisting of special centres in ordinary schools sought factual information on the service they received from educational psychologists, speech therapists, and physiotherapists. In addition to our own informal observations that went on throughout the project as and when appropriate, we engaged a researcher to carry out structured observations in four of the integration programmes. This entailed a week's observation in each location covering both classroom and playground.

Detailed case studies were conducted on 42 pupils selected from the different programmes to give a range of special needs, ages and extent of integration. Information was sought from their parents by both questionnaire and interview on their attitude to the integrated placement, their contact with the school and other agencies, and so on. A social development profile was devised for these pupils, covering various aspects of adjustment, independence, relationships with others and so on. This was completed twice by teachers with a nine-month interval to give information on pupils' social and emotional development.

PART TWO

First Steps

Chapter Three
Alternatives to Segregated Special Schools: Models in Practice

The challenge of educating pupils with special needs in the ordinary school can be met in many ways. In this chapter we look at different ways of describing the range of possibilities and put forward a schema within which the various arrangements can be located. We go on to discuss why LEAs chose to develop alternatives to segregated special schooling and how they opted for particular models of provision.

Models of provision

It will be clear by now that integration does not refer to a single form of provision. Educating pupils with special needs in ordinary schools poses a challenge which can be – and is – met in many ways. One can contrast the situations of a pupil at a special school attending an ordinary school part-time and a pupil attending an ordinary school full-time on an individual basis. There are many intermediate arrangements where specialist resources are provided in different ways within the ordinary school for groups of pupils.

Various writers have described these different possibilites. The cascade system (Figure 1) described by Deno (1970) is regularly cited. It was one of the first models to carry over into organisational structure the assumption that whatever different-from-the-mainstream kind of setting is judged necessary for a given pupil it must be based on *learning variables* and not clinical labels. It offers a model for a complete special education service. The tapered design reflects the numbers of pupils at the different levels (in American in the late sixties). Also, at each successive level the need for specialised facilities on a long-term basis is greater. The strength of this model is that it is based on assessement of

Figure I: *Range of special education provision (Deno)*

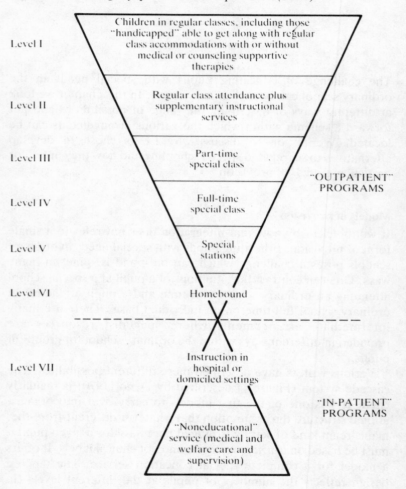

Level I

Children in regular classes, including those "handicapped" able to get along with regular class accommodations with or without medical or counseling supportive therapies

Level II

Regular class attendance plus supplementary instructional services

Level III

Part-time special class

Level IV

Full-time special class

"OUTPATIENT" PROGRAMS

Level V

Special stations

Level VI

Homebound

Level VII

Instruction in hospital or domiciled settings

"IN-PATIENT" PROGRAMS

"Noneducational" service (medical and welfare care and supervision)

educational need rather than traditional categories of handicap. Its orientation is one of tailoring treatment to individual needs rather than sorting pupils into pre-defined categories. Pupils are given supplementary instruction (Level II) or placed in a special class full-time (Level IV) because of an identified need for extra teaching, a highly structured environment or whatever, not because they are blind or physically handicapped or educationally subnormal.

Following on Deno, there have been various more detailed efforts to categorise special educational provision in terms of educational arrangements instead of categories of handicap. These are usually structured in terms of degree of separation from the mainstream. They imply a continuum from total segregation to the absence of segregation and pick out the main points along this continuum. Two examples are given in Figures II and III, from respectively Cope and Anderson (1977) and Gearhart and Weishahn (1976). These represent two efforts to schematise the range of special educational provision and outline the different forms integration can take.

Cope and Anderson's schema is notable for its relevance to the British context. Though devised with the physically handicapped in mind it can be applied more widely. The Gearhart and Weishahn schema is American in origin, and it is instructive to compare the two for the contrast offered and the illustration of the fact that any schematisation of services will reflect the prevailing range of provision and conceptualisation of special needs. It can be seen that the main difference between the two is that the American model offers a finer discrimination in terms of services *within* the ordinary school. This can be taken as a reflection of the greater diversity of service delivery within American special education. There has been greater pressure to educate pupils in the mainstream, and there has been more experimentation and a greater diversity of provision as a consequence. In Britain by contrast, the main alternatives so far to special schooling have been either special class placement or placement in the ordinary school with relatively little specialist attention. The reason for the paucity of alternatives are, as Cope and Anderson point out, largely historical: heavy investment in special schools discouraging the search for alternatives; a related under-resourcing of special classes when they were set up; and a presumption that such classes led to social isolation.

Figure II: *Range of special educational provision (Cope and Anderson)*

Suitable for *individual* PH children, placed in their *local* school.

1 — Ordinary class, no special help.

2 — Ordinary class + ancillary help on the care side.

Suitable for *groups* of PH children placed in a *selected* (adapted or purpose-built) ordinary school in which extra ancillary help, and speech and physiotherapy is provided.

3 — Ordinary class as base, + 'resource room' part-time

4 — Special class (base) part-time, ordinary class part-time.

5 — Special class full-time.

6 — Day special school formally linked (e.g. same campus) to ordinary school.

7 — Day special school, no such link.

8 — Residential special school

Figure III: *Range of special educational provision (Gearhart and Weishahn)*

Ordinary class placement, no additional assistance	1
Ordinary class placement with consultative assistance only from specialist educator	2
Ordinary class placement with consultation and specialist materials from specialist educator	3
Ordinary class placement with assistance from peripatetic specialist teacher	4
Ordinary class placement with withdrawal into resource room	5
Placement 'shared' between special and ordinary classes	6
Special class in ordinary school	7
Special class in separate day special school	8
Hospital/homebound service	9
Residential school	10

A further point emerges from considering the two schemas. This is that it is only in an imprecise way that one can speak of a continuum here. Whether it is couched in terms of separation from the mainstream, degree of association with handicapped peers, nature and amount of resources or whatever, one can do no more than point to an overall trend. There will be a clear line of progression from one end of the spectrum to the other but the direction may be reversed at intermediate points. For example, a pupil in a special class full-time (level 5 in Cope and Anderson's schema) may be more segregated and in receipt of more specialist resources than a pupil at a special school who attends ordinary school part-time (level 6). A pupil based on an ordinary class but withdrawn from time to time (level 3) may be more isolated from the mainstream than a pupil based in a special class but spending a great deal of time outside it (level 4). Gearhart and Weishahn do not really get round this. They offer a finer discrimination at one part of the spectrum. Referring to the special educator's involvement in an ordinary class placement, they show a continuous progression from level 2 (Consultative assistance only) through level 3 (Consultation and specialist materials) to level 4 (Assistance – presumably teaching/ treatment – as well as consultation). As well as overlooking ancillary involvement, which may or may not be present at each of levels 2, 3 and 4, they make no mention of the comparable refinement that might be made for withdrawal provision (level 5) that would entail considerable overlap with categories on either side.

The outline we propose seeks to get over these difficulties by acknowledging the multifarious nature of provision and accepting that any scheme of categorisation will have lots of overlap. It follows the others in its general outline of progression from integration with the mainstream to separation from it. Because of the many overlaps however and the fact that pupils at a given level may be either more or less 'integrated' – whatever criteria are invoked – than pupils at a different level, no effort is made to develop a hierarchy. A given type of provision involves different possibilities and organisational forms, and the important consideration is to be aware of the possibilities within a given organisational form. There are some similarities to the Cope and Anderson schema but differences arise partly from the fact that theirs is concerned primarily with the physically handicapped whereas ours reflects a wider range of provision.

Figure IV: *Range of special education provision*

A   Ordinary class, no support.
B   Ordinary class, support for teacher,
      support for pupil within class, care support.
C   Ordinary class, withdrawal for specialist
      work.
Di. Ordinary class as base, special centre part-
      time.
  ii. Special centre as base, ordinary class
      part-time.
E   Special centre full-time.
F   Special school part-time, ordinary school
      part-time.
G   Special school full-time.

As far as integration is concerned, the provisions of interest are types B to F. Type A (Ordinary class, no support) may be integration of a sort but it is not in general a means of meeting special educational needs. Unless a teacher has had some relevant background experience or is particularly favoured in some other way, the likelihood is that special needs of any complexity will go unmet, if not unrecognised. Type A is at best integration by default and for the present should be discounted as a means of meeting special educational needs.

The distinctive characteristic of type B (Ordinary class with support) is that resources are dispersed and brought to the pupil instead of being concentrated in one place to which many pupils with special needs are gathered. In general, the pupil attends a local – though not necessarily the neighbourhood – school. Here extra support over and above what peers receive is given. In the case of a physically handicapped pupil this may mean the constant presence of an ancillary helper; for a pupil with impaired hearing or vision it can mean occasional or frequent visits from a peripatetic advisory teacher depending on the severity of the sensory impairment; a pupil with a speech or language problem may be visited by a speech therapist. The ancillary helper will attend to pupils' care needs, frequently outside the classroom of course, but may have an instructional function as well. This can range from supervising walking exercises for a disabled pupil or implementing a programme of exercises drawn up by a physiotherapist, to working in the classroom to instructions from the teacher or speech therapist. The visitors may have a specific teaching purpose, sometimes tied in with ongoing diagnosis and assessment, or they may confine themselves to working with the teacher or ancillary. In other words, they have the option of working directly with the pupil, or working with staff to improve skills, increase sensitivity and so on so that they can deal more effectively with the educational problems that arise.

On the face of it this is the least segregative of all ways of meeting special needs. The pupil receives all the help he or she needs and is never separated from peers. Some cautions are necessary however. Receiving a high level of support within the classroom in full sight of one's peers can be intrusive and segregative in the extreme. It can in some instances serve to underline how different a given pupil is. Secondly, it is common experience that pupils' needs go unmet in this situation either because the needs are not recognised or, more commonly, because the requisite support is simply not available. If specialist resources are scarce, the implications of a dispersal policy must be considered. It may be noted that this type of provision was the subject of research by Anderson (1973). The general conclusion was that it was suitable for many severely physically handicapped pupils at primary age provided they had no specific learning difficulties.

Type C (Ordinary class, withdrawal for specialist work) operates to a resource model and allows for two main possibilities: withdrawal to a resource facility which is a permanent part of the school; and withdrawal for specialist help provided on a peripatetic basis. Which one applies usually depends on the numbers involved, the former occurring if there is a group of pupils in need of help, the latter if there is only one or two. This form of provision is relatively uncommon in this country. Type D (Ordinary class part-time, special centre part-time) encompasses the more usual form of integration in Britain, viz unit or special centre provision along with placement in an ordinary class. It is necessary to distinguish arrangements that have a special centre as base from those that have the ordinary class as base, since there are important differences of attitude as well as organisation associated with them, though the amount of 'integration' may be identical in both cases. Type E (Special centre, full-time) in many cases does not merit being bracketed with integration since pupils may be as isolated as if they were at special school. In some cases however there is a social contact and joint use of resources.

These three types of integration arrangement (C, D, E) usually entail a centralisation of resources in designated ordinary schools. In this respect they are intermediate between the dispersal of B where resources are brought to any ordinary school as required and the more total centralisation of F and G (Special schools). Groups of pupils who exhibit special needs are directed toward schools that have been specifically chosen as the location for the requisite resources. Depending on the particular needs there will be modification to the physical fabric of the school (e.g. installing ramps, lifts and differently textured flooring, modifying toilets and widening corridors, acoustically treating certain classrooms), and the development of a specialist area, class or department, within the school, appropriately staffed and resourced. Concrete details on the working of these different forms of provision in this country are hard to come by, partly because of the limited number of examples, partly as a result of the lack of systematic description and evaluation. As noted, type C (Ordinary class, withdrawal) is comparatively rare in Britain. Jones and Berrick (1980) offer a recent description of a resource model at work in a secondary school. Cope and Anderson (1977) report on research into the different types of unit or special centre provision in so far as physically handicapped pupils of primary age are concerned. Jamieson *et al.* (1977) have discussed various organisational approaches to the integration of vision impaired pupils. Garnett (1976) gives an account of ESN pupils attending a comprehensive school. The DES surveyed special units for hearing impaired pupils (1967) and for pupils with a variety of handicapping conditions (1972). The companion volume provides detailed descriptions of 14 different integration programmes that encompass a range of models of provision between them.

Type F (Special school part-time, ordinary school part-time) usually entails pupils who are placed in a special school and on its roll attending an ordinary school for part of the school week. (There are instances too of the reverse movement where pupils from an ordinary school attend a special school for a specific purpose, usually for a limited period.) This can be for various reasons: wider curriculum opportunities; better facilities for practical subjects; social contact and the general normalisation of experience. This arrangement combines access to the mainstream with availability of the specialist resources of the special school

It also is a relatively new departure in this country, though a good deal of experimentation is taking place.

Why integration

The research project on which this book is based incorporated examples of different kinds of integrated provision. Here we want to look at the reasons in practice why LEAs sought to develop alternatives to segregated special schooling. It is clear that within society at large and the education system in particular there are many pressures toward educating as many pupils as possible in the ordinary school. These were outlined in chapter one. The general factors such as, for example, the movement to desegregate minority groups can be very pervasive but they do not account for changes at a particular time and place. What we want to do here is to look at particular reasons why given LEAs opted to develop or expand their integrated provision.

Within the various authorities examined several distinct reasons for developing alternatives can be discerned. Two stand out in particular. The first is where an authority has articulated a policy for meeting special needs which embraces the principle of integration. This is not to say that all pupils will be educated in the ordinary school but that a plan is developed setting out the possibilities. Drawing up such a plan forces attention on the range of options and can lead to an awareness of new forms of provision. In one authority where it was decided that each secondary school would accommodate most pupils with special needs of various kinds within its catchment area it became clear that available resources and existing arrangements within the schools could be combined in rather different ways to lead to quite different forms of provision. Policies were not always formally worked out of course. One authority had had a comprehensive statement of policy for many years which was updated regularly. Another had a detailed plan for the different categories of pupils and was implementing it systematically across the authority. By contrast, a smaller metropolitan authority with a compact administrative structure while pursuing clear objectives and maintaining a wide range of provision did not possess a formal policy statement.

The second main reason for opting to educate pupils within the mainstream of education was an attempt to overcome existing inadequacies – either provision was lacking or it needed to be improved. This applied in several instances. In one authority all physically handicapped pupils had historically been provided for in an all-age special school. When a new head teacher was appointed in 1969 he quickly found pupils who, in his opinion, "could have managed in ordinary school". This, together with his conviction that prolonged special schooling only led to "multiple problems at 16 . . . they were pretty well educated but they hadn't really had the experience of relating to other people", led to his seeking to transfer pupils to their local schools. In the event, problems over access and other factors led to a decision to concentrate the transfer in a single school. In another LEA the impetus derived from the working of a Child Development Unit, a multi-disciplinary assessment facility for pre-school children. Over a period of two years this unit identified a group of children, some 34 in all, who although not considered intellectually handicapped were nevertheless retarded because of speech and language problems. The authority was faced with the problem of developing facilities for these children whose need for specialist attention was not being met under existing pre-school provision, and was unlikely to be met subsequently under existing schooling arrangements, whether ordinary or special.

A third authority, prior to the late 1960s, had little or no special education facilities of its own. Here it was a case of developing from scratch. There was no network of special schools in existence so the new arrangements quite naturally encompassed a range of integrated provision. Two other much larger authorities, while they could avail of residential provision, both within and out-county, were concerned to extend 'home' provision, and this too was done in an integrated mode. Provision for pupils with moderate learning difficulties in another authority offers an interesting variant. Special schools had been developed at primary level, on the assumption that extensive specialist remediation early in the child's educational career would remove any need for comparable provision at secondary school. Accordingly, pupils transferred on to ordinary schools, being placed either in ordinary classes or in remedial streams where these existed. The requisite resources for this bold move were lacking however and it was not successful. One LEA officer indeed described the results as "disastrous". As a consequence, the LEA embarked on a crash programme of day units attached to ordinary schools.

These then are the two most common factors behind attempts to mainstream. There are others. In particular, we identified: parental pressure; individual initiative; and a desire to experiment. The influence of parental lobbying could be discerned in several of the integration programmes we studied. For example, in one authority where physically handicapped children are integrated from infancy, an LEA official's summary judgement was that "the impetus has been parent-oriented . . . in conjunction with medical officers". Elsewhere, pressure was brought to bear by the local branch of the Society for Mentally Handicapped Children when Education assumed responsibility for those with severe learning difficulties in 1971. Parents took encouragement from the fact that the authority already had an innovative system of 'special opportunity classes'. In a third authority, profoundly deaf pupils had had to be sent out of the authority to continue their education at secondary stage. Growing parental concern at this was partly responsible for the LEA's decision to develop links between a school for the deaf and a neighbouring comprehensive. The authority had some unit provision, catering primarily for partially hearing pupils and operating on a withdrawal principle, but this was considered inappropriate for the profoundly deaf.

The consequences of individual initiative and vision are readily apparent throughout special education in this country. The practice of integrating primary age physically handicapped children in one authority reflects, in part, the strong convictions of a particular medical officer. She views this particular form of handicap as "purely a management problem" unless there is associated brain damage. Consequently, she considers there is no need to separate very young children from their families and indeed opposes it vehemently – "it is criminal to compound handicap with emotional separation". When residential placement was the norm for physically handicapped pupils she encouraged and supported parents who wanted their child to go to ordinary school. She also liaised with the schools, persuading them to give it a try and generally helping them cater for physically handicapped pupils.

A further example of the effect of individual initiative concerns the individual integration of severely and profoundly deaf pupils. An academic involved in the education of the deaf and the head of the school for the deaf combined forces to set up this programme. The former drew on experience of integration programmes in other countries and pointed to findings from surveys of units for partially hearing pupils he had conducted which demonstrated the poor attainments and limited social interactions of pupils attending them. The latter spoke of "the stigma that commonly attaches to special schools" and pointed out that "those with a hearing problem (should be) the last to be placed together . . . it is a negative situation in living terms . . . One slowly becomes abnormal . . . out of phase with community and behaviour patterns". The programme was in a sense experimental, to discover to what extent those with *severe* hearing loss can be integrated on an individual basis.

Another programme which illustrates this experimental aspect concerns a specialist resource developed in a comprehensive school. This provides for a varied clientele – pupils with learning problems, the physically handicapped, the mildly hearing impaired – and operates, quite unusually, to the 'resource room' model. Although the conviction held by those who were instrumental in setting up this provision is that every school should provide for all pupils within its catchment, perhaps the most notable feature is that it is regarded as an experiment on which to base future policy: "(Previously provisions) have tended to reflect the interests . . . of an individual head and the response of the authority to meet these . . . (we're) using (this) as a touchstone for county policy." (Principal educational psychologist). Close monitoring and analysis of this particular programme would provide detailed information to guide the further development of integrated provision in the authority.

Reasons for choosing particular forms of integration

We propose here to take each of the three basic organisational formats in evidence among the LEAs we studied: (i) individual integration whereby the pupil attends a school within the home neighbourhood and specialist attention is delivered on a peripatetic basis; (ii) special class or department, which may be largely self-contained or may operate along 'resource room' lines; (iii) special school as home base/resource centre. For each one we consider the reasons authorities gave for choosing the particular format.

(i) Individual integration

There were two such examples, catering respectively for the hearing impaired and physically handicapped. In each case particular individuals with strong convictions about the principle and practice of integration had exerted pressure on the authority to follow this particular course of action. These persons took the view that it was the right of every pupil to attend his or her local school – and that this was an implicit avowal of the pupil's 'normality'. Secondly, they argued that mainstreaming was educationally and socially superior. Thirdly, in both cases the numbers involved were fairly small so individual integration was organisationally feasible and would not lead to assimilation problems.

(ii) Special class or department

As noted, the special class or department was the most common format adopted. A variety of reasons were advanced by officials within the LEAs who had opted for this particular format. In some instances it reflected the need to provide for a *group* of pupils with special needs. This was so in one urban authority where a head teacher of a school for physically handicapped pupils identified up to 50 secondary age pupils who, in his opinion, were not being adequately provided for; in a second authority where a specialist assessment centre identified some 34 pupils over a period of two years whose overall development was retarded as a result of speech and language difficulties; and in a third where the LEA was concerned to initiate an area facility for children with severe learning difficulties. It also applied in an authority that had special schools for primary age children with moderate learning difficulties but little specialist provision at secondary stage. Finally, one authority had sought to apply the principle that every secondary school should have a specialist facility capable of meeting the educational needs of *all* pupils within its catchment.

Closely related to the above are two other considerations: certain handicapping conditions (notably, sensory impairment and communication disorder) require a concentration of resources; and specialist interventions in these cases may need to be intensive and maintained for a fairly lengthy period. Thus officials in two LEAs justified their choice of special classes on the grounds that without them there would be insufficient specialist help – particularly as regards speech therapy – and insufficient resources. If six children were scattered across six different schools the speech therapist or teacher of the deaf could not possibly provide the extent of individual and small group attention that could be given in a single morning if the pupils were in one place. Teachers of the deaf in one LEA were particularly adamant that if a pupil was to overcome the enormous educational handicap that severe or profound deafness generated, there was the most pressing need of prolonged specialist attention early in life to establish foundations for later learning.

A further reason that can be identified is individual preference. Thus, in one authority the then assistant education officer (special education) was extremely enthusiastic about the unit model, as long as certain safeguards were built in. It was most important that there should be the possibility of flexible exchange with the parent school. A unit or special centre allows the possibility of assimilation into the host school yet at the same time serves as a safeguard should a pupil being integrated meet with unexpected difficulties. Elsewhere a related argument was advanced. It was held that any group of pupils with special needs will exhibit a variety of such needs; further, that these needs may vary at different stages in pupils' school careers. A special centre is a flexible structure where such variations in needs can be easily handled. For example, a newcomer can spend all his or her time within the centre but can easily transfer to the main school when judged appropriate.

Closely related was the point made in one location, that integration – here meaning functional integration – was not necessarily appropriate for all pupils. Consequently a special centre needed to be large enough for it to be educationally viable for those pupils who spent little or no time in main school. Of course, a particular provision can be justified on several grounds. In the instance just quoted the need for some form of grouping was also a matter of hard economics – it was not possible for all, or even many, of those pupils' local schools to be suitably adapted to accommodate them.

(iii) Special school as base

Two of the programmes involved links between a special school and an ordinary school. Both involved secondary age pupils – with impaired hearing in one case, physical handicap in the other.

In some respects this can be viewed as the ideal arrangement: all the various strengths and safeguards which the special school – unlike many special centres – can offer; and ready access to the 'normal' environment and the broader facilities (e.g. curriculum, teaching resources) of the ordinary school. In fact this was the basis on which their proponents argued. There are potential costs to this arrangement of course – costs which stem from the fact that there are two separate establishments involved. Which school does the pupil relate to? Who assumes overall responsibility? How is the joint curriculum worked out and administered when there are two sets of staff involved? These and related issues can present considerable working difficulties.

Adopting this particular format stemmed in one case from the need for extensive medical and therapeutic resources, especially for the young physically handicapped child, rather than from any particular educational reason. The head teacher declared quite firmly, "There is no justification for this school on educational grounds. . . You have grouped scarce medical resources so that children are not going to miss too much (education) time" (eg in attending clinic appointments). As special educators "our real expertise is in making allowances for and overcoming the difficulties that these children have". Consequently, by secondary school age, when for many PH pupils the need for medical and therapeutic intervention will have lessened, there is a need to find some means of enhancing their educational opportunities. In the second example, the school for the deaf had retained pupils to the age of 12 at most. The majority then transferred out of county for their secondary schooling. Faced with mounting pressure from parents, the authority and the school were forced to consider alternatives. Developing a specialist secondary resource locally was not possible either on educational or economic grounds. Some form of joint enterprise with a mainstream school offered a solution.

Those involved in these examples spelled out the following advantages as they saw them. First, pupils had the possibility of following a wider range of academic subjects and receiving more extensive specialist subject teaching than could have been provided by a special school of itself. Secondly, retaining the special school as 'home base' was a valuable safeguard if something should go seriously wrong. The pupil could easily be withdrawn with a minimum of administrative fuss. Thirdly, special education staff were on hand to provide any necessary back-up for either pupil or ordinary teacher. Fourthly, in any negotiations with the ordinary school, the special school head would operate from a position of equal status – unlike a teacher in charge of a special centre who is under the jurisdiction of the head. This was held to be particularly important in the event of disagreement or disputes.

Fifthly, specialist support and back-up can be guaranteed on a continuous basis whereas a special class or peripatetic service can be crippled when a key member of staff leaves. Sixthly, not only was there ready access to a range of support services from the special school (eg physiotherapy, speech therapy, counselling) but the special school had the necessary status – and negotiating experience – to be able to arrange for or acquire less common specialist treatments. Seventhly the special school would have its own financial budget. Not only would this be on a more generous scale than that of the ordinary school, but it allowed of much more flexibility than did a special class which administratively was a department of the main school. Should a head not be particularly disposed toward a special class, it may find itself having to operate on a shoestring. Such problems do not arise in a special school which can guarantee that integrating pupils are well-resourced.

Chapter Four
Initiating a Programme of Integration

This chapter focuses upon the practical steps involved in establishing and maintaining a programme of integration. First, a suitable location must be determined. Then an approach must be made to the school about the possibility of its accepting pupils with special educational needs. The main part of the chapter documents the preparation – of school staff, pupils and their parents – to be done before a programme commences. Especially when seen in the light of what can go wrong, this suggests areas where improvements can be made. Finally, there is a brief consideration of what is entailed in monitoring and developing a programme of integration once established.

Selecting a location

It should be noted at the outset that there is a very real difference between integration which comprises pupils feeding out from a special school – which may be regarded as a means of enhancing pupils' education – and where it entails making full-time provision for pupils within an ordinary school, irrespective of how this is actually achieved. The two latter instances – a special class or department, or individual placement with peripatetic support – carry perhaps the greater risk, although the stakes are higher. It is these that we examine initially.

A critical factor in the choice of a 'suitable' school concerns the head teacher. The place that any new provision will occupy in a school will depend on the head's understanding of it and commitment toward it. The head is in a key position to foster any new development within a school – in the way of negotiating with outside agencies, allocating resources internally, shaping staff attitudes and generally facilitating its growth in the early days. It was clear from many comments that people did attach a great deal of importance to the role of the head. Indeed, some respondents felt this was the crucial factor. One authority, when canvassing for a location for a unit for partially hearing children, was pleased to find a school where the head teacher was "a very progressive sort of person". In another case, it was stipulated that what was wanted was "a roundness of character in the head in looking at problems and needs of children". Specific experience in special education was not generally required – though when present it was considered an asset – but rather a known capacity to respond sensitively to pupils' differing needs. In several instances schools were rejected from consideration because the head lacked enthusiasm or was not judged to possess the requisite qualities.

Given this, one would expect that candidates for headship appointments would be fully informed of special provision already in the school or due to be introduced to it, and that their views on it would be sought. We encountered several instances however where this had not happened. One newly appointed head of a small primary school discovered on taking up his post that the school was just about to acquire a language class for children with communication disorders. Though this had been planned for some time no mention was made of it at the time of the interview. While he was not opposed to the siting of the class at the school, he felt – not unreasonably – that it was a significant development within the school and should have been discussed with candidates for the headship.

Leaving aside such apparent oversights, it would seem reasonable to expect that the head be given full information on any proposed development and how it will relate to the school. Unless lines of responsibility are clearly laid down there is risk not only of confusion and conflict but also of limited commitment on the part of the head. As one head in this situation put it, "they are not *my* children". Another head sought clarification from the LEA on the extent of his authority over and responsibility for a special class in his school – "I would like to have it in black and white where I stand with this unit". Repeated failure to get a clear statement had left him somewhat dissatisfied.

Schools were selected also because they had "the right ethos" or were considered suitable along various different dimensions. For instance, various schools which housed provision for children with severe learning difficulties in one authority were considered to practise "good infant methods (of teaching)". A comprehensive school to which physically handicapped pupils were transferred after attending their neighbourhood primary schools was described by an LEA official as "the premier secondary school" in the district. Schools may be suitable in the sense that they have a stable staff and are not experiencing serious problems with their existing pupils, or in that they are centrally located and do not present particular problems of transportation. Finally, with some forms of special need the physical suitability of the school is critical. Thus physically handicapped pupils who are integrated individually in one authority generally attend their neighbourhood schools. It is perhaps fortunate that in the main these schools are physically suitable: most are on one level, and access is possible to any part of the premises; and no substantial modifications have proved necessary in any of them.

The notion of the 'good' school did not always pass unchallenged. Education officials in one authority spoke disparagingly of the lack of enthusiasm that heads and staffs in a number of primary schools had shown when they had visited in connection with the possible establishment of a new class for communication disordered pupils. Many of these teachers had seemed mainly interested in the able, middle-class pupil and did not wish to have handicapped or problem pupils cluttering their classrooms. The teacher in charge of an existing infant unit was able to reinforce this with an anecdote of her own. She told of a child whose need for specialised language treatment had diminished to the point where they contemplated transferring him back to his local school. In the event this school was not prevailed upon to take him because it was perceived to be over-concerned with standards of behaviour and educational attainment. Although the boy's behaviour was relatively 'normal' it could be rather erratic at times, while his educational performance although markedly improved was well below the norm for the school.

Similar points were made elsewhere about language classes and provision for pupils with learning difficulties. If the school had a certain number of low ability pupils then pupils with special needs were less likely to stand out as totally different. One authority sought to establish provision for pupils with learning difficulties in selected schools. In parts of the authority school catchment areas were relatively affluent and many schools set a premium on high academic performance. For the same reasons these schools were rejected from consideration in some instances.

What other grounds for selecting a school did we come across? A school may already be dealing very capably with pupils of its own who are experiencing educational difficulties. This was the case in a school which contained an unofficial 'language unit'. It was also true of a comprehensive school where the initial batch of pupils with moderate learning difficulties put up for transfer was perceived by the head teacher to be very similar to the school's existing low ability pupils. Again, a school may be considered appropriate because it contains a specialist facility of some kind, even though this may not be directly related to the particular needs of those pupils proposed for entry. For example, one physically handicapped pupil was placed in his local school because it contained two special classes which provided variously for delicate or mildly physically handicapped pupils and for those with moderate learning difficulties. In some cases schools had been chosen by default, in that they were the most acceptable of a number of generally unsatisfactory options. Thus in one school at which a large department for pupils with moderate learning difficulties had been located, the teacher in charge when asked why this school had been chosen thought that it reflected the disinterest shown by other head teachers in the area. The necessary space was available at this school and the head was not unwilling.

In conclusion, a word about the special schools engaged in building links with adjacent mainstream schools. Clearly, the choice of mainstream schools is likely to be circumscribed in the case of an already established special school. Our sample contained one such instance, a school for the deaf. Here the obvious choice was a comprehensive school close by. It helped that there was already a small link with the comprehensive (certain senior pupils came over to the special school as part of a 'community service' course), and that the head teacher of the comprehensive believed in integration. Where a special school is newly built then the choice of location, in theory at least, is much greater. One such example is provided by an all-age school for the physically handicapped. Here, an authority anxious to facilitate integration canvassed the views of the heads of all its comprehensive schools prior to deciding on a location for the new special school. The location eventually chosen offered space between two ordinary schools, one primary, one secondary. Moreover, the head teacher of the comprehensive was very positively disposed toward the principle of integration and had previous experience of integrated provision.

Approaching the school

The responsibility for the initial contact is usually the province of educational administration. Informal discussions and negotiations will generally precede a formal invitation to participate. The point of contact in the school is the head in the first instance who is left to involve and consult with staff as appropriate. It was our impression that relatively little prior consultation went on, and indeed teachers commonly had little expectation of being consulted. This could lead to negative attitudes, as when a teacher complained on behalf of colleagues about a provision that "had been forced on them whether they were interested or not".

As an example of a more constructive approach we describe the procedure used in one authority where hearing impaired pupils are being integrated on an individual basis. Selecting schools is handled in an individual fashion by the head teacher of the school for the deaf. Once he has a pupil in mind, the first task is to sound out the authority on the suitability of the pupil's local school. If there is no encouragement to go ahead then the matter will not be taken any further. Assuming a favourable response, he visits the school, outlines what is entailed and weighs up the head's reaction. "At this stage all I'm looking for is a sympathetic hearing." An opportunity to meet the pupil is then arranged. Beside conveying certain basic details to his colleague head, the head of the school for the deaf is concerned to appraise the quality of the school and the likelihood of general support for the placement. He is convinced of the importance of the latter and emphasises that all staff should have a say in the matter, not just the head and prospective class teacher. Next he will address the staff, giving them basic details but also the opportunity to question him about the purpose of the venture and how it will work in practice.

Assuming everything is favourable thus far, staff will be invited to visit the pupil concerned in his or her current provision, examine records and discuss any anxieties with specialist teachers. The final decision on whether to accept a pupil is left to the school. The head of the school for the deaf retires from the scene – "I want to hear what the decision of the staff is". He sees no point in trying to persuade or cajole; school staff must agree to take the pupil because they actively want to.

In this example, officials of the LEA have little involvement, being content to leave arrangements to those most closely engaged in the education of the deaf. The same holds true in another authority where physically handicapped pupils attend their local schools, though in this case there were no systematic procedures. Although the local school was automatically considered as the first option, it would sometimes be rejected because of the amount of physical alterations necessary or because staff in another school were judged to be more receptive. In the early days of the programme, representatives of Area Health joined with Education staff (notably the adviser for special education and an educational psychologist) in approaching a school, assessing its suitability and generally overseeing the placement. In the course of time these roles were taken over exclusively by Education staff. The most comprehensive approach we heard of here concerned a small infants school where – largely at the behest of the head – discussions were pursued on several occasions between head teacher, community physician, adviser for special education, educational psychologist and class teacher. It is unlikely that this would have occurred had the particular head not pushed for it. Committed to encouraging open discussion among his staff, he had been made aware of considerable anxiety – and in a few cases open hostility – when the idea was first mooted. He was anxious that this should be aired at officer level.

In some authorities educational psychologists are the de facto policy makers – usually in the absence of an adviser for special education. Thus, in one authority the possibility of setting up a language class in the infant school was initially proposed to the head teacher by the principal educational psychologist with whom she had a good working relationship. He in turn was operating on behalf of two colleagues, one a speech therapist, the other a consultant paediatrician. A number of children had been identified who, it was felt, "even with regular speech and fair cognitive ability were not going to succeed" in the ordinary school if they only received periodic attention from speech therapists. The head teacher verified that she had agreed to participate in the experiment, which she regarded as "a shot in the dark", largely because of her prior working contact with the psychologist.

However, the picture was not always positive. There were a number of instances where little or no consultation had gone between representatives of the parent authority and officials of a given school, where the potential difficulties had not been explored or the necessary back-up services considered. In several cases this led to enduring negative attitudes. While consultation can be overdone so as to inhibit action and people can use the lack of consultation as a convenient justification of their underlying hostility, there can be little doubt that well-judged consultation should be part of the initial overture to a school. Not merely is it courteous and professional to do so, but it can also draw attention to potential pitfalls in good time and lead to positive attitudes and a sense of involvement in what is proposed.

Preparing a school for integration

What is entailed in preparing a school to receive pupils who have special educational needs? We identify three major areas: preparation of staff; preparation of parents of pupils already attending the school; and preparation of the pupils themselves. (There is, in addition, sometimes a need for certain physical adaptations. This is discussed in chapter 10.)

(a) Preparation of staff

In order that the teaching of pupils with special needs is done most effectively, school staffs need certain basic information concerning the handicapping conditions and the likely educational consequences. They should be informed of agencies within the wider community to whom they might turn for advice or assistance. It may be necessary to adopt measures to counteract negative staff attitudes based upon misinformation or misperceptions. These are matters we return to and develop in subsequent chapters. (See chapters 7 and 19 in particular.)

Much can be done at the outset to ease the take-up of a

programme of integration. It was readily apparent that where integration had been carefully planned, definite benefits accrued. Take one small metropolitan authority, for example, which decided to build up unit provision for the hearing impaired. A new set of classes was opened in three different schools as an initial cohort of pupils moved through the educational system. In each case, the head teacher went on a week-long induction programme at the Department of Audiology in Manchester, designed with the concerns and responsibilities of the ordinary school head in mind. Each one spoke very positively about this experience. It had provided some basic knowledge about deafness and an insight into how this affected a child's education. More importantly, it alerted them to possible difficulties and areas of tension which could so easily arise but which might with a little foresight be avoided. They referred to such matters as the relations between the main school and special education staff and the amount of time that hearing impaired pupils should spend in ordinary classes.

They were particularly preoccupied with the first of these. "I don't think methods are as important as relationships" was one comment. A second referred to "the illusory cushy number" – that specialist teachers only had a small number of pupils to deal with – "It's important (this) be dispelled". Two of these head teachers had insisted that special education staff make some small teaching contribution to the main school – "It (helps) overcome the problem of the bolshy (ordinary) teacher". At the same time it was considered to "keep them in touch with normality". As regards the second aspect, the amount of time spent integrated, the view of one head was that "integration sometimes can be not necessary and not even very desirable". There were times when a pupil's need for extensive specialist attention and support must come first and this should not be jeopardised out of feeling obliged to have him or her spend lengthy periods in the ordinary classroom for sake of a formal commitment to integration. What mattered was that pupils were incorporated into the general life of the school wherever possible – "acceptance is the thing".

It would appear to have been the authority's intention that the individual head teachers would pass on their knowledge, information and insights to their respective staffs. This might have been judged impractical and in the event did not always occur. In the absence of any corresponding training for his staff, one head had arranged for the school to be closed for a day's in-service training. Staff were addressed by a range of experts in the education of the deaf, had a chance to voice their concerns and fears, and generally gained an understanding of how deafness can impede pupils' education. One aspect considered particularly useful was the invitation to heads of other schools that already contained hearing impaired pupils to talk about their experience – "teachers will listen to other teachers".

Preparation of school staff can also be taken as the responsibility of special education staff who are in situ and consequently in the best position to determine the anxieties and limitations of their non-specialist colleagues when dealing with special pupils. One head of a special centre who organised a course of five lectures for his colleagues also saw it as his task to communicate knowledge and ideas in casual conversation. This contrasted with another teacher's policy of giving colleagues a minimum of detail so that they would not be put off by the difficulty of the task: "Tell them very generally what they are going to need to know . . . don't innundate them with details." The remark of a colleague appeared to support this strategy: "Teachers of the deaf have to be very careful about making themselves special . . . We have always got to appear a bit ignorant . . . (in order to) elevate the classroom teacher."

We encountered a number of examples of careful advance preparation. One was where hearing impaired pupils attended their local schools on an individual basis. Here, the organiser of the programme makes a series of presentations each year on different aspects of the education of hearing impaired pupils. These cover common problems of deafness and their functional effect, details of equipment used, and information about specific skills such as lip-reading. These sessions are open to all staffs of schools which contain such pupils. This is in addition to the general address given to any school which accepts a hearing impaired pupil for the first time.

In a different authority the head of a primary school, when asked to accept a specialist resource for visually impaired pupils, took it upon herself to win the commitment of her staff – "If you accept a challenge it's up to you". Before the specialist resource opened she made several visits to existing special centres within the borough, discussed practical issues with a wide range of practitioners with experience of teaching the visually impaired, and searched out relevant literature. She arranged opportunities to discuss and communicate the knowledge she had derived and the insights she had had with members of her staff, as well as encouraging them to air their anxieties and concerns. In addition, various teachers visited special schools, and some went on a DES course on developments within special education at a local teachers' centre.

In a third authority an integration programme was established linking a school for the deaf and a neighbouring comprehensive school. Here too preparation remained largely in the hands of those most closely involved. The aim was to work toward pupils' assimilation into the ordinary school and foster feelings of competence among ordinary teachers. A teacher of the deaf with responsibility for liaison between the two schools was appointed one term before the first pupils started. She spent time with the head and various heads of department, giving information, seeking to reassure, clarifying what was intended from the venture, answering questions, and arranging for those who expressed interest to spend some time in the school for the deaf. Two other matters that were considered crucial were getting across the notion that ordinary teachers had a definite contribution to make – "let them feel they are partners" – and having teachers of the deaf accompany integrating pupils to lessons in the early days.

Useful lessons for future implementation can also be learned from past omissions. So it can be instructive to look at a few examples where there was little initial preparation. In one comprehensive school which made extensive provision for physically handicapped pupils there was very little in the way of an initial induction of ordinary teachers, either before the special department opened or subsequently. (This was partly because it was assumed this would not be necessary since pupils being integrated would all be of at least average ability.) In point of fact, some 50 per cent of those teachers who responded to a questionnaire stated that they did not know enough about handicap and felt that they needed better information. It was quite some time before this need was generally recognised, by which point the feeling was that it was too late: teachers were perceived to be too fixed in their ways of thinking about and reacting towards the physically handicapped for training to have much effect.

In another authority where physically handicapped children are placed individually in their neighbourhood schools, there was no initial induction or in-service training of any kind. In fact this has been a major limitation of the programme to date. On occasions something was retrieved from the situation, though in an ad hoc way. In one primary school, for example, where there had been little initial planning and no briefing of either head teacher or staff, the head took it upon herself to read around the subject and communicate some basic information to her staff. Elsewhere, the contribution of mothers of handicapped pupils – informing teachers of medical and management aspects – proved critical time and again. In one school a mother had worked alone; in another she has been supported by a community physician. These were accepted to be stopgap measures, the more so as there were sometimes glaring gaps in the information communicated and there was danger of misperceptions and incorrect handling procedures being passed on.

(b) Preparation of parents

Educating a sizeable number of pupils with special needs in an ordinary school must lead to changes within the school. It may be judged necessary to make a formal announcement to parents with children at the school and engage in some preparation. Apart from the courtesy of letting them know of an important development in the life of the school, such steps can help allay anxieties and scotch rumours that their own children may miss out because of the presence of the handicapped. It may seem odd that a development that extends the school's educational possibilities should be seen in terms of a threat to standards, but these concerns are widespread and should not be taken lightly. More positively, parents can come to endorse the work of a special centre and lend their support to it if appropriately involved from the outset.

There was little evidence in the majority of programmes visited of efforts to inform parents in advance. Where there was preparation however it tended to be extensive. One primary school was exemplary in this regard. The head teacher maintained that "parents can do a great deal of harm through ignorance . . . If you can answer their fears then they are always ready to support". Accordingly, some months before the first visually impaired children were to start she called a meeting of all parents of existing pupils. She and the educational psychologist made a joint presentation, including relevant slides, and asked parents for their support. She felt their action had been amply rewarded – "the parents are very much for it". Besides being committed to the right of these children to attend an ordinary school, the local parent-teacher association raised considerable sums of money for the purchase of specialised resources.

Another head took a different line. When the first special class was being planned for her school she sent a letter to every parent informing them about it and reassuring them that it would not lead to any lowering of standards. If any parent was concerned he or she was invited to visit and discuss it. This approach was subsequently revised when the class became established. Now the parents of each new intake meet up on one or more occasions. They are told about the special class and can visit it if they so desire. The head claimed that there had never been any objection; rather, parents would say, "What a good idea". . . "that's the way it ought to be". Another school in the same authority has recently adopted a similar approach. Here a coffee morning is held for mothers of the new intake to which parents with children in the special class, the children themselves and their teachers are all invited.

It should be noted that there is a counter-argument to the effect that formal advance preparation only singles out pupils and militates against their eventual acceptance. A number of heads claimed that they preferred to introduce special provision in a low-key way and refrained from making a formal announcement so that pupils with special needs would not have a distinctive identity. Some heads made a distinction in the terms of type of special need: they might make formal preparation in the case of type of 'less stigmatising' handicaps such as sensory impairment or physical handicap but would certainly refrain from doing so where provision for maladjustment or learning difficulty was concerned.

(c) Preparation of main school pupils

Preparation of pupils already at school tended to be limited. One school had a unique opportunity in its CSE Community Studies course. This contained a term-long block on Handicap, consisting of a general introduction to handicap followed by a more detailed look at specific conditions – mental, physical and sensory. Some pupils with physical handicaps themselves take the course. The teacher involved claimed she had not been aware of any embarrassment on the part of either these or the able-bodied. The latter had responded favourably and were considered to have developed a matter-of-fact attitude to handicap which led to ready acceptance of physically handicapped peers when they joined the school in large numbers.

A more informal approach obtained in another comprehensive school attended by pupils with severe learning difficulties. Here, a number of main school pupils came into contact with the pupils who had special needs through taking a CSE Child Care Course. Otherwise pupils learned about those less fortunate than themselves through direct association – there were opportunities for them to help out informally within the special department. Additionally, some non-examination pupils from the main school spent time within this department where they engaged in various practical activities, such as working on clay modelling with one or two pupils there.

A more definite line was taken by the head teacher of a comprehensive school attended by hearing impaired pupils. Anxious not to overplay matters, thereby making them stand out more, yet convinced that positive action was necessary, his approach had been to prepare pupils "very gently through the medium of assemblies". Two primary heads also saw assemblies as a natural opportunity for seeking to influence pupils' attitudes. One of them remarked: "I told them stories about handicapped people, about the kind of problems they have, about the ways in which they will need help". Her counterpart took the line that different children have different gifts and disabilities – some can't walk very fast, others can't learn very easily. Accordingly, there is a need to help them, be kind to them. She noted that this had to be done carefully and in a relaxed, non-formal manner – "It mustn't be a forced situation".

This was taken further in two secondary schools. In the first, which houses a special department for pupils with moderate learning difficulties, the teacher in charge had at first maintained a low profile because he did not want staff and pupils from the main school to perceive the department as something special. Subsequently however he was prevailed on by a number of main school staff to address first year pupils. These teachers "felt they couldn't explain" what the department's function was. They felt that pupils "needed reassuring", particularly as some of them had come from a feeder school which contained a special class that operated as a segregated unit and they were accustomed to seeing pupils with learning difficulties as quite different from themselves. The teacher in charge eventually agreed with this and addressed the first year pupils. He began by talking about handicap in general: people have all sorts of difficulties – some can't ride a bicycle very well, others can't read or write very well. "Our job is to help those who need it." The presentation lasted for about twenty minutes. There was great enthusiasm at what this had achieved. Several pupils came up at the end and asked if they could have help with their reading or number work. The following year a different approach was tried. Each first year form was invited to visit the department with their teacher. They were shown around, informed of its purpose, met staff and chatted with the pupils who were already receiving assistance, were told that they would be welcome any lunchtime to come in and use the facilities (eg, pool tables) and that if they met any difficulties with their schoolwork then they could come over and ask for help.

Another teacher in charge of a similar special department described an explicit preparation she had carried out in respect of a pupil with epilepsy. She had gone along to the form in which the boy would be placed, described his condition and what could happen, and even had a pupil simulate a fit so that the others in the class could practise what to do. When the boy came and had his first – fairly mild – fit the reaction of classmates was one of some disappointment that he had not remained unconscious long enough for them to carry out all their procedures!

We conclude our look at getting a scheme of integration under way by recapitulating the various stages of preparation involved.

- An appropriate school must be selected – appropriate in regard to such factors as internal organisation, attitudes of head and staff, physical suitability (possibly given certain modifications), staff stability, and location for transport purposes.
- The head teacher needs to have a good understanding of what is entailed, be positively disposed toward it, and be in a position to give time and effort to initial planning and early implementation.

– Staff of the school must be consulted for their views on accepting such pupils and also given information and guidance. They will need to know what is entailed in the proposed venture and how they will be affected by it. They will need information on the special needs that the proposed pupils have, the implications for lesson content and teaching practice, and the existence of outside agencies which may be able to offer assistance. Some such preparation of staff should be done in advance of pupils' entry into the school and should involve all staff.

– Pupils should be informed along the lines described – in a matter-of-fact, sensible but sensitive manner. They should be helped to see that individuals differ in many ways and that special needs are not the uniquely distinguishing characteristics that they are often supposed to be. They should be encouraged to accept and have contact with those less fortunate than themselves.

– For their parents it is appropriate to call a meeting at which the new development is explained and they have an opportunity of raising matters which worry them. The chance for them to meet with both parents of pupils with special needs and the pupils themselves is also a help – in some such forum as an open day for all new entrants.

What can go wrong

As will be clear from the above, initiating an integration programme is fraught with difficulty and things can very easily go wrong. This is all the more likely when new ways of working are being developed and there is little experience of existing practice to draw on. We want to document here some of the deficiencies in practice that we encountered, deficiencies it should be noted that are far more evident with the benefit of hindsight; as one head involved in an integration programme since the early '70's pointed out: "Everyone is ignorant of what is needed initially".

1. Pupils arrive before the necessary physical alterations have been made.

Certain physical alterations – ramping, toilet adaptations and so on – are usually necessary in order to accommodate physically handicapped pupils. These are generally of a minor nature, yet frequently we found pupils had been in school for considerable periods of time before the requisite alterations were carried out. Toileting arrangements were a particular problem and some pupils had to make do with inadequate facilities. The necessary alterations were generally simple and relatively cheap to effect. What was lacking in some instances seemed to be an awareness of the needs and a coordinating agency to ensure that needs were identified and any necessary work carried out in good time.

2.   School staff were not informed.

There were several instances where head teacher and staff of schools chosen to house some form of special provision had not been informed of the fact beforehand. Apart from the failure in courtesy, this is hardly conducive to good relationships or assimilation of the pupils with special needs into the school, not to mention functional integration. One school which subsequently received a language class for children with communication disorders received no advance information. The staff heard vague rumours about some form of special provision but had understood that it would be concerned with children of ethnic minorities. They had not anticipated receiving children who exhibited behaviour problems nor children whose language problems were so pronounced. The adjustment to expectation made necessary did not help the early assimilation of the language class.

In another case the head of a comprehensive school claimed to have first learned about plans to locate a sizeable special department at his school through a chance remark made by an LEA official. Being favourably disposed toward integration he had not seriously queried the matter. He was subsequently to regret this. All manner of difficulties arose: he felt he was being urged by the parent authority to promote integration and yet the authority had failed to specify the purpose behind the proposed integration, or how it might be achieved; little account was taken at first of the fact that the school was already overcrowded and under-staffed; and actions which were carried out were frequently done without prior consultation – for instance builders arriving unexpectedly to carry out building works.

3.   The nature and status of the programme was not made clear to those involved in it.

Some teachers remained uncertain after several years of running a programme whether it was a stable part of the authority's provision or an experiment that might be terminated at short notice. Some teachers were quite aggrieved at the way they had been continually left in the dark on this matter: "We would like to know exactly where we stand". One teacher implied that the failure to communicate clear guidelines resulted from the authority's own uncertainty about the purpose of the programme: "I wonder how much they are setting up integration because it is the expected thing to do and how much . . . because they have thought it through".

4. Initial support was not maintained.

Once the provision was established, LEA officers who may have played a central role in establishing it tended to retreat into the background. Their presence was less necessary and they had many other commitments on their time. In some cases the retreat was total however. Staff never saw them again except perhaps when showing visitors round 'their' provision and they felt isolated and unsupported as a consequence. A few were quite satisfied to be left to develop the programme without interference, but most would have welcomed a continuing indication of interest and support on the part of the authority.

Monitoring the programme

It may be thought premature to include monitoring arrangements here but it is important that thought be given at the outset to the monitoring both of individual pupil's progress and the development of the programme as a whole. Even when a programme has been planned in detail and implemented with care, there is a limit to the amount of planning that can be done before it starts. It will be necessary to monitor the programme in action not only to ensure that it is on target and objectives are being met but also to take account of emerging developments. The adequacy of support for ordinary teachers, the amount of classroom integration that is possible, the need for involvement of external agencies – these and many other factors need to be scrutinised in the light of experience. Numerous examples could be cited where initial arrangements were seen with hindsight to be quite inadequate. In order to become aware of these and respond to them in a constructive way it is necessary that the programme is subject to continual monitoring and evaluation.

Such monitoring can be done by people outside the school or by staff actually working within the programme. Ideally, external and internal perspectives would combine to form a coherent overview. It is unlikely in many cases however that there will be people available outside the school who have the requisite time and expertise. The study of LEA advisers by Bolam *et al.* (1978) suggests that the advisory service can offer only limited help in this regard, while other agencies are even more restricted. In effect, if sustained monitoring is to be carried out the chances are that it will have to be done within the school.

Such internal monitoring is subject to certain weaknesses but has a number of strengths as well. Staff may be too immersed in the local situation and have difficulty in putting it in perspective. They may be too busy doing the job to find time to reflect on how they are doing it. They may lack the expertise or the means to monitor the programme in any systematic way. On the other hand, their closeness to the programme gives them an advantage over any outside evaluator. They have an intimate knowledge of its working, and if they are doing a review for their own purposes they should be free of the temptation to highlight the successes and gloss over the weaknesses.

Self-evaluation by schools has grown in popularity in recent years and a number of authorities have developed schemes for carrying this out. Self-evaluation documents have been produced that detail how the exercise is to be done, specify questions to be asked and information to be gathered. These documents are frequently used in a context of accountability. The other context here however has to do with the *development* of a programme and the gathering of information that will foster that development. While this may go hand in hand with generating accountability data, it is a separate enterprise and one that is more closely related to the teachers' professionalism. In certain cases indeed, as when things have gone badly wrong or there are difficulties in personal relationships, it may be best pursued away from the public gaze and demands for accountability.

What can be borrowed from the self-evaluation movement however is the importance of having a structure to guide the monitoring process. This will help to make it more systematic, guide observation and reflection, and draw attention to features that might otherwise be overlooked. Moreover, such a structure can provide a means of standing outside the immediate situation and asking the questions about it that an outsider would ask. When this perspective is combined with the intimate knowledge of the local situation that permits detailed answers to the questions, the result can be a reflective awareness of the developing programme that will not only keep it on course but will also ensure that emerging opportunities are availed of in a positive way.

Since educating pupils with special needs in an ordinary school has implications for the whole school the questions to be asked must correspondingly range over the whole school. An outline of some of these questions is given in Hegarty (1980). Thus, the questions to be asked cover: staffing – specialist teachers, ordinary teachers, ancillaries, external specialists and training; teaching and curriculum planning; pupils' social and emotional development and their interaction with peers; the practicalities of accommodation and transport; home/school contact and parental involvement. It is planned to give a more detailed account of these in a pamphlet which will be published separately.

PART THREE

Staffing

Chapter Five
Staffing of Special Centres

The central resource for an integration programme is its staff. When integration takes the form of a special centre attached to an ordinary school, as in most of the programmes we studied, the staff of that centre occupy a key role. So in this chapter we discuss the staffing of the special centres in our study before going on in the next to consider the roles carried out by the individuals in post. We begin with an account of staffing levels, and then report on various characteristics of the teachers and ancillaries in these special centres. We also consider the selection criteria advanced by which suitability for working in special centres was determined.

The material in this and the subsequent chapter is based primarily upon interviews with 52 teachers. These interviews varied in length and duration, some of them extending over more than one session. Certain specific information of a basic kind was obtained from everybody; where the situation warranted it or where matters of particular interest arose, more detailed information was sought. Supplementary details came from head teachers and other staff and from our own observations.

Staffing levels

The distribution of staff and pupils in the special centres is given in Table I. Three comments are necessary about this table. First, many of the programmes under study were in a state of development and changed considerably during the course of our study; any simple description must consequently be a compromise. We have elected to report the circumstances that obtained midway through our study. Secondly, the staff/pupil ratio varied very considerably from programme to programme and the ratios presented here can in no way be regarded as normative.

Table I: Pupil numbers and staffing levels of special centres

Type of special need and age range covered	Number of pupils	Staff	
		Teachers	Ancillaries
Moderate learning difficulties			
1 (primary)	40	3	1
2 (secondary)	65	5	1
3 (secondary)	67	4	1
Severe learning difficulties			
4 (primary)	35	5	4
5 (secondary)	13	3	1
6 (infant)	17	2	4
7 (infant)	7	1	2
8 (infant)	8	1	2
9 (infant)	6	1	1
Hearing Impairment			
10 (infant)	15	4	3
11 (junior)	23	4	2
12 (secondary)	28	6	2
Visual Impairment			
13 (primary)	14	3	2
Physical Handicap			
14 (secondary)	40	6*	5.5
Communication Disorder			
15 (primary)	19	2	2
16 (infant)	6	1	2
17 (infant)	6	1	1

* Five further posts were added to this school's staffing establishment, taking account of the eventual target of 60 pupils with physical handicaps.

Doubtless, people who work in similar situations will want to see what staffing arrangements other people are working to and make comparisons with their own situation. It should be emphasised however that the staffing complements in the various programmes correspond not merely to the special needs being catered for but to a variety of local factors as well. These include: the extent of existing provision; different relationships with the parent schools; and differing conceptions of the job to be done and demands to be met. Thirdly, in some instances only an estimate is feasible, based on full-time staff and pupil equivalents. This arises in various ways: special education staff may have teaching and other commitments in the parent school, or indeed staff of the parent school may spend time in the special centre; and main school pupils may spend a considerable proportion of their time with special centre staff for remedial or other purposes. In some cases where people are specifically appointed to carry out tasks that cross the divide between special centre and parent school there is no clear line between the two sets of staff.

As would be expected, the provisions for pupils with severe learning difficulties, communication disorder and visual impairment all had high staffing ratios. They compared favourably with the ratios suggested in Circular 4/73. Such high ratios can be seen as a direct response to identified need, together with a determination on the part of LEA officers and/or head teachers that, at least as far as staffing is concerned, these new forms of provision would not be to the children's detriment. Some of the other provisions have higher ratios than one might expect, ratios indeed that compare well both with Circular 4/73 and with those obtaining in special schools. Again this could sometimes be attributed to identifiable local factors: LEA policy to make generous staffing provision; particularly determined head teachers; special centres which were building up to establishment slowly, or falling below assigned quotas of pupils.

The only dissatisfaction expressed came from some staff working with pupils with moderate learning difficulties. On the face of it, the ratios did not seem untoward. Two considerations need bearing in mind however: these schemes were all in early stages of development; and the staff in question often had additional duties involving pupils other than those to whom they were formally assigned. On both counts the simple ratios reported are deceptive. Initial organisation, curriculum development and – in some cases – public relations work can absorb a great deal of time. Implementing a programme of integration can generate a great deal of extra work that makes conventional estimates of teacher/pupil ratios misleading.

As well as special centres we looked also at some programmes of integration whereby individual pupils were being placed in classes in ordinary schools. These involved physically handicapped and hearing impaired pupils respectively. For the former it was LEA policy to provide a welfare assistant where necessary. This had been interpreted relatively generously by the LEA: many of the pupils we saw had the services full-time of a welfare assistant, while others – usually in schools where there was more than one pupil in question – received extensive help from a welfare assistant. As regards the hearing impaired, they were directly assisted by 'support teachers' working under the supervision of teachers of the deaf. The amount of support time available in this way varied with the individual pupil's age, extent of hearing loss and educational need. Moreover, support teachers did not always confine themselves to the hearing impaired pupils but made their services available to the other pupils in the class. Again, the allocation of time was generous, each support teacher being engaged for a maximum of two hearing impaired pupils. In all there was the equivalent of 6.1 full-time teachers, three of whom were qualified teachers of the deaf, for the 12 pupils in this programme.

Quite different considerations were raised in those programmes involving links between ordinary and special schools. This involved four locations, dealing respectively with physically handicapped, hearing impaired, developmentally delayed and learning disabled pupils. These programmes had different objectives and ways of working. The amount of staff time committed to the integration component of the programme varied accordingly. In each case a specific time allocation was made. The nature and adequacy of this are discussed below.

Not surprisingly perhaps, there was relatively little dissatisfaction over staffing ratios. As noted, the staffing arrangements in our sample seemed quite generous. This apparently had not always been the case, however. We learned of several instances where a great deal of effort had been necessary to bring staffing up to a level considered acceptable by those involved, though this was by no means a general problem; as mentioned, several authorities held very positive attitudes toward staffing.

The fact that schools and individuals had in some instances to struggle quite hard to attain what they considered a reasonable staffing level does raise important issues. When this happens, the ratio achieved will depend on (a) the individual concerned knowing what an appropriate staffing level would be, and (b) his or her ability to persuade and exert pressure. As regards the first of these, the individual teacher is very dependent on past experience of meeting special needs and where this is limited may be unaware of the possibilities; he or she may in consequence be happy with a staffing ratio which precludes undertaking certain activities simply because of lack of awareness. Clearly, the person on the spot should have a say in deciding on the staffing needs of a given situation, but it should not be so dependent on the individual that important possibilities are neglected through this person's lack of experience.

While an informed advisory service can play a crucial role here, there are steps that the individual teacher or school can take to compensate for lack of knowledge. As part of the planning of a resource centre in a primary school, one head teacher made enquiries from a neighbouring special school as to appropriate staffing levels (and many other matters as well). In other cases heads or teachers-in-charge visited a range of existing provisions while engaged in planning their own.

Assuming an appropriate staffing level has been determined, there remains the problem of implementing it. This is ultimately a matter for decision by the Education Office. If an authority is totally unwilling to agree to a requested staffing level or to improve on a staffing allocation, there is very little that the individual teacher or school can do. Our experience suggests however that total intransigence is relatively rare and that defeatist attitudes are unwarranted. Officers do respond to overtures, decisions can be reversed, sometimes even policy can be changed. We encountered several instances of schools achieving good staffing levels by persisting in their demands for more staff and refusing to give up until their requirements were met. This can be a drawn out process, entailing arguing one's case repeatedly and to different people, enlisting support from various colleagues, sometimes putting the case in terms of the school as a whole and not just the special centre.

This does raise a broader issue to do with the allocation of scarce resources in general (i.e. not just staff). Education authorities do not, on the whole, have formal policies that would guide such allocation in detail. Indeed many would argue that such policies are not in any case feasible except in very broad outline. Given this, there is serious danger of inequitable distribution. There was evidence to suggest that on occasion those who shouted loudest or were most persistent got disproportionately favourable treatment. This can have serious implications when there are tight financial constraints. Attitudes on this matter varied enormously. One teacher summed up his stance thus: "I'm concerned for *my* children – it's up to others to fight the battle for theirs". Another quite rejected this view, regarding it as "a law of the jungle" where only the fittest survive. There would seem to be a strong case for developing procedures that give everybody the fairest deal possible regardless of their campaigning skill, nuisance value or whatever.

Teacher characteristics

The teachers in our sample varied enormously in personal characteristics, in backgrounds and experience and in their motivation for taking up this work. There was no clear career pattern by which teachers elected to work in special centres. While certain features emerged as highly desirable, one would be hard put to construct an identikit teacher for the job! What they did share perhaps was an enthusiasm for the job and a level of motivation that went well beyond what might have been expected. The evidence presented below suggests too that their training and commitment to on-going training were well above average.

Predictably perhaps, the sample was skewed in terms of sex, containing three times as many females as males (13 male and 39 female teachers out of a total of 52). Only two male teachers were working in primary schools. There was a more even distribution between the sexes in the secondary schools, something regarded as important by many heads of department. In one secondary school, for example, there were only two male teachers (one of whom left during the course of our study) out of a staff of seven; this was perceived as undesirable, putting extra pressure on the sole male remaining.

We did not collect data on age but the group as a whole was quite young. This is worth noting in the context of occasional comments about the lack of flexibility of some older teachers. One head of a school which contained a small number of individually integrated pupils felt there was a clear division between his staff simply in terms of age; the older ones while sympathetic in principle were unaware of the real problems and for that reason less able to respond, while the younger teachers who would have had at least a token introduction to special education in their initial training were more aware of the highly individual needs of such pupils.

The major professional characteristics examined had to do with teacher training and previous experience. Teacher training is discussed in chapter nine. Here we note that teachers in our sample had engaged in a wide variety of training courses. Out of 52 teachers, 9 had concentrated or taken a major option on some aspect of special need in initial training while 31 had taken courses of at least a year's duration covering various aspects of special and remedial education. (It should be noted that 17 of the latter taught pupils with sensory impairment where training was obligatory.) Staff had also taken a great many short courses, largely out of their own initiative.

As regards previous teaching experience, four groups of teachers can be identified: those who had taught in special schools only; those who had taught in ordinary schools only; those who had taught in both special schools and ordinary schools; and those with no previous teaching experience. The distribution of teachers in our sample across these groups was as follows:

Special school only	13
Ordinary school only	22
Special school plus ordinary school	6
No experience	11

i. Most of the teachers who had taught only in special schools worked with either hearing impaired pupils or those with severe learning difficulties. They had acquired specific training or had built up experience with these pupils. Some were appointed because they possessed the experience and skills that were needed to supplement the teaching strengths of a particular set of staff.

This can be assumed to have implications for integration. The pupils may need highly structured teaching which is best provided by teachers with appropriate training and experience, but if the integration opportunities are to be availed of staff must have appropriate skills there also. We note below the defensiveness in respect of lack of ordinary teacher training expressed by some teachers. The same defensiveness can arise from lack of ordinary school experience. (It may be added that many of these teachers were quite young and did not have children of their own of school-going age.) In point of fact, opportunities for integration were poorly availed off in those locations where the majority of staff had no ordinary school experience. This was for a number of reasons but one major one was the limited background of the teachers.

This is not a criticism of these teachers so much as of the situation in which they found themselves. Many were in our judgement doing excellent work but would themselves readily acknowledge the problems arising out of this limitation in their professional background.

ii. The largest of these sub-groups comprises those whose teaching experience was confined to ordinary schools. Apart from eight who had taught for two years or less, most had considerable experience. Seven of the 22 were still in the schools where they had done most of their teaching, having either transferred to a special centre when it opened or returned to one after training.

Most had worked as classroom teachers in the ordinary way, sometimes with a particular interest in pupils with special needs, until – for various reasons – they became involved full-time with such pupils. For a few however this mainstream experience had been far from ordinary, and served as an excellent apprenticeship for specialised work with pupils who had special needs. We provide case histories which illustrate this.

Henry is a teacher in his early forties who has charge of a secondary department for pupils with a range of learning difficulties. Originally he trained as an ordination candidate but he transferred to teacher training, taking a Certificate of Education in English and Biblical Studies. His first teaching appointment was in a secondary modern school where he taught mainly Religious Education. Over a three year period he found himself moving toward working with the remedial pupil. He was subsequently appointed to the remedial department of a comprehensive school and during the next three and a half years worked his way up to being second in the department. His next appointment was as head of department in another comprehensive school. During this period he studied on a part-time basis for an Advanced Diploma in the Education of Children with Special Needs. After a further three years he transferred to his current position.

Catherine is teacher in charge of a special resource for children with impaired vision. She began teaching "many years ago"! Untrained at first, she quickly undertook teacher training. After a break from teaching when her children were growing up, she returned to teaching initially in a part-time capacity and later on a full-time basis. She began at her present primary school some 10 years ago.

What was described as a "major challenge" arose with the introduction of team-teaching when a new head teacher took up appointment. At first Catherine had found this extremely difficult since her long experience was of being in exclusive control of her own classroom. She persevered however and grew to like the new approach. This was to prove critical subsequently when visually impaired pupils were dispersed throughout the school. At the time however, its significance was that it encouraged her to feel that she could adapt to altered circumstances and embrace new challenges.

Shortly afterwards, the possibility of the school accepting visually impaired children was raised. Although "the question of special education had never arisen" for Catherine before, it appealed to her and she "expressed interest" to the head teacher. She believed that she was in a strong position to promote the assimilation of these pupils into the school as a whole because she had been at the school for a long time and enjoyed good relationships with all members of staff. She was duly appointed in this capacity and went away on a year's secondment, taking a Diploma in the Education of Children with Special Needs. When the existing teacher in charge retired she took over as the only qualified teacher of the visually impaired in the school.

This group of teachers would seem to be in a stronger position to promote integration. This was indeed borne out by our observations, though the picture was not clearcut. These teachers who had been ordinary teachers in the same school where they now worked as special educators were in a particularly good position to build close relationships between the special centre and the main school and to further the academic and social assimilation of their pupils.

iii. The small group of six teachers with experience of both ordinary and special schools would seem to be the most suited of all to the task in terms of their background. This was not particularly supported by our evidence however. Most did not now teach the kind of pupils they taught in special schools, though the experience undoubtedly helped. Moreover, some had put their ordinary school experience quite behind them and made no direct use of it.

iv. Finally, there were those who had had no previous teaching experience, the majority young teachers in their early twenties but also a small number who had trained as mature students. This group of 11 teachers was concentrated in a small number of schools. In three schools with large departments catering for pupils with special needs they constituted half or virtually half of the departments' staffs. In one school they taught in the main school for one third to one quarter of their time, in accordance with school policy. In the others they had little or no contact with the main school and had no opportunity to become acquainted with normal classrooms.

Besides teaching experience, a few teachers offered other relevant experience. One teacher now working with severely retarded children had for several years run a playgroup for multiply handicapped children. Another had run an ordinary playgroup and found that a useful experience. A third, also working with the severely retarded, had trained initially as a nursery nurse and worked with such children in this capacity for five years, before training as a teacher. A fourth teacher had worked for a number of years as a teacher counsellor and had been involved in work with parents.

We enquired briefly into people's reasons for choosing this work. Three patterns emerged: deliberate choice; availing of opportunity; and fortuitious circumstances. These are somewhat rough-and-ready categories since all these teachers had at some stage made a definite decision to work with pupils with special needs. It might be argued in any case that choice – especially career choice – is to a degree a function of available opportunity.

This first group includes those whose training and career pattern suggest a clear orientation toward special education. They were trained in special education and some had a good deal of experience with pupils with special needs. A number however were working with pupils whose problems and needs were quite different from those with whom they had experience. This group included practically all of the teachers whose experience was confined to special schools and approximately half of the teachers with no previous teaching experience. (Incidentally, it would be incorrect to assume of the former that their presence in ordinary schools is necessarily indicative of a strong commitment to integration. In some cases it seemed to reflect simply that an opportunity was available when a special school appointment was not to be had or when a special school was reorganised.)

The second group – in some ways the most interesting – includes many who had considerable experience of teaching ordinary classes and, for a variety of reasons, made the transition to teaching in special centres. The most common situation was where a special centre was opened within their school; in some cases volunteers were encouraged from existing staff, in other cases contact with pupils based in the centre led to an interest in them and their needs. Sometimes this development occurred simply through contact with slow learners in ordinary teaching. These teachers typically had been in the profession for a number of years and in some cases had built up an impressive experience of different kinds of expertise by means of part-time and short courses, with occasional secondment. Not all were long-serving teachers; some, particularly in practical subjects, made the transition to special teaching quite quickly. In several instances this was attributed to the policy of concentrating slow learners into the practical subjects. One art-trained teacher for example traced the origins of her interest in slow learners to her secondary modern teaching days, where the academically recalcitrant were 'encouraged' to take up art.

The third group consists of those, who by their own admission, have ended up doing this work without it ever having been their intention. Sometimes a family move had made it necessary to accept whatever teaching appointment was available; sometimes young teachers were unable to obtain any other appointment; and on occasion this work initially presented a convenient part-time return to a teaching career which had subsequently become a full-time commitment.

Selection criteria

One of the first things that has to be done when an integration programme is being mounted is to select staff. This may entail appointing new members of staff, as when a new centre is set up in a school; it may mean selecting existing staff for new duties, as when a special school establishes links with an ordinary school; or it can involve assigning extra tasks to teachers, as when pupils are integrated on an individual basis. We present a number of dimensions invoked by teachers and administrators, report some views on them and develop some of their ramifications.

Two preliminary reservations need pointing out. First, there are practical constraints which frequently limit choice; redeployed teachers may have first claim on new opportunities, whatever their suitability for the work; there may be only a few teachers who are available for extra duties; and the pupils being integrated will be of a given age and may need to go into one or other of a very small number of classes. Local constraints abound and it is impossible to ignore them. Equally however they should not be given undue weight; we encountered a number of instances where individual determination and ingenuity circumvented apparently immovable constraints.

Secondly, there is little point in offering a straightforward summary of the criteria as reported to us. The requirements vary with age of pupil, the nature of their special needs and a whole host of local factors. Also, the relationship between what people do and say they would do in this area is far from simple! This is not necessarily because they seek to conceal their practice but because of the difficulty in articulating it. Interviewing prospective candidates and making appointments is not an exact science, and it is far from easy to elaborate on the intuition, tacit understanding and so on that are key elements in the process. Moreover, people vary in what they take for granted. For instance, none of our informants gave as one of their criteria that the person appointed should have a basic regard for children, and only one stipulated the ability to communicate well with children and young people. It would be wrong however to assume that these qualities were not required by them. It is very likely that they regarded them as so fundamental as not to need mentioning.

Training came up as a major consideration, both in respect of detailed knowledge and skills and in respect of general background. Views on training were far from unanimous. A majority were in favour of having as much specialist training as possible. One head teacher described himself as "qualifications mad". Another had not been so convinced of the need for qualifications until she had seen what was being achieved by members of her staff who had additional training. A sizeable number felt that too much importance was customarily attached to training. A good grounding in basic teaching was what was needed – "what I want is good infant teachers". This fits in with the frequently expressed desire for teachers who were free of preconceptions and could be moulded into effective members of the team once they had started on the job – "we do our own in-service training". (Sometimes a pretty unjustified claim.) This suspicion of training tends to be found in experienced heads whose only experience has been with mainstream children where the specialist may indeed be much less useful than the experienced teacher – "You could have a very knowledgeable specialist but one who doesn't know about norms for ordinary children, or about teaching".

Even when no specific comments were made about training, many people required skills of various kinds, some of which would imply specialist training. Most of them might be regarded as the fundamental skills of teaching. It was clear however that something more than average teaching skills were being required, whether in the way of using them more precisely or being more explicit and reflective in their use. They included the following:

a. Capacity to individualise instruction: in the context of groups of pupils with widely differing problems and needs, it was felt important that teachers should be able to prepare and work to individual programmes.

b. Ability to teach basic skills; this of course is something that would be expected of any primary teacher but not perhaps in quite the same way or in the same detail as required from teachers of pupils with special needs.

c. Ability to analyse teaching sequences: one head described it in terms of "the ability to plan a programme, analyse it, assess what went wrong with it, ask how can I improve it". These are activities doubtless that other teachers will engage in as well but in a more general and less explicit way.

d. Detailed record keeping: this is another example of the detail that is required over and above what an ordinary teacher would do.

A variety of other skills and competencies reflecting personality and experience as much as training were called for. One of the most frequently mentioned was the capacity to fit in to a new situation and work as part of a team. This is because the job is a team one with a need to exchange information, adapt teaching practice, develop joint approaches so that pupils receive a consistency of treatment, and so on.

Besides the specialist teachers, there will be a range of other professionals involved – outside specialists, ancillaries in the classroom and teachers from the main school. If these various inputs are not to fragment the pupil's educational experience, care will have to be taken to unify their contributions and ensure that they work together harmoniously. There are various qualities associated with this, such as the capacity to handle adult relationships; to be socially and professionally acceptable; and to be able to imbue other people with enthusiasm for new tasks.

Ancillaries

Ancillary staff in the special centres we visited had a wide variety of backgrounds. Few had received any specific preparation for the work they were doing. A majority had received nursery nurse training though its relevance to working with special pupils was generally felt to be limited. Out of 36 staff some 24 had been through some form of professional training. Most of these (17) had taken the National Nursery Examination Board (NNEB) course. The remainder were Norland-trained (a further qualification for nursery nurses) or were, by way of exception, nurses or teachers who opted to work as ancillaries rather than be unemployed.

There was a tendency for the younger ancillaries to have obtained formal qualifications, whereas the unqualified personnel tended to be older women, many of them mothers whose families had grown up. A few had had some prior contact with children or adults who had some form of special need. For example, one had been an area playgroup organiser. Some of the playgroups had contained mentally retarded infants. Another had worked in a playgroup for handicapped children for over five years. A third had helped develop playgroup provision for disabled infants and was a founder member of the local association for riding for the disabled. A fourth person had become involved in a swimming club which contained polio victims. A fifth had had a very diverse background: a year in an ordinary day nursery followed by over three years in the nursery department of a school for the physically handicapped. Next she spent a year in a multi-disciplinary assessment centre helping out in a general capacity before transferring to her present post in a class for communication disordered children.

The local authorities covered by our project varied in the extent to which they required classroom ancillaries to be professionally qualified. In one authority for example it was LEA policy to employ only qualified personnel. Two other LEAs though not possessing a stated policy tended to employ only trained personnel, which suggested that they operated a de facto policy. By contrast a fourth authority gave no indications of preference and was content to employ mothers who had had first hand experience of bringing up children.

Chapter Six
Specialist Teachers and Ancillaries in Integration

Specialist teachers and ancillary staff are the major resources for an integration programme. If they are to constitute an effective resource it may be necessary to develop new ways of working and acquire new roles not previously carried out. In this chapter we examine the working of staff in integration programmes and detail the various roles taken up by specialist teachers and ancillaries. By specialist teachers here we mean teachers who had a specific function in respect of pupils with special educational needs. They were usually on the staff of a special centre but, as we shall see below, they can also belong to a special school staff or might even be the subject of a one-off appointment to promote integration. We begin by looking at the various roles carried out by teachers attached to special centres and then discuss other roles associated with integration – working as a support teacher, transferring or returning pupils to the mainstream, providing specialist assistance via the class teacher and maintaining oversight of an integration programme. Finally, we consider the roles and deployment of ancillary staff.

Special centre staff
The role of the teacher or teachers staffing a special centre is characteristically a multi-faceted one. This is particularly true of the person in overall charge whose role is likely to be a good deal more complex than that of others in the centre. The discussion here is directed toward the former since the work of the teacher in charge will encompass the sorts of activities carried out by other staff. Also, many centres consist of a single class and just one teacher who has to carry out a wide variety of tasks.

There were numerous components in the role in fact. Not all were present in every case but the job did tend to be complex and demanding, and in terms of daily routine and professional demands very different from that of the average classroom teacher. These various activities are only sketched in briefly here since most of them are discussed in more detail elsewhere in this book.

i.   Teaching pupils with special educational needs

Clearly this will be the primary concern – unless, by way of exception, the centre is of such a size as to necessitate the teacher in charge working almost full-time in an administrative capacity. (To our surprise this did happen in some instances). This teaching role is examined in the chapters on the curriculum.

ii.   Monitoring and recording progress

Monitoring pupils' progress and recording it systematically should be an integral part of the educator's teaching activity. As discussed in chapter sixteen, it can be done in many ways from standardised testing to loosely structured diaries. One can include here teachers' involvement in case conferences where they contribute to the assessment of pupils' progress.

iii.   Teaching pupils from the parent school

In three of the programmes that we studied, the special centre was formally committed to providing some form of service to pupils from the parent school. In two instances the area of expertise of staff from the centre was in the field of learning difficulty. This being the case it was relatively straightforward for them either to assist staff from the main school who were experiencing problems in dealing with pupils who exhibited specific learning difficulties or to assume responsibility for these pupils themselves. In the third instance, the field of specialism was physical handicap. Here the connection is perhaps not so readily apparent. A prime expertise of such staff however is in dealing with learning difficulties, and it was in this respect that they were able to contribute to the parent school.

At a fourth location – a large department attached to a comprehensive school and providing for physically handicapped pupils – it was accepted that those pupils in the department of low academic ability would experience very little classroom integration. It was policy in the school for staff of the special department to have teaching duties in the parent school and for some main school staff to teach in the department. It was recognised that the special department was in a position to provide a specific service to the school. Also, staff were conscious of the possibility of the non-integrating pupils becoming an outgroup in the school. A possible solution to both problems that was being explored was to have a remedial curriculum jointly planned and put into operation by remedial teachers from the main school and their colleagues from the special department.

iv. Administrative duties

Although in most cases the person in charge of the special centre had considerable teaching duties, there was commonly a heavy administrative load as well. The problem was acutely felt in the smaller, one or two-teacher centres where the person in charge of necessity had a full-time teaching role with administration over and above this. Some found that administration occupied an inordinate amount of time, in spite of their efforts to keep it to a minimum. One teacher reported that it had to be fitted in almost entirely out of school hours.

By administrative duties here we mean both the routine aspects –registration, ensuring regular attendance and checking on absences, ensuring that any equipment needed is available and maintained in good working order, requisitioning stock, arranging visits outside school, routine correspondence, maintaining records, receiving visitors – and the more fundamental ones – determining how the centre is to operate, how staff are to be deployed, planning the timetable, negotiating for additional resources and so on.

The following outline of a typical day in the life of one teacher in charge of a unit for hearing impaired pupils will not be typical for everybody, but it does illustrate the varied tasks carried out:

08.50 – 09.30	registration; collecting dinner money etc, (on the appropriate day)
09.30 – 10.30	working with a less experienced member of staff; sorting out practical difficulties; helping with classroom organisation; providing individual or small group work.
11.00 – 12.00	liaison and consultation with head teacher of parent school; general administration; individual tuition;

checking hearing aids, basic audiometry; carrying out reading tests.

13.30 – 15.00   receiving visitors; liaising with outside agencies over curriculum redevelopment that is taking place; taking children out on visits; teaching – "I am timetabled to teach some afternoons but I often have to drop this because something comes up"; organising visual displays; generally checking on unit routines; visiting parents at home.

v.   Disseminating information to staff of parent school

Where there is an active programme of integration going on, even if only a small number of pupils are involved, the ordinary teacher will need to be given certain basic information about pupils' conditions and how these might influence their educational functioning. Passing on this information is usually the responsibility of the person in charge of the special centre. This can be done informally in the staffroom, through formal meetings or by circulating information sheets.

vi.   Monitoring integration

When pupils divide their time between a special centre and ordinary classes there is need of somebody to maintain a watching brief. How are they progressing? Have they been accepted by the class? How is the teacher coping? Can a given pupil's integration programme be extended or does it need to be curtailed?

vii.   Responsibility for training

There are two aspects to this: improving the skills of specialist staff either informally, through casual interaction or in some more formalised way; and seeking to further the knowledge and skills of staff of the parent school. Both aspects are discussed more fully in chapter nine.

viii.   Involvement with outside agencies

Involvement with agencies outside the school can take various forms. It may simply be a matter of general liaison with the educational psychologist, a consultant paediatrician or a specialist social worker. The teacher may be part of an assessment team responsible for monitoring pupils' progress. He or she may work to instruction from some outside agency, such as speech therapy or physiotherapy, carrying out specific exercises in the therapist's absence. There may be regular opportunities for discussing general issues associated with educating pupils who have special needs or for formulating educational policy. There may be specific purposes in view: working with a psychologist to improve assessment procedures; collaborating with a psychologist and speech therapist to formulate individual programmes of work; liaising with employers and careers officers to set up work experience placements and jobs.

ix.   Taking on the roles of other agencies.

"I do speech, audiology, psychology – am always present at testing . . . I do things a parent ought to do like taking a child to the dentist . . . This is (perhaps) taking away the role from the parent but if we didn't do it it wouldn't get done . . . (I'm) a social worker, a welfare officer (eg chasing up grants), taxi service, school nurse, substitute parent . . . Perhaps we overstep the mark because there is no-one else to do it . . . Very often teaching comes near the bottom of my list and yet my job is to educate these kids."

Most teachers find themselves donning the mantles of other colleagues on occasion, if rarely to this extent. Sometimes there is no problem other than finding the time. There can however be a real dilemma for teachers here between ignoring a need for which the requisite specialists are not available and attempting to meet it themselves without possessing the requisite background or training.

x.   Contact with parents

As discussed in chapter 20, there was a great deal of home/school contact. It took many forms, ranging from open days and meetings at schools to home visiting and the use of home/school books. It served a variety of purposes: providing personal support for parents and helping them deal with management problems; liaising with professional agencies on their behalf; involving them in their children's education; and facilitating the exchange of information and understanding between home and school.

Support teacher role

One way of providing the necessary specialist expertise in the ordinary classroom is to appoint teachers in a support role. This happened in a number of integration programmes involving hearing impaired pupils. Staff were recruited and trained to support pupils in ordinary lessons, thereby enabling them to follow the main school curriculum.

Our first example comes from a school for the deaf which has placed twelve hearing impaired pupils in ordinary schools. These attend classes in their different schools as individuals, supported by three teachers of the deaf and four (3.1 full-time equivalent) support teachers. The latter are qualified and experienced teachers who do not possess a specialist qualification in hearing impairment but have received some specific training for the programme by means of lectures and apprenticeship arrangements.

The support teacher's primary role is to provide back-up for the work of the class teacher, by helping the hearing impaired pupil to understand lesson content and carrying out appropriate preparatory and follow-up work. Discussion with support teachers elicited the following detailed role components:

i.   providing assistance in the classroom by, for example, ensuring pupils understand announcements and instructions and grasp information provided.

ii.   reinforcing lesson content by going over it outside the classroom and providing additional explanation and practice.

iii. reinforcing the specialist language work carried out by teachers of the deaf by spending time in conversation and helping pupils with their reading.

iv.   facilitating and promoting the pupil's assimilation into the particular class and into school life generally by encouraging hearing pupils to include him or her in classroom activities, explaining some of the things that cause difficulty and intervening over misunderstandings or instances of minor aggression.

In conjunction with the teacher in charge and the teachers of the deaf, they are also concerned with

v.   establishing and maintaining sound professional links with class or subject teachers.

vi.   maintaining contact with the home.

Staff sought to provide the requisite support *within* the classroom, withdrawing pupils as little as possible. This entailed gauging when to intervene with explanation or reinforcement and when to stay in the background. Teachers were conscious of the danger of directing pupils' attention away from the class teacher to an excessive degree and creating a lesson within a lesson. Sometimes work was unfinished at the end of a lesson and this might be taken up in a withdrawal period subsequently. In individual cases, pupils were withdrawn from music and radio broadcasts with specific speech and language work substituted. One pupil was withdrawn from a subject where the teacher spoke very unclearly and seemed to have difficulty in coping with having a hearing impaired pupil in class.

There were particular difficulties at secondary level. Priority was given to supporting lesson content (as opposed to reinforcing the work of the teacher of the deaf). The amount of support possible was necessarily restricted: "You pick up the essence of the lesson and (decide) what you can leave out". It would be impossible to cover all lesson content satisfactorily so teachers must set priorities. The aim was to convey the essential content of the lesson while maximising the pupil's understanding of it.

Various strategies were described. One teacher sought to cover one lesson of every subject each week. A colleague tried "to cover half the lessons during the week . . . I support not only for that particular lesson but to get the drift of the rest of the week". In her view it was "a waste of time to support completely". (While true in the case of two pupils she supported, it cannot be assumed that this will necessarily be so in every case.) There is also the danger of over-supporting, leading to a situation where the pupil becomes over-dependent on the support teacher; this also runs the risk of "isolating . . . rather than integrating (him)". This particular support teacher described how when a pupil first took up a subject she would support totally but pull out as quickly and as far as possible consonant with the pupil's needs being met. Thus, for one of her two pupils, a fifth former, she was present within the classroom for three out of four periods of social studies; all four periods of geography; and three from five periods of mathematics (the boy was of average ability, at best). She withdrew him for four periods of English each week; and a further period was taken with a small group for whom she provided remedial English.

At a comprehensive school which had two support teachers for four hearing impaired pupils at the time, with a fifth due shortly, each teacher allocated her time across all four pupils on the basis of the subjects she felt most able to deal with. Thus, for Marisa one of the teachers was present for two double periods of biology and one double period of maths. Her colleague 'supported' a further two double periods of maths inasmuch as she was present at the beginning and end of any lesson where new content was being introduced, specific tasks set or some form of test taking place, and approximately 60 per cent of Marisa's English, something which the subject teacher felt was "absolutely essential". Here, support took a number of forms: the class might work as a single unit with the support teacher acting as interpreter, taking notes of the key elements and reinforcing these at a later stage; it might be split into smaller groups with the support teacher taking her own group of pupils including Marisa; or it might be an oral lesson where the teacher asked questions and pupils responded or where pupils read out passages from books or from something they have written. It was acknowledged that Marisa's presence limited to some extent the amount of oral work that was done.

The support teacher's crucial role as a mediator may be noted, primarily between the hearing-impaired pupil and the class teacher but also between the pupil and the teacher of the deaf and between the pupil and other pupils. This meant that tact and flexibility were required – "You've got to make yourself acceptable" – in addition to teaching competence. It also meant that while their work was crucial it was secondary to that of the class teacher. One noted that it was "a passive role for most of the time", while another commented that "you are never in control of the situation . . . you're just backing up somebody else's work, never really teaching them anything (of your choosing)". The support teacher did not have her own class and did not determine what was to be taught. This did not mean of course that the job was passive in itself. The task of selecting what should be reinforced from a lesson or set of lessons and presenting it in a form appropriate to the needs of a hearing-impaired pupil within the constraints of a conventional lesson was a continually demanding one that required a high level of resourcefulness and professional comepetence.

A second example comes from a programme where secondary age pupils with severe and profound hearing loss attending a school for the deaf received part of their teaching at a nearby comprehensive school. This was for PE/games and all practical subjects – art, woodwork, pottery and home economics. Initially, integration was confined to two afternoons a week and the 11 pupils involved were accompanied by one of two teachers of the deaf. The aims at this stage were to foster links between the two schools and ensure that subject teachers did not feel imposed upon, rather than to provide explicit support for pupils.

At the outset the teachers of the deaf sought to withdraw from lessons as soon as their full-time presence was no longer required. This was achieved quickly in games and PE, but their presence in other subjects has proved to be more lasting. They seek to attend one in every five craft lessons. This was a facilitating rather than a teaching role. They concentrated on general advice to subject specialists and assisting both parties – teachers and pupils – with communication. One teacher of the deaf noted how one of the most common difficulties subject teachers experienced, especially in the early days, was ensuring that even basic communication had been effective: "(They) didn't realise how little our children were getting from what they were saying . . . I don't think they were aware of what the problems of deaf children were for a long time". To this end teachers of the deaf had exerted themselves in informing, advising and guiding subject teachers on the most appropriate means of communicating knowledge in their subject. Within lessons the preference was for a generalist role. One teacher of the deaf found from experience that the most useful role she could adopt in craft lessons was to offer general assistance to the class as a whole. In home economics, where new vocabulary presented considerable difficulty, her efforts had to be more focused. To avoid spending too much time within class explaining lesson content and risking setting up a lesson within a lesson, pupils subsequently were timetabled for one period a week of lesson reinforcement back in the special school.

A further development took place in the second year of operation. As the number of hearing impaired pupils increased, including some of lower ability, two teachers were appointed on a part-time basis to the staff of the comprehensive school to provide support. These did not possess specialist qualifications in deaf education. They were assigned particular responsibility for the lower ability hearing impaired pupils and were charged with providing support within the classroom – unlike the teachers of the deaf who tended to support back at the special school. Part of the reason for this difference was that the pupils in question had greater need of immediate support, provided *during* a lesson and not at some time subsequently.

The detailed deployment of these teachers had not been finally resolved. Both of them were acutely aware of the lack of training; one had considerable problems in communicating with her pupils. Staff were predisposed against providing extensive individual support – as in the previous example – on the grounds that "as soon as you have a support teacher going in on a permanent basis then integration (in the way of social assimilation) stops . . . the children form a nucleus around the support teacher" (teacher of the deaf). The hope was that subject teachers, support teachers and teachers of the deaf would in time form a complementary team, but this was still to be realised.

Transferring pupils to the mainstream

It is well known that few pupils transfer from special schools to ordinary schools. One of the reasons for this may be that the transfer process is more difficult and needs more attention than is commonly supposed. We describe first an example where a detailed procedure had been worked out for transferring pupils from a special school to ordinary schools, and then a special class which was deliberately organised to facilitate pupils' return to their own neighbourhood schools and had evolved guidelines for achieving the latter.

The special school – which we shall call Meadow View – has an explicit diagnostic and assessment function for children of preschool and primary school age who exhibit severe behaviour problems together with learning difficulties – with customarily a major difficulty in the area of communication. The aim is "to understand the nature of (children's) problems, treat those problems, and try to get them back in ordinary school as soon as we can" (head). Following upon assessment, a detailed programme related directly to the developmental needs of each child is devised and applied within the school. Typically, children spend from one to three years before eventual full-time departure. Of 26 children who have passed through, 12 have successfully transferred to ordinary schools while the remainder have gone on to some form of special education, including special classes.

The procedure for transferring a pupil commences with the identification of a suitable candidate. This judgement is made by the head of Meadow View in discussion with his staff. The characteristics that typically indicate readiness for transfer include: distinct improvement in a child's understanding of language; good expressive language; the beginnings of concept formation; indication of an ability to 'make out' in the social sense; and a reasonable level of independence. Since the school's teaching approach follows closely specified objectives staff are able to indicate levels of development precisely. The intention is always to route the child towards the neighbourhood school. To this end Meadow View seeks to maintain at least nominal contact with the local school of every child it accepts.

Over the past three years a procedure for preparing the local school has been developed. This is followed in all instances, though the particulars will vary with the individual case. We illustrate this procedure by describing two examples:

Freddy had attended his local school for a time before being excluded, ostensibly on the grounds of extremely poor behaviour. He spent twelve months at Meadow View before it was decided that he might transfer back. The procedure was initiated by inviting his parents to the school to discuss the progress he had made and possible future placement. They agreed that an approach should be made to the local school, and offered to visit the head teacher to discuss this with her. The head teacher proved extremely wary about having Freddy back – fearing a renewed outbreak of disruptive behaviour. The parents' visit was followed up by a visit from the head of Meadow View requesting that Freddy might make a weekly visit to the school.

With certain misgivings, the head gave permission and phased visits over a period of a term commenced (these visits were in fact interrupted by illness, on the part of both Freddy and his prospective teacher). On the initial visit Freddy was accompanied by his teacher from Meadow View and the deputy head. This was little more than a courtesy call. It was followed up with an invitation to the head teacher of Freddy's local school and his prospective teacher to visit Meadow View for lunch. On the next occasion that Freddy and his teacher visited the school he spent 1½ hours in his prospective class. At this point the decision as to whether to continue the process of transfer was left to staff of the local school. They agreed to this and on the next occasion Freddy attended for a half day. He was left with his prospective teacher and classmates. By this stage, full transfer was imminent.

A second example comes from a written account by a teacher from Meadow View explaining the procedure she followed with another child, John.

I visited with John on approximately four occasions. The first two visits were only about one hour's duration and the class teacher was happy for me to stay in the classroom with John and help with story time, etc. During playtime John was put in the charge of a responsible child and observed from inside the school to make sure there were no problems. On the next visit I stayed in the staffroom while John joined his class and on the following occasion I took another class whilst their teacher was on a course. On this occasion John stayed for school dinner and readily copied what the other children did as regards collecting his food, etc. He coped admirably. These visits occurred during the latter half of summer term and it was felt that John was ready to start school with the new intake in the September. After John had been in school two weeks the school was contacted to check on his progress and later during the term I visited to see how he was faring.

A number of points may be made about the transfer procedure. First, Meadow View staff emphasise that when a child visits the local school he or she is on trial; furthermore, that staff of the school have the ultimate say in whether or not the child transfers. Their approach to a school is along the lines of, 'We would like you to help us with the further assessment of this child. We think he/she might be ready to transfer. Could you give us your opinion in your situation?'

Secondly, great importance is attached to advance preparation: the child's prospective peers – otherwise he or she may be treated as a curiosity; the parents of the child being transferred; the parents of children already at the school (one of the potential problems is adverse parental reaction arising out of fears that their own children will start imitating the speech of these children); and the teachers of the school concerned, pointing out the areas of improvement and stressing that if there are serious problems the transfer will be stopped.

Thirdly, the transfer is effected in a highly informal manner: "It can't be done through an official set of procedures . . . you need a direct link with the people responsible for treating the child subsequently". Accordingly, one of the main advantages recognised by one Meadow View teacher was that ordinary schools were "being invited to help a child . . . they are not being imposed on by a system". Fourthly, some information about the child is made available to the ordinary school though details are deliberately restricted, apparently in an effort to encourage schools to reach their own conclusions about the child rather than take on, perhaps unquestioningly, views and attitudes that may relate to a condition that no longer exists.

Our second example refers to a language unit which comprises two special classes for children of primary age with speech and language disorders. While the transfer procedure adopted here has certain similarities with that of our first example, there are notable differences. The procedure again commences with the identification of a likely candidate for transfer. The decision is based on such factors as improvement in speech, to the point where the pupil can communicate fairly readily; being relatively independent of the teacher in classroom work; evidence of emotional maturity and overall stability, and the capacity for satisfactory social interaction with age peers. The decision is taken by the teacher in charge in consultation with the speech therapist and educational psychologist who serve the language unit and the head and class teacher of the receiving school.

Generally speaking, pupils transfer to their local school though occasionally a school within the wider neighbourhood will be chosen because it is regarded as more suitable in some respect. There is a deliberate policy of maintaining a link with the local school of any pupil taken into the language unit. This is achieved through an unusual practice whereby all pupils spend four days at the unit and on the fifth attend their neighbourhood school. When it comes to implementing the transfer procedure the school will already be relatively familiar to the pupil. The actual transfer is phased over a period of months. The pupil concerned starts attending the neighbourhood school for two days each week. This is later increased to three days a week, and in the end full transfer is effected.

A crucial part of this exercise is the liaison between teachers in the language unit and class teachers in the receiving schools. This is important in ensuring that pupils make a smooth transfer and in guaranteeing continuity in the work they are doing. It is helpful if class teachers are given an overview of the particular problems an individual has had and any aspects of them that have current teaching implications. Class teachers may benefit from receiving an outline of the specialist work the pupil has been doing. Also, if there are good personal links they will be more prepared to ask for help should they need it subsequently and will be more at ease in doing so.

Providing specialist attention via the class teacher

A major reason why more pupils with special needs cannot be educated in ordinary schools is that class teachers lack the requisite skills or do not have appropriate teaching materials. This suggests a further role for the specialist teacher that is highly relevant to integration, viz assisting class teachers to cope better with pupils in their classes who have learning difficulties. In the example we describe here teachers from a special school sought to help pupils who had difficulties in ordinary schools *through* their class teachers. They remained in their own classes following programmes of work drawn up by the specialist teacher but implemented by the class teacher.

This programme involves four teachers from a special school (for pupils with learning difficulties) who are timetabled to spend part of the week working in ordinary schools nearby. Each works in a maximum of two schools. The typical procedure is as follows. The school psychological service notifies the school of a pupil who is having difficulties. A teacher from the special school visits the pupil's school to conduct the assessment. This will typically comprise criterion-referenced assessment and discussion with class teacher, head teacher and educational psychologist. The specific area(s) of weakness thus identified are 'treated' by setting specific tasks, agreed jointly by the visiting teacher and the class teacher, to be completed on a weekly basis. This will involve using some of the learning resources developed within the special school. Each week the visiting teacher returns to discuss progress with the class teacher and agree on further work.

Such intervention is not without its risks, not the least of which is the possibility of the ordinary teacher handing over responsibility for a pupil to the visiting teacher or alternatively feeling resentful at the latter's intervention. The visiting teachers are in fact very careful to emphasise that it is a joint venture, and they are not coming to dictate to school staff how they should teach. They seek a balance between helping ordinary teachers to develop their skills in teaching pupils with learning difficulties and giving the impression that they themselves have all the answers. 'We mustn't lose sight of the original intention: monitoring progress of the children is the most important role of the visiting teachers, they should have very little contact with the children themselves. We have to be very careful that we don't sacrifice quality for quantity and abandon the central position of classroom teachers'. (From a written account by a teacher involved in the programme.)

The intention all along was for the *joint development* of plans of work involving visiting and class teachers. Pupils' progress would be monitored by the visiting teachers. Although in the early stages it was accepted that the latter would work closely with individual pupils, they hoped to be able to reduce this direct contact, with the class teacher gradually assuming responsibility for setting the weekly objectives and providing any individual assistance that proved necessary. (The learning resources in use are so designed that a pupil should be able to use them with the minimum of attention from a teacher or ancillary.) In the event the visiting teachers have found it less easy to reduce the direct contact than they had envisaged. This was due to the numerous other demands on class teachers' time and the fact that they were following a different curriculum and teaching approach for the majority of their pupils.

This intervention carries far-reaching implications for ordinary teachers' approaches to learning difficulties, in regard of both teaching content and its transmission. Given such ambitious objectives a great deal is demanded of the visiting teacher. Not only must he or she be skilled in diagnosing the particular problem or problems that a pupil is having, but must also be able to determine how to go about providing the necessary remediation. At the same time the class teacher must be encouraged to feel that he or she has an active part to play. This may entail a didactic or at least persuading role: getting the teacher to see the need to modify teaching content or approach, helping him to simplify learning tasks and implement a suitable programme of work geared to the individual pupil's needs.

Maintaining oversight of an integration programme

Implementing an integration programme of any size is not just a question of placing pupils with special needs in ordinary classes. As we have been at pains to point out, there are implications for the school as a whole. Implementing a programme and monitoring its development must then be seen in a broad context. The skills of liaison and administration required for this task are very different from the teaching and other skills associated with special education. We illustrate these by reference to a number of locations where staff were formally assigned an overseeing responsibility.

The first comes from a campus-sharing arrangement between a comprehensive school and a school for the physically handicapped. Responsibility for liaison was given over to two senior teachers, one from each school. Staff of both schools were informed of the arrangement and told that any matter concerning a pupil with special needs should be raised first with the appropriate liaison person. The special school teacher had a substantial amount of time (about one third of the timetable) set aside for this work. Tasks carried out included attending to administrative details, resolving problems, dealing with pupils' anxieties and generally ensuring that they were benefiting from joining ordinary classes. A lot of time needed to be devoted to relatively trivial matters – sorting out discrepancies because information about timetable alterations or changes or rooms had not been passed on or dealing with a lift that is out of order or an electric wheelchair that has broken down. The liaison teachers were also involved in the formal assessment of pupils' progress and participated in round-table discussions at which placements were reviewed. They were consulted about selecting subject options and were also responsible for devising an interim programme for use during the examinations period each year when the normal timetable of the comprehensive was set aside.

A further example comes from a primary school which had a special centre for children with impaired hearing. One of the main school teachers was given a post of responsibility to develop links and improve communication between the special centre and the main school and have general oversight of the integration activities. The teacher appointed saw her role as follows: liaising with the teacher in charge to decide which ordinary classes hearing impaired children might join – a child with severe deafness, for example, she would "try and direct . . . to a teacher who was well used to having these (hearing impaired) children"; providing reassurance for her colleagues; and arranging specialist guidance and advice as necessary. She made a point of talking to all members of staff who were involved every half term to check on whether things were running smoothly and if they had any particular concerns. In this example time was not formally set aside for the work, and it had been fitted in when possible.

In both these examples it will be appreciated that interpersonal skills are at a premium and may be more important than the possession of specialist expertise. The individual concerned must be able to relate effectively to colleagues and enlist their co-operation. If this is not done there is a danger of unco-ordinated development. The personal qualities required for the task were detailed as follows: ability to establish rapport with others: capacity to listen sympathetically – ". . . allow discussion rather than just go in with the answer . . . not always push their own point of view"; having an eye for protocol – "go through the right channels", at least in the first instance; tactfulness; and patience –"I'd rather take longer than push so hard that I upset the staff and made them resistant to the whole idea". One of the persons involved considered it important to have, and to be seen to have, status. "You have to have authority that is recognised . . . (to be) in a position to influence things". When this is lacking "they (teachers) are not going to come to you for help if they are aware that it has to go up the ladder".

Roles carried out by ancillaries

All of the integration programmes we studied availed of the services of ancillaries. Sometimes they occupied peripheral roles; in other cases they were crucial to the integration programme and it could not have taken place without them. They were usually employed initially in a general helping capacity, with particular emphasis on providing physical care, but tended to be used in a great variety of ways. We outline these different roles here – care, education, working as a para-professional and general. In the following section we discuss a number of general points bearing on the deployment of ancillaries.

i. Care

Looking after the well-being of young children is a duty strongly associated with nursery nurses and other types of classroom assistant in British primary schools. However, this duty takes on added importance when the children concerned have special needs. Many of them will require a level of supervision and attention that no teacher could possibly expect to provide without detriment to her teaching responsibility. There are some pupils whose needs are such as to warrant *constant* supervision and assistance. These include the severely physically handicapped, pupils with severe learning difficulties and those with marked sensory impairment.

All the special centres in both primary and secondary schools which we visited had ancillary workers whose primary responsibility was the care and wellbeing of pupils with special needs. The need for physical care is perhaps most apparent with the physically handicapped, for obvious reasons – dressing, toileting, walking and feeding. This side of the job is well illustrated in the following description of a typical day's work provided by two welfare assistants employed in a special department for physically handicapped pupils attached to a large comprehensive school:

08.50	Put out electric wheelchairs. Check that toileting and washing facilities in working order.
09.00	Taxis begin arriving. Meet and transfer children from taxis to wheelchairs (or walking aids). Remove and store outdoor clothing.
09.20	Round up the pupils who have lessons in main school first period. Transfer to internal transportation (the school is split-site which necessitates a mini-bus shuttle service) and escort pupils to their respective classrooms. (This may entail pushing wheelchairs and/or accompanying those who have to negotiate the lift.)
09.30 – 10.15/ 10.15 – 11.10	Either remaining with pupils within main school and providing general assistance (eg taking notes, assisting with practical work) or undertaking general duties within special department (eg helping with activities, dealing with a fit, toileting).
11.10 – 11.25	Morning break. Setting out school milk, straws, tissues. Returning pupils to special department if that is where they are scheduled next period; transporting others from department to main school. Supervising play. Toileting.

12.20	Lunch. Return pupils to special department. Serve lunch. Sit with pupils and assist with feeding as necessary. General supervision. Toileting.
13.15	Round up those pupils who will be in main school and oversee transportion.
13.25 – 15.15	As per morning lessons.
15.15	Return pupils to special department. Toileting as necessary. Transfer pupils from electric wheelchairs which remain at school into their own chairs. See pupils off the premises. Arrange sterilisation of toileting apparatus. Clean and lock away equipment. Put electric wheelchairs on overnight charge.

From this timetable and from discussion with the assistants it was evident that they were extremely busy – and this was in a context where ancillaries were not particularly engaged in providing educational support within the classroom. In this example, because of the number of pupils present (up to 40) the department has a full-time nurse and a part-time physiotherapist. The ancillaries therefore have a *general* caring role.

A related activity which ancillaries elsewhere engaged in was promoting independence – particularly in the areas of mobility and feeding. The first of these will be dealt with more fully later. The latter is a problem associated mainly with blindness, physical handicap and severe learning difficulty. Each condition may necessitate a slightly different emphasis in the remediation attempted. For example, with physical handicap the difficulty may stem from poor fine motor control and the solution is simply to engage in painstaking practice. In the case of a child with severe learning difficulties there may be no physical difficulty in feeding but the connection between eating utensils and food may not be appreciated. A behaviour modification programme implemented by an ancillary on a daily basis may effect improvement.

ii. *Education*

Many ancillaries contributed to their pupils' education, both indirectly by carrying out tasks that freed the teacher to engage in teaching and directly by engaging in teaching activities themselves under a teacher's instruction. These contributions took various forms: preparing teaching materials and other learning resources; hearing children read; marking work set; helping pupils during practical work; acting as amanuensis; conversing with children and thereby providing an extra source of language practice; supervising general activities, and thereby allowing the teacher to work with individuals; and working on language programmes with individual children.

These various roles were not universally carried out. Much depended on the attitudes and ways of working of teachers. Where ancillaries did extend themselves beyond a purely caring role however, this served to enhance children's education in numerous ways, especially in the degree of individual attention that became possible.

Ancillaries working in a special centre for hearing impaired infants participated in creative activities, where the teacher of the deaf acknowledged that "they have a very important language role". Two ancillaries working in a centre attached to a comprehensive school were timetabled to spend part of each day on 'resources work' – organising and putting up displays in the school, cataloguing books and tidying the library. Another ancillary working with junior age children with hearing impairments was commended for her ability to talk to the children and encourage their response: "She understands the children; she has a marvellous knack of talking to them in a normal way". In the classroom this ancillary worked closely with the teacher. The class was usually split into small groups; while the teacher of the deaf was providing individual attention she might be "checking story writing, checking number. It is work that previously would have been covered . . . it is helping the teacher so that he can have more work time with individual children . . . do more specialised language work". She also accompanied hearing impaired pupils to main school lessons, acting as interpreter as necessary and executing aspects of a support teacher's role.

Several ancillaries took individuals and small groups for cooking and general domestic skills. While this would always be under the general responsibility of a teacher, they frequently ran these sessions in an autonomous way, deciding themselves what to cover and how it should be done. In one case this role extended beyond pupils with special needs since the ancillary took a mixed group of hearing impaired and hearing pupils for one period of cookery a week and for a further period of art and craft.

Assistance in practical work was especially important for pupils with visual impairment or physical handicap. One ancillary enabled a blind child to engage in craft work and use implements such as knives that without close supervision would have been too hazardous. Pupils with poor fine motor control benefited from individual assistance in home economics and science. Those who tired easily and lacked strength might have part of the task done for them. In a few cases ancillaries acted as note-taker or amanuensis for pupils who though intellectually able had extreme difficulty in writing.

iii.   *The ancillary as para-professional*

Some specialist services are in short supply because of the shortage of trained personnel. Speech therapy and physiotherapy are cases in point. One tactic in this situation is to make use of untrained staff such as ancillaries. They can be given a general introduction to the specialist skill in question, ideally even some training, and then carry out some work in the specialist's absence. This would usually be a programme of work specifically devised for implementing by the ancillary and regularly monitored by the specialist.

We encountered several examples of effective practice in this regard. The first concerns a welfare assistant who has assumed increasing responsibility for speech therapy at a centre which caters for pupils with moderate and severe learning difficulties. About one seventh of her week is devoted to this. This came about because the number of pupils in need of speech therapy was such that taking them to a clinic was not feasible. The ancillary, who had been accompanying them, broached the possibility of the speech therapist coming to the school – an invitation which was readily taken up. The therapist at first paid visits weekly but pressure of other work reduced this to fortnightly. The next step was to involve the ancillary more deliberately. The therapist invited her to sit in on some therapy sessions explaining what she was doing and why. Then she had the ancillary take sessions herself, working to her detailed instructions and in her presence so that she could correct as necessary and offer constructive criticism. From carrying out specific exercises worked out by the therapist, over time the ancillary has come to take the majority of sessions herself and contributes to the content of programmes worked out for individual pupils. She spoke of what she did as a blend of therapy and teaching – "A lot of it is language development . . . concept stuff . . . not just clear speech".

Our second example concerns a system developed for delivering physiotherapy to physically handicapped pupils placed in their local schools. This is described in more detail in chapter 8. It too was born out of necessity in that there were too few physiotherapists to provide for all the pupils in need of their attention. Accordingly, they turned to the classroom ancillaries with specific exercises to be carried out daily with individual pupils in between their own visits (weekly, monthly or termly, depending upon extent of need). These exercises could be simple walking exercises or practising transfer from a wheelchair to splints. A more detailed example is given below. This is the programme worked out for a junior age child suffering from cerebral palsy, with spastic extension paralysis:

a. rolling side to side
b. practice sitting on side of mattress (hips abducted, feet plantigrade)
c. balance reactions long sit
d. prone lying, head and shoulders raised – forearm support
e. sand and water play – sitting, leaning forward or prone, encourage hands into midline. No weight bearing.
f. supine lying – knee flexion onto chest; repeated movement to break spasm of quads on hip extensors
g. hands by side, rolling pelvis from side to side with knees bent
h. knees bent, dorsi-flexion of feet.

In addition, the ancillaries play an important part in observing how a child is progressing physically. In what ways is he or she responding to treatment? Is this appropriate? What are the outstanding difficulties? This was described by one physiotherapist as invaluable "reinforcement . . . another pair of eyes". They could watch out for the more obvious signs – bad posture, the sudden appearance of a limp, apparent worsening of a particular condition. Anything more specialised – eg shortening of a limb – could of course only be noted by a trained person. This was valuable in that pupils' physical condition could be monitored continually and remedial action put in train far sooner if anything did begin to go wrong.

iv.   General

Ancillaries occupied various general roles that though less tangible or easily described were important none the less. Some of this came from the fact of being an adult who was outside the authority structure in the school. In several cases the ancillary was the only member of staff who had had children of her own. When coupled with the fact that the ancillary was somewhat older than teaching staff, this may have enabled pupils to relate in a different way to her.

A few comments may be illustrative. One ancillary claimed to have developed "a sort of special relationship with them (children) . . . a more caring relationship . . . I'm not a teacher so I haven't got the discipline problem . . . I can allow a little more talking, be more affectionate . . . I can have a more friendly approach . . . I think I bring a lot of fun into it". The notion of mother figure, of friend and confidante, was echoed in the comments of another ancillary in a centre which served secondary age pupils with moderate and severe learning difficulties. Speaking about a teacher whose class she worked in for almost half the week, she remarked, "Sally is the authority and I'm the one that can be a little bit softer . . . can sit in the corner and talk to them".

Deployment of ancillaries

i.   *The individual or the group?*

When an ancillary has a particular responsibility for a given pupil there is a dilemma – whether to restrict attention exclusively to that pupil or, while providing the necessary support, at the same time seek to help out across the whole class. The ancillaries in our sample generally opted for the latter on the grounds that over-involvement with one pupil could lead to his or her becoming too reliant on them. Furthermore, it was considered that this would hinder assimilation into the group. Having an adult with the pupil at all times means that everything is mediated through the adult. By contrast, when this presence is more occasional the pupil has the opportunity to relate to peers and to act and develop independently.

ii.   *Need for a more clearly defined role*

We have indicated above the range of activities in which ancillaries can be engaged. There would appear to be no general agreement on which of these they ought to engage in or how they should divide their time between them. Some teachers and therapists saw their roles strictly in helping terms while others sought more initiative and encouraged them to develop their skills and contribute to pupils' education in whatever way they could. Ancillaries were sometimes confused, to say the least, when they worked with teachers who viewed their roles and made use of them in very different ways. It would seem clear that efficiency as well as good morale would be best served if the ancillary's role was clearly spelled out.

Joan worked as an ancillary in an infant school for three years looking after two physically handicapped children. She was keen that her involvement should not be limited to providing physical care. The teacher concerned welcomed this and encourged her to hear children read, mark books and generally help out in the classroom. When the two moved up to junior school however Joan found herself having to fit in with a teacher whose perception of the classroom ancillary was much narrower. In the beginning she was obliged to confine herself exclusively to her two charges. Even more difficult to take had been the fact that the teacher assumed complete responsibility for the children's welfare – "I used to do everything for them in the other school – now the (teacher) does it all". The situation changed eventually, not without an element of confrontation, and on a subsequent visit Joan was operating more independently and helped out generally within the remedial class.

iii.   Informing the ancillary

There was evidence to suggest that classroom ancillaries were not always given the best information needed for them to carry out their duties to best effect. This was so in regard of initial briefing when a child first started at a school and details passed on subsequently. Given the ancillary's crucial importance – particularly for the very young child – this is unsatisfactory. Perhaps most disturbing was that very often this lack of information was at its worst in the circumstances where it was most needed – when pupils with special needs attended their local school on an individual basis. Here both teacher and ancillary may lack relevant experience and it is all the more important for the fullest possible information to be passed on.

One ancillary commenting on having learned of a child's problem indirectly through her mother remarked, "We didn't even know she had dislocated hips". She wondered what other important details had still to emerge. Another spoke of the anxiety she felt at not having received even a minimum of details, and certainly no reassurance that her handling of the child was correct. She was unsure why the girl was in splints. Furthermore, she had no notion of how much daily exercise she needed. A third described how she had been given a list of the various conditions pupils were suffering from together with brief instructions on handling them. Her greatest problem was again a lack of confidence in her own ability – "I feel she (child) could do more if only I knew how to do it or if I was doing it right". This apprehension which many referred to is perhaps the strongest reason for providing some advance preparation. As one ancillary stated, "When I arrived I hadn't a clue . . . I was really nervous, apprehensive".

iv. The ancillary in the secondary school

With increasing integration of pupils with special needs, classroom ancillaries are now being appointed to secondary schools. Here they come into contact with teachers who are not used to having another adult in their classrooms – even though that person is not present in a teaching capacity, and is not a fellow teacher. This can lead to tensions and downright intransigence – "over my dead body" was one teacher's response to a suggestion that an ancillary join his class.

Difficulties arose in one school where a physically handicapped girl was accompanied by an ancillary who had supported her in primary school. The latter continued as before, sitting in on many of the lessons and providing constant assistance. This led to objections from teachers about her presence, alleging that the girl was being over-protected, was not being allowed to work on her own or be assimilated into the main body of the class. They also perceived the ancillary to be encroaching on their own territory. The latter, for her part, maintained that subject teachers were sometimes unaware of the tremendous pressures they were placing on the girl when demanding that a particular piece of work be undertaken. With hindsight, much of the difficulty that arose could have been avoided by sensible advance preparation. It would seem that the purpose behind the ancillary presence was not communicated to teachers. This meant that there was a certain resistance from the very beginning. This was exacerbated by the ancillary's failure to realise the need to adapt her approach to the very different situation of a secondary school.

v.   *The absence of a career structure*

Given the increasing complexity of the tasks that ancillaries carry out, it is unsatisfactory that there is no career structure of any kind for them. Their position is fixed irrespective of how imaginatively or innovatively they carry out their job, or how much responsibility is assumed. In some locations a special class or department was effectively getting the services of a teacher 'on the cheap'. (Indeed, in two schemes qualified teachers who could not find employment were working as classroom ancillaries.) At present if any ancillary wants promotion her only option is to retrain and do some other work.

Chapter Seven
Integration and the Ordinary Teacher

Pupils with special needs are increasingly more visible within the mainstream of education. This has major implications for teachers in ordinary schools who must expect to contribute to their education. This whole book is predicated on the notion that integration affects the whole school and so there are implications for teachers throughout, especially in chapter 9 on Training, the chapters to do with the curriculum and teaching and chapter 19 on Perceptions and Attitudes. There are various other matters relating to the ordinary teacher's contribution to integration programmes that are not dealt with sufficiently elsewhere and we address these here. (By 'ordinary teacher' we mean simply any teacher who does not have a specialist role in relation to pupils with special needs. This is a negative designation and we would not wish to imply that this diverse group of individuals is ordinary in any other sense!)

We begin with an account of the knowledge of special needs that teachers in the schools we visited had and their competence, as reported by themselves, to handle and teach pupils with special needs. If ordinary teachers are to play an effective role a certain degree of support must be provided; this will entail at least good lines of communication between specialist teachers and ordinary teachers. Some maintain that this only marks a beginning stage and that a thoroughgoing integration programme should entail far closer links between the two groups of staff. We consider some arguments for and against staff integration before, finally, noting teachers' views on the impact of the integration programme on their school.

Much of the discussion here is based on a questionnaire completed by ordinary teachers in the schools we visited. The questionnaire is reproduced in Appendix C. It was sent to staff in 22 schools; these included all schools catering for groups of pupils with special needs and a selection of these running individual integration programmes. (In the latter case, where secondary schools were concerned, only those teachers who taught the pupil(s) were asked to complete the questionnaire.) In all 413 questionnaires were sent out and 247 returned – a response rate of 60 per cent. The information obtained in this way was supplemented by interviewing a selection of teachers, both individually and in small groups. In only a few instances was this a formal interview for the specific purpose of supplementing the questionnaire data; our presence in the schools gave many opportunities to talk to teachers both formally and informally on a wide range of matters, including the topics under consideration here. Further relevant information came from talking to heads and specialist teachers.

Knowledge of handicap

Teachers' understanding of special needs is important both for the relevance to teaching and for the impact on attitudes. Much research has been conducted on the relationship between information about handicap and attitudes held (eg La Bue, 1959; Murphy *et al.*, 1960). Warren and Tutor (1966) reported a significant correlation between attitudes held by professional workers, among others, and their educational background or work experience. Kutner (1971), having surveyed research into teacher attitudes concluded that 'there exists a considerable residue of fear, hostility and aversion', implicitly because of a lack of understanding, among possible factors. However, the relationship between acquiring knowledge and attitude modification is far from direct. Haring *et al.* (1958) found that while an in-service workshop resulted in significant improvement in teachers' knowledge and understanding of exceptional pupils, it did not automatically lead to increased acceptance of integration. Only teachers from schools which contained pupils with special needs showed significant increases in their acceptance of integration. This prompted the conclusion that 'information about exceptional children may be more likely to promote positive attitude change in teachers having concurrent involvement with handicapped children than in teachers without such involvement'. This sentiment was echoed by Harasymiw (1976). Having conducted an in-service training designed to provide teachers with new knowledge about handicap and classroom expertise, he cautioned that although such a programme made teachers less anxious about involvement with pupils with special needs, 'a more prolonged procedure of familiarisation with various disability groups may be needed to modify underlying social biases'.

Turning to our sample of teachers, we found that the majority of those responding to our questionnaire had relatively little knowledge about special needs when the integration programme started in their school. Table 1 gives the distribution of responses to the question: *How would you describe your knowledge of handicap prior to your contact with these pupils?*

Table 1:	Initial knowledge of handicap				
Non-existent	Poor	Fair	Good	Very Good	Total
43	91	72	29	7	242

Over half of the teachers described their knowledge of handicap as non-existent or poor. Note that if the responses are scored on a one to five basis, the mean response is approximately 2.4, ie midway between poor and fair.

Teachers involved with the physically handicapped tended to assess the extent of their knowledge about physical handicap as fair or better than fair. By contrast, proportionately more of the teachers dealing with pupils who exhibited learning difficulties than with any other category except perhaps hearing impairment rated the extent of their knowledge as low. This is a little surprising since one might expect basic teacher training to equip them to some extent to teach these pupils.

Teachers reported a considerable increase in their knowledge of handicap from the time when they first encountered pupils with special needs through to the present. Table 2 gives the corresponding distribution of responses.

Table 2:	Subsequent knowledge of handicap				
Non-existent	Poor	Fair	Good	Very Good	Total
3	30	109	87	13	242

148 *Educating Pupils with Special Needs in the Ordinary School*

Scoring the responses as before a mean score of 3.3 (as compared with 2.4) is obtained (ie the level of knowledge is between fair and good). This reported increase in knowledge was attributed by teachers to two sources in particular: direct experience of pupils with special needs – mainly teaching them; and interaction – largely on an informal basis – with persons more knowledgeable (eg special educators, educational psychologists, speech therapists). These and other training strategies are discussed in detail in chapter 9.

Earlier we referred in passing to the influence that a specialist facility can exert. The relationship between the support available to the ordinary teacher and the attitude subsequently held toward pupils with special needs is complex. Whether or not the specialist facility sees itself as having a training function – and not all of those contained within our study did – its presence alone provides a basic reassurance which most teachers felt they needed. Moreover, it serves an important function as a safety-net in dealing with the more problematic cases. Thus, staff in one comprehensive school which contained a well-integrated programme for pupils with learning difficulties noted how it was always possible to refer to the special centre pupils they felt incapable of handling themselves.

Competence

Teachers' competence in handling and teaching pupils with special needs is a function of numerous factors: general teaching skills; perceptions of the pupils and attitudes toward them, the precise nature of the pupils' needs; the teaching context and the kind of support available. In this section we look at the adequacy of teachers' knowledge and develop some points relating to teaching and generally dealing with pupils with special needs.

Some American research into teachers' perceptions of their competence paints an unprepossessing picture. Gickling and Theobald (1975) found that only 15 per cent of 183 teachers questioned agreed with the following statement: *'The regular classroom teacher feels he/she has the skills to help special education students'*. Only 10 per cent of a group of teachers who would shortly be involved with such pupils agreed that teachers in elementary education in general had the training and competence necessary for meeting the needs of 'educable mentally retarded' pupils (broadly corresponding to pupils with moderate learning difficulties in the UK) when supportive services were *not* available. More significantly, after a year's experience of mainstreaming, no significant change had occurred in teachers' perceptions of the competence needed to teach these pupils, in the continuing absence of supportive services. More of the teachers (32 per cent) agreed that the knowledge and skills of elementary teachers would suffice if supportive services were provided. Interestingly, this research was conducted prior to the implementation of PL94-142. Has this made any difference? Gottlieb and Many (1979) asked 54 ordinary teachers whether they felt they had the necessary skills to teach educable mentally retarded children. Sixty-three per cent replied that they did not. What of our own sample of teachers?

We posed the following question of teachers:
Do you feel you know enough about handicap to deal with the pupils you come across? Their responses are given in Table 3:

Table 3:	Adequacy of knowledge			
	Adequate	Non-adequate	No view expressed	Total
	134	96	17	247

Thus, 54 per cent of respondents – and 58 per cent of those expressing a view – felt they had sufficient knowledge. Very often their accompanying comments underlined that this was only *given the circumstances they found themselves working in.* The latter is a most important qualification. Their estimates of the adequacy or inadequacy of their knowledge reflected two things: (a) the existence of a specialist facility on site and its relationship with the parent school; (b) the demands made on them as ordinary teachers.

In only one programme – involving the individual integration of physically handicapped pupils – was undue concern expressed by teachers about the extent of their knowledge. This was in spite of the fact that a majority of teachers in four different schools felt that they had at least a fair knowledge of the handicap in question.

There was repeated mention of the complexities of the various physical conditions, and of how these might affect pupils' educational development; the physical limitations that different conditions imposed; and the need to counteract related emotional problems which some pupils displayed. No in-service training had been arranged for the teachers, nor was there any advisory support. In two other locations where there were fairly self-contained classes for hearing impaired pupils, teachers were particularly concerned about the difficulty they experienced in understanding what hearing impaired pupils were saying; also how best to approach teaching them, and how to ensure that they grasped at least the essentials of lesson content.

In several cases the fact that teachers felt insufficiently informed on pupils' special needs reflected a degree of isolation on the part of specialist staff. Not only were the latter less visible in the school and less obviously available as a resource for ordinary teachers but there were also few oppportunities to discuss matters or pass on specialist knowledge. This again would support the importance of the special centre and its staff playing an active part in the life of the school.

Turning to the demands made on ordinary teachers, it is clear that the precise role they adopt will depend on the degree of specialist expertise available in the school. One teacher made a distinction between the 'general course of teaching' and 'specialist teaching'. Most teachers felt reasonably confident about their level of expertise with regard to the former but turned to special education staff for the latter. Our impression was that the level of knowledge of ordinary teachers were generally fairly skimpy, and that it only sufficed – if indeed it did – because of the presence of specialist teachers. There was a tendency throughout for ordinary teachers to leave full responsibility for the educational development of pupils with special needs in the hands of specialist staff.

These observations receive further context from teachers' responses to the question:
How important is it in your view to have specialised knowledge of handicap when dealing with these pupils?
Responses were post-coded into three groups: specialised knowledge essential or very important; desirable, somewhat important or important in some circumstances; and not important.

This gave the following distribution:

Very important	Somewhat important	Not important	No answer	Total
116	94	29	8	247

It will be seen that the great majority of these teachers saw it as important to have specialised knowledge of handicap when dealing with pupils with special needs. Most of those who regarded it as unimportant qualified this by saying that their particular teaching involvement did not necessitate it – 'Not for the ones I teach' – or that there was sufficient specialist expertise at the school –'Specialist help is readily and closely available'.

Teachers recognised that their *teaching* competence as far as pupils with special needs were concerned was limited. This is discussed in more detail in chapter fifteen and we confine ourselves to a number of summary observations here. Teachers were insufficiently informed on the educational implications of given handicapping conditions and needed to develop their awareness of pupils' potential. Related to this was the problem of knowing what to expect of and demand from pupils. This spilled over into discipline problems and knowing how to handle untoward behaviour. There were specific teaching difficulties – structuring material appropriately, and making necessary adjustments to teaching approach. The uncertainty often related to lack of advice and support: 'I was never told how to teach Sammy . . . never given any advice . . . I wasn't confident in myself to plan out a course of work . . . I thought it was better to let him join in everything rather than try and do something special'.

Support for the ordinary teacher

The most evident form of support available to teachers was the transmission of basic information on individual pupils. Advice and guidance were also available but this was less frequent. For the most part contact and liaison were informal. Many special educators intimated that they did not wish to appear 'too pushy' or 'scare teachers off' by representing the teaching of pupils with special needs in such a way that it was seen as something highly specialised. Nevertheless we came upon many instances where teachers would have welcomed much more in the way of basic information. Opportunities for formal and focused interactions or 'professional discussion' were relatively few. This may have been a consequence of specialist teachers' concern to minimise the impact on colleagues of teaching pupils with special needs in order to guard against negative reactions on their part. It may have been due to an – generally mistaken – impression that ordinary teachers would not have welcomed such interaction. It may also signify their failure to realise the extent of the latter's need for guidance and assistance.

When information on individual pupils was communicated to ordinary teachers it was generally quite limited. Typically it amounted to a form with the individual's name and condition, perhaps a reference to the home background, intellectual ability, possibly an indication of attainment and any additional details it was considered that teachers ought to know. This outline information was sometimes added to in informal discussion. The ordinary teacher might be told that more specific details could be obtained, either upon request to specialist staff or through consulting school records. The limitation of this was that the onus was placed on the ordinary teacher who might not have the time or the inclination to seek out the information but could have benefited from receiving it.

There were numerous instances where some teachers appeared to be far better informed than others. This presumably was a reflection of their having taken the trouble to find out more by consulting central files or pursuing questions with specialist staff. We enquired, by means of the questionnaire to teachers, whether they considered they received enough information about any pupils with special needs that they taught. Responses were as follows:

	Adequacy of information transmitted		
Too little	Enough	Too much	No response
75	118	2	52

A majority of those responding said they received enough information, but a significant minority – nearly 40 per cent – claimed to receive too little information. Teachers' comments, which were verified by our own enquiries in the schools, highlighted the general absence of a coherent *system* for ensuring that information was communicated effectively to all relevant parties. The proportion of positive responses must be seen in the context of remarks about the presence of a specialist facility on site: pupils with special needs were perceived to be the responsibility of colleagues, and they were content with far less information in consequence.

The presence of specialists was not always sufficient, as testified by particular dissatisfactions expressed in four locations. In one authority which contained classes for infants with severe learning difficulties, there was repeated mention of the limited professional interactions between specialist and ordinary teachers in a number of schools. (The amount of time the children spent in ordinary classes was restricted.) Where pupils are 'shared' between two schools a new set of potential difficulties comes into play. In one such location there was a general feeling among staff of the ordinary school that while sufficient support was forthcoming in an emergency, with regard to more routine collaboration there was 'a paucity of co-operation over specific handicaps' and generally very limited interaction. Each school had co-opted a member of its staff in a liaison role, responsible for co-ordinating the programme of integration. This seemed to work well but it did not extend to bringing teachers from the respective schools together – something that various subject specialists requested. In other locations the tendency of a special centre to function in a self-contained way was remarked upon. Another area of difficulty widely noted was how to find time for liaison and support. This was more often a characteristic of secondary schools where the sheer size of the school and the pressures of the examination syllabus frequently combined to make it difficult for staff to get together.

Two further considerations may be noted. First, some forms of special need were seen as quite removed from the ordinary teacher's experience, and if teachers were to cope with them they needed a good deal of specialist support. Thus, teaching pupils with sensory impairments or language disorder required more explicit guidance and support than did teaching pupils with learning difficulties. There was some similarity between the latter group and the school's existing slow learners, whereas pupils with severe communication disorders were quite new to them. Secondly, again and again school staff reported having been denied access to information on a pupil on the grounds of medical confidentiality. The transmission of information in this area does raise particular problems, that medical personnel were not always minded to solve. One authority did make progress by introducing a card index system whereby brief medical details on any pupil could be made available to school staff without infringing medical confidentiality.

Support made available for the newcomer to the staff of a school is worth mentioning in its own right. Only one school operated a system for ensuring that new staff were at least as well informed as the colleagues they were joining. It was policy in some cases to avoid placing pupils with special needs in the classes of newly appointed teachers, especially if they were probationers, until they became accustomed to the school. Where newly appointed teachers did have contact with pupils with special needs they were likely to receive as much or as little information on them as did colleagues. They frequently missed out however on the general introduction to the special needs in question that their colleagues had received when the programme started. We found no instances where the initial in-servicing had been repeated – despite the fact that at one school staff turnover in the four years subsequently was estimated to be at least 50 per cent.

Finally, we turn to the support forthcoming from agencies outside the school. Details on the nature of the service provided are given in chapter eight. Here we restrict ourselves to two general observations. First, very often the service that outside agencies were able to provide was seriously restricted by the shortage of skilled personnel. This was particularly true of educational psychologists and speech therapists. These professionals often found themselves struggling against case overload. In order to manage their work, priorities had to be identified and in some cases only the most urgent matters could be attended to. Thus, pupils referred for psychological assessment were seen – though often only after a considerable wait – but teachers' calls for guidance on curriculum matters or practical suggestions with regard to handling pupils generally went unanswered.

Secondly, where outside agencies did become involved in schools, their involvement typically stopped short of contact with the ordinary teacher. There were two notable exceptions to this, both involving teacher attendance at case conferences. In both instances teachers spoke appreciatively of how they had had the chance to make their own comments and to meet outside specialists face to face. Generally however, psychologists, speech therapists and others tended to communicate with the teacher in charge of a special facility, even though this person was not always in classroom contact with the particular pupil(s) in question. A similar finding is reported from America in Project PRIME (described in chapter 2). This found that special class teachers were 'much more likely than regular class teachers to be provided certain critical services such as special materials and teachers' aides'. One conclusion drawn from this was that the 'disproportionate availability of supportive services to special education teachers can hardly be expected to increase regular teachers' acceptance of integration' (Baker and Gottlieb, 1980, p.16).

Staff integration

Specialist staff are usually assigned to a special centre within a school and spend much if not all of their time there. There are various tasks they can carry out in the main school however: accompanying pupils with special needs into ordinary classes; engaging in team-teaching with staff from the parent school; exchanging classes with an ordinary teacher; and generally helping in the ordinary classroom. This situation poses an odd dilemma. On the one hand, participating in the life of the main school and making a contribution to the education of all pupils can enhance the acceptability of the special centre and its pupils; 'showing willing' in this way can be crucial in winning the co-operation that is essential if there is to be real co-operation. On the other hand, specialist expertise and skills are scarce and some argue that dissipating them in this way is not justified, even if the staff in question also possess the requisite teaching skills needed in the parent school. Pupils with special needs require specialised assistance and teaching if their learning problems are to be overcome, and this should be the priority for special educators.

Teachers' views on this matter were sought by means of the question: *What are your views on staff integration? Should specialist staff be encouraged to have some ordinary classes – and main school staff have a function in the units?*

The proportion of ordinary teachers in favour of greater flexibility of teacher deployment, both as regards themselves and specialist teachers, outnumbered those who were opposed to the idea by three to one. Some qualifications need to be made however. First, some teachers would seem, from their accompanying comments, to have responded to the first part of the question – should specialist staff have a teaching involvement with mainstream pupils? – rather than the second. The ideal situation, as they saw it, would be for pupils with special needs to join their teaching groups but with far greater involvement from specialist teachers, rather than that they themselves should teach in the special centres. Secondly, it is necessary to take account of the differences between primary and secondary education. Whereas at primary level it is relatively straightforward for a special educator to make a relevant contribution to the educational development of the ordinary pupil, at secondary level the emphasis on subject specialisms and the constraints set by examination-oriented syllabuses make such contribution more problematic.

Teachers identified three conditions that should accompany this more flexible deployment of staff. First, such an arrangement should not be obligatory. This was generally the case in practice. Only one school operated a policy whereby any newly appointed member of staff had to accept the possibility of being deployed in part within the special department. Secondly, it was pointed out repeatedly that there was need at the very least of a specific induction into the particular handicapping condition, possibly even some more extensive training. Thirdly, there was a feeling that any exchange of staffs should not relate to the core curriculum, however defined, but should be restricted to less central matters.

What benefits and costs did ordinary teachers envisage arising out of integrating members of staff? On the positive side, it was considered that this could widen horizons, eg by giving ordinary teachers a broader range of educational concerns and skills than they might otherwise encounter. As one teacher put it, it would be beneficial 'in understanding different teaching situations and informing on differing approaches in teaching specific academic and social skills'. Having members of staff from the parent school teaching partly – or even wholly – in the special centre was widely regarded as a valuable means of winning the acceptance of members of staff generally. (In at least two locations staff from parent schools were deliberately encouraged to make this transition.) The other main benefit was the greater understanding among both specialist and ordinary teachers of the demands each made on pupils with special needs; this could lead to greater cohesion amongst staff. A small number of teachers commented from a general standpoint: that 'if integration is wanted it has to operate at all levels' (ie it should not be restricted simply to the pupils).

Most of the comments opposing staff integration came from teachers working in secondary schools and referred either to the central importance of subject specialisms or to the sheer impracticability of managing staff integration at this level. It was frequently claimed that subject specialists had opted for secondary schools precisely in order that they could teach their subject – preferably to pupils with some examination potential. Some pointed out that just as their skills lay in this area, so special education staff and not themselves should teach pupils with *special* needs. 'What is the point of training people to specialise in handicapped and then putting them in main school', was one teacher's view. Another observed, 'A specialist (in some aspect of handicap) has been trained for his or her particular job and . . . it would be wrong to bring in amateurs'. A third took the view that 'special treatment all of the time is what these pupils need'. These teachers were of the opinion then that *not* having subject specialists concentrating almost exclusively on their particular specialism made little sense. A further view was that teachers with a strong academic orientation would not be greatly interested in teaching pupils with special needs and would not take the task seriously, or alternatively that they would not be very good at it. Mention was made too of practical matters such as the time pressures occasioned by having to get through the syllabus or the cuts in staffing levels.

Instances of staff integration were fairly rare. The most notable were the comprehensive school already mentioned, where a condition of employment was a willingness to contribute toward the teaching of the special department, and a primary school where a special resource for pupils with impaired vision had been dispersed throughout the school. In the first case six staff are formally assigned to the special department but all have some teaching commitments in the main school. Some indeed belong to other departments in the school. In return, a number of main school staff teach within the department. Staff in the second school were grouped into teaching teams, usually comprising one specialist (in vision impairment) teacher and two others. Children were grouped for teaching purposes according to the principles of team teaching: each teacher taught pupils with vision impairment, and no teacher taught only these pupils.

The impact on the school

An integration programme can affect the school in many ways. Here we look at the changes in their own schools that teachers picked out as significant, in response to the question:

What changes in the school have resulted from the presence of these pupils? (We are equally interested in positive and negative aspects.)

This provoked a large number of responses, mostly positive but some critical and showing a keen awareness of the difficulties.

By far the most common observations related to the improvement in pupil attitudes toward peers with special educational needs. This was noted by some teachers in every school. The vast majority of those who reported changes commented on increased understanding, awareness, sensitivity or helpfulness towards pupils with special needs on the part of the main body of pupils. 'The idea that physical handicap equals low intelligence is fading amongst students.' 'A certain fear is probably dispelled.' 'The others no longer regard these children as freaks.' 'Greater tolerance and acceptance.' Some staff commented on how attitudes had developed from initial unease and embarrassment to a natural acceptance: 'Staff and pupils are more aware of each other now in a way that escaped us before.' 'They are accepted now whereas previously they may have been shunned.' 'A near-complete acceptance of those physically abnormal now – much changed from the first year when they were pointed out by some children.' 'Students now speak directly to people in wheelchairs and not to the people pushing them.' 'The ability in both handicapped and able-bodied children to get over the embarrassment of dealing with one another.' 'The handicapped pupils are now individualised – and are no longer merely handicapped people.'

A smaller number commented on the easier relationships

enjoyed by pupils with special needs as they grew in confidence and became used to being part of the mainstream environment. There were benefits too for pupils already at the school. Many teachers could think of pupils who had gained a sense of purpose from assisting and/or striking up a relationship with others less advantaged than themselves. 'It has brought out the better side of the characters of children who can be a problem otherwise' and 'Normal children who were previously "unnoticed" become involved in helping and befriending', were two typical comments. Closely related was the increased motivation which these pupils sometimes demonstrated. As one teacher observed, 'What used to be the lowest ability pupils are motivated now they see "poorer" children than themselves in school'.

Other comments related to the educational benefits. The expertise and curriculum materials generated by the integration programme constituted a resource for the school as a whole. The greater visibility of outside specialists and sometimes the easier access to them were noted. The effect of all this was to enhance the education the school offered to all its pupils. There were many comments relating to teachers' improved capacities for dealing with learning difficulties of whatever kind throughout the school. A further benefit was the increase in communication and professional interaction between staff; the greater contact necessitated by the integration programme did sometimes spill over into the professional life of the school more generally.

There were material gains as well. One school gained a new staffroom for the benefit of all staff. Elsewhere, there were mentions of lifts being installed, a swimming pool, improvements to the fabric of the building.

These gains were not without cost. Certain organisational aspects were now regarded as more problematic, especially timetabling and the allocation of classrooms. Free movement about the school could be seriously hindered by the presence of disabled pupils. Coping with a broader range of pupil behaviours was widely held to be a source of concern. One teacher noted that 'the general atmosphere around the school' had become 'less calm and more noisy'. In some schools the presence of pupils with erratic or disruptive behaviour was perceived to have aggravated discipline. Ensuring that the same, or similar, discipline procedures were applied to all pupils was sometimes difficult to achieve. There were problems within the classroom too arising out of the need to incorporate one or more pupils with special needs into teaching arrangements geared to the majority.

In summary, ordinary teachers can play a key role in the education of pupils with special needs. Their knowledge and skills may be limited but these can grow. We see in a later chapter that attitudes likewise can develop from an initial reluctance and even hostility to positive endorsement of an integration programme. A crucial factor is the availability of appropriate support for ordinary teachers. This will entail effective liaison and good lines of communication between special education staff and their colleagues. When this happens the net result is an extension of the educational strength of the school as a whole.

Chapter Eight
External Specialists

Meeting special educational needs involves many professionals from the health and social services as well as from Education. Their roles and the sort of service they can provide are affected by moves toward integration, as by other structural changes in special education. These are considered in some detail here for LEA advisory staff, educational psychologists, speech therapists and physiotherapists and, more briefly, for doctors. This is followed by an account of issues arising in multidisciplinary working.

There are many other professional groups involved in special education – social workers, school nurses, careers officers and so on. Time did not permit a detailed study of all of these, and in any case several professional groups were not represented at all or only very sparsely in the integration programmes we studied. This might support an argument about the dearth of specialist provision – which was regularly advanced – but does not permit detailed discussion on our part. It may be noted that the scarcity of social workers and the difficulty of securing social services involvement was the subject of particularly frequent comment; as noted in chapter 5, this led to an engagement in social work by teachers that was considered by the teachers and their superiors to be excessive, albeit necessary.

Advisory staff

Although all education authorities employ officers in an advisory capacity there has been little systematic study of the structure and functioning of advisory services. Bolam *et al.* (1978) commenced their study of LEA advisers and educational innovation by noting how sparse the literature is on educational advisers and inspectors. Their study produced a good deal of detailed information that serves as background here.

There was considerable diversity as to who precisely within an LEA was engaged in advisory work and how they were styled. Bolam *et al.* found that 22 different titles were given to advisory staff in their sample, generally based upon one of three words – adviser, inspector and organiser. Advisory duties were also undertaken by a wide range of other staff – assistant education officers, educational psychologists, wardens of teachers' centres and even education librarians. Staffing levels and mode of organisation of advisory teams also varied considerably. This diversity is reflected in special education services. Some LEAs employ an adviser specifically within the area of special education. Others possess advisory teachers who are specialists in a given field of special need such as hearing or vision impairment or in a particular subject area such as home economics or science. In some instances there is no adviser for special education but an assistant education officer whose remit is or includes special education or a principal educational psychologist with an advisory function.

In broad outline, the work of the advisory service is to advance an authority's educational provision at two levels: that of the school, and of the authority. It is charged with stimulating, advising and evaluating educational activities in schools and reporting on these to the authority. Bolam *et al.* sent questionnaires to a sample of advisory staff and identified from the returns the following main features of the advisory role:

i.   Assisting in staff appointments
ii.   Advising individual staff about personal or professional matters
iii.   Evaluating probationers and other staff
iv.   Advising in a single school or college on major organis-ational or curriculum changes
v.   General inspection
vi.   In-service education and training
vii.   Planning and implementing LEA wide curriculum projects
viii. Advising on the design, furnishing and equipping of schools and colleges
ix.   Reporting to the authority
x.   Administrative and clerical tasks.

For our purposes two of the findings of Bolam and his colleagues may be noted. First, although visiting schools occupied a good deal of adviser's time, visits to any given school were rarely part of a regular cycle (unless a probationer was concerned). Over 80 per cent were special purpose visits of one kind or another. While the variety of these purposes was considerable, twice as many were concerned with personnel matters as were concerned with advising on classroom teaching.

Secondly, advisory staff typically face a tension between the professional and administrative aspects of their role. Bolam *et al.* refer also to the 'Janus' dimension that has them facing in two directions simultaneously – toward teachers and schools and toward policy makers and administrators. In their professional or advisory role they try to improve educational standards through their advice to teachers and schools and, reciprocally, they advise policy makers and administrators about the needs and problems of schools and teachers. In their administrative role they inform teachers and schools about policy and administrative decisions and evaluate their performance. The tension involved between these two roles was resolved in practice by stressing one at the expense of the other, by becoming either administration-oriented or teacher-oriented; 'the attempt to give equal priority to both produced intolerable role strain' (op.cit., p222). Whether advisers turned to administrators or to schools depended on many factors but especially on their position in the hierarchy; those in senior positions were more likely to be adminstration-oriented while subject specialists were more likely to retain their orientation toward teachers.

Organisation of the service

Where advisory services were available to the integration programmes we studied they were supplied in various ways: assistant education officer plus adviser; either assistant education officer or adviser on their own; or educational psychologist. In several cases no advisory service was available. This was attributed to staffing shortages or to the fact that the advisory staff in post did not have the requisite background or skills. Two authorities were well served, having both an assistant education officer (special education) and a special educational adviser. Many had only one or the other or had people in post with a nominal responsibility for special education alongside numerous other tasks. When there was only one person this tended to be an assistant education officer rather than an adviser, a reflection perhaps of the fact that the involvement of LEA officers tended to be administrative rather than advisory in nature. In two cases much of the advisory role was taken on by the head of the school psychological service.

The tasks carried out by advisory staff are discussed in detail below but a few general points may be made first. The involvement of advisory staff was primarily at the outset of the integration programme when LEA officers were making the case for new provision, selecting and possibly adapting a site, appointing staff and generally getting the programme off the ground. When the programme was established the involvement was far less, sometimes to the openly-voiced dissatisfaction of teachers but justified by advisers on grounds of priorities and other calls on their time. Related to this was a tendency to stress the administrative as opposed to the advisory dimension of the job. Advisory staff had relatively little to do with the day-to-day running or the professional content of the programme, again despite the many calls of teachers for such involvement.

A number of general constraints on the operation of advisory services can be noted. Apart from staffing shortages *per se* and the associated workloads, many officers were unable to devote themselves exclusively to special education. This was particularly so at assistant education officer level, with one combining responsibility for primary and special education, another exercising a dual function as assistant education officer (special education) and inspector, while a third was responsible for nursery provision, school meals and transport in addition to special education. Advisers were more often in a position to specialise though by no means invariably so; thus in one authority the function was carried out by the infant adviser.

The constraints arising from a necessarily limited background bore more heavily on advisers. Even when there was a specialist adviser in special education in post, such a person would be experienced in certain forms of special need only but would still have to act over the whole field of special education. Other advisers, as noted, did not have a background in special education and were at a particular disadvantage. This latter was more often the case with assistant education officers. While some had relevant experience in teaching or educational psychology, most did not. One assistant education officer acknowledged that his role was that of "a collector . . . a focus of collected wisdom . . . reflecting the opinions of people" he was more or less obliged to accept on trust the suggestions and recommendations of the advisory team. "I am an administrator and look to them for specialist knowledge of special education." This is all very well when there are advisory staff in post with the requisite experience and skills. When there are no specialist advisers however, not only must the administrative function predominate but it runs the risk of not being informed by the expertise that a specialist adviser would bring to bear.

While the presence of both administrators and specialist advisers enhanced provision there were some attendant problems as well. The mere existence of a plurality of staff gives no guarantee that they will be actively involved in schools. One well staffed LEA for example seemed to be unduly preoccupied with policy formulation and general administration in relation to the effort devoted to meeting the needs voiced by school staff. It can also occur that in an administratively complex service teachers do not know who to turn to for advice and guidance. Finally, it may be noted that there was very little systematic effort to avail of the specialist expertise residing within special schools for advisory purposes.

Content of the service

We identified eight major role components of the advisory service that bore on the integration programmes we studied. There is considerable overlap with the more general range of tasks described by Bolam *et al.*, though in some cases they are described rather differently. Not all of the tasks were held in common or given equal importance, as will become apparent.

i. Staffing

Appointing staff to work in integration programmes was a task that generally fell to advisers, whether it involved new recruitment or redeployment of existing staff. In carrying out this they would follow established procedures within the authority, except perhaps when an existing member of staff was being redeployed. In the latter case the school typically would have a greater say. Apart from appointing or participating in appointing staff, advisers also had a concern for determining staffing levels, creating a career structure and providing motivation and encouragement.

a) *Staffing levels* Responsibility for determining staffing levels was evident throughout. Staffing levels were generally arrived at by reference to official guidelines on pupil/teacher ratios – DES Circular 4/73 on Staffing of Special Schools and Classes. In a few cases staffing ratios were deliberately enhanced to take account of the demands of integration. Thus, agreement was reached in one authority to provide extra staff to a comprehensive school which accepted physically handicapped pupils part-time on the basis of one teacher for every eight pupils, while an integration programme for hearing impaired pupils achieved a staffing ratio of one teacher to two pupils. Officer support was more evident with regard to ancillary staffing levels. Thus, in an authority where physically handicapped pupils attended schools in their home neighbourhood the officers concerned had secured agreement from the Education Committee that wherever necessary an individual pupil would be allocated a personal welfare assistant. In another authority catering for children with severe learning difficulties in special classes attached to ordinary schools the assistant education officer responsible had been insistent on the need for a generous adult to child ratio, which in practice has meant one teacher and two assistants to every nine children.

b) *Career structure* Teachers working within integration programmes are frequently disadvantaged in terms of career opportunities by comparison with colleagues in both special schools and ordinary schools. They do not have the promotion possibilities available in special schools, while they are often seen as peripheral to the ordinary school to which they belong and lacking in experience of 'ordinary' pupils. One assistant education officer sought to address this problem directly by appointing teachers in charge of special classes at a relatively senior level – scale 2 initially, moving to scale 3 "as soon as they have shown they can do the job" – and maintaining a career structure for them within the mainstream of education. Two teachers in charge of special classes in this authority had indeed gone on to take up primary school headships. Another authority was exploring the possibility of creating more advisory teacher posts which would give career opportunities to staff from special centres while enabling their specialist expertise to be used more widely.

c) *Motivation and encouragement*   While one assistant education officer stressed the importance of "showing the flag" and maintaining the authority's interest in a programme in a public way, most others made no mention of it. This may have been because they took this part of their role for granted, but in many cases it seemed more likely that it was at the bottom of a long list of other priorities and was neglected in consequence. The importance of such an involvement was readily acknowledged at the outset of the programme but the tendency was to withdraw completely at an early stage. "Unless the school squeals one doesn't really react." The assumption was that the programme was working successfully unless something untoward came to attention – "No news is good news". This was clearly unsatisfactory in some cases where schools felt that they had been lumbered with a problem: the authority was only concerned with administrative placements and had no thought for the long-term needs of pupils or the school. Staff complained that they were so far from getting encouragement that they often did not know where they stood in the eyes of the authority, being unsure for example whether they were a stable form of provision or an experiment that could be discontinued at any time. Whether these perceptions were well-founded or not their effect on morale was clear – and the lessons for advisory staff equally so.

One authority tackled this problem in a novel way. After opening a new provision – a specialist resource for various groups of special pupils – a steering group of professionals with relevant experience was set up to monitor the operations of the resource and to contribute to its further development. The group consisted of a specialist adviser, principal psychologist, medical officer and the teacher in charge. Its continued presence and active involvement would appear to have played an important part in sustaining the initial impetus.

ii. Advice to schools

Two different aspects can be distinguished here: advising on teaching and other curriculum matters; and advising on organisational and operational matters. The former has to do primarily with the individual teacher, whereas the latter is more general, bearing on the special centre or the school as a whole.

a) *Teaching and curriculum matters*   There was very little evidence of advice in this area among the programmes we studied – despite repeated calls from teachers for such guidance. One of the better examples came from an authority which contained an advisory service. There was a good staffing level and the special education adviser had a fair degree of involvement with classroom teachers on a variety of matters – acquiring specialist resources (both learning materials and technical aids to learning), informing teachers of new developments and so on. There was also the occasional involvement of specialist subject advisers, something that was rare elsewhere. One example cited was of the adviser for home economics offering guidance on what pupils with a physical handicap could be expected to do in this area and how they could be helped by modifications to cookers and other equipment.

b) *Organisational and operational matters*   There was evidence of greater involvement in this area. For example, one officer who had helped establish special classes for children with severe learning difficulties had had a large say in how these classes operated, their relationships with the host school and the amount of integration. He arranged for the teachers to have one day a week free from teaching to enable them to meet parents, prepare materials and make professional visits. A special class for language disordered children closed down every Friday at the suggestion of the assistant education officer and the children attended their neighbourhood school.

iii. Policy formulation

While some officers especially those at more senior level regarded the formulation of policy as an important part of their work, others were not involved in this at all. Officers in one authority indeed appeared to view policy as their proper domain; policy formulation was highly formalised and inputs from, for example, the school psychological service did not seem to be encourged. A less formal approach obtained in a smaller authority where policy was also very much in the hands of the assistant education officer (special education). His priority upon taking up office had been to formulate a plan for special education, developing services in a coherent way rather than maintaining odd items of provision that had grown up in an ad hoc way. Thus, the dispersed nature of services for the hearing impaired necessitated peripatetic teachers, so he set about building up an appropriately qualified peripatetic team.

One assistant education officer declared that his responsibility was not formulating policy so much as translating agreed policy into actual provision. As an instance, when the local child development unit identified a number of children with significant speech or language problems and discussion with the relevant professionals (speech therapist, educational psychologist, medical officer) led to a decision to press for a language class, it fell to him to take the case to the education committee. When agreement was secured he had to find a suitable location, organise the necessary resources and liaise with the various agencies who had to be involved. Another assistant education officer had policy formulation as part of his brief but lacked the professional background that would have enabled him to make a substantive contribution to it. In effect, his role was one of sieving and articulating the views of the advisory service.

iv. In-service training

Organising in-service education and training activities is traditionally the responsibility of advisers. Few of the training initiatives described in chapter nine however emanated from advisory services. This reflects in part the lack of relevant expertise and in part the lack of time and the effective priority given to in-service training. What involvement there was tended to be at the level of *facilitating* – assisting with the logisitics of course organisation, providing cover for staff, arranging secondment in the case of longer courses and so on. There was general dissatisfaction with the state of affairs on the part of both school and advisory staff. There was clear need of specific training geared to integration programmes in many locations. A number of advisory services were grappling with this problem and some initiatives were being planned.

v. Liaison

As noted earlier, advisers provide a bridge between schools and the LEA. In the integration context they serve as liaison agents in two further respects, viz between Education and other agencies, and between different departments within the local authority. Other agencies will typically be Area Health and Social Services. Their involvement in the education of special pupils is all the more important when the latter do not attend a special school where the full range of special services and continuity of specialist oversight might be more readily available. Establishing and maintaining channels of communication are often the responsibility of advisory staff. Thus, the senior adviser or assistant education officer will often be the first point of contact within Education for professionals from other agencies. In many cases he will also be charged with convening multi-disciplinary case conferences for placement and review purposes.

Liaison between different departments in a local authority is also important in integration. The most commonly cited contacts were with Building and Transport. The former arises from the need to adapt buildings in favour of physically handicapped pupils. In times of financial constraint this can be extremely important since a fixed budget can impose limits on the extent of integration that is feasible well in advance of educational considerations. Transport too becomes important in integration and indeed, as noted elsewhere, was commonly one of the problematic aspects of officers' work.

vi. Administrative duties

Most assistant education officers and some advisers saw their role largely in administrative terms. This occurred even when people fought against it: "I am forced to take a more detached role (from the schools) than I would like . . . There is an enormous amount of admin and that has to take precedence". The term 'administration' can of course cover many things, extending from routine clerical work to servicing case conferences and committee meetings to executing decisions taken.

Discharging financial responsibilities may be regarded as a particular administrative duty. Assistant education officers were commonly responsible for managing the special education budget. In some cases officers were allocated funds to be used at their own discretion. This enabled them to provide additional resources for integration programmes that might not otherwise be available.

One adviser instanced using this fund to purchase low vision aids and a modified typewriter while another acquired specific curriculum materials. It should be stressed that the sums available in this way were small in relation to the number of schools and range of purposes they had to cover.

vii. Crisis intervention

As noted earlier, many officers felt constrained to work to a 'no news is good news' principle and their direct contact with the school tended to be in a trouble-shooting or crisis intervention role. The examples we encountered involved personality clashes or conflicts arising out of unwavering commitments to different modes of working. When positions get entrenched or disagreements become too intense to be resolved within the school, the involvement of an impartial expert from outside the school may be necessary. In two cases the difficulty centred on the integration process itself and different degrees of adherence to it. The advisory staff in one case decided that restoring staff relations within the school should take precedence over any further extension of the integration programme and accordingly concentrated their efforts on the former. In the other case the difficulties did not lend themselves to easy resolution and continued until the departure from the scene of one of the protagonists.

viii. Monitoring of progress

Advisers were in the past seen as the guardians of educational standards and they engaged in general inspections in pursuit of this role. More recently, the inspectorial function gave way to an advisory one, though the current calls for accountability have turned the tide a little. We came across no examples of officers or advisers engaged in any systematic monitoring of integration programmes. Some acknowledged that they did not have the requisite specialist expertise while another admitted that, for lack of time, "We do not pay even remote attention to it". Again, a principle of negative evaluation was frequently espoused – if things were not working out we would hear about it. Some officers claimed to be more positive in that they were kept informed by teachers in charge or educational psychologists and that these latter in any case were fully apprised of what was going on so that a further line of monitoring on their part was unnecessary.

Educational psychologists

Almost all LEAs employ educational psychologists and many have a well developed school psychological service. There is no statutory definition (in England and Wales) of the duties of educational psychologists though they are concerned for the most part with children and young people who have special needs. It may be noted that the Warnock Committee did not hold with the practice in some LEAs whereby the school psychological service provides a special education advisory service. While there is overlap with the role envisaged for advisory services, and while the psychological service contributes a great deal to special education, its contribution should be distinct and should be made from an independent base.

The Summerfield Report (1968) constitutes the major official study into the duties, training and supply of educational psychologists. It recommended a ratio of psychologists to school population of one to 10 000. The Warnock Report recommended in view of additional demands in recent years and extra requirements arising out of its own proposals that the target should be at least one psychologist to 5 000 children and young people up to the age of 19. The average ratio prevailing in England and Wales recorded by Warnock is in fact one to 11 000, though there is considerable local variation.

On the basis of a survey of practice then current, Summerfield noted that educational psychologists engaged in two main types of activity: the psychological assessment of individuals; and treating children within child guidance clinics and elsewhere (not notably schools).

Two more recent reports provide further details on general working patterns. Wright and Payne (1979) conducted a study of the school psychological service in Portsmouth in the mid 70s. As part of this educational psychologists kept full diaries of all their activities over a two week period (in 1975). A cluster analysis of the activities yielded seven categories of work which are given in Table I below along with the proportions of time spent on each.

When these psychologists were asked what aspects of their work they valued most, the four items chosen most frequently were:

i.   locating handicapped children with special needs, making assessments and recommendations for special educational treatment in normal or special schools when appropriate;

Table I: *Categories of work for educational psychologists in Portsmouth, 1975*

		Percentage
1.	Individual assessment with children, and work with parents and health personnel	24
2.	Treatment, case reporting and all work for children in the care of the social services department	17
3.	Administration and general advisory work mostly with head teachers in schools	17
4.	Team discussions re action concerning individual children	14
5.	Travelling	13
6.	In-service training and professional meetings, including working parties and policy development	8
7.	Undertaking research and also personal development time	7

ii.   spending time making an individual assessment of school age children in school, observing, carrying out a personal interview and testing;

iii.   making regular visits to schools or being readily available to teachers elsewhere to discuss general problems of pupils' behaviour at school and organisation and curriculum as it might affect pupils' behaviour;

iv.   in-service training: organising in-service training programmes and talks for teachers and others concerned with children including parents, to pass on skills in the assessment and management of children.

A national study, covering England and Wales, is reported by Wedell and Lambourne (1980). Table II gives the percentage of total time given over to various (predetermined) categories of work by educational psychologists other than principals. (Rounding-up errors conflate to give a total of more than 100 per cent.)

The two sets of data are not directly comparable but various points of contact can be noted such as the predominance of individual assessment and treatment and the limited involvement in in-service training or research.

Table II: *Time spent by educational psychologists on various*
categories of work

	Percentage
Assessment, diagnosis and placement recommendations, including related administration and case conferences	41
Indirect treatment (conducted through other agents such as parents, teachers or nurses)	15
Administration	13
Meetings on matters of provision, planning and policy	10
Direct treatment of personally conducted programmes	9
Training others	5
Organised data collection	4
Professional development	3
Other activities	1

Organisation of the service

A large part of the work of school psychological services has been geared toward pupils with special educational needs: viz the identification and treatment of individual pupils with learning and adjustment problems. Changes in the way that the needs of such pupils are met must inevitably affect psychological services. Current moves toward integration represent one such major change which in this country takes many forms and is at various stages of realisation. In this section we examine the involvement of educational psychologists in this process and document some of the ways in which they have responded.

Information was gathered on the workings of school psychological services in 13 LEAs in so far as they related to the integration programmes under study. This was to find out how psychological provision for the integration programmes fitted into the overall concerns and operations of the service, and whether any changes in the latter had been necessitated by the former. We sought details on the psychologist's involvement in a programme – how much time was devoted to it, how this time was spent, what roles were carried out. We also sought to form an impression of how adequate this service was perceived to be.

The nature and extent of psychological provision for the integration programmes varied widely. Three broad patterns could be identified: close structural involvement of a psychological service; psychologists adopting particular roles as a result of integration; and psychological provision continuing very much as before. These differences commonly reflected the constraints and exigencies of the local situation and the particular form of special educational need being dealt with. It should not be assumed that a given service is at fault because it shows little or no change in the existing pattern of working to take account of integration. The lack of change may be due to sorely limited resources; to the fact that other needs are judged more pressing; that the service is already somewhat ahead of its time; or that integration is not judged to require new styles of working. It is necessary to be quite clear on this since, although innovative working was often promoted by far-sighted and energetic individuals, the absence of innovation should *not* necessarily be taken to imply a service of poor quality.

In terms of the three patterns identified, in fact very often psychological provision *did* continue as before with little or no change of any consequence. A majority of the school psychological services examined either found it unnecessary or were unable to effect significant changes, and sought to meet the needs of integration within existing patterns of operating. The main activity engaged in was individual assessment, usually for the purpose of initial placement. While there were some attempts to provide teachers with knowledge and background information specific to given conditions, a large number of integration programmes received no added psychological inputs beyond what they would have had anyway and did not enjoy a special or enhanced relationship with the psychological service.

The practice of integration more often had an effect upon individual psychologists. In seven authorities we found instances of psychologists having adopted various roles as a direct or indirect consequence of integration. These are discussed more fully in the next section, but included: assuming responsibility for staff development; participating in a multi-disciplinary team effort to ensure that educational programming and assessment of progress went hand in hand; helping to identify an appropriate clientele for a specialist facility and clarifying the nature of their learning difficulties; working with parents; involvement with pre-school children; and advising an authority on provision for hearing impaired pupils by providing a rationale for their integration and identifying limitations in the existing provision.

The third pattern of involvement in integration programmes – to which we have given the term 'close structural involvement' – was apparent in three LEAs. Here, a senior or principal educational psychologist engaged in – and indeed in certain instances assumed formal responsibility for – the development of forward policy on behalf of the authority. In one case the principal psychologist was also senior adviser for special education; in the other LEAs there was no adviser for special education, while the assistant education officer (special education) tended to operate solely as an administrator. This meant in effect that there was a de facto extension of the psychologists' sphere of operations. In two of the three authorities the particular provision under study functioned for all pupils within the authority, as opposed to a given area or set of schools within it. This meant there was need of a person who could command an overall view of special educational provision within the authority and knew what constituted appropriate placement in each.

Content of the service

We identified many components of the psychologist's role and discuss here those that have a particular bearing on integration.

i.   Diagnosis and assessment and
ii. Placement and decision making

These two components are discussed together because they are closely linked and form part of a continuous process. Various actions are subsumed within this process. The psychologist may operate alone or in close collaboration with professionals drawn from other specialist services, the concern of each being to appraise and to comment upon a child from the background of a particular specialism. The psychologist may undertake assessment within a clinical setting or more frequently nowadays within the 'real life' context of school or possibly even in the home. The psychologist may place a high premium upon formal test results or may eschew their use in favour of less formal data based on observation, pupils' work and so on. Specific decisions about educational placement are in some cases a foregone conclusion (for example, where a child is very severely handicapped, or where there is a policy of integrating children but only one form of integrated placement). In other cases there are several options and the psychologist can play a key part in matching a given pupil's needs with the placement options available.

iii. Monitoring progress

Monitoring progress is discussed in detail in chapter 16 and we confine ourselves here to outlining some examples that involve psychologists. The first concerns a team of professionals offering specialist support to two language classes. Educational psychologist, speech therapist and class teacher work as a close team to monitor and support the work of the classes. Initial assessment is the province of the psychologist and speech therapist working together in a clinical setting. There are twice yearly case conferences when the circumstances of every child are reviewed. In advance of these the psychologist will appraise each child's functioning and contribute toward the case notes that are prepared jointly by the professionals involved.

A second example concerns a system of rating profiles developed by an educational psychologist in an effort to structure teachers' observations and make them more systematic and comprehensive. The profiles seek to combine ideas from published developmental scales and general psychometric experience with the categories teachers use in describing pupils anyway. They cover the five areas of general presentation, independence, language development, social development and learning aptitude. (The children in question were infants with severe learning difficulties.) A third example comes from a more informal means of monitoring progress (in use with visually impaired pupils). This includes twice-yearly assessment meetings chaired by the educational psychologist. Though the latter does not have specific expertise in visual impairment, he sees a role in terms of ensuring children are progressing educationally by focusing discussion and asking critical questions of teachers.

iv. Informing classroom practice

Despite being one of the areas of greatest demand from teachers, educational psychologists spent little time expanding on their assessment and developing their educational implications or giving classroom guidance to teachers. Some examples of formal inter-disciplinary working are given below but very often what teachers wanted was something that was immediate and informal. Their expectations may on occasion have been naive: they wanted to know 'what was wrong' with a pupil and how could it be 'cured'. Their reasonable expectations however were frequently not met. They were either told what they already knew – "merely confirmed what I had thought all along . . . that he has problems!" – or were given technical statements that they did not understand. (One member of the research team had an uncomfortable experience with a head teacher who was fulminating on the – absent – psychologist and demanded of the hapless researcher that he 'translate' the psychologist's report.) In some cases information did not reach the school at all. A comprehensive psychological assessment was carried out on all entrants to a centre for pupils with severe learning difficulties but little detail from this reached the teachers.

Teachers were even less well served in respect of classroom guidance. If integration meant that they had pupils in their classes that they might otherwise have expected to be transferred to special schools, they needed appropriate advice and support. Educational psychologists acknowledged the importance of this but pointed to referral case loads and other work that prevented them from giving time to it. If they did engage in it this was usually to assist with management problems rather than the conduct of teaching. One psychologist while regretting this justified it in terms of priorities. The numerous demands on his time allowed of limited engagement only in classroom work. If a particular pupil's disruptive behaviour could be contained with psychological assistance, the teacher could at least get on with teaching the rest of the class.

v.　Inter-disciplinary working

Educational psychologists attached great importance to inter-disciplinary working. Several pointed out that they were well placed to further this through their teaching experience and their contacts with the different professional agencies. They were able to carry out a facilitative role through being able to "cut across departments". One psychologist spoke of himself as "a lubricator, a facilitator . . . I know who to contact about what . . . I can facilitate communication on certain problems".

As far as participating in inter-disciplinary work was concerned, this was confined mostly to assessment, either through conducting joint sessions or participating in case conferences. This is described in Chapter sixteen. A few limited examples of inter-disciplinary activity focused on developing programmes for individual pupils were encountered. Thus, in two different locations the psychologist met with the class teacher and the speech therapist to examine the implications of assessment information on children with communication disorders and develop individual programmes of remediation. In one case the psychologist contributed to developing a detailed profile for structuring both teaching and assessment and joined with the others in working out the profile in detail for given pupils.

vi.   Determining admission criteria and procedures

A particular form of interdisciplinary working related to the admission of pupils to integration programmes. Many did not have clear-cut admission criteria, whether in terms of type or severity of special need catered for, and the effort to develop agreed criteria and a procedure for implementing them was an ongoing enterprise. The psychologist regularly made a contribution to this by giving an overview of related provision available locally, outlining what pupils with given problems required from a psychological standpoint and analysing what they were likely to receive from the integration programme. This was often carried out in conjunction with other professionals. Thus, speech therapists would have an independent perspective on language unit provision and what pupils were likely to benefit from it. In several cases there were substantial differences of view which took a good deal of time to resolve.

Admission criteria must of course be embodied in admission procedures. The psychologist is in a key position to influence practice here. One example will be described in detail where the psychologist, faced with the task of instituting a more formal procedure, did so by giving teachers a major role. The programme was a special centre for pupils with moderate learning difficulties in a comprehensive school. Initially, selection for the centre had been rather ad hoc, based largely on IQ scores supplemented in some cases by discussion between the teacher in charge and the class teachers in the feeder primary schools. The psychologist was concerned that more attention should be given to individual needs. Teachers were asked to administer particular attainment tests and provide specific information on pupils' backgrounds, medical histories, patterns of school attendance and so on. Further information was gathered through the psychologist spending time in school talking to and working with teachers and ancillaries, concentrating especially on pupils' approaches to learning. There would then follow a case conference, involving psychologist, class teacher and teacher in charge of the special centre, at which the circumstances of potential candidates would be considered. As well as giving a better picture of pupils' abilities and needs, the more detailed assessment undertaken in this way provided detailed information relevant to curriculum planning.

vii.   In-service training

The various training initiatives described in the following chapter regularly involved psychologists as speakers or workshop organisers. In one case the school psychological service had assumed responsibility for in-service training of all staff in special classes for children with learning difficulties. This entailed organising a training day once a term when all the special classes were closed. (Details are given below.) In addition, training sessions with the needs of these staff in mind were organised on a weekly basis after school.

Apart from this example, psychologists' involvement in training was informal and directed to making teachers more reflective about their work. Several psychologists attached considerable importance to making teachers more aware of the implications of special needs. One for instance paid regular visits where his concern was to guard against complacency and introduce an element of rigour into teachers' informal and often casual appraisals of pupils, by asking probing questions and raising broader issues; he sought to "act as a sounding-board" and offer "the outsider view". He saw the psychologist as a generalist: his was the sole profession with the necessary training, experience and background to allow of "a child overview". Others too sought to carry out an animating role by getting teachers to reflect on their practice and amend it as necessary.

viii.   Working with families

Some psychologists made a point of visiting the homes of special pupils. This provided an extra source of information in rounding out their assessments and enabled them to advise parents and inform them on the educational options open to their child. There was one example of formal working with families. This involved the application of the Portage model of service delivery described below in chapter 20. Educational psychologists have traditionally attached low priority to working with pre-school children but the school psychological service in one area was instrumental in getting the Portage model adopted and contributed much to its development and running.

ix. Research activities

Educational psychologists receive a basic grounding in research methods as part of their training. This enables them to evaluate the research literature and inform teachers of relevant developments. This was not widely engaged in but one psychologist at least took it very seriously. He sought to analyse and digest relevant findings and disseminate them to teachers. He also worked to inculcate a research attitude in teachers to get them to "look rather more critically at what they are doing".

He conducted his own research into the language development of all pupils in the authority's units for the hearing impaired. This was to provide evidence relating to the oral v. manual issue in deaf education and the possible need to move away from the authority's total reliance on oralism.

x. Advisory tasks

As noted, educational psychologists took on various advisory functions either formally as when a psychologist was also adviser for special education or informally when particular advisory roles were thrust upon individual psychologists. The most notable of these was policy formulation. In at least five authorities, psychologists had made specific contributions to policy on integrated provision. This role is implicit in various examples cited above: determining the nature and extent of coverage of an integration programme through laying down admission criteria; the advocacy of the Portage model; and gathering data relevant to different ways of organising education for the hearing impaired.

Speech therapists

Speech therapy services have been the responsibility of Area Health authorities rather than local education authorities since 1974. Consequently those speech therapists (along with physiotherapists) who work in schools operate within a different administrative context and to different lines of authority from their teacher colleagues. The individual therapist will report to a principal or area speech therapist and will normally work from an Area Health clinic. Even if she spends much of her time in schools her professional resources and contacts with fellow therapists will tend to be at the clinic.

The training and work of speech therapists were reviewed by the Quirk Report (1972), which also recommended staffing levels. There are two routes of entry into the profession: three-year diploma course and four-year degree course. The latter which is becoming more common provides the dual qualification of teacher and speech therapist. Apart from teaching, one can distinguish three roles exercised by speech therapists: diagnosis; clinical treatment and therapy; and counselling. These roles are exercised in respect of both children and adults. Where schoolchildren are concerned they often entail working with families and close collaboration with teachers.

Organisation of the service

The speech therapy services available to the integration programmes in our sample fell into two types, depending on whether the programme was a specialist language unit or not. As could be expected, the language units enjoyed a much closer and more intensive relationship with speech therapists than did the other forms of provision. These latter received limited or no speech therapy. Where it was available it was usually insufficient. In only one school in this category were teachers satisfied that the needs of children were being met. This particular school had the services of a therapist for half a day a week and relations between teacher and therapist were very positive. Of the other schools in receipt of speech therapy, only one received weekly visits from a therapist. The more usual arrangement was for a therapist to come along for a fixed period of time at regular intervals – fortnightly, monthly, etc – and see whichever children were presented. In a small number of cases the therapist visited only on request – at infrequent intervals.

A considerable number of schools had no access to speech therapy. In some cases school staff felt this was unsatisfactory as some children were in clear need of speech therapy. In others it was our view that individual children would have benefited from the attentions of a speech therapist on account of clearly evident language problems that were not being dealt with by the school.

The language units, as one would expect, had close working relationships with their local speech therapy services. One unit was allocated seven sessions (three-and-a-half days) a week while the other two had one full day each. Particularly in the case of the former the speech therapist was effectively a member of the unit staff. In one case there had been difficulties arising out of insufficient liaison between Education and Area Health. This meant for example that the requisite number of speech therapy sessions was not costed into the Health budget and provison for that year was less than it could have been. In all cases of course the therapist allocated to a particular unit remained responsible to Area Health through her Principal. Some reservations were expressed about this: heads and education officers were uneasy about people working in schools for lengthy periods who were not employed by Education and over whom the LEA had no control. These were usually expressed as generic fears however, and as potential dangers, rather than in relation to specific instances of complaint. Moreover, these comments when made were not confined to speech therapists but embraced all staff working in schools not employed by Education.

There seemed to be few problems of this kind in the language units we studied. One therapist expressed a view that her intensive involvement in a language unit did set her apart a little from her colleagues. Not only did she work with children in a different way and in a different setting, but her orientation and frame of reference were increasingly at odds with theirs. More generally, there was a feeling that greater knowledge of the school system would be an advantage for speech therapists working in this way. (This too was a theme that kept recurring for medical and paramedical staff.)

Content of the service

The work of speech therapists varied greatly depending on whether the provision in question was a language unit or not, and the two situations are considered separately here.

Language units

While the service provided depended on the amount of time

available – one day a week in the case of two of the units, two and a half days (later three and a half) in the third – there were a number of significant elements in common. All the therapists were involved in placement and monitoring meetings, assessment, treatment and programme development. There were other roles too, depending on the priorities and needs at a given location.

The speech therapist was in all cases an important member of the initial placement committee and of case conferences. In one instance the therapist made a point of bringing tapes of children's language to case conferences to illustrate particular problems. This seems a commendable practice in view of the many comments made about 'paper children': professionals were uneasy at the extent to which they and colleagues were being called upon to reach decisions on children with whom they had little or no current involvement and whom they may not even have met. (The likelihood of this happening increases the more multidisciplinary assessment becomes the practice.)

With regard to work undertaken in schools, the speech therapist was clearly seen as the language expert. This is not to derogate from the competence and skills of the teachers, but merely to acknowledge the absence of suitable training for language unit teachers. (A positive development to help right this situation occurred during our study with the setting up of a one-year course leading to the Diploma in Language Remediation Studies at Reading University.) While teachers had some general knowledge concerning children's language development, they lacked the specific detailed knowledge. As one teacher put it, "I know the rungs of the ladder as far as education is concerned; the rungs of language development I leave to (the speech therapist)". It should be stressed however that the working involvement between teachers and therapists was not entirely a one-way process: one speech therapist who attached a great deal of importance to working with teachers saw part of her job as examining "how the use of language impinges upon educational progress".

The speech therapist's role as language expert can be broken down into the following sub-roles:
- initial diagnosis and assessment
- developing and revising individual programmes
- providing day-to-day expertise
- liaising with and providing information on the broader community.

The speech therapist will have had contact with the child prior to his or her placement in the language unit, whether through one of the pre-school agencies or through a school referral. Her specialist contribution to initial assessment will reflect the use of tests, such as the Reynell Developmental Language Scales, the LARSP profile, the Edinburgh Articulation Test and so on. The issue of what were the appropriate criteria for placing a child in a language unit was debated throughout our study. Psychologists, teachers and speech therapists all had their own perspective on this. As far as speech therapists are concerned, they have an overview of the provision available for pupils with speech and language difficulties, and will be guided by this in deciding whether their diagnosis of a particular child's difficulties does in fact suggest a language unit placement.

None of the speech therapists we spoke with regarded diagnosis and assessment as a once-for-all activity. Assessment was a continuing feature, depending crucially on inputs from the teacher and related to the detailed work that the child was doing with both therapist and teacher. In two of the units individual programmes were worked out for each child. Following upon detailed initial assessment, long-term aims were arrived at which were broken down into short-term aims with a time scale of weeks. A programme of specific activities would then be drawn up, designed to achieve these aims and suited to the specific needs of the individual child. Given the continuous assessment, both therapy techniques and long-term aims could be modified in the light of a child's progress. The speech therapist sought to involve the teacher in developing these programmes, though the actual involvement seemed quite limited in some instances. In the third unit the speech therapist worked along with the educational psychologist and the teacher to develop individual curriculum profiles for each child. This exercise was in process during our study and while it seemed a very promising development with significant implications for both assessment and teaching it was not fully operational; only a small number of profiles had been completed by the end of our study.

The speech therapist played an important role through being constantly available as an informal source of specialist knowledge. Having access to distant experts is one thing; being able to talk to them on the spot when a problem arises and being able to demonstrate the problem rather than having to describe it is quite another. This is particularly important when a child's problems seem complex or resistant to treatment. If the specialist is to hand, she can join with the teacher in trying different approaches, abandoning or adapting various tactics as the child's response indicates.

This role is also one that may have personal significance for the unit teacher. As her work moves away from that of teaching colleagues, sometimes becoming qualitatively different, she may lose the sense of belonging to a community. This can be redressed in part by close collaboration with the speech therapist who will share her concerns and appreciate the nature of the work rather more than teachers in the parent school.

Various other roles adopted from time to time included liaising with persons in the broader community, talking to parents, and visiting children's original schools. These roles are not entirely dependent upon the speech therapy role and reflect in some measure the fact of being an expert who is independent of the school. By virtue of belonging to a community of experts on language development and disorder, the speech therapist can help to build a bridge between that world and the world of the school. This gap can seem at times to be impassably wide to the individual unit teacher. One therapist saw her role partly in terms of a facilitator, almost a Named Person in the Warnock sense. As well as furthering liaison with local agencies, she felt that she was also in a better position to write for information to specialist agencies such as the Wolfson Centre or the Hester Adrian Research Centre. Much of this external liaising was done by the teacher in charge of one of the units. Quite possibly this will become increasingly commonplace as teachers in language units are more appropriately trained.

Some differences emerged with regard to visiting parents. One of the units had close relationships with the parents who tended to identify the unit with the teacher rather than with the speech therapist. The other two units had little contact with parents, and such contact as existed was through the speech therapist. One therapist felt that there was insufficient contact with parents and would have liked to be in a position to work more closely with them. Considerable dissatisfaction was expressed over the amount of contact with parents. In one authority the speech therapist was assigned half a day a week for making contact with parents and schools. Her declared intention was to see all parents individually in order to establish rapport with them, develop more meaningful case histories, reinforce correct language patterns and gather informal information on the home enviroment.

In one authority it was policy to maintain contact with children's previous schools, and to this end they spent every Friday back in their respective local schools. The speech therapist here paid regular visits to all the schools, sometimes on her own, sometimes accompanied by a teacher from the language unit. The intention was to spend time with the class teacher, but frequently it was necessary first to spend one or more visits with the head teacher. In one school it was claimed that four visits had had to be made before the teacher from the language unit gained access to the classroom! Whatever these local difficulties, the idea was not so much to advise as such but rather to get over to the class teacher an idea of "where the child is at, what I think he might be doing". A further aim seemed to be to communicate a sensible view to the teacher of the child's actual and likely progress. These visits were also of course for the purpose of gathering information; the process worked both ways – "we want to find out how the child is coping".

Finally, a word about how the various therapists undertook their work in the schools. One therapist identified three patterns: withdrawing children for intensive treatment; working with a group of children, frequently in the company of the teacher; and working with individuals in a group. Another made a point of seeing each child individually for a short time on the occasion of each visit. This therapist worked in a corner of the classroom so that the teacher was aware of what was going on. The latter had a good idea from this what the therapist did and was acquiring skills of her own. The third therapist, with rather more time than the others, devoted the greater part of her time to individual treatment in a withdrawal situation. She still had a good deal of time however to spend in the classroom, an opportunity which provided useful information on children's working language. Given the greater time available for individual treatment, her aims were to promote development where it was lacking and to remedy inappropriate learning. All the therapists spent some time talking with the teachers; in one case half an hour discussing each child at the beginning of the day, in another it was over lunch, while in the third case this was an activity that permeated the week.

It is worth noting that in two of these cases the speech therapist devoted part of each weekly visit to seeing children who were in other classes in the parent school. (This did not apply in the third case since the unit was independent of the school at which it was located.) In one case the therapist spent time in the school's nursery and a further five minutes or so with a child in the junior part of the school. In the other the therapist was regularly seeing two children from the parent school plus a third in a reception class. It is highly unlikely that these children would have received the same frequency or continuity of speech therapy if the language unit had not been located at their school, or that their teachers would have acquired the same awareness and understanding of their problems.

Programmes other than language units

As noted above, speech therapy services for integration programmes in this category were sparse and often insufficient. Two examples will be given, both relating to provision for pupils with severe learning difficulties. The first relates to special centres at two neighbouring schools, one junior, one secondary. The junior school reported weekly visits of half a day each plus ready access when needed. Considerable time appeared to be given over to working with teachers and ancillaries; developing therapy programmes in a collaborative way; advising and giving information; and obtaining feedback from teachers. Positive comments were made about the flow of information from therapist to teachers, and there was general satisfaction with the service provided. The secondary school likewise received weekly visits. One of the more significant developments here, described in detail in the previous chapter, concerned the structured collaboration between the speech therapist and a welfare assistant. This involved a detailed work programme drawn up by the therapist and carried out and monitored by the assistant.

The second example comes from an authority which had special classes for infants with severe learning difficulties in four schools. The situation obtaining in respect of speech therapy was as follows:

School 1   The speech therapist visited once a month. This was felt to be insufficient. The teachers (there were two special classes in this school) would have liked the services of a speech therapist for most of their children, while the therapist described herself as merely an adviser!

School 2   The speech therapist came every three weeks to plan a speech therapy programme, "more in an advisory position"; she devised a programme for the teacher and her assistant to carry out between visits. While this was useful it was judged inadequate by the teacher. The need expressed was to have people such as speech therapists "on tap" so that they could be called on whenever specialist assistance was required to clarify a particular child's learning difficulty.

School 3   The speech therapist visited every two or three weeks. She assessed the children once a year on the Reynell Developmental Language Scales. She would then inform the teacher about areas where the children were experiencing difficulties and show how they might be met. The teacher was given a list of things to do with each child. One example was of a girl who needed to be introduced to the Paget Gorman signing system in the view of the therapist. She proceeded to instruct the teacher in this technique and the latter then taught it to the girl.

School 4   No speech therapy provision was available to this school.

Physiotherapists

Physiotherapy services are also the responsibility of Area Health authorities. The majority of physiotherapists work within the National Health Service and are employed in hospitals. Some work outside the hospitals in health centres, patients' homes and schools. Trainees require State Registration in order to enter the profession. This is obtained on successful completion of a three-year training course, embracing practical and academic studies, and gaining membership of the Chartered Society of Physiotherapy. As part of a health care team, physiotherapists use their special techniques to help patients who are physically disabled by injury, illness or medical condition to lead as active and normal a life as possible. In schools they contribute to the assessment and development of the physical skills and mobility of pupils with special needs.

Organisation of the service

Physiotherapy is a highly specialist intervention appropriate for quite specific problems which only a relatively small proportion of the school population can expect to face. Given this, one would not expect it to be widespread throughout the educational system. This is indeed the case. The main need for physiotherapists is in those schools and special centres which provide for pupils whose primary handicap is a physical one. Our study contained three such examples.

The need for physiotherapy is not confined to such schools and centres. In a number of other schemes there was the occasional pupil who, in addition to perhaps severe learning difficulties, also had a physically disabling secondary condition. The more severe cases were receiving some physiotherapy, though often this was only after persistent pressuring and campaigning by a teacher or parent. There were many other pupils who were not receiving any physiotherapy and yet who by common consent could have benefited from it. For example, one infant with severe learning difficulties had received physiotherapy while in hospital. The physiotherapist later visited the child's special class to see him in a 'real life' setting and review progress. The boy's movements were in fact quite uncoordinated and progress was relatively unsatisfactory. The physiotherapist devised some exercises for the boy and instructed staff in carrying them out. In due course the boy improved to a point where he was able to walk unaided. Staff in the school pointed to a number of other children with similar co-ordination problems who also seemed likely to benefit from physiotherapy.

In a similar class in the same authority another child received monthly visits from a physiotherapist, exercises again being left for the teacher and ancillary. This service did not extend to other children in the class. In another authority, at a special unit for pupils with severe learning difficulties (which included a 'special care' section), staff had extreme difficulty in obtaining physiotherapy – "we had to fight to get any physio at all" (teacher in charge). For a time the teacher had taken children to the nearest hospital department some 15 miles away. Eventually a physiotherapist was made available for one day a week.

The delivery of physiotherapy across the integration programmes we studied varied in accordance with the particular organisational format: large groupings of physically handicapped pupils (eg, special schools or specialist departments) on the one hand, small centres or individual integration on the other. The former had regular access to physiotherapy provision, sometimes on a quite generous scale – though it was not always perceived as such by those involved. The latter – as has already been noted – commonly had very little, though a significant development occurred in one area during the course of our research which is of sufficient interest to merit detailed consideration.

First, with regard to the large groupings, two locations were involved. One was an all-age special school for the physically handicapped where some pupils at secondary stage attended an adjacent comprehensive school on a part-time or full-time basis. There were 135 on roll, of whom 103 were, according to the senior physiotherapist, in need of regular physiotherapy. This was provided by a team of two physiotherapists and an aide plus an occupational therapist. The school contained excellent resources for both general and specific therapies, including a hydrotherapy pool. All physiotherapy was done in the special school and pupils in the integration programme returned there for it. Convenient times could not always been found and the amount of physiotherapy some pupils received was less because of this. The second location was a special department for 30/40 secondary age physically handicapped pupils attending a comprehensive school. Physiotherapy was provided here by a physiotherapist who spent the equivalent of three days a week at the school. This was quite inadequate in her judgement. Though pupils' need of formal physiotherapy was reduced at this stage – all were aged 13 plus – there was too little time to carry out the independence training and other programmes she perceived to be necessary.

One authority in our study had opted for the individual integration of physically handicapped pupils. A major problem was that for many years after the programme started no physiotherapy was available in the schools. One set of parents made their own arrangements with a hospital-based physiotherapist but most of them were unable to do so or were unaware of the continuing importance of physiotherapy after their child had been discharged from hospital. This was a major weakness of the programme, and pupils' needs in respect of toileting, physical activity and equipment maintenance were poorly met in consequence.

The difficulty arose partly from the national shortage of qualified staff, exacerbated in this instance by the altered conditions of service following on local government and health service re-organisation in 1974. A further complication was the dispersion of pupils across a generally sparsely populated county with difficult communications. This had several ramifications: no-one in the local schools had much idea of the nature of the handicap and the need for physiotherapy in many cases; there were too many pupils too widely spread for ready monitoring; and traditional modes of physiotherapeutic provision did not lend themselves to meeting the needs of pupils dispersed in this way.

This gap in provision was eventually resolved with the introduction of a peripatetic community physiotherapy service in September 1978. Three part-time physiotherapists were appointed, and charged with serving the needs of all physically handicapped pupils in ordinary schools. (Some had a responsibility for pupils in special schools as well.) Twelve months later they were seeing a total of 59 pupils attending ordinary schools. Clearly, given their part-time employment and the other demands on their time, it would be unrealistic to expect them to offer an intensive service for all pupils. The team's response to this constraint has been to delegate much of the routine work to classroom ancillaries, who are responsible for the welfare of the more severely handicapped among the pupils.

Content of the service

The discussion here is based on the three integration programmes involving physically handicapped pupils: an individual integration programme, a special department in a comprehensive school and a special school/ordinary school link. The first of these is crucially different from the other two in the present context since it did not involve groups of pupils in need of physiotherapy. Thus, it raised the dispersal problem associated with integration in a very direct way; moreover, school staff were not versed in physical handicap, and the physiotherapist was coming in as the sole expert.

Roles undertaken

Physiotherapists dealing with groups of pupils (second and third programmes above) worked in the same general way as their colleagues in segregated special schools, though with some modifications to take account of the integration context. Staff made mention of the following role components: assessment; providing treatment; liaising with other professionals (notably medical consultants); informing teachers of pupils' capacities and advising them on general handling; advising and working with parents; promoting greater independence in pupils, including providing practice in general orientation and road-training skills; and encouraging an acceptance of the handicap. In addition, the physiotherapist in the special department reported an advisory involvement in regard of occupational therapy.

The importance of contact with parents was emphasised by her counterpart in the special school. This was due in part to pressure of work: neither she nor her colleagues could provide the necessary therapy for all pupils so there was a need to determine priorities. Her solution was to concentrate on hydrotherapy at school where the facility was available, and to seek to educate parents so that they themselves could provide 'land therapy'. Added justification for this course of action was that formal physiotherapy would cease at the end of compulsory schooling, so that the onus would fall on parents or on the young people themselves. "You have to educate them to look after themselves . . . If you don't . . . a lot of them have the attitude, 'I'm handicapped and I don't have to do it', and this leads to atrophy . . ."

The physiotherapists in the first programme adopted a rather different approach. This was forced on them by the dispersion of the pupils and the lack of specialist knowledge of physical handicap in the schools where they worked. They were appointed in fact as community physiotherapists. The key difference lay in the amount of delegation: physiotherapists sought to work through welfare assistants and drew up programmes for them to carry out rather than always providing treatment themselves. This was stressed by a research physiotherapist involved in the early days: 'The physiotherapist undertaking this work must be prepared to be adviser and teacher rather than pure practitioner. It will not be possible personally to carry a full treatment load daily for many children.' They continued to see pupils individually – for assessment, for some routine treatment and for all technical work such as post-operative physiotherapy or where a child was being trained in using new orthoses. Any sustained formal physiotherapy was scheduled for a hospital department outside school hours.

The main components of the physiotherapist's role here were: treating individual pupils; training and working with ancillaries; and monitoring equipment. Each physiotherapist visited the pupils she was responsible for on a rota basis, usually every few weeks or termly with review cases. More frequent visits – two or three times a week – were arranged for those in need of more intensive treatment.

The standard routine on an initial visit is for the physiotherapist to see the pupil alone initially, and later in both the classroom and general setting of the school (corridors, toilets, playground, gym, etc). She will check for any problems of physical management that the pupil presents, and for any difficulty with mobility experienced or likely to be experienced. Sitting in on PE lessons is regarded as particularly crucial, to see whether the pupil is included or not, and to advise on routines or activities he or she could cope with using existing or perhaps additional equipment. In the classroom the therapist concerns herself with assessing such matters as what would be the best form of movement. Would it be less disruptive if the child crawled around? Would a rollator (an aid to walking) be an obstruction?

By the close of the visit the therapist will have worked out specific reinforcing exercises for the ancillary to carry out informally on a daily basis. Seeking minimum disruption to the pupil's education is paramount. The exercises are presented on workcards and explained to both ancillary and teacher. These may be walking exercises, practising transfer from wheelchair to splints or specific physical exercises.

Subsequent visits by the therapist typically comprise a period of individual treatment for the pupil, which the welfare assistant always attends – a form of ongoing induction; discussion of any problems that may have arisen with teacher and/or head; possibly some guidance on specific exercises; advice on miscellaneous aspects – the pupil's posture within the classroom or the appropriateness of classroom furniture; and concluding with the checking of orthoses and wheelchairs to ensure they are in proper working order.

The physiotherapists working in this integration programme attached great importance to their training function. The class teachers and ancillaries had no specialist background in physical handicap yet they were in sole charge of the pupil for practically all of the time. The therapists encountered a lack of knowledge and gross misperceptions. "The teachers are not aware of the physical and psychological needs . . . they are frightened, they don't know how much to ask of a child." They pointed to the over-protectiveness, the lack of awareness of what pupils *could* do, the failure to realise the physiological importance of daily standing and exercise on the bladder, bowels and soft tissues, the lack of maintenance of equipment.

One member of the physiotherapy team identified three issues commonly raised by school staff. First, they wanted to know when physiotherapy exercises should be carried out, and for how long. Secondly, was there a need for any specialist equipment and, if so, where could this be obtained? (In general all that was needed was a private space, a soft floor, a mat and chair. With some conditions use could be made of a school's gymnasium apparatus. The therapists found parallel bars particularly useful.) Thirdly, what was the nature of the pupil's physical condition? (A remarkable degree of ignorance prevailed on this score even after the pupil had been in school for some time.) The physiotherapists sought to enlighten ancillaries and teachers on these various matters in the course of their visits. This was done on an ad hoc basis, as and when the opportunities arose. It was clear that much benefit followed from this: to staff in the way of better understanding, increased skills and more realistic attitudes; and to pupils through having a more normal experience of schooling.

Constraints associated with integration

A number of difficulties associated with providing integration in integrated settings emerged. While these were definite constraints that in some cases reduced the quality of service that could be provided, there were advantages or at least opportunites associated with many of them as well.

(a) Education took priority over physiotherapy – in a way that physiotherapists claimed had not obtained in some special schools where they had worked. "We try to fit in with breaks and things for the children who are fully integrated." Lunchtime was the main opportunity at secondary level. In some cases this meant cutting back the amount of physiotherapy a pupil recieved because it was felt that he or she could not physically cope with the demands of the integration programme *and* therapy. Thus, one boy had to drop three lunchtime physiotherapy sessions and five hydro-therapy sessions a week. The pressure on time is well illustrated by the case of Peter, a teenager suffering from muscular dystrophy: "Dressing and undressing Peter takes half an hour and he only has an hour's session. This leaves half an hour to do all the things that should be done for muscular dystrophy kids . . . giving him time to lie flat every day for quarter of an hour, pool work and breathing exercises." In one programme there was some pressure from consultants to provide more physiotherapy. Staff felt that they had to resist this: "You've got to think of the overall child . . . you can't do it (provide the ideal amount of therapy) *and* turn out thinking people . . . you've got to get a happy compromise".

(b)   The difficulty of controlling the environment of a large mainstream school made for difficulties in developing independence. One physiotherapist described how in a special school it was relatively straightforward to set up a gruelling routine for a pupil to encourage self-reliance and to build physical stamina. However, in a mainstream school "(the able-bodied) fall over themselves on the whole to make themselves helpful" – for example by opening doors – thereby defeating the purpose of the exercise. A further constraint arose from the time pressures occasioned for example by the need to move around the school quickly at change of lessons. This meant that there was "a tendency to whip them into a chair so that they can be pushed around because it's quicker rather than making their own way". On the positive side, pupils had the opportunity of learning to cope with a normal environment where everything was not designed to accommodate them.

(c)   Disabled pupils could more easily become 'lost' in a large secondary school. This meant that greater responsibility must fall upon the individual pupil. For example, spina bifida sufferers are prone to develop pressure sores and constant monitoring of physical conditions is essential.

(d)   There was often insufficient space available for general exercising. (This was particularly mentioned in the larger, secondary schools.) One therapist referred to exercises in manoeuvring which were extremely difficult to do. Another told of how she had provided therapy at home for two pupils because there was insufficient suitable space at school. Also, some ordinary schools lacked the necessary facilities that a special school could be assumed to have. One example given was of a boy who had to remain in his wheelchair all day because there was no hoist available in school. Mention has been made of parallel bars, which were seen as particularly useful in strengthening the arm muscles and other exercises, as well as being an aid to walking.

(e) Many pupils had to travel considerable distances to school in transport that followed circuitous and slow routes. Inevitably, this was further time lost to many out-of-school activities such as swimming or horse-riding.

(f) Many staff, teachers as well as physiotherapists, commented on how parents, mothers especially, persisted in 'babying' their physically handicapped sons and daughters. Whereas in residential special schools there was an unbroken period of at least five days within which to inculcate proper habits of independence, some physiotherapists found that in integration programmes (as in day special schools) the actions of over-protective parents made consistency of treatment more difficult to achieve. On the other hand, there was better access to parents and the possibility of working regularly with them in their homes.

(g) One therapist felt that sometimes specialist attention which would be provided automatically in a special school went by the board in the ordinary school because no-one realised the need for it. Referring to the need for intensive and realistic independence training in early adolescence (covering such matters as domestic living skills, mobility training and hobbies), she instanced a 'living skills' programme which one school had devised but which in her view was virtually useless. In cooking for instance, "about all she (pupil) has to do is mix the food": cooking ingredients were always laid out for her and put away after use, the washing up was done for her and, much of the equipment was at the wrong height.

Use of ancillary staff
There were sharply contrasting views on the use of unqualified ancillary staff for providing physiotherapy. Those opposed to their

use pointed to the potential danger and the possibility of pro-fessional negligence, while those in favour pointed to staffing shortages and claimed that ancillaries could be deployed effectively. Indeed, there was virtue in this necessity to the extent that the use of ancillaries made it possible to integrate the physiotherapy input into educational activities.

The danger arose from the possibility of injury or damage to the individual being treated or of improvement being delayed as a result of unskilled handling. Many of the exercises and activities carried out may seem simple and easy to follow, but their importance and position in a sequential programme of treatment may not be appreciated by somebody lacking an adequate theoretical and practical background. Likewise, warning signals or signs of deterioration may not be noticed in good time. Consequent on this is the possibility of legal action for negligence. We were given to understand that there are precedents for legal action being taken as a result of physical injury.

On the alternative view, the prevailing staffing shortages demanded new approaches. Without accepting that untrained aides should be employed as a cheap substitute for professionally trained staff, it was argued that ways could be devised of giving aides a real share in the work. How this was achieved in practice has been described above. Essentially, it involved close working contact between the physiotherapist and the aide, whereby the former prepared detailed workcards, demonstrated procedures and monitored progress regularly. The content of this working was moreover confined to routine activities for the most part.

The physiotherapists felt that delegation was facilitated by the fact that much of the treatment could be routinised and did not require the formal exercise of their specific skills. Beyond that, they pointed to advantages in the arrangements. Instead of physiotherapy being confined to a set hour, the aide could ensure that the pupils would "do it little and often". This prevented boredom and meant that relevant activities could be carried on throughout the school day. The ancillary can pick the time to do exercises that is least disruptive or that fits in with what other pupils are doing. This will apply particularly to PE but to other activities as well, and can lead to therapy becoming an integral part of the school day in a natural way.

While we are not in a position to discuss the technical details of physiotherapy practice that may underline this conflict of views, it would seem that the attitude to professional skills is at the core of it. Both sides accepted that there was much that required the exercise of professional skills and could not properly be delegated, though they would probably not agree on how much of the physiotherapist's work this constituted. One side was more concerned to maintain professional standards however and ensure that physiotherapeutic expertise was not diluted or abused, while the other was concerned to disseminate skills and finds ways in which ancillaries could contribute.

Doctors

The discussion here includes clinical medical officers (formerly school medical officers) and consultants, principally paediatricians but including others such as neurologists, audiologists, ophthalmologists and orthopaedic specialists.

Aside from the specifically medical function, the clinical medical officer can carry out a number of important tasks in integration programmes. These include educating school staff on the nature and possible implications of difficult conditions, and guiding them through the intricacies of the health services and on occasion short-circuiting cumbersome official procedures. Medical officers can carry out an educational function in virtue of their medical background and detailed understanding of physical handicaps. This is particularly important where physically handicapped pupils are concerned. In many cases nobody at the school had any prior knowledge of the handicapping conditions they were dealing with, and if the medical officer did not supply information staff were likely to remain uninformed. One medical officer arranged to meet with the school head when an integrated placement was being proposed and sought to explain the nature and implications of spina bifida, cerebral palsy or whatever, and discussed the management of the pupil in detail. Subsequent visits were made with the intention in part of informing other members of staff. It was a source of general regret that it had not been possible to develop this role and execute it more systematically. Some teachers complained at having received very little information, while one medical officer's experience was that information was often not transmitted from one teacher to the next when a pupil changed classes. Elsewhere, in a school with a large department for physically handicapped pupils the medical officer made a point of talking to staff periodically; although some teachers here had had experience in dealing with physically handicapped pupils this was still very useful. In several locations medical officers were invited to contribute to in-service training activities.

In general, this educational role for medical officers was endorsed by school staff and some medical officers; their professional knowledge and expertise constituted a valuable resource for integration programmes and much could be gained from drawing on it more heavily and systematically. A note of caution however was sounded by several educational staff. They pointed out that some medical officers tended to make or imply educational judgements which were beyond their competence but which were accepted by teachers and ancillaries because of the medical officer's status. Thus, a medical officer might refer to a severely handicapped child as 'bright' and lively, meaning that he or she was alert and responsive by comparison with hospitalised peers; a teacher interpreting this remark within the school setting could easily relate it to academic potential and build unrealistic expectations on it.

The intricacies of the health services can be daunting to those outside it – and, we gathered, to some within it as well. This can be a drawback in integration programmes. Special school staff will build up a network of relationships with appropriate medical staff over a period of time and will have a point of contact for any new situations that arise. Staff involved in integration programmes especially if the numbers are small will not have the same opportunity; they may not know who to approach or what steps to take to ensure that a service is provided. Medical officers can play a major role here by familiarising school staff with the services available locally and the procedures for gaining access to them. More importantly, they can act as intermediaries on behalf of the school. Their knowledge of the system and the people in it enables them to achieve results that teachers on their own could not. One medical officer pointed out how she knew everybody in the local health service, who would move quickly, who would be able to do what was requested, and so on. Another was able to "short-circuit the system" through her contacts with medical colleagues and acquire medical services for pupils being integrated that would otherwise have to wait on protracted bureaucratic negotiations.

If the presence of pupils with special needs in a school leads to more frequent visiting by medical officers this can be considered a gain for the school as a whole. Other pupils about whom there is some question can be seen informally and at short notice. Teachers' worries can be allayed without waiting for the annual medical inspection, and if any action is necessary it can be initiated quickly. The regularity of contact means that the medical officer is a familiar figure in the school and that information on relevant health services is far more accessible to teachers than it otherwise would be.

Consultants will naturally be far less in evidence in schools. In point of fact many will visit special schools but were generally found to be reluctant to visit special centres attached to ordinary schools, apparently because of the smaller numbers but also, it was claimed, because the latter were simply outside consultants' frame of reference in many cases. This also could be considered a drawback to integration programmes. One teacher in charge of a special centre (for primary age pupils with severe learning difficulties) was so convinced of this that she prevailed upon the paediatricians in the area to hold clinics *at the school*. The pupils were drawn from a wide catchment area so a number of paediatricians were involved. Each came on a regular basis, at intervals of a month or thereabouts. In the course of a visit they would see the pupils for whom they were responsible – in one case this included some main school pupils suffering from epilespy – and spend time in discussion with teachers as well as parents. This development was enthusiastically received. Teachers acquired a better understanding of the medical background, the role and effects of drugs, and so on; doctors became more aware of the realities of the classroom; and parents felt more at ease and better able to ask questions in the relatively secure environment of the school as opposed to that of a hospital. Also, the pupil did not have to miss a day's schooling in order to keep a medical appointment. The net result was to further the development of a common policy between teachers, parents and the school on "the way you should be going with a child".

The importance of doctors having a good understanding of what went on in schools was stressed repeatedly. One educator spoke only partly in jest when he castigated consultant ophthalmologists of his acquaintance for being "concerned only with eyeballs".

Many teachers expressed concern about medical colleagues' inadequate grasp of educational matters. They themselves might have a limited grasp of medical factors but then they were not given to handing down medical opinions and nobody would take any notice if they did! Some doctors had quite decided views on education however and did not hesitate from making educational pronouncements – which *were* listened to because of their status. Quite aside from any misinformation that might be circulated, especially to parents, in this way, teachers needed guidance on the educational and classroom implications of physical conditions. If doctors were to provide this in any depth they had to have a good understanding of educational practice. Involvement in case conferences provides a further context: the more informed doctors are on the educational setting the better able are they to relate the specifically medical factors to the other perspectives being advanced and contribute to a multidisciplinary view of the pupil.

A final point relates to the passing on of medical information. Doctors are bound by a strict code of practice designed to protect the confidentiality of medical information. One does not have to take issue with this code to regret the frequent failures in communication that were reported. Chazan *et al.* (1980) found in a recent study of services for parents of handicapped children under five that confidentiality was often used as an excuse for failure to communicate. Our experience strongly corroborates this. While doctors were properly guarded about confidential information, teachers were commonly left without information which they should have had – sometimes getting it in garbled form from the parents. Teachers reported numerous efforts to obtain information, only to be ignored or even brushed off. One teacher sought to ascertain of a boy who had been seen by various consultants whether his poor handwriting might be associated with neurological impairment; repeated enquiries produced no information whatsoever. A spina bifida girl in a country school was admitted to hospital on an emergency basis one day. Her teacher rang the hospital out of concern and to volunteer any information that might be of use. Not only did she fail to elicit any information on the girl's condition but was given clearly to understand that she had no business contacting the hospital.

Interdisciplinary working

The Warnock report regards the development of close working relationships between professionals in the different services concerned with children and young people with special needs as central to many of its recommendations, especially those concerned with assessment and educational provison (16.1). The case for coordination of services and interdisciplinary working is clear: the child or young person is one, whereas the services are many and based on distinctions that are to a degree artificial. The individual does not have a medical problem and a *separate* educational problem. The different problems are inter-related and in the individual's experience may not even be seen as different problems. The problems or the different aspects of a problem must then be tackled in a concerted way. When these problems are such that a single individual cannot be expected to have all the requisite knowledge or skills, the involvement of a range of different professionals becomes necessary. One might add the advantages of having second opinions and sharing perspectives that are made available. When problems are complex this can be important within a single discipline or professional approach as well as across disciplines.

Several instances of interdisciplinary working have been given in this chapter and others are detailed in chapter 16 on the monitoring of progress. These examples are encouraging as examples of what can be achieved. The more important consideration however is that such examples were few in number and relatively limited in scope. The emphasis was on assessment, with some excellent practice in the way of joint assessment and multi-disciplinary case conferences. Concerted *treatment* was little in evidence however, apart from occasional examples of joint working between ancillary staff and individual professionals such as physiotherapists or speech therapists. Assessment meetings might issue prescriptive recommendations but these were seldom sufficiently detailed to sustain direct work with the individual for long. One LEA officer pointed to the urgent need for "treatment that matches the fineness of diagnosis" and called in effect for a multidisciplinary *service* where diagnosis, assessment and treatment were all informed by relevant expertise from different professional backgrounds.

Achieving genuine interdisciplinary working is not easy and

indeed would appear to be beset with difficulties. We have referred to comments about 'paper children' and professionals' unease about being party to discussion and decisions on pupils not known to them. Some professionals regarded many assessment meetings as a waste of scarce professional time and viewed the trend toward ever larger and more representative case conferences with disquiet and alarm. Such gatherings were an inefficient and cumbersome way of exchanging views and reaching decisions. They made for considerable delay: one head noted that whereas previously a decision could be taken and action initiated within a matter of days it took six weeks or more to assemble opinion. Finally, they were interdisciplinary in name only.

This last consideration is what concerns us here since it brings the central problem into focus. However desirable inter-disciplinary working may be, it is not to be achieved simply by sitting people from different backgrounds down together. Means must be found of enabling professionals to communicate with each other and to do so at a professional level, avoiding the two extremes of using language and concepts not accessible to colleagues and resorting to commonsense exchanges. Clearly, 'talking at' colleagues in abstruse jargon is not the target but neither is it discussion that stays at the level of common sense. Though the latter may be useful in limited ways, it is not interdisciplinary working. That requires that the people involved interact as *professionals* contributing something that is specific to their professional background but which is also accessible to other professionals. This would seem to be more difficult than is commonly supposed. In addition to the possible need for retraining and new orientations to the exercise of professional skills, it may require also the development of new conceptual frameworks that facilitate the required exchanges. Teachers, doctors, speech therapists, physiotherapists, all work within their own framework, using the language and set of concepts appro-priate to that framework and making distinctive observations and inferences. Relating these different frameworks to each other is a considerable task; unless its scale and complexity are more generally appreciated it is likely that interdisciplinary working will continue to be unsatisfactory and will fail to contribute as much as it could to the education of pupils with special needs.

Summary

In this chapter we have considered the roles of various professionals external to the school. Advisers carry out numerous roles in respect of integration programmes, relating to policy, staffing and general oversight. The principal involvement was at the outset of a programme when advisory staff were usually closely involved. Advice as such tended to be limited on account of advisers' lack of time and/or specialist knowledge. In some cases this was of little consequence as there were well-qualified staff in post. Many teachers however did need advice or access to people with expertise, and when this was not available the educational provision that they could offer suffered as a result.

Educational psychologists likewise exercised many roles, some of them overlapping with the work of the advisory services. Individual assessment and placement decision making were major concerns of course but there were many signs of collaborative working and a concern to remediate learning problems through indirect intervention. Thus, there were several instances of educational psychologists either organising or taking part in in-service training activities geared to integration. They contributed to the monitoring of pupils' progress, sometimes in sufficient detail to guide classroom practice. In one case this monitoring took on a specific research orientation. Psychologists helped to develop admission criteria and procedures to govern entry to integration programmes and offered general advice on running them. These roles were not widespread of course. To the extent that they occurred at all they were an indication of a welcome shift in the educational psychologist's role from assessing and recommending placements to a more comprehensive engagement with pupils' learning and behaviour problems that took in the environment in which these problems occur and teachers and other staff who work with the pupils. This engagement, which entails an ongoing concern for pupils and collaboration with other staff, is of paramount importance in integration programmes. When present, it helped to make up for deficiences in the advisory services. All too often however it was not present, and, whether through pressure of time or preferred mode of working, educational psychologists were not in a position to give integration programmes the depth or continuity of service that would have been desirable.

Speech therapy provision varied in quantity and nature depending upon whether the integration programme was a language class for communication disordered pupils or not. Though therapists were generally in short supply, provision for language classes was relatively good and therapists exercised a wide range of roles in collaboration with teachers. Speech therapy services otherwise were sparse and frequently insufficient; physically handicapped pupils and those with severe learning difficulties in particular tended to miss out on requisite specialist attention.

By comparison with other agencies, the need for physiotherapy services is restricted to relatively fewer pupils, mostly the physically handicapped and some of those with severe learning difficulties. For these however the need can be acute and the absence of appropriate services a serious drawback. Apart from the problems occasioned by the shortage of trained staff, integration made for difficulties through the lack of time for physiotherapy in the ordinary school day. This was particularly the case at secondary level when physiotherapy could not be integrated into other activities as readily as at primary level and was often effectively confined to lunchtime. A development of great interest, though not without its critics, is the use of ancillary staff to provide physiotherapy by implementing programmes drawn up for specific pupils by a physiotherapist.

For these different professionals and others whose roles have been examined more briefly, it is clear that integration requires new ways of working for the benefit of special pupils. In particular, there is need of close collaboration with colleagues, sharing information, viewing pupils' problems in a comprehensive light, disseminating skills and generally moving toward interdisciplinary working. These new ways of working have to be developed in a context of staff shortages – a recurrent feature throughout the services involved – which could moreover be exacerbated by the demands of integration programmes. There were opportunities as well as difficulties. This was particularly true of ancillary staff whose deployment in integration programmes offers an important means of extending scarce professional skills.

In conclusion, integration programmes may well necessitate a formal concern for interdisciplinary working over and above what is required in special schools. The latter commonly had staff from different professional backgrounds in post and have regular access to others. This can make for a *de facto* interdisciplinarity through the sheer physical proximity and good personal relationships. Such opportunites are often lacking in integration programmes. The speech or physiotherapist is not on site, the educational psychologist is an irregular visitor, and the medical consultant is a distant personage. In this situation it is all too easy for the visiting specialists to be just that and for their understanding of and work with a pupil to have no bearing on what the class teacher or ancillary does. It is necessary then for those involved to have deliberate thought to how their different professional contributions come together for the benefit of the individual pupil.

Chapter Nine
Training

Educating pupils with special needs in ordinary schools leads to considerable demands on teachers and other staff. Specialist teachers need in addition to their specific assessment and teaching skills to be able to work with other teachers and secure their co-operation, liaise with outside agencies, involve parents and generally carry out the various functions described in previous chapters. Main school teachers have to deal with a wider ability range than before. They may find that their training and experience are insufficient and need to be supplemented. Ancillary staff can contribute to integration programmes in many ways but do so most effectively if they have been given appropriate training. The various external specialists have important roles to play as well but some of these may be unfamiliar ones that entail new ways of working on their part. In all of these cases there is need of training in order to ensure that pupils' needs are met and that the advantages of being in an ordinary school are availed of.

It is worth noting that integration programmes almost by definition entail a dispersal of staff, pupils and resources. This has implications for training and staff development to the extent that the advantages claimed for special schools in this respect are not available. Special schools, it is argued, provide an important locus for research and development work in special education and have been responsible for much pioneering work. The concentration of expertise, resources and pupils with complex problems provides a stimulating environment as well as an experimental situation where alternative approaches to particular problems can be tried out and evaluated. It is sometimes claimed also that the special school is a valuable training ground for teachers entering special education: it provides easy contact with more experienced colleagues and a supportive environment in which theory can be translated into practice or gaps in training remedied. This may be an idealised account of what special schools actually do but it is clear that a good special school can create an educative milieu for its staff that a small special centre cannot. Integration raises new and distinctive problems of training; the needs are if anything more varied and new ways of meeting them must be found.

In the long term the answers must be sought in initial or early in-service training. If a majority of teachers are likely to encounter pupils with special needs in the course of their teaching careers, initial teacher training must take explicit account of this. Nisbet *et al.* (1977) carried out a survey among newly qualified teachers in Scotland and reported that 58 per cent felt inadequately prepared for teaching slow learners. Noting this finding, the Warnock Report observes that there is no reason to think that a similar survey in England and Wales would produce different results. Specialist options must be available for teachers who intend to work in special centres. Whatever special schools may have been able to do in the way of inducting teachers without the relevant specialist training, most special centres are not in a position to do this and depend for their proper functioning on the availability of suitably trained teachers. Classroom ancillaries generally possess the NNEB or Norland qualifications if they are trained at all. These are geared toward working with normal infants and as they stand are not an adequate preparation for working with pupils with special needs. As for external specialists, some of the roles forced on them as a result of integration are new ones for them and require an orientation and skills not present in their training or previous experience.

While we acknowledge the importance of initial training it is not our primary concern here. We report some data on the initial training that staff had received but are more interested in arrangements for on-the-job training. Even if initial training of teachers, ancillaries and other staff was revolutionised overnight there would still be need of training for staff already in post or changing responsibilities as well as appropriate induction for those entering work. In this chapter we outline some possibilities in practice whereby this training can be provided.

We commence with a brief look at the training that staff in our sample received and the training needs expressed, and then detail the different models in action by which these needs can be met. The main focus is on teachers since they are the professional group primarily responsible for educating pupils with special needs in ordinary schools but it is not confined to them.

Training received by staff

Our remarks here are addressed primarily to teachers and, to a lesser extent, ancillary staff. We did not enquire in any systematic way into the training customary within their own profession. This might or might not have contained components relevant to integration but we are not in a position to comment in detail. What has emerged is a number of clear training implications, relating to knowledge and skills that ought to be made the subject of training or induction where they are not already so. These are discussed in the following section.

Teachers

The key staff in integration programmes are those teachers who have a major responsibility for pupils with special needs. The teachers in our study were involved in programmes of very different kinds. As discussed in chapter 5, there was considerable variation in their relevant professional backgrounds and they brought a wide range of professional and personal experience to bear on their work.

Most of the teachers in our sample had been through ordinary teacher training, with the exception of a small number of teachers working with pupils with severe learning difficulties. These latter few had all acquired the (now defunct) NAMH Diploma. The teachers in this small group were uneasy that they had had no formal preparation in dealing with ordinary children. While they considered the course as excellent in terms of meeting special educational needs, its focus on deviance and the lack of teaching practice in ordinary schools were considerable drawbacks. In particular, it was no preparation at all for teachers with a concern to promote integration. (The lack of any training orientation toward integration and making optimal use of the opportunities presented by it was not peculiar to this group. As discussed elsewhere, this was a marked feature of many of the programmes studied.) Some of these teachers displayed a certain defensiveness with regard to their mainstream colleagues. There was a feeling that they were not proper teachers and could only deal with a very small group of children. "*They* say you can't call it teaching" (teacher speaking of her mainstream colleagues' perception of her work). Some main school teachers had the – mistaken – impression that certain of their colleagues in special centres were not qualified teachers, and felt in any case that they could only teach in "purely 'S' circumstances".

The greater number of teachers in our sample received no specialist inputs relating to handicap during initial training or regarded them as too cursory to be of real use. There were mentions of occasional lectures, booklists being distributed and brief course components on handicap, particularly among the younger teachers, but the general consensus was that these inputs were too slight and made little difference to their capacity to do their jobs. As noted above, ordinary training – and teaching – came first for many of them, and involvement in pupils with special needs developed subsequently.

Many of the teachers, including those working in secondary schools, were junior trained. There were clear pedagogical advantages to this, in that much work with low-achieving secondary age pupils is at a basic level and may well be at – or even below – junior school work. There is a danger in emphasising the similarities however. An average or bright nine-year-old and a backward fourteen-year-old who function academically at the same level will need to be taught and handled in very different ways. The age difference entails many other differences – relationships with adults, physical maturity, social and emotional development, appropriate behaviour and so on. The teacher who is junior trained and junior oriented may need new skills and a considerable change in attitude when dealing with secondary age pupils, of whatever academic level. Moreover, secondary schools are academically and organisationally very different from primary schools, and the junior teacher may not be as well-equipped to promote the integration of pupils with special needs as colleagues with secondary experience.

Specialist training was acquired subsequent to initial teacher training by the great majority of teachers in our sample. Apart from three holding the NAMH Diploma, only six concentrated or took a major option on an aspect of handicap in initial teacher training. (All figures refer to the 52 teachers described in chapter 5.) Most of these had taken a course on teaching mentally handicapped children. All 17 teachers working with hearing or vision impaired pupils had taken the appropriate professional qualification or were due for secondment to take it. A further 14 teachers had taken courses of at least a year's duration covering various aspects of special and remedial education; these led mostly to diplomas though some were of degree standard.

Teachers had set about these training courses in various ways. A small number had been able to avail of secondment to follow full-time courses. A number of others applied for secondment while our study was in progress with considerable success; despite the limited secondment opportunities over the period in question, it is our impression that as a group these teachers fared quite well. Many more had taken or were in the course of taking part-time courses, either entirely in their own time or being released from teaching on one day a week. It is interesting to notice that in at least one instance a job was advertised with the stipulation that the person appointed should be willing to undergo training. (This training was in the event provided: the equivalent of a year's full-time course spread over three years.)

The great majority of these teachers had taken one or more short courses. Some teachers were assiduous in seeking out suitable courses and had attended a great many. These took place after school or at weekends, though sometimes entailing a week's absence from school. Many courses were organised by colleges of education or by education departments within other higher education establishments. Other courses and conferences were organised by the DES, individual LEAs, the Spastics Society, the National Council for Special Education and other bodies. The content covered in these courses was exceedingly diverse and included speech and language disorder, music for the mentally handicapped, remedial reading, structured play, Makaton (a signing system), aspects of speech therapy, movement therapy and much else besides.

As far as ordinary teachers are concerned, it would seem reasonable to suppose that the limitations of initial teacher training are even more marked since they are less likely to have had an orientation toward special education. We have seen in chapter 7 that more than half of the teachers responding to a questionnaire described their knowledge of handicap prior to the integration programme as poor or non-existent. Some 15 per cent described it as good or very good. Other evidence however suggested that this estimate was a little high, possibly reflecting the self-report nature of the data.

Ancillaries

The most common qualification possessed by ancillary staff in our sample was the Certificate of the National Nursery Examination Board (NNEB). (This is a qualification in nursery nursing, usually obtained following a two-year course in the development and care of young children.) This was possessed by rather more than half of the sample. In one authority NNEB training was required in order to obtain appointment as classroom assistant, while in several others it was considered desirable. Of those ancillaries who were NNEB trained, only the recent graduates had had any specific instruction on handicap – and that usually amounted to very little. While many found the training useful in a general way, the common feeling was that it was not geared to the work they were doing, and that there was need of much more specific instruction. This feeling was corroborated by teachers and LEA officers who acknowledged that they looked for NNEB training not because it was of great relevance but because it was virtually the only form of training that might reasonably be expected. A small number of ancillaries had Norland training; this is an alternative form of training for nursery nurses and is broadly similar to that provided under the auspices of the NNEB.

A small number of ancillaries had undergone all or part of relevant training courses such as nursing or teaching. These were women who were unable to find employment in their own profession or who found it convenient, because of family commitments, to have a local job that was tied to school hours. Others had no formal training but were mothers who had had experience of bringing up their own children; this tended to happen when ancillaries worked with one or two pupils as opposed to being attached to a special class or department. It may be noted that the vast majority had had no experience of handicap before taking up their present appointment. The exceptions were four who had minor involvement with handicap in a general way, eg a week's voluntary work in a special school.

Training needs

The training needs posed by integration could be identified by analysing the tasks carried out by the different people involved, relating them to the training they received in any case, and noting areas where further training specific to integration is required. As we have seen above, teachers find themselves carrying out many unaccustomed roles not covered in any training they have received. More generally, integration places a high premium upon interdisciplinary working and sharing of professional skills – physiotherapist devising a programme of exercises to be carried out by teachers or ancillaries, psychologist helping teachers structure their observation of a child or conducting assessments jointly with other professionals, teacher working with parents, and so on. By systematically detailing these various tasks and relating them to the training received by the professional groups in question a formal account of the training needs occasioned by integration could be derived.

An alternative to this formal approach is to ask the participants to describe the training needs they perceive and to note the training implications of their comments about their work. This is broadly the approach followed here though it is subject to the limitations that the untrained may lack awareness of what they should know and be able to do.

Specialist teachers

The training requirements for certain groups of teachers are quite specific. Those working with hearing or vision impaired pupils are required to take a recognised course of training within three years of commencing such work. There are no statutory requirements for other teachers but the need for training geared to the problems posed by particular handicapping conditions seemed to be gaining wide acceptance. This was especially the case in respect of pupils with severe learning difficulties, where many of the teachers had done extended courses or were planning to do so. The scarcity of relevant training for teaching pupils with speech and language disorders was also the subject of regular comment.

Outside formal training courses and the specific increments of knowledge and skill they provide, there were many references to general competencies. These have been discussed in chapter 5 under 'Selection criteria' and can be recalled briefly here. Broadly speaking these were of two types: teaching skills, eg analysing teaching sequences, individualising instruction; and non-teaching, eg disseminating information, collaborating with others as part of a team.

Ancillaries

The purpose of ancillaries is primarily to assist others, so one has to ask: How much training is necessary for them? We have seen that few had training relevant to the work they were doing. Some were unconcerned about this, even seeing a benefit in being free from preconceived ideas – "You don't dwell on the child's disability but take them for what they are". Others inclined to the view that the job was such that the requisite skills could not be taught but had rather to be acquired by experience – "You've got to be there gaining it for yourself, it's not something you can be told about". In point of fact, the ancillaries expressing this view had been 'trained' on the job by a more experienced ancillary already in post and had not been left to learn by trial and error.

The opposite view predominated however which held that some advance preparation would be useful. The general feeling was that it was insufficient to be left alone to work out things for oneself. This could lead to quite alarming incidents, particularly with physically handicapped children. We heard of ancillaries having to be instructed by parents on how to handle their children. One ancillary called upon to change a colostomy bag had no idea what to do and had to work to the pupil's instructions! The danger in this is that bad habits and incorrect ways of working may be perpetuated. Ancillaries referred to the lack of confidence that came from knowing so little: "When I arrived I hadn't a clue . . . I was really nervous, apprehensive". This meant also that less was being done for the pupils than might otherwise have been the case: "I feel she could do more if only I knew how to do it or if I knew I was doing it right". Again, it could be difficult to know when to take a firm line: "It would be handy to know just how much pain they feel and how much is kidology". It should be mentioned that the ancillaries themselves often had a clearer idea of their own need for training than many of the teachers and other professionals working with them, who sometimes inclined to the view that little or no training was necessary for them.

Ordinary teachers

Teachers were asked by means of questionnaire (Details in Appendix C): *Do you feel a need for any formal training to help you deal more effectively with these pupils?* Answers are summarised in the Table below:

Table	*Teachers' need of training*		
	Yes	No	Unanswered
	87	98	62

The high number of null responses is attributable to the fact that many of the teachers had little or no contact with the special pupils in their schools. Of those answering, it will be seen that just over half did not feel there was a need for formal training. The most common reason cited for this was that there was specialist help on site: the specialist staff in post were capable of providing any expertise required. Others referred to their limited involvement with special pupils or said that 'they should be treated like any pupil', so that special training to enable one treat them different was unnecessary. Those who argued for more training sought two things in particular: more information on handicapping conditions, especially those of a physical or sensory nature, along with details on matters such as checking hearing aids, lifting pupils in wheelchairs, and coping with fits; and a better understanding of the educational implications of these conditions, along with an insight into the teaching that the pupils were receiving. There were several mentions of the confidence that followed from training; teachers lost the fear of not being able to communicate with hearing impaired pupils, for instance, and became more relaxed in relating to special pupils generally. Others felt they needed training in specific aspects of their job, eg providing careers guidance for pupils leaving school.

Others

Judging by remarks from teachers and from some professionals themselves, the other professionals involved in integration programmes faced two main difficulties: their own lack of knowledge about education; and the relative novelty, as well as the sheer difficulty, of interdisciplinary working. Individuals and professional groups varied in their familiarity with the education system.

Some such as educational psychologists were well versed in it while medical and paramedical staff operated from quite a different base and, especially if their involvement with Education was limited, could lack important perspective. Some professionals commented on this, noting their ignorance of the educational context and their limited grasp of the overall situation of a pupil for whom they were supplying particular specialist inputs. One pointed out that outside his own specialism he was a layman and had no more brief to intervene or give opinion than anyone else, nevertheless frequently finding himself in the position of having to make such intervention. Teachers also commented on this – to an extent that might dismay some professionals – pointing in particular to the lack of awareness of classroom realities. This might be in reference to educational psychologists who conducted assessments and made educational prescriptions without confronting the learning tasks at which pupils were failing or medical and paramedical staff who diagnosed and treated them as if the classroom did not exist. Such practices were by no means universal nor, we suggest, do they raise insuperable training problems. It does take effort to switch from one professional context to quite a different one but it is not impossible. In addition to the possession of basic information, what seems to have characterised those who achieved it successfully was an openness of attitude and a readiness to learn from others while exercising one's own skills.

This awareness of educational realities is indeed an aspect of the much larger problem of interdisciplinary working. The difficulty of achieving interdisciplinary working has been noted. Many professionals are by training, established procedure and experience geared to working within the confines of a particular professional practice, without taking any substantive account of adjacent professionals. If the barriers are to be knocked or at least have some holes made in them, the question of training must be tackled. Professionals must take from their training an awareness of colleagues' domains and how their own relates to them. They must develop collaborative attitudes toward the sharing of information and joint working where appropriate and acquire the necessary skills.

How training needs were met

In this section we report on a number of ways in which staff involved in integration programmes sought to develop their understanding of special educational needs and acquire or improve their command of relevant skills. In their comments on teacher training, the Warnock Committee tended to concentrate on formal full-time courses and their part-time equivalents. While these are exceedingly important many teachers will not be able to avail of them even if suitable courses are available and their local education authorities can facilitate their attendance. We concentrate here on what can be done at local level without major expenditure of resources. Four broad approaches can be noted: attendance at courses; professional interaction with colleagues; contact with the pupils themselves and the experience of doing the job; and reading. Before discussing the first two of these in some detail, we offer a few observations on the others.

Contact with special pupils was regarded as most important, both by specialist teachers and their colleagues, in developing competence. When the former had had prior experience, for example in a special school, this was a considerable asset, just as its absence was a drawback for the others. We have noted above how diffident and even incapable many ordinary teachers felt when faced with special pupils for the first time. When asked about any growth in their knowledge about handicap, they referred to contact with pupils more than any other factor. Two thirds of the teachers replying to our questionnaire affirmed a growth in their knowledge. This was attributed to various factors, as noted in chapter 7, but in the great majority of cases teachers made specific mention of contact with pupils. Sometimes this was offered as a plain statement of fact – 'obviously through personal contact', 'front-line experience', 'through talking with them, eating with them and mixing normally in their society', 'one constantly learns from one's association with one's pupils, whatever their condition'. Some became aware of pupils' strengths and weaknesses through observation. On the strengths – 'from realising that they are capable of giving more, in many ways, than I realised', 'actually seeing an improvement in reading, writing and spelling ability', 'by observation of what they can manage in class and also group activities', 'as time has passed I have had the opportunity to observe their development higher up in the school', 'seeing handicapped pupils interacting with normal pupils'. On the weaknesses – 'I have come to realise their limitations', 'from increased contact a deeper understanding of their inability to cope with normal routine', 'I have realised some of their difficulties, eg manipulation skills, and difficulty they find in expressing themselves', 'having a handicapped child in the class for a year made me more aware of how much more care and attention was needed'. A small number noted specific benefits that accrued from teaching pupils with special needs, referring to 'direct contact with these pupils in a teaching situation', 'continuous contact in the classroom situation' or 'practical experience of working with a deaf child'. Others pinpointed the educative factors as having to cope with physically handicapped pupils in a practical situation, learning to communicate with them in 'their language' by translating ideas and words so that they understand, gearing work to suit their level, trying to teach them at the right level for them and maintaining their interest.

Surprisingly few teachers made mention of reading as a relevant factor. Those who did were clear that they had learnt much in this way and only regretted not having read more and sooner. There was a general call for guidance in this respect. Teachers often did not seem to know what to read or where to turn for information. We ourselves were regularly asked for recommended readings. It is reasonable to suppose that the circulation of suitable reading lists, and giving thought to making books and pamphlets accessible would pay rich dividends. In one school we noticed that the head of the special department took care to place suitable literature in the school staffroom that would serve to introduce staff in a general way to the problems faced by pupils in the department.

Courses

Attendance at courses is clearly a major source of training, much used by staff in our sample. We noted above how numerous teachers sought to further their professional development by taking appropriate courses. These were courses organised by colleges and other agencies external to the school or LEA. In this section we look at courses devised and laid on at local level. These tended to be custom-built with local needs in mind and drew upon local resources, though not exclusively so. It is clear that the organisational possibilities are many, and the examples described by no means exhaust the range.

Example A

The first example comes from an authority which catered for infant age pupils with severe learning difficulties in special classes attached to ordinary schools. Some of the teachers had had specialist training but the majority did not. In order to cope with the training needs, these classes along with the opportunity classes for moderately retarded pupils were closed for one day each term and a course of professional training organised at a local teacher training college. These were open to all teachers and ancillaries in the classes, the heads of the schools to which they were attached and some special school staff. The general format was that a theme for the day was chosen and speakers were invited to present matter relevant to this theme. Visual material was sometimes used and there were some discussion groups.

The range of topics covered was varied. They include: support services; teaching of early language, communication and attention skills; dimensions of parent/teacher involvement; early development of number concepts; vision – assessment and perception; people in groups – use of drama techniques to explore aspects of working in groups; problems of diet and feeding in the handicapped child; portage; language disordered children and provision for them; monitoring systems in special education; causes of retardation; development of intelligence – learning and teaching applications.

This innovative approach to in-service training was much appreciated by those who took part in it. The primary benefits were the professional content and the opportunity to meet others. On the negative side, there was not enough time to meet with others according to some teachers: there was a certain conflict between the situation created by having distinguished outside speakers and the need to have time for practitioners to sit and discuss among themselves. Another difficulty was that, while laudable in theory, mixing ancillaries with other staff did not always work very well since material of different kinds was required.

Example B

A second example comes from a secondary school with a large special centre catering for pupils with learning difficulties. The initiative here came from the school. There was an extensive integration programme and many staff in the main school taught special pupils so that staff in the special centre considered they had a duty to provide their colleagues with opportunities to learn more about special needs. In the first instance, it was planned to cater specifically for the staff of the school, its feeder primary schools and the associated special services. In the event colleagues from neighbouring secondary schools making similar provision expressed interest and invitations were widened.

The course consisted of five meetings held after school at weekly intervals. These followed a traditional format of 45 minutes lecture by a visiting speaker followed by questions. The speakers were all from the authority – advisers, psychologists, a teacher. Experience suggested that this was 'an unnecessarily drab way of transmitting knowledge and sharing views' and staff felt that workshop activities carried out in small groups would have been more profitable. Topics for the first course comprised: special education in the mainstream school; management of children with learning problems; core curriculum; teacher-based assessment of pupils with learning difficulties; and management of pupils with behaviour problems. Attendance at the meetings was good, reaching 50-60 (and including about a quarter of the host school staff), and the reception was fairly enthusiastic.

Example C

A third example comes from a campus where physically handicapped pupils were integrated part-time from a special school into a comprehensive school. The original idea was that comprehensive staff would benefit from having a talk by the head of the special school prior to the arrival of the pupils. This developed into a course of lectures held at lunch times except on one occasion when the speaker could only come after school. They took place on alternate weeks at the two schools. Because of the timing of the lectures and because the content was perceived as specific to that campus attendance was restricted to the staff of the two schools. It was acknowledged subsequently that there was nothing comparable in the locality and that many teachers and other staff could benefit from it.

The course comprised eight lectures on various aspects of physical and sensory deficit and the associated educational problems. Topics covered were: introduction to physical handicap;

visual handicap; auditory handicap; the delicate child; the physically handicapped child in the classroom; integration in practice;
problems of programming the handicapped child into the secondary school timetable; the Warnock report. Speakers were drawn
from the two schools and from outside agencies. Attendance at the
talks was moderate, with proportionately more coming from the
special school than the comprehensive.

Example D

In another authority a course planned initially for classroom
assistants working in special schools was extended to assistants in
all schools 'who are working with or interested in children with
special learning difficulties'. It was organised on a regional basis
within the county, which is a largely rural one, and comprised ten
hour-long sessions once a week after school. These sessions are
generally taken by teachers and other local professionals involved
with special education. Topics included the role of the nursery
assistant in preparing materials, maintaining records and so on,
the value of play, visual aids, aspects of physiotherapy.
These courses are held in different special schools within
their respective localities. Attendances at the early ones were
reported to be good despite the distances that some people had to
travel. The courses on offer in the different areas seemed to differ
considerably. They were generally welcomed in spite of being a
little general.

It was acknowledged that these courses were only a first step
and that more specific instruction was needed for ancillaries
working with physically handicapped pupils. A physiotherapist
working in the area outlined the sort of content that could usefully
be covered in a short (2/3 days) course:
1. Toileting – needs and techniques
2. Dressing
3. General handling – lifting, putting on shoes and so on
4. Day-to-day maintenance of wheelchairs, calipers and so on;
   fitting and adjusting; looking out for sores and pressure points
5. Keeping records.

Example E

In an authority where severely and profoundly deaf pupils
attended ordinary schools on an individual basis, the head of the

school for the deaf runs short courses for teachers in receiving schools. These comprise three evening lectures on the basics of hearing impairment and deaf education. They sought to give teachers an understanding of what hearing impairment means in practice, an introduction to the technicalities of causation and measurement, maintenance and use of hearing aids, communication with hearing impaired pupils and practical teaching tips.

Example F

A final example comes from an authority which has instituted handicap awareness courses for its teachers. Two experienced teachers have been seconded from their schools for one day a week to organise these courses. Each course runs for five consecutive Fridays. The first four days consists of lectures and discussions on different aspects of special education and the support services available to teachers. These presentations are made by local Education and Health personnel. On the fifth Friday they visit special educational establishments in the morning and come together for discussion on the visits in the afternoon.

This development arises directly from the Warnock recommendation (12.12) that short in-service courses on special educational needs should be taken by the great majority of serving teachers. Each course takes in 30 people, and it is anticipated that before long every primary school will have at least one teacher who has taken it. (It is envisaged that this would be the minimum requirement for them to act as a Named Person in their school.)

There are a number of general points to be made about organising courses of this kind. First, there is the question of location. If it is organised and presented within a single school or campus, it can be 'customised' for the specific needs of that location. Also, it is easier for staff to attend. On the other hand, considerable resources and efforts go into a well-organised course, and it would be unfortunate if others were unable to benefit from it. Also, it is commonly found to be beneficial to share experiences and perspectives with colleagues from other locations. A central consideration, which did not surface in our examples, is the extent to which a school-based course might enable staff translate training material into classroom practice in a co-ordinated way.

Secondly, there is a balance to be found between formal presentation where staff learn new things and less structured interaction where they explore ideas with colleagues and exchange details on practice. This will obviously depend on the content matter. Teaching a signing system will require a more didactic approach than discussing the timetabling implications of integration. The dilemma is a familiar one in running short courses, but it acquires a particular edge in the integration context where so many teachers are working in isolation. They run single classes within ordinary schools and have little opportunity for professional exchange with colleagues doing comparable work save when they go on courses. In this situation the bringing of staff together in a professional context may be as important as any formal course content.

A third consideration relates to the logistics of attendance. Should the course be held during school time or outside of school hours? Clearly, it is easier to require attendance in the former case. In some cases this is done by the simple expedient of shutting the school for a day and devoting it to in-service training or by closing special classes on one day each term. It was more usual to hold courses after school however or, exceptionally, over lunch time. This applied especially to courses for ancillary staff and was a particular problem there to the extent that a sizeable number of ancillaries are mothers with schoolgoing children of their own. The appeal of the job for them is that it ties in with school hours, and it may not be feasible for them to attend courses after school.

Professional interaction
1. Formal collaboration

Interdisciplinary or co-operative working can help to develop professional skills in many ways. A particular aspect of such working is when specialists formally adopt a role of instructing colleagues or otherwise developing their skills. This can be a result of a deliberate policy to adopt such a role or because the needs of given pupils can only be met if certain specialist skills are widely available. We describe four examples here, two where special school teachers worked with colleagues in ordinary schools, and two where therapists enabled ancillary staff to carry out professional programmes.

Example 1a The first example comes from a special school for pupils with moderate learning difficulties that established close liaison with neighbouring schools. This is described in more detail in the accompanying volume. Briefly, the purpose of the liaison was to assist teachers in ordinary schools to teach those of their pupils who had particular learning difficulties. Teachers from the special school were timetabled to spend part of their week in ordinary schools working collaboratively with class teachers. If a pupil presented teaching problems the special school teacher would conduct his own assessment, relate it to the class teacher's perception of the problem, and in conjunction with the class teacher work out an appropriate educational programme for the latter to implement. This might be based on curriculum material developed in the special school or it might draw on commercially produced materials. Contact was regular and frequent: the specialist teacher would visit each school he was working with for at least half a day each week.

This collaborative working was not set up as a means of providing in-service training. The purpose was to meet pupils' needs, and to do so in a way that ensured they remained in their neighbourhood school. To the extent that it was successful in achieving this however – and considerable progress was reported on the part of individual pupils – it did so by changing teachers' attitudes and developing their skills and by effecting relevant changes in the schools. In particular, teachers referred to being better able to analyse teaching and learning difficulties, to individualise instruction, to devise appropriate learning tasks and curriculum materials, and in general to reappraise their teaching strategies for all pupils. This development in competence went along with the emergence of positive attitudes toward pupils with learning difficulties and the institution of changes that benefited them, such as timetable adjustments and more flexible use of ancillaries. Such collaborative working is fraught with difficulty and it is critically dependent on good relationships and mutual respect between those involved, but it can be a most fruitful source of professional development and means of disseminating specialist skills.

Example 1b   A second set of examples arose in programmes where pupils were being transferred from segregated provision into ordinary schools. A diagnostic and assessment school we visited returned about half of its pupils to ordinary schools. Language classes and other special centres drawing from a wide catchment area sought to return as many of their pupils as possible to their own neighbourhood schools. We have described elsewhere the expedients adopted to ensure that this process was successful. In some cases it included an important element of training for the ordinary school staff, though the opportunities presented were not always taken by the specialist staff. The tendency was to concentrate on making a smooth transition for the pupil. The process of transition might go on for weeks or sometimes months, and it was important to ensure that the pupils could cope with belonging to two different institutions. As far as the class teacher was concerned, the specialist would concentrate on reassurance, emphasising the newcomer's normality and his similarities to other pupils rather than any difference from them. This is understandable but to be regretted when it means that the teachers are left uncertain as to how best teach a given pupil. Besides information on the nature of any problems or difficulties, class teachers may need curricular suggestions, advice on teaching approaches and so on. Some class teachers complained that they had been left in the dark, while in those instances where even a rudimentary amount of training was incorporated into the transition process the results were positive. In one school for example, the specialist teacher joined in the work of the class, taking over a teaching group so that the class teacher could observe her ways of relating to pupils. In another school, by contrast, a class teacher was relieved from her class in order to have undistracted discussion with the specialist teacher when the latter came to visit. This was considered less useful by some parties.

Example 1c A third example comes from an authority where severely physically handicapped pupils attend their neighbourhood schools. A peripatetic physiotherapy service was inaugurated to meet their physical needs. Since it was neither possible nor practical for the physiotherapist to treat each pupil on an extended basis, it was necessary to delegate much of the work to the classroom assistants. This necessitated training and reorientation for the latter since they lacked the requisite skills and indeed often handled pupils in inappropriate or over-protective ways. Details on how the programme operated are given in earlier chapters. As far as equipping the assistants to carry out the work was concerned, the physiotherapists followed a number of procedures. The assistant was always present when the physiotherapist saw the pupil and so could observe how the professional handled the pupil, learning in what ways he or she should be treated as normal and where particular care should be taken. This also enabled the physiotherapist to sensitise the assistant to potential sources of trouble such as posture or pressure points, and draw attention to the adjustments needed to wheelchairs, calipers and so on as the pupil developed. These sessions, focussed around the particular pupil in the assistant's care, gave opportunity to ask specific questions, get reassurance on matters of concern and so on. In most cases the therapist would then draw up a set of exercises for the assistant to carry out in her absence, visiting periodically to resolve any problems, monitor progress and develop the programme further. These arrangements seemed to work well: classroom assistants developed skill and competence in dealing with physically handicapped pupils; what they received was not a grounding in physiotherapy but it did mean that the everyday handling of the pupils in question was informed by physiotherapeutic understanding and based on good working practice in physiotherapy.

Example 1d Our final example involves the collaboration between a speech therapist and a classroom assistant, also described below. This took place in a comprehensive school catering for pupils with a wide range of learning difficulties. The need for speech therapy was far greater than the service could provide by conventional means. The therapist sought the assistant's involvement by having her sit in on therapy sessions, explaining what she was doing and why. Then she had the assistant take the session herself, working to her detailed instructions and in her presence so that she could correct and amplify if necessary. In this way the ancillary developed a competence in carrying out specific speech therapy exercises and in time took the majority of sessions with pupils on her own.

2.   Working together on a common professional task

In a context where many teachers and other professionals work for the most part on their own, collaboration on a common task can be a valuable source of professional development. This is another aspect of the multi-disciplinary working whose importance we emphasise throughout this book. Such collaboration can encompass many tasks. The examples we give here refer to curriculum development but the training benefits to be derived are not confined to this area; with appropriate changes they are just as available for carrying out a range of other tasks (eg dealing with behaviour problems).

Example 2a   The first example comes from a language class and involved collaboration between teacher, speech therapist and educational psychologist. In addition to a good deal of general contact and co-operation, made possible by generous staffing, the three set themselves the task of developing an assessment profile for the children. This is a set of categories, broken down in fine detail, for 'reading' a child in terms of educational possibilities. It leads to individual programmes with objectives and means for obtaining them spelt out precisely. (Details are given in chapter 16.) The class teacher monitors the programme in action and reports back so that it can be modified and extended.

The profile, comprising ten categories from background information to social/emotional skills, took a good deal of time to develop. Staff met regularly on a weekly basis, gradually refining the profile as they tried it out in practice. Staff were agreed that the exercise itself, as distinct from any outcomes, was useful: it increased awareness of their own, and others', distinctive professional contributions, and facilitated communication among them; it sharpened their perceptions of pupils' problems and ways of dealing with them; and it gave clear demonstration of the difficulty and benefits of tackling problems systematically.

Example 2b   A secondary department for pupils with learning difficulties embarked on a major programme of curriculum revision and development with the arrival of the new head of department. It was a large department, some seven teachers strong. The intention was to break down the various areas of the curriculum – language, reading, number, social studies and practical social skills – into finely-graded component parts. All members of the department were involved, each being assigned a specific task to be undertaken in conjunction with one or more colleagues. The ad hoc working parties formed in this way were to report back to the group as a whole. Though the exercise was abandoned after it had run for several months and the outcomes in terms of curriculum development were limited, some staff at least benefited from having to analyse the content of their teaching and present it in a rational way to their departmental colleagues.

3.   Having contact with expertise

Having access to people with expert knowledge and developed skills is another important source of training that is generally relevant in integration especially when pupils are being integrated on an individual basis. One teacher in the latter situation affirmed that she did not want to go on courses or engage in formal training: she would only have the pupils in question for a year or maybe two and then they would be the responsibility of somebody else in the school, so what she wanted was access to an expert when she needed one. The purely functional approach to using expertise that might be implied here may beg some questions about recognising needs, effective collaboration and so on. Where professionals are prepared to work in an appropriate manner however there are spin-off training benefits for their colleagues. Observing experts in action, being able to put questions and engage them in dialogue, seeing how they respond in specific situations which are familiar to one, are all educative experiences. The practice of integration would seem to offer particular opportunities in this regard because of the range of services and different professionals that may be involved with a given pupil.

Most of our examples here relate to particular sets of individuals who evolved an appropriate form of working between them but we encountered at least two situations where there was a formal arrangement instituted or sanctioned by the authority. In one case the authority's three special centres for the hearing impaired were engaged in revising their curricula. The exercise – and teachers' competence – was considerably enhanced by drawing on the guidance and assistance of specialists in curriculum development employed by the authority. A maths adviser worked with the teachers of the deaf in order to sensitise them to the mathematical needs of their pupils and help devise appropriate learning materials. Staff from the authority's reading resource centre collaborated in the assessment of pupils' reading problems, collection of suitable reading material and so on. Another integration programme, also dealing with hearing impaired pupils, had teachers of the deaf as the source of expertise. Pupils were supported individually in ordinary classrooms by teachers who had done a short course – within the authority – on the basics of deaf education. A further element in the training of the support teachers was that they were attached to teachers of the deaf for a period of time, observing them in action, and seeing how they handled pupils and so on.

The more usual example of this form of training was when a particular professional worked in such a way and so exercised his or her skills that colleagues learned something that added to their understanding of a pupil's problems or improved their skills in handling them. At one secondary special centre for pupils with learning difficulties the educational psychologist made a point of having the teacher in charge (also the parents) present when he assessed a pupil. This served various functions directly related to the assessment but it also helped the teacher. Besides adding to her understanding of individual pupils and their problems, it taught her a good deal about testing: applicability and use of different tests; administration and interpretation; and piecing together information from tests and other sources to compile a comprehensive educational assessment.

A speech therapist working in a language unit could only spend one day a week there and had no separate withdrawal area but made a virtue out of these necessities: by seeing children and treating them in a corner of the – admittedly large – classroom she was able to give the teacher a very clear idea of what she was doing with the children. Allied to a speech therapy programme that was worked out in fine detail, and generally close co-operation between the two people involved, this meant that the class teacher became quite adept in speech therapy skills and was able to integrate the specialist work into her own work in the classroom.

Another school took advantage of the presence of a language class by giving the teacher in charge a responsibility for language development across the school. Before the class was set up this teacher had been on the staff and, according to the head, "was already interested in language development in the general sense". It made sense to capitalise on her growing expertise, hence the brief for language development. This comprises advising other teachers about language materials, selecting books and equipment, and on occasion discussing problem children – "so-and-so isn't speaking clearly and what can I do about it". This role is carried out largely in an informal way, by means of casual staffroom exchanges and so on. Where necessary, this teacher will intimate that a given child might benefit from formal speech therapy.

The most common example at this level comes perhaps from the interaction between teachers and classroom ancillaries. A number of the latter testified to having learned a great deal from being in the classroom the whole time, observing what the teachers did, the way they related to pupils, how they handled different situations, the learning activities they set up, and so on. It was clear too, both from comments made by teachers and our own observation, that many of these ancillaries had learned a great deal; they had moved beyond the traditional rather limited role of classroom assistant and were making an informed and independent contribution to the education of pupils with special needs.

Finally, mention can be made of the role of informal contact in the staffroom, before and after case conferences, and otherwise. This can serve the valuable function of making a body of expert knowledge or a professional domain less remote. This hardly counts as training and the explicit gains in terms of increments of knowledge or skills may be slight. Changes in attitude and orientation can be significant however. This has particular relevance to integration. Busy professionals who dash in and out of schools, confining themselves exclusively to professional tasks and interacting only with senior members of staff, may fail to realise how alienating such a profile can be to the ordinary teacher. Many of the latter have little effective idea of the visitors' professional domains and tend to assume, if they think about it at all, that they are irrelevant and have nothing to offer them. Informal contact can be a means of righting these perspectives by alerting teachers to relevant areas of expertise and ways in which they can be helped to meet pupils' needs better. Effective professional contact does not depend on good interpersonal relationships but it can be facilitated by them.

If professional development is to occur in this way certain pre-requisites may be noted. The most important relate to the experts and their attitudes to professional working and to colleagues. In the first place, they must be confident in the exercise of their professional skills to a point where they can without distraction assess or treat a pupil in the presence of other people, if necessary subsequently explaining or justifying their course of action. Not only must they be free from attachment to arcane mysteries that must be preserved intact from the uninitiated – an attitude that has by no means disappeared – but they must also have both the commitment and skills to communicate with colleagues. Our experience would suggest that a principal difficulty that professionals face in this area is developing an awareness of the contexts in which colleagues work and orienting their communication toward them. Teachers commented on how various professionals seemed unaware of the realities of classroom life or had difficulty in getting beyond technical language in describing pupils' problems. One can note – and we observed instances of this – that the kind of contact we are describing here can help the outside experts also through making them more aware of pupils' everyday situations and the contexts in which teachers work. The onus for professional development in this way does not fall entirely on the outside expert. The teacher and the ancillary must be receptive and open to new ideas and ways of working, prepared to question their existing practice, and willing to learn from somebody whose experience is different from and possibly in terms of classroom practice more limited than their own.

4. Team teaching

Team teaching – an arrangement whereby two or more teachers pool both classes and resources and plan educational activities in a flexible way for the group as a whole – is not peculiar to special education and indeed seems to have had limited currency there, but it does offer particular advantages in the education of pupils with special needs in ordinary schools. Viewing the latter as an extension of mixed-ability teaching underlines the need for expanding teaching skills. Team teaching affords one way of doing this. In general terms, it forces teachers into more conscious planning, detailing of objectives and spelling out of teaching methods and resources; it provides the opportunity to observe colleagues' teaching – an educative experience that is all too rare; and it leads teachers to focused conversation on individual pupils. If one of the team is a special educator these activities and interactions will help other members of the team to meet special needs better.

Our first example comes from a junior school which has a resource centre for visually impaired pupils. The school operates a team teaching approach based upon vertical grouping. It is divided into four areas – nursery, infant, lower and upper junior – each with its own team of two or three teachers. As there is a great deal of integration most teachers teach visually impaired pupils. Initially, when the special centre was being built up and there was only one specialist teacher, each team had one of its number assigned to liaising with specialist staff. Subsequently, there were three specialist staff in post and these were attached respectively to the nursery/infant, lower junior and upper junior teams. Among the advantages accruing from this arrangement was an improvement in the skills of main school staff in dealing with visually impaired pupils. Previously some may have been "willing but not aware of how much extra attention the visually handicapped children required". Hand in hand with this gain in competence from seeing the specialist teachers in action and participating in team teaching went increased confidence and greater willingness to have visually impaired pupils in teaching groups.

Another example comes from a secondary school that operates a special resources department for pupils with a variety of learning and behaviour difficulties also working to a resource model. Team teaching is accepted practice in the school and the functioning of the special resources department takes account of this. It also provides training opportunities. The situation is still evolving and has yet to reach a steady state, but it would seem that a number of training advantages are available: subject specialists and staff from the department work together to provide appropriate work for individual pupils – an activity that expands competence in mixed ability teaching; staff from the department have given demonstration lessons on how to teach particular groups; and staff are available in a general consultative role, based on their training and experience in dealing with pupils who have special educational needs.

5. Visits and meetings

One of the weakness of a locally administered educational system is the potential for isolation and lack of awareness of relevant developments elsewhere. This is frequently commented on as a characteristic of British education. Our evidence is that it certainly applies within special education, particularly where integrated ventures are concerned. Indeed, it is all the more likely to hold in the latter case because the number of staff involved in a special centre will be far fewer than a typical special school staff; this means that the reservoir of experience will be probably more limited and also that it will be more difficult to arrange for staff to make visits or go on courses.

There are many possible examples here and we shall confine ourselves to a few. The first concerns a teacher appointed to a language unit who was – fortuitously – in post for two terms before any children arrived. This time turned out in fact to be extremely valuable, not least because of the training opportunities it afforded. Among other activities, the teacher in question was able to pay visits to existing language units and to a special school catering for pupils with communication disorders. This was useful both in terms of specific professional content and organisational details. It may be noted that such visiting is less easy to arrange – and much less likely to take place – unless the time for it is available in this way or is otherwise made available.

In our conduct of the research project we found great curiosity about developments elsewhere and eagerness to learn as much as possible about them. Indeed we acted as information brokers in a small way, describing relevant forms of provision and ways of working and putting people in touch. As part of our project activities we organised weekend conferences specifically for people working in the integration programmes we were studying. By common consent these were judged to be educative occasions but they also led to a great deal of fruitful contact subsequently which in some cases looked like developing into lasting exchanges. Staff from one authority that was building up provision for physically handicapped at secondary level visited a comprehensive school that had been making such provision on an extensive basis for some time. The two situations were very different and there was no question of copying the provision, but the visit was considered useful for highlighting the issues and drawing attention to problems and for the first hand experience it gave of an actual working provision. Another school which had pioneered curricular and organisational innovations was visited by a number of colleagues from other authorities, in one case returning the visit and developing a mutually useful set of exchanges.

A further example comes from an authority with close on a dozen special needs departments in comprehensive schools. Once a term the heads of the departments met at the authority's in-service training centre for a full day. These were loosely structured and did not have formal programmes. It was considered useful however to spend time with colleagues in a comparable position in other schools exchanging notes and experiences, discussing common problems, hearing about innovations and so on.

Summary

Two facts emerge from looking at training in these integration programmes. First, many programmes are operating without the benefit of appropriately trained staff and there is much need of training. Secondly, a great deal can be done to meet this need at local level by flexible and imaginative use of available resources. The need for training was evidenced in the sheer absence of relevant training for teachers, ancillaries and other staff documented above, in the repeated calls from staff for training to increase their knowledge and develop skills, and in our own observation of pupils' needs going unrecognised because of lack of awareness on the part of staff or unmet because of lack of competence. As for providing the training, we have described a great many approaches that require little more than ingenuity, flexibility and goodwill. These are all actual examples, and there is no reason why the majority of them could not be adapted for use elsewhere.

It might be felt indeed that many of these examples were doing no more than articulating good professional practice. Working with colleagues on common professional tasks or participating in team teaching in such a way that all staff involved learn from each other is not something that should only happen when there is a concern for training. When these various activities are conducted in a fully professional way they frequently have as an integral part of them an interactive element that constitutes training for those involved. It will be noted that most of the examples are grouped under a heading 'Professional interaction'. This is because of a common thread running through them that has to do with attitude toward the exercise of professional skills. This is an attitude of openness and collaboration, of willingness to share skills and learn from others, of acknowledging mistakes and building from them, of commitment to discussion and public shared activities. It is the antithesis of clinging to professional mystiques and demarcation lines.

Apart from the manifest training benefits, this attitude and the specific activities associated with it achieve other positive effects. The gains in knowledge and skill are important but the indirect effects may be even more significant. New patterns of working and relationships between people are set up; structural changes in a school or service agency are effected; staff develop and maintain a sense of the urgency and challenge of teaching special pupils, and are helped to shake off the 'remedial pupil/remedial teacher' image that regrettably has sometimes prevailed.

It may be of interest to recall the American experience of complete integration cited above (Gruenewald and Schroeder, op.cit.). Great importance was attached to training there and numerous strategies were used. The authors give a rank ordering of the forms of staff development and training that were found most effective in helping teachers and other professionals develop the knowledge and skills necessary for successful integration (from most effective to least effective):

- on-the-job training acquired while working with an individual student integrated into his/her class
- team teaching with a special educator a class of regular education with several handicapped students integrated into it
- through curriculum development efforts where regular and special educators are jointly developing adaptive curriculum
- building in-service programmes which focus on philosophy, characteristics of handicap and assessment strategies
- formal course offering sponsored by the school district (exchange courses)
- continuing education course work at the university level.

These various approaches take us beyond the limits – of eschewing formal training and concentrating on local initiatives – that we have set ourselves here. We have confined our discussion to practice within a small number of locations but consider it worthwhile to document this in detail for the interest and variety of practice uncovered. There are other relevant initiatives however, some of them highly developed. Thus, the Education of the Developmentally Young (EDY) project at the Hester Adrian Research Centre has produced a disseminable training course for professionals working with profoundly handicapped children.

The course which is described in Foxen and McBrien (1981) deals with (a) assessment and recording of behaviour, (b) selection of educational/developmental task areas, (c) basic behaviour modification teaching skills. The Teaching and the Severely Subnormal (TASS) project carried out at Huddersfield Polytechnic in conjunction with the Hester Adrian Research Centre is concerned to develop and evaluate a short self-instructional course for teachers of the mentally handicapped. The aim is to assist the teacher to run effective short structured sessions with individual children or with small groups of children. Finally, mention may be made of the new Open University course 'Special needs in Education' (E241) which will be available from 1982. This is the University's first full course on the education of handicapped children and is described as 'a general introduction to the field drawing on many disciplines and approaches: psychology, sociology, economics, history and politics'.

It should be noted too that there is a body of knowledge and experience in other fields to draw on in organising training activities or promoting staff development. The format adopted must match training requirements: workshops will be preferred to lectures for some purposes while private reading may be the best option in other cases. On occasion the need will be to bring colleagues together in a professional context that is free of normal working commitments and is otherwise relatively unstructured. When organising a training activity thought must be given to the *training* skills involved. These will generally be second order to the skills being developed and it must not be taken for granted that those providing training possess the requisite training skills in addition to the primary skills. Being a good teacher or speech therapist does not necessarily mean that one is versed in communicating one's teaching or therapy skills. This is particularly relevant to more loosely structured activities such as workshops where the absence of skilled leadership can lead to much time-wasting – and loss of enthusiasm for the training enterprise.

A further consideration is that training based on local initiatives must of necessity depend on creative response to the conjunction of individual needs and opportunities. Special education in ordinary schools is currently in a dynamic state, and new responses will have to be made as new situations emerge. The burden of creativity must rest with the individual group at local level. We offer, as illustrative of the sort of responses that might be made, a few further examples of possible practice. These are not current practice and may seem far-fetched to some, but practitioners with whom we discussed them endorsed both their relevance and feasibility.

1. Give every teacher and ancillary say three days for professional activity a year, of which at least one might be devoted to special education training. Of course many teachers do more than this, but a formal requirement would extend the awareness of special needs to teachers that present approaches do not reach by obligating them to give some thought to special educational needs.

2. Utilise teachers of proven quality and experience as consultants and animators in other schools, either in setting up or reviewing integration programmes. Such people will have direct *current* experience to draw on and other teachers are more likely to listen to them. Incidentally, carrying out such an assignment could contribute in a unique way to the professional awareness and development of the individual concerned.

3. Shut schools down for training days. This would provide a means of reaching all staff with a custom-built training package assembled in the light of specific local needs. (It would also enhance pupil attitudes!)

Finally, it should be made clear that our stress on the role of local initiatives in meeting training needs should in no way be taken to imply that local initiatives are sufficient on their own. There is a great deal to be done at national and regional level and utilisation of available resources being advocated here need not depend on the implementation of national plans, but they can only supplement and not replace them. Indeed, there would be a danger in a proliferation of local training initiatives in the absence of the professional core that must come from formal training. There are a body of knowledge and a set of competencies that must be acquired; if the formal training to transmit them is missing then other training activities will lack a professional context and be subject to the vagaries of common sense and received wisdom. Just as thoroughgoing commitment to educating special pupils in ordinary schools entails changes in the ordinary schools, so teacher training must be organised to take account of the shift in the ordinary teacher's role. It is in the context of this understanding of teacher training that the various approaches to further training described in this chapter take their place.

PART FOUR

Practicalities

Chapter Ten
The Physical Environment

> The Council would urge that . . . the development and testing of new educational ideas will recognise the intimate relationship that exists between the physical environment and educational possibilities . . . Educational aims, and the environment within which they are to be realised, must be considered together as aspects of the total purposes of education. (Newsom Report)

This chapter is concerned with the physical environment of the school and its relevance to the education of pupils with special needs. The topic is important not merely because the physical appointments of the school are often critical to integration but because of the links between the physical environment of the school and the educational needs it is to serve. Architectural features do not on their own determine what the school can do but they have an influence on it, not least where pupils with special needs are concerned. Many special schools have the benefit of purpose-built accommodation, the absence of which in the ordinary school is sometimes seen as presenting insuperable difficulties to integration. The challenge for the ordinary school that would educate pupils with special needs is to do so in buildings that must cater for all the pupils.

Importance of the physical environment

One of the more common objections to educating pupils with special needs in ordinary schools is that the buildings are unsuitable or even dangerous. The difficulties are usually couched in terms of the physically handicapped – wheelchairs blocking up narrow corridors, whole areas of multi-storey buildings out of reach, extra hazards in the event of fire and so on. There are problems too with pupils who have other handicaps, though these are less frequently articulated. Some schools are overcrowded even without the addition of another group. Other premises lack the flexibility to facilitate the range of teaching approaches that may be required for pupils with special educational needs. Some large comprehensive schools are considered to be so impersonal that certain pupils have difficulty in coping with them, though it is arguable that such problems reflect school organisation rather than buildings.

It is clear that these objections must be taken seriously. Before looking at them however, a broader context may help. Consideration of the physical environment tends to focus rather narrowly on the fabric of the school building. Access, mobility, sanitary arrangements, all raise obvious problems and may dictate specific modifications to the building. This is only part of the problem however, and perhaps the easy part. Providing an appropriate physical environment for educating pupils with special needs in the ordinary school extends far beyond ramping and toilet adaptations. These basic considerations are important – and we have seen instances where the failure to attend adequately to them resulted in problems that were quite disproportionate to the relatively little effort involved in solving them – but they are only a first step.

There are two reasons why this broader approach is necessary. First, there are links between the physical environment of the school and educational functions. Secondly, if one takes seriously the notion that educating pupils with special needs in ordinary schools is something for the whole school, the implications for the physical environment of the school and how it is to be used are correspondingly widespread. It may be noted that these are also reasons for taking seriously the concerns about accommodation and physical constraints that are commonly voiced.

Much has been said and written about the effect of the physical setting on the nature of the school and what goes on within it. The relationship is however problematic. On the one hand, there are those who posit a very close link between architectural form and educational function; not only are different kinds of space needed for different kinds of work, but the nature of the space itself affects the behaviour patterns of teachers and pupils. On the other hand, some emphasise the human contribution and insist that the atmosphere of a school is created by staff and pupils rather than the physical setting; they point to situations where schools and individual teachers have tackled unsuitable locations and managed to create highly effective working environments from them. A good illustration of the opposing arguments is provided by the case of open-plan schooling. There was widespread debate about the effects of open-plan schools and this led to a spate of evaluative studies in the early '70's. From a welter of conflicting evidence it emerged that while architectural features were seldom a decisive influence they did have a considerable effect on teacher and pupil behaviour, on relationships within the school and on general school organisation. This is perhaps what common sense would suggest and may be taken as a conclusion that is relevant to physical arrangements in general and not just to open plan. The network of interactions that go to make up a school is subject to many influences, social as well as physical, so that the effect of architectural and design features will always be achieved within this broader context.

The second reason for locating the physical environment in a broader context is in accord with the wider notion of integration being advocated in this book. Educating pupils with special needs in ordinary schools is something for the whole school and not simply a question of slotting in individual pupils or groups of pupils. There are two aspects to this. First, specific provision for the handicapped may inconvenience other pupils or necessitate new systems within the school. The siting of specialist accommodation, movement of pupils between lessons, provision of support within the classroom, are all cases in point. If the changes involved are conceived only from the side of pupils with special needs, it is possible that they will operate to the detriment of other pupils. Moreover, if they are imposed unilaterally, there is every likelihood of resentment and other negative attitudes. Secondly, if integration is seen in a comprehensive way with implications for the education of all pupils with special needs, then the physical arrangements must allow for this. Thus, if individual or small group work is adopted as a common strategy, it is important to have appropriate space available. If there is judged to be need of extra craft or domestic science work, it may be necessary to provide extra equipment if the school's equipment is being fully utilised already.

A further reason for taking the physical environment seriously in the case of integration is the possible effect on morale. If a primary classroom is so crowded that the teacher has difficulty in moving around it, let alone organise the children into groups for different activities, then introducing a child in a wheelchair may be the last straw. The individual teacher faced with this situation tends to make the best of it. Outright refusal or industrial action is rare especially when faced with a child who has special needs. There can be negative consequences however. We have seen resentment on the part of teachers who felt they were being taken advantage of. They were concerned to do the best for every child and sought to minimise the effects of unsuitable space. When inadequate accommodation persisted however and there was no serious effort to put it right, they felt short-changed by the authority and in some cases became highly sceptical about integration. Particular exception was taken to having to spend a lot of time in getting basic matters put right. The contrast in attitude when suitable accommodation was available from the outset was striking.

The problem for integration

Special schools which are purpose-built for specific groups of pupils will incorporate a range of features designed with their needs in mind. Thus for the physically handicapped, access to every part of the school will be available as a matter of course. Doors and corridors will be wide enough to permit easy passage of wheelchairs; raised threshholds and doormats will be avoided where possible; light switches will be at convenient heights; floors will be non-slip, handrails available as required, and so on. It has been pointed out to us that even new special schools do not always match ideal requirements. Frequently it is the first such assignment on the part of the architect and important lessons from experience may not be applied. We do not have any first-hand evidence of this. Several special school heads however who had been involved in building programmes had strong views on the matter and felt there was a case for extending the design team. The experience of people who had worked in special schools would complement the team's skills in important ways.

Whatever about the foregoing and the occasional defects in special school design, there is no doubt about the shortcomings of ordinary schools in terms of physical suitability. The situation has improved with the passage of the Chronically Sick and Disabled Persons Act (1970). This requires of persons providing buildings for schools (and many other purposes) that

'in the means of access both to and within the building, and in the parking facilities and sanitary conveniences to be available (if any), they make provision, in so far as it is in the circumstances both practicable and reasonable, for the needs of persons using the building who are disabled (Section 8.1).

There are of course exceedingly many circumstances where it has not been judged practicable or reasonable to make the requisite provisions, particularly in respect of older buildings. The main impact has been on new and substantially adapted buildings. In any case, while the legislation was framed in terms of the disabled in the broader sense[1] the tendency in practice has been to interpret it in terms of the physically handicapped. Finally, it is concerned with basic physical provision – access and toileting –and not with educational requirements, and so has nothing to say on teaching arrangements or the other aspects of a school's activity that can be affected by the physical environment.

A further consideration is that the physical provision suited to the ordinary school will not be the same as that made available in a special school. The context, educational needs and general constraints are all different. Even if it were possible, one does not want to reproduce the physical environment of the special school in an ordinary school. That is not what integration is about. Educating pupils with special needs in the ordinary school requires changes and modifications but not a total transformation. Features of special school premises will be adapted in parts, if not all, of the school. This must be done carefully however and taking into account the needs of the school as a whole. There are a number of possible disadvantages if this is not done. First, the differences between pupils with special needs and their peers may be accentuated if the physical arrangements are obtrusive. This may be inevitable if there is a sizeable group of pupils with special needs in a given school. There is no point in disguising their special needs but it must be recognised that the existence of a large area

---

[1] The Act refers to the definition given in section 29 of the National Assistance Act 1948 – 'persons who are blind, deaf or dumb, and other persons who are substantially and permanently handicapped by illness, injury or congenital deformities or other such disabilities as may be prescribed by the Minister'.

within the school for their exclusive use increases the likelihood that these pupils will be seen primarily as 'the handicapped'.

Secondly, too much adaptation removes one of the benefits of being in an ordinary school, viz the opportunity to make out in a 'normal' environment. Some schools of course are very far from normal in any sense of the word and are sufficiently taxing for middle-aged staff, let alone pupils with mobility problems. One multi-storey Victorian school perched on a Welsh hill-side was considered best suited to young goats and those undergoing Olympic training! There is a benefit however in exposing pupils, with support as necessary, to physical environments that were not designed with their needs in mind. Having to cope with them is valuable learning experience that will stand them in good stead outside school. Thirdly, the needs of all pupils must be balanced. Changes that would benefit a particular group may be to the detriment of other pupils. Introducing one-way movement round the school's corridors may be readily accepted but changing a form room or the siting of specialist lessons may be less so. Providing suitable withdrawal areas, eg for specialist language work, can pose difficulties in a school where space is already at a premium.

Particular aspects of the physical environment

In this section we want to look at specific features of the physical environment that emerged as significant. These are grouped in terms of the basic functions of school, viz education, contact between pupils, and other miscellaneous purposes. In order for these to be achieved, certain physical requirements must be met: pupils need to get into school and move about within it before they can benefit from its educational and socialising opportunities. It is well to remember that the basic physical requirements have importance only in this instrumental way. They are often the most obvious manifestation of the changes needed to accommodate a programme of integration and can be critical to its success or failure, even its feasibility. Moreover it can be difficult to carry them out and get them right. None of this however should deflect attention from the central consideration of pupils' educational wellbeing.

Basic physical requirements

Some pupils will be precluded by their physical condition from doing certain everyday activities – getting into a school building and moving around in it, using its sanitary facilities, having a means of escape in case of fire. They are also likely to need facilities for medical inspection and treatment. These various needs can be met in part by appropriate management of the school but they will in general entail some structural alterations.

This is not the place for architectural or building guidance which is to be found in the appropriate professional literature. Mention may be made of two documents of interest to the layperson: 'Designing for physically handicapped children' by Goldsmith (1975) and Design Note 18 from the DES (1979). Goldsmith's article is an architect's contribution to the book by Loring and Burn (1975). It considers the nature of the environment required by physically handicapped pupils and makes a number of specific recommendations. Though concerned primarily with the design of schools for the physically handicapped much of it is relevant to provision in the ordinary school as well.

The DES Design Note 'Access for the Physically Disabled to Educational Buildings' is a brief document containing design guidance for those concerned with improving access to educational buildings, especially schools. It refers in particular to those in wheelchairs and those disabled people who are ambulant with or without aids. It seeks to help those responsible for designing new buildings or adaptations to existing ones to meet the requirements of the Chronically Sick and Disabled Persons Act 1970. Seven elements of provision are identified and detailed design guidance is offered in respect of each.

1. Parking facilities

There is a need for a suitably sized setting down area or collecting bay in a convenient position close to the most appropriate point of entry to the school. The size of area required will depend on the numbers of pupils and whether they arrive in coaches, mini-buses or cars. In exposed situations, sheltered provision for waiting should be considered. The arrival and departure points should be easily accessible from the internal circulation routes within the building.

One school we visited had well-designed arrival facilities at the main arrival point – sheltered provision for loading and unloading, slip-resistant surfaces and adequate lighting. The school's other site however was not similarly equipped. Indeed the transport carrying physically handicapped pupils was not able to get right up to the doors so that pupils had to go a certain distance by themselves. This meant that, in the absence of a covered way, they could get quite wet, especially those in electric wheelchairs.

2.   Approach and entrance

The aim should be to provide a level or suitably ramped approach from the public footpath to the school entrance and from the school to external play areas. Level approaches are preferred where possible. If ramps are required they should reach certain minimum specifications in terms of gradient, width, length, provision of handrails and kerbs. External steps may be required in addition to ramps to facilitate the ambulant disabled who would have difficulty in negotiating long ramps. On exposed sites weather protection should be considered.

Some form of ramping was provided in all the schools we visited that had non-ambulant pupils. In most cases these were perfectly adequate, but there were some problems due to specifications not having been met or ramps placed at inconvenient points. On two sites where physically handicapped pupils had lessons in demountables around the campus the ramps that gave access were so steep that pupils had difficulty in negotiating them and had to rely on other pupils to push them up and down.

A physically handicapped girl in a wheelchair attended her local school. A ramp was provided and initially thought to be adequate, although it had been built at the back of the school by the service entrance to the kitchen because there was not enough space at the front of the school. However, difficulties emerged in practice. The playground was at the front of the school and access to it via the ramp meant a trek right round the school, so that at break by the time the girl had made her way there and back there was very little time left for play. Also, it became an isolating factor since nobody else needed to use this exit and she was separated from the others while moving around.

3.   Door and doorways

Doorways should be wide enough to permit easy passage of wheelchairs. Doors should have appropriate handles at convenient heights and if possible incorporate a vision panel (in safety glass); where used, door closers should be correctly tensioned. There should be adequate clear wall space to the side of the door by the door handle to aid the wheelchair user when approaching and opening the door. Raised thresholds and doormats should be avoided. Where lobbies are provided either at the entrance or within buildings, adequate spaces must be provided for wheelchairs between doors.

Schools varied in the extent to which they met or found it possible to meet these requirements. A large school particularly if it is old cannot easily make all the changes that may be necessary. The main problems seemed to be with thresholds and negotiating doors independently. In some cases there was not sufficient wall space adjacent to door handles and wheelchair users could not negotiate doors independently as a result. Swing-doors were also a barrier when closers were incorrectly tensioned. Thresholds were a particular problem with several demountables where ramps had been installed without taking them into account. In some cases pupils had to be helped over them by other pupils. As well as causing an obstruction, this led in one location to a certain amount of buffeting and horseplay.

4.   Internal changes of level

Pupils need to gain access to accommodation on different levels within the school. This will entail the provision of internal ramps, lifts or occasionally additional staircases. As well as meeting the requisite specifications, these must be sited with care in the school so that on the one hand they are easily accessible and on the other are not obtrusive and do not create a hazard for other pupils.

Some of the schools we visited had experienced insuperable difficulties in the matter of internal changes of level. For example, one such change – in a new school – was effected by means of a short and narrow flight of stairs. If a ramp of sufficient width was installed it would be too narrow to cope with the volume of traffic and the ramp would in any case have to be unacceptably steep. There were a number of problems with lifts – cramped and inconveniently sited so that long journeys were necessitated. One school had an initial problem with minor vandalism and pupils joy-riding so that the lift was not available for bona fide users.

5.   Sanitary provision

Depending on the number of disabled pupils, there is need of one or more W.C. compartments accessible to wheelchair users of either sex. These should be sited so as to provide quick and easy access from teaching areas. On a very large or split site more than one W.C. compartment would be required regardless of numbers. These must meet various specifications in regard of minimum dimensions, doors, fittings and support rails. Consideration should also be given to the provision of incinerators or other disposal arrangements.

The standard of sanitary facilities in the schools we visited left a great deal to be desired. Some were perfectly adequate; indeed the standard of the better ones highlighted how poor some of the others were. The problem was not confined to the physically handicapped – there were two examples of self-contained special centres for other groups of pupils with far too few facilities for the number of pupils or none at all so that a long walk across the playground was necessary – but they were most acute there. Substandard facilities tended to occur in schools that were catering for a single physically handicapped pupil particularly if the building was old and the special facilities could only be provided by reducing existing facilities.

In all cases the basic essentials were provided. The shortcomings came with the supplementary provisions which were either skimped on or badly done: no storage space; guard-rails missing; bench for changing at wrong height and too narrow; heating insufficient for changing children; inadequate disposal arrangements. Finally, it may be noted that physically handicapped pupils tend to occupy sanitary facilities for longer periods than other pupils and the Victorian decor that is a feature of some school toileting areas is something they could be spared.

6. Facilities for medical inspection and treatment

There is need of a suitable room for treatment and withdrawal. This must provide access to wheelchair users and be conveniently located near an adapted W.C. In most schools use is made of an existing medical room where there is one for this purpose.

7. Means of escape

Adequate arrangements must be made for emergency escape. This entails management as well as design considerations since the way in which a building is used can determine how safe escape may be effected. Multi-storey buildings pose the most serious problems since the use of lifts for escape purposes in case of fire will not

normally be possible. A number of alternative measures are suggested:
- transfer on the same level to an adjoining fire compartment of greater safety
- link bridges on same level to adjoining blocks
- the provision of lobbies adjacent to stairways with at least half-hour fire resistance
- external ramps to ground level.

The choice will depend on the form of the building, the number of disabled pupils and the nature of their disabilities.

When schools took Fire Regulations seriously, as they necessarily had to when there was a sizeable number of disabled pupils, they found great difficulty in complying with them. Two multi-storey secondary schools adopted a similar procedure of creating fire zones in the upper storey by means of fire doors and minor structural alterations. A fire breaking out in one zone could be confined wthin it for a definite period of time so that pupils could be transferred to an adjacent zone and thence to safety or kept there until fire services arrived. Fortunately, there had been no occasion to test these arrangements. Some staff did observe that waiting in a fire zone or safety cell while fire raged about one could be an extremely trying experience for disabled pupils and could occasion considerable distress or even panic.

Another school, of modern design, did not permit the creation of self-contained fire zones within reasonable cost limits. None of the other possibilities was judged feasible either. The result was that non-ambulant pupils had to be excluded from the upper storeys of the building.

For obvious reasons of cost, it is not possible to make major adaptations to cater for one or two pupils. This means that the initial choice of school is restricted, being effectively limited to single storey buildings with existing escape routes that can be adapted to cater for a disabled pupil. Fire doors and door closers need to be reviewed closely since they could impede the unaided escape of a disabled pupil. Attention must also be paid to corridor width and the number of pupils likely to use the corridor in case of emergency. Some older schools would seem to be courting disaster in this regard; a wheelchair could be a major obstruction in a narrow corridor in an emergency, and if there is no direct egress from classrooms a fire could lead to disaster.

Curriculum considerations

If the purposes of educating pupils with special needs in ordinary schools are to be achieved, two conditions are necessary: they must broadly speaking have the same curricular access as their peers; and specialist provision to meet their needs must be available. These are governed by various factors, as discussed throughout the book. Here we look especially at those arising out of the physical environment.

The main problems over access to the curriculum arise with the physically handicapped, particularly at secondary level. If physically handicapped pupils cannot gain access to parts of the school it may be necessary to relocate some classes. As well as adding to the complexity of timetabling, this can create practical problems for the class teacher and impose constraints on the other pupils. If a room is designated as a particular subject room, eg geography, and contains the resources needed for teaching it, it is an inconvenience at the least and possibly a waste of resources not to hold geography lessons in it. Teachers either have to carry lots of materials around with them or make do without them to the possible detriment of the lesson. It may be noted that feelings of territoriality come into play here and some teachers do not take kindly to other subject specialists teaching in their rooms.

More serious problems arise over access to rooms with practical equipment which cannot readily be moved – science laboratories, craft rooms and language laboratories. If pupils cannot gain access to such rooms the school cannot seriously claim to be providing them with a full curriculum. (Modern languages may be an exception in view of the conflicting claims over the need for language laboratories.) If pupils can gain access there are questions of safety and adaptations to equipment to consider. Fear for pupils' safety in science laboratories and craft workshops were voiced for various groups – hearing and vision impaired, physically handicapped, and mentally retarded. It is prudent to be aware of the risks but one must not exaggerate them to a point where pupils are protected at every turn. Here too our experience was that teachers initially erred on the side of caution, sometimes unwilling to let pupils near lathes or handle chemicals. One teacher worried that deaf pupils were greatly at risk in the craft workshop since they could not hear the machinery and moreover could not be given a shout of warning. These fears would seem to be unjustified for the most part however. Teachers who gave pupils scope while exercising normal standards of care found no problems. One metalwork teacher noted that pupils with learning difficulties not only treated the machines with respect but took pride in being able to use them confidently. Nobody had any accidents to report, and it would seem as if undue caution over safety is unwarranted.

The question of adapting equipment raises the issue of over-protectiveness in a different way. In some cases adaptations are necessary simply to enable pupils to use equipment, for example if they are too weak to operate controls or cannot reach them. Benches, worktops and sinks may be at inconvenient heights or designed in such a way that wheelchair access is difficult. Storage space may be inconveniently located so that a pupil cannot see an operation through from start to finish unaided. Various adaptations and special pieces of equipment will be needed to facilitate the blind and partially sighted. We came across examples where the failure to make requisite adaptations did narrow pupils' curricular experience, while in other cases it merely made it more difficult for them to participate. Some teachers argued in the latter case that the world outside school would not be adapted for them and it was best that they started learning how to cope with it while still at school.

There is a balance to be achieved between promoting independence and exposing pupils to the curriculum. The primary purpose of science teaching is to promote scientific thinking, communicate relevant knowledge and develop experimental skills. This can be done in ways that are more or less conducive to independent action. It would seem inappropriate however that the development of independence should become the primary goal, as happens when adaptations that would enhance a pupil's experience of the subject are rejected because they separate him from the 'normal' environment. To do this is in fact to limit his access to the curriculum. Besides access to the school's curriculum, some pupils will need specialist provision as well. The main difficulty we encountered here related to withdrawal facilities. Thus in several classes for pupils with speech and language difficulties facilities were inadequate for speech therapy – either no separate area available outside the classroom or a thoroughly unsuitable one. It may be noted that speech therapists generally required an area that was quiet and free from visual distraction, ideally with a mirror at pupil level. The accommodation difficulties facing speech therapists in many schools have prompted a number of authorities, backed by the Association for All Speech-impaired Children (AFASIC), to provide speech therapy from a specially constructed mobile van which travels from school to school. First reports from users were very positive, and this could be one answer to a particular accommodation problem.

Many teachers besides those working in language units needed withdrawal space for individual or small group work. Visiting professionals likewise needed facilities for assessment and treatment. Open-plan accommodation that was not sufficiently diversified seemed to cause most problems here. One language unit was initially in an open-plan area and had to be moved to a hut to achieve a more controlled and less distracting environment. Others commented variously on noise levels and the absence of quiet corners.

A final point about the suitability of teaching accommodation refers to the constraints that may follow from the presence in a class of pupils with special needs. In one school with little spare space in its classrooms one girl's wheelchair blocked off the aisle and prevented pupils from moving about. Where classes had to be relocated because of problems of access, some pupils were consistently deprived of access to specialist rooms as noted above. In one school relocating meant for the most part using huts away from the main school building. These were not up to the same standard as main school classrooms, being cramped, equipped with older furniture, hot in summer and cold in winter, and generally uninspiring. Classes with disabled pupils found themselves spending a disproportionate amount of their lesson time in these surroundings.

The social context

The physical disposition of a school can affect the opportunities for socialising and the nature of social contact between pupils in important ways. This is obviously so in the case of physically handicapped pupils but it comes into play for other pupils as well. We propose to look at this here in terms of play areas, meeting places and lunch arrangements.

1. Play areas

All pupils need places in a school where they can relax over chosen activities, whether this is physically letting off steam, chatting with friends or taking part in organised club activities. If some pupils do not have access to such places – and no compensatory adjustments are made – then they do not participate fully in the social life of the school.

A first prerequisite is sheer physical access, hence the importance for physically handicapped pupils of ramps and easy routes from teaching areas to play areas. This should not mean that they can reach a special playground or part of the school playground but that they have ready access to all of it. Given access, the playground should be suitable. This can mean different things. For example, two schools with language units had no grassed area to facilitate boisterous play; with many pupils who were hyperactive and/or clumsy this was considered a serious drawback. In one of the schools moreover it was not possible to use the playground for ball games so a further outlet for excess physical energy was missing. Another school had the converse problem of too much grassed area and not enough hard surface so that pupils were confined to an area that was too small in wet weather. Cramped playgrounds were a problem in several schools. An area that was barely adequate might become inadequate with the arrival of a group of pupils with special needs because of the extra numbers and because of the latter's needs. If conditions are cramped, wheelchair users may have little room to move about in; the disabled ambulant, the blind and partially sighted may be physically at risk; and some pupils may be disoriented and unable to cope. It must be remembered also that pupils already at the school may feel with some justification that their facilities are being reduced if an already small playground is cluttered up with wheelchairs.

Some schools catering for groups of pupils with severe learning difficulties had two playgrounds, a general one and one specifically for the special group. In one case this was justified in terms of the use made of the special playground and its equipment as an extension of the classroom – the pupils in question were of infant age – and anyway care was taken to ensure that the pupils spent at least one playtime with the others. Another school dealing with older pupils considered that the disparity in social development and forms of play activity between their pupils with learning difficulties and the main pupil body was too great to permit meaningful playground interaction. Having a separate playground certainly prevented interaction of any kind. It also served to underline the distinctness of the group and reduce the likelihood of meaningful interaction if contact occurred in other ways.

Needless to say pupils need access to indoor leisure areas as well. Crowding can be a particular problem here, with the difficulties mentioned above being intensified. There can be other considerations too. Club activities will need to be organised in rooms to which physically handicapped pupils can gain access. One sixth form common room which was otherwise suitable had low level casual furniture so that wheelchair users could not easily join in card or board games.

2. Meeting places

Providing meeting places is of course a prime function of the school's leisure areas. This can assume particular importance when the school is catering for a group of pupils with special needs. There are two contrasting considerations. On the one hand, if these pupils are to participate equally in the life of the school they must be free – and *feel* free – to congregate where other pupils gather. On the other hand, there can be advantages in developing the special centre as a place where pupils with special needs are 'at home' and mix with friends both from the special centre and the main school.

If the special centre is to carry out this function the requisite space must be available. In fact, three schools that we visited sought to establish the special centre as a focus of social activity for pupils from the special centre and the main school alike. This worked reasonably well in two cases but not in the third, partly because of space considerations: the take-up by main school pupils of the activities laid on was so great that staff physically could not cope in the available space.

One special centre has open-plan areas for cookery, art and library. This doubles up as dining area and meeting place at lunchtime. It has a pleasant, even cosy atmosphere by comparison with the rest of the school. Pupils from the main school congregate there to play table tennis, chess and other games – on tables of a convenient height – or just 'hang about'. There is also an open area by the swimming pool separated from it by a glass partition. This provided an ideal space for more boisterous activities such as hand football (an exceedingly hazardous looking game – with considerable potential for disablement – that is much enjoyed by physically handicapped and able-bodied alike).

Another school is able to create space by folding back partitions that separate teaching and craft areas in the special centre. There is space to set up a pool table and play other games. Again, the comfortable and relaxed atmosphere of the space created in this way makes it a focal point for pupils throughout the school.

The implications for social interactions of having such spaces is discussed below. There are potential drawbacks but it seems clear that their existence provides an opportunity for social contact that is not available in other schools.

3. Lunch arrangements

It it is judged desirable that all pupils take lunch in common, this should not be ruled out or made difficult because of inappropriate accommodation. This happened in fact in a number of instances.

An infant school which was to receive a special class had a fairly cramped dining area. As the special class had only eight pupils it was just about possible to squeeze them in. A second class arrived two years later and it simply was not possible to accommodate them as well. Rather than having these pupils eat alone the first class stopped having lunch in the main school and both had lunch together – in isolation from the main school – in the special centre.

It was not the lack of space so much as the pressure resulting from seeking to feed a large pupil body in the shortest possible time that constrained pupils in other locations. A large comprehensive school sought to get through three sittings in an hour; it was felt that slow moving and clumsy physically handicapped pupils would clog up the system, so they had separate eating arrangements.

Miscellaneous factors

A number of further factors bearing on the physical environment are grouped together here. These are either not particularly related to the categories above or else cut across them.

1. Position of special centre in school

The siting of a special centre within a school can affect an integration programme in important ways. In some cases there will be no choice but even if there is not it is well to be aware of what can be at stake. An awareness of the drawbacks can lead to a reassessment and perhaps the discovery of alternative options where none had been thought available.

The most obvious difficulties relate to physical separateness and the barriers it creates. If a special centre is placed in an isolated position the opportunities for contact are reduced. For example, a special class housed in a hut across the playground from the school did not permit casual contact between special class and main school pupils and was in any case quite cut off in bad weather. Generally, the likelihood of social contact is reduced if pupils from the main school and special centre have consciously to make a journey in order to meet. Academic contact can be hindered also because of distance or perceived separateness. When the special centre is physically separate pupils feel they are going *out from* the centre if they have a main school lesson, and conversely efforts to use special centre teaching accommodation for main school pupils must contend with a certain resistance to going *into* the special centre. By contrast, arrangements were made in another school where a new special centre was built to re-locate the head teacher's office in the centre. The main entrance to the school also led past the special centre so that it became a familiar and accepted part of the school.

Physical isolation can also lead to *perceptions* of separateness which are even more damaging to integration because of their implications for how the special group is seen. One head teacher discussing the relationship between the school and the – quite separate – special centre said: 'They are two completely different things . . . in one sense it is completely detached from the school'. Referring to pupils in the special centre, another head observed: "They are not *my* children . . .". These are perhaps somewhat extreme examples but the general point was made by many teachers who insisted on the importance of having the special class or centre sited in a central position in the school: there would then be lots of to-ing and fro-ing past it; it would be visible and noticeable; it would be seen as part of the school, not an appendage to it tucked away in a corner; and pupils based there would be accepted as part of the pupil body, not regarded as outsiders who happened to be housed at the school. A special class in an old infant school was deliberately placed in a classroom in the heart of the school rather than in a demountable in the playground which would have offered superior but isolated accommodation. 'They could have gone into a super unit in the yard – and be completely cut off there!' The physical isolation was not consi-

dered a problem for the ordinary class which used the demountable instead.

There were some advantages in being isolated. It was quieter
and gave an element of privacy. Teachers pointed out that they
could let some young children out of the classroom on their own
that they otherwise might not have done because of the danger of
being buffeted or knocked over in the corridor.

2. Staffroom for special centre

Most of the larger special centres had their own staffroom in the
centre. This can clearly serve important functions. Apart from
providing a natural gathering place for teachers who work closely
together and share common concerns, it facilitates the exchange of
information on pupils and curricular arrangements; provides
teachers with a convenient work place and storage facilities;
fosters team spirit; and enables pupils locate teachers readily.
Some teachers pointed out that they had far greater and more
regular need than main school teachers to discuss particular pupils,
and congregating in their own staffroom after school provided an
ideal opportunity to do this. Indeed they claimed they were
invariably the last to leave!

Despite these considerations, it is clear that the existence of
separate staffrooms does create barriers. Wherever they existed
they were extensively used by special centre staff – and hardly at
all by main school staff. In many schools special centre staff never
went to the main school staffroom or mixed with colleagues there.
(This was not peculiar to them; especially in large schools, staff of
other departments formed their own enclaves as well and rarely
used the main staffroom.) This tended to cut them off from
colleagues and operated to the detriment of integration programmes. The personal and professional relationships that foster
integration are less likely to develop. Opportunities for communicating knowledge and information and shaping attitudes are lost.
Special centre staff are less aware of the problems that main school
staff face and the situations that pupils from the special centre are
entering.

Schools generally did little to combat these problems. Either
they seemed to be unaware of them or they judged it imprudent to
intervene in an area that related to teachers' social presence in the
school. One school was able to re-locate the main school staffroom

in the special centre when building works were carried out. This led to greater contact though for other reasons only limited benefits followed. Another school sought to get round the problem by ruling that kettles were not allowed except in the main staffroom! This worked wonders and the majority of staff did in fact congregate in the staffroom. The school's departments, including the special centre, all had their own department meeting and work rooms, thereby demonstrating that the undoubted need for the latter does not have to rule out a more general level of contact between staff.

3. Accommodation for parents

If a special centre attaches importance to having parents visit, some conscious thought must be given to the physical arrangements. Teachers who have been working in a school for some time tend to forget how cheerless if not repelling the building may seem to a casual or first-time visitor. Even new and well-appointed buildings can be confusing through sheer size and lack of signposting. Getting lost in a building and having to be ushered through a maze of corridors are not conducive to feeling at ease. When parents reach the special centre it helps if there is a quiet and comfortable spot where they can wait if necessary and a room where they can talk with teachers in private.

One school which attached a great deal of importance to work with parents and involved them effectively in a number of ways had a large comfortable staffroom next door to the office of the head of the special centre, both conveniently sited near the main entrance. Regular coffee mornings were held for parents here. They felt at ease in the staffroom and knew they could wait there if they wished to see a member of staff or had an appointment with the head of the centre.

Setting up integrated provision

Our main discussion of the factors involved in initiating a programme of integration is contained in chapter four. Here we want to look at factors arising out of the physical environment. These are grouped under: choice of location; consultation with relevant parties; and getting necessary alterations carried out.

1. Choosing a location

If a particular facility is intended only for pupils within a school's catchment area the question of choice does not arise. Frequently however special educational facilities in ordinary schools have to serve a broader catchment area than that of the school in which they are based.

Some such as special centres for those with visual impairment or communication disorder may cover the whole of an authority. In these cases an initial decision must be where to locate the special centre. There are many factors to consider. The discussion above of basic physical requirements, curricular considerations and the social context, raises pertinent issues. We advance three further considerations here, bearing respectively on the location of the school, its neighbourhood, and the amount and nature of the space available within it.

If pupils are to attend from outside the normal catchment area for the school, consideration must be paid to travelling arrangements. Journeys can be long because of distance or urban traffic; if more than one pupil is being transported a circuitous route may be necessary. This can mean pupils being in taxis for lengthy periods, in some cases as much as 1½ hours before they arrive at school each morning. In order to cut down on excessive travelling time it is desirable that a centre be sited roughly in the middle of the area it is to serve, provided this fits in with available travel routes – a centrally located site may not be the most convenient if it is not well served by public transport. Also, if the centre is conveniently located for ease of access by the pupils it will be equally convenient for parents to visit the school.

In one area a special centre (for secondary age pupils with moderate learning difficulties) is sited at a comprehensive school in a housing estate on the edge of town. Transport poses no problems for those within the school's own catchment area but it raises considerable difficulty for the others. The school is served by a local bus for housewives on the estate to go shopping in the town centre but there are no direct or even suitable indirect bus routes to the school from many of the outlying districts served by the centre. Pupils who were otherwise quite capable of finding their own way to school had to travel by special transport because of this. So an opportunity for promoting independence and normality had to be foregone.

Another consideration sometimes advanced is that the school chosen should not be in a blatantly difficult part of town, on the assumption that a special centre is less likely to flourish in such schools and also that some parents of children with special needs would be unhappy to see their child attend them. There is some evidence to support the latter but the former is rather more questionable. Certainly, schools in favoured areas tend to have active – and fund raising – parents associations, and home/school contact is easily established. A great many factors must be taken into account however in setting up special centres. If there are links between the demographic characteristics of schools and their suitability for providing special facilities for pupils drawn from a wide area, the picture is by no means simple and clearcut. As against the view that schools in difficult areas should be avoided, one teacher reported on the basis of canvassing a number of schools in order to site a language unit that schools in favoured middle class areas tended to be resistant to the idea. Another teacher who ran a language unit was quite happy with her inner city ethnically diverse school where infants with specific language problems did not stand out as being grossly different from their peers, even if the language models were not as good as they might be in another school.

As far as parental reluctance is concerned, this is not a negligible consideration since so much can depend on it: attitudes to service providers; perceptions of the child's needs, the education he is receiving and what the future can hold; the nature of home/school contact and the willingness to work cooperatively with the school. One secondary school described by its head as having one of the worst intakes in town and possessed of a tough reputation offered the only facilities for pupils with certain special needs over a wide area. Some parents were unhappy about their children attending this school and indeed had fears for their safety. In the event, the expected catastrophes did not materialize and succeeding generations of parents had less cause for anxiety. The lesson to be learned from this perhaps is not that parents have no need to be anxious – sometimes anxiety over a projected placement is an exceedingly rational response – but that teachers can by careful endeavour ensure that untoward incidents do not happen and that the pupils' educational needs are met appropriately.

Finally, a key factor in deciding on a location is the amount of space available. It can be exceedingly difficult to find a suitable school with the requisite space, so there is a tendency to use locations which are unsuitable in many respects but happen to have spare space. For instance, a group of physically handicapped pupils were placed at a school with a split-site campus; speech impaired children some of whom were hyperactive were placed at a school with no grassed area to play on; children with moderate and severe learning difficulties starting school from age three were placed in schools that had no nursery provision so they had no age peers; pupils with severe learning difficulties were placed at a school so formally organised as to make integration extremely difficult.

One understands the reasons for these placements. In times of economic stringency it is important to avail of readymade facilities; frequently the choice is between an unsuitable location and none at all. It is unsatisfactory however that so often a question asking why a particular provision was sited where it was elicited the simple answer that 'there was space available'. The constraints imposed by restricted budgets cannot be ignored but equally they do not remove the need to assess critically the facilities on offer. If attention is paid to the criteria by which space can be assessed, there is less likelihood that a thoroughly unsuitable location will be accepted just because it happened to be there and available.

2. Consultation

When setting up a specialist facility it is sensible to consult with any available persons who possess relevant experience. This is as true of the physical arrangements as it is of the other aspects of provision. There is a tendency to leave building and adaptation works especially if they are major to the architects' department. When this occurs it is to be regretted. If an integration programme is to be an integral part of the school and not a foreign body attached to it, then the accommodation for it must be designed with the school as a whole in mind. This is clearly not a job for the architect only. Sound functional design depends on accurate analysis of the needs a building is to serve. In the absence of direct experience such analysis tends to be speculative. In any case, these needs and the activities associated with them are to an extent still emergent, in that integrated provision is a relatively new venture in this country. There are schemes of integration however that have been running long enough for the people involved to have built up a solid understanding of how such provision works. These are educators for the most part, teachers and advisers, rather than architects. So if the analysis of special needs and the design of accommodation are to be based on experience, ways must be found of incorporating educators into design teams.

Our evidence suggests that this does not always happen. We encountered several examples where the experience of special school staff was ignored, despite the fact that the integration provision was designed to supplement or replace special school provision in the area. More generally, teachers were rarely consulted about the design or adaptation of accommodation in which they would be teaching or which would have far-reaching implications for the school.

A new special school with facilities for integration was to be built to rehouse pupils from the local rundown special school. Prior to the relocation to the present site, the staff had worked on designing a new school for some two years. Not only were they not consulted in the kind of school that was eventually built but their plan was ignored by the authority.

A large department was being built in a comprehensive school to accommodate the upper age range of physically handicapped pupils from the local special school. Even though one of the teachers from the special school was designated head of the department, neither he nor anybody else in the special school was consulted over the design with the result that facilities were cramped, worktops and tables at the wrong height and so on.

A related problem is when building designs are repeated without reference to the lessons of experience. Significant improvements can be effected by consulting those who have worked in the buildings and experienced at first hand how well they serve their purposes.

One authority built a special school for the physically handicapped on the same campus as a comprehensive school. After a number of years it was decided to replicate this provision elsewhere in the authority. The new special school was built to exactly the same design as the first, and a valuable opportunity was lost thereby to capitalise on the experience of the staff at the first school. There were numerous small changes that could have been made that would have been to the advantage of both staff and pupils.

3.   Getting alterations carried out

Ensuring that necessary adaptations were carried out, to an adequate standard, sometimes caused problems. Likewise, necessary resources and facilities were not always provided. In order to acquire adequate accommodation and resources head teachers commonly had to engage in extensive negotiations with the authority. This took a great deal of time, particularly as it was not usually possible to delegate – "the office doesn't give the same attention to a unit head as they do to the head". Heads sometimes resented the amount of time they spent agitating in this way – "it takes my time out of all proportion". They felt too that they were working in the dark to a certain extent. They lacked the requisite experience and did not know what was available or what level of provision the pupil should have, sometimes appreciating deficiencies only with hindsight. "Until you know what is wrong, you don't know how to put it right".

Three physically handicapped pupils, two girls and one boy, attended an infant school. Basic alterations such as ramping were done before they started. Great difficulty was experienced however in providing adequate sanitary facilities. One of the girls needed to be changed several times a day while the others had colostomy bags which needed regular attention. For a whole year the girl was tended to on the staffroom floor. At the insistence of the head alterations were eventually made but only on a piecemeal basis. First, the girls' toilets were adapted but another battle was necessary before requisite alterations were made in the boys' toilets. Further practical difficulties arose, and it was a long time before the system ran smoothly. Not only did it all take a great deal of time and effort but it also provoked much needless acrimony.

It is clear that providing an appropriate physical environment for integration programmes is not a simple matter, and everybody –pupils, teachers, education officials – would benefit from the adoption of more systematic procedures. There is need of local insight and professional experience from elsewhere as well as architectural and design expertise. The alternative is learning by discovery – and resigning oneself to inadequate provision since the lessons of hindsight cannot usually be applied except in other buildings.

Chapter Eleven
Costing Considerations in Integration Programmes

And I say to you: Make unto you friends of the mammon of iniquity.

Luke 16,9.

Decisions on educational provision rest on many factors. In an ideal world perhaps the only consideration would be the needs of pupils. If an individual's educational and other related needs were clearly identified one would be assured that the necessary resources would be made available. This does not happen however, for various reasons. Some are clear-cut such as the shortage of particular specialists. There are more pupils in need of speech therapy and physiotherapy than there are trained personnel to provide it (in the labour market at any rate – there is a sizeable number in retirement). Others are less easy to understand and seemingly more intractable such as our failure to avail of existing resources and manpower. The coexistence of groups of unemployed teachers and nursery nurses and large numbers of pupils whose needs are not being met as effectively as they might be is a case in point.

What underlies these and many other considerations is the question of costs. It is clear that financial constraints govern the nature and extent of educational provision in many ways. This is so whether people acknowledge it or not. Indeed our experience suggests that the less one acknowledges them the more constraining they are: those teachers who paid explicit attention to them and consciously 'worked the system' were generally better resourced. It is understandable that many teachers pay limited attention to the cost aspects of their work. The financial arrangements of even a modest scheme of provision can be quite complex, and teachers generally lack relevant accounting experience. In our experience also, they tend to have little interest in the finances of their schemes – apart from getting the most out of them. Educational, not financial, considerations were quite properly uppermost in their minds.

Costs are important determinants of educational provision however. Whether or not a particular form of provision is implemented or implemented on a scale sufficient to give it a chance of succeeding will often depend on financial considerations. This is not to say that educational decisions can be based on cost criteria alone. Equally it is idle to take the view that the education of these pupils should be determined entirely by educational considerations, to the exclusion of economic considerations. Educational resources are scarce, and those required in special education are in some instances exceedingly rare. This scarcity is at any given time in part a function of society's commitment to providing resources to meet special needs. It is always possible to argue for more resources – and many people see this as a legitimate part of their function as special educators – but the fact remains that economic constraints persist, and loom larger. The job in hand has to be done within these constraints, and this in consequence means decisions about allocating resources.

Our purpose here is to draw attention to the cost implications of educating pupils with special needs in ordinary schools and this chapter discusses various concepts and approaches to costing which teachers and administrators dealing with integration programmes should find useful. It also outlines a simple accountancy structure for looking at the monetary costs of integration programmes. Working out the costs accruing to a form of provision may be difficult and there is no question of dispensing with the detailed treatment of costs that an accountant or financial administrator would provide, but it is important for others to have a good understanding of the cost-incurring elements and their order of significance. If educators are more sensitised to the detail of costs, they will be better able to monitor their use of resources, decide on reallocation of them and generally utilise them efficiently. They will also be able to specify the resource implications of proposed innovations and support their arguments for them with quantitative data. If necessary they should be able to comment on cost comparisons between different forms of provision, eg between special schooling and different forms of integrated placement. (It should be noted that such comparisons are fraught with difficulty and are usually best avoided.)

We start by drawing attention to the identification problem, deciding what should count as a cost and what can be ignored. This is followed by a section on measurement, discussing how to assign values under the different headings and including a checklist of the costs that may be incurred. Finally, there is a note about interpretation and the problem of making cost comparisons. The exercise is necessarily limited through being carried out in the abstract since the detailed purposes to which a cost analysis is put affect it in important ways. There are some general principles however that have wide applicability and it is useful to consider these.

Identifying the inputs

The first task is to identify the inputs to the programme. It may seem a simple matter to agree on the components of an integration programme that incur cost but there are many problems. Certain major items stand out such as staff costs and major building works, though even here there can be difficulty. As illustrated below, major building within a school may require the school as a whole to be 'reconstituted'; this entails additional expenditure beyond that required just for the new building, so that the gross building costs for an integration facility are greater than the facility on its own requires. Likewise, staffing for an integration programme may include an enhancement of main school staffing, so that the increase in staffing may not be entirely attributable to the programme.

What is required is a detailed description of the programme in terms of factors which incur cost or the utilisation of resources. Three main problems can be identified. First, there are various cost-incurring elements whose financial implications may not be realised. Examples might be the time spent by the head, increased involvement on the part of the school psychological service, extra open evenings and greater home/school contact. These could all be important factors in an integration programme. They could also be costed in terms of staff time and resources used. It may be the case however that no extra *money* is involved since the head is not paid any more (unless the school's group size is altered or a special allowance is paid) or the psychological service absorbs the new work by rearranging priorities. To the extent that factors such as these are integral to the success of a given scheme a way of taking account of them must be found. This may well not be in monetary terms but in terms of costs of a different order: the head has less time to spend on the rest of the school; referral queues at the school psychological service lengthen, and so on.

It hardly needs stressing that the financial costs are only part of the cost of a formal educational provision. Just as educational decisions cannot be made on cost criteria alone, any assessment of the cost of a scheme of integration must take account of a range of factors, some of which can be expressed in direct monetary terms, some can only be costed indirectly or in terms of some other units, as in the examples above, and some such as patterns of relationships do not lend themselves to quantification at all. It is for the person making the assessment to identify clearly the factors of each kind and the actual costs to be assigned them preparatory to deciding how costs of different order weigh up against each other.

Secondly, there is the problem of apportioning costs between the integration programme and the main school. This is all the more difficult if there is extensive integration and the new provision becomes an integral part of the school. Many pupils formally assigned to the special centre will be receiving part of their education within the main school. The special centre may provide a service for pupils not formally assigned to it. This will release other staff from certain duties or simply improve the education offered to the pupils in question. There may well be a policy of staff integration whereby special centre staff take main school classes and vice versa. In all these cases the distinction between special centre and main school becomes blurred with the result that the costs incurred by them are interwoven. If it is required to identify them quite separately very detailed information must be obtained on how the school works in practice – allocation of pupils to teaching groups, deployment of staff, utilisation of classrooms and resources and so on.

A further complication is the fact that an integration programme will not be receiving inputs from Education only. There may well be intensive medical and paramedical support, which will be a charge on Area Health, and social worker involvement, which will be a charge on Social Services. These bring in further costing formulae, as well as difficulties of retrieval. Typically, the involvement of Health and Social Services personnel will not be full-time so that the charge on a particular provision in receipt of service must be obtained by apportionment. Even if this can be done readily for direct costs, there will be difficulties with indirect costs unless the different services take account of overheads in similar ways.

Assigning values

Having established what is and is not to count as a cost, the next step is to measure them and assign actual values to them. This is theoretically straightforward once the cost-incurring elements have been clearly identified. In practice there are problems. The requisite information is not in the hands of those who run the integration programme. It is not even in the hands of the school. It has to be extracted from the LEA, and possibly the Area Health Authority and the Social Services Department as well. We say 'extracted' advisedly since the costs of individual institutions are not readily available, and those of sub-sections of institutions even less so. Knight (1980) points out that even within Education there is no agreed format for school costing, so that comparisons between one school and another are difficult to make. Moreover, information on school costs is geared to treasurers' estimates rather than the management of institutions. This means that the information available may not be what is required. To get at costs in a usable form it may be necessary to engage in a complex reconstruction exercise.

Details on standard procedures for allocating educational expenditure can be found in the 'Form of published accounts of local authorities' published by the Chartered Institute of Public Finance and Accountancy (CIPFA) – formerly the Institute of Municipal Treasurers and Accountants (IMTA). Four general headings are used:

Employees
Running Expenses
Debt Charges
Revenue contributions to capital outlay.

Employee costs cover salary and related costs and training

expenses both of teaching and non-teaching staff, and their total costs make up the most significant item of expenditure. (These costs are critically dependent on pupil-teacher ratios.) The main detail is under the heading of Running Expenses. For primary and secondary education as well as special education the following represents a simplified abstraction.

Premises
    Repairs, alterations and maintenance
    Fuel
    Furniture and fittings
    Rent and rates
Supplies and Services
    Books
    Educational equipment
    School stationery and materials
    Office equipment
Transport
    This is primarily for staff transport
Establishment expenses
    Printing and office costs
    Travelling, subsistence and conference costs
    Insurances
Agency Services
    Contributions to non-maintained schools
    Contributions to jointly maintained schools
Miscellaneous expenses
    Fees and expenses
    Provision of board and lodging
    Provision of transport between home and school
    Educational visits
    Provision of transport other than between home and school.
                                                (From IMTA, 1969)

This outline and the more refined schedule from which it is taken do allow a detailed allocation of educational costs. Its very detail however means that it has much redundant information and is needlessly complicated as far as the educator is concerned. Also, it contains only part of the information required to cost a programme of integration. Further breakdowns may be required to cover LEA administration and the school psychological service, as well as any charges accruing from Area Health and Social Services involvement. The above is moreover an accounting tool rather than one geared to the detailed analysis and management of individual institutions. Some costs are irrelevant to a scheme of integration while others need further refining. The cost of maintaining grounds for example will probably have no bearing whereas staffing costs and curriculum expenditure may need greater refining than in standard analyses if the integration programme is to be costed accurately.

In place of the CIPFA schedule we offer an alternative, rather simpler schedule below. This is not an alternative in accounting terms. Its aim is to enable the (financial) layman to examine an integration programme in financial terms, or at least sharpen his analysis of it, by identifying the areas where costs specific to integration are being incurred or can be anticipated along with an idea of the order of cost. It is not worked out in fine detail since the forms of integration vary widely. It is used in the following chapter to structure the discussion of the cost-incurring elements of the integration programmes studied.

1. *Staff and professional services*
This will be the main source of expenditure. Costs will be incurred under three headings:
i.   Salaries and wages, plus NHI and Superannuation
ii.   Training expenses
iii. Other staff-related costs, including travelling.
These costs will be incurred variously for the different categories of staff involved. It is convenient to group them as follows:
A   Staff employed wholly or mainly for the integration programme.
  – teachers
  – welfare assistants
  – others, including therapists, nurses and general assistants but excluding drivers.
B   Staff with part-time involvement.
  – other teaching and support staff from the school
  – external staff (Education), including peripatetic teachers, psychologists, advisers
  – external staff (other services), including speech therapists, physiotherapists, medical and nursing staff, social workers.

2. *Premises*

This includes both teaching and non-teaching accommodation, the latter covering everything from mobility and care arrangements to swimming pools.

i.   new purpose-built accommodation
ii. major adaptations to existing buildings
iii. minor alterations, such as ramping, adapting toilets
iv. furniture and fittings
v.   operational costs – this is narrower than Running Expenses above, being confined to items such as rent and rates, fuel and electricity and building maintenance where there has been new building or substantial adaptation.

(NB: Any capital expenditure involved would first have to be converted into a recurrent annual equivalent before being included in this format. This equivalent will normally be a loan charge and must be separately and clearly identified. The task of reducing capital costs to annual equivalents in this way is of course a technical one and not for the layman.)

3. *Resources and equipment*

i.   books and other printed resources, including tests
ii. educational equipment, including language masters and tape recorders
iii. adapted equipment as required for physical education, craft subjects, domestic science, science and music
iv. stationery and other consumable materials
v.   handicap-specific items, including wheelchairs and other mobility aids, typewriters adapted as required, low vision aids, hearing aids.

4. *Transport*

This is a separate heading both because it is important in integration and because it is frequently problematic and in need of close scrutiny.

i.   to and from school, including escorts
ii. travel during school day, in split-sites or when schools are collaborating
iii. trips and extra-curricular activities.

5. *Miscellaneous*

This is for items of significant expenditure not covered elsewhere. Increases in school administration for instance may not be covered entirely under staff costs, and it may be necessary to include a figure for office costs.

As noted, this schedule is not intended to be an accounting tool nor is its function to provide the basis for cost comparisons. Its purpose is to help in identifying the costs in an integration programme or, for future planning purposes, the costs likely to be incurred if a given programme is implemented.

Interpreting the results

Having assigned figures to the agreed headings, one is faced with the task of analysis. How to interpret the results? What do the figures mean in terms of the needs being met and the amount of resources being consumed? One should be clear that there are no simple answers here, and certainly no right or wrong ones. There are no formulae for decreeing what should be spent on different categories of pupils or what a particular form of provision should cost. This is not to say that there are no cost criteria. What this exercise does is to make explicit the costs incurred by an integration programme so that when costs are joined with other factors that bear on decision-making they can be discussed with some precision. Also, if monetary comparisons are to be made between, eg special schooling and different forms of integrated provisions, it offers a means of specifying the costs of the integration options.

There are a number of considerations that must be borne in mind when examining the costs. The net figure finally arrived at may represent the cost of running this particular programme, but how meaningful is it in terms of implementing comparable programmes elsewhere? There are perhaps three questions to answer here. First, how much of the cost is attributable to integration and how much to peculiarities of the local situation? Secondly, how much does it reflect the state of development of the project? Thirdly, to what extent is it a net cost in respect of the pupils in question? These questions are important since many costs are idiosyncratic to place and time and because these pupils would incur some educational costs in any case. This means that the figure in question may not be representative of the form of provision unless these other factors can be disentangled and discounted.

What is required in the first instance is to identify those factors in the local situation that affect costs idiosyncratically and estimate their contribution to the total. Accommodation and transport provide fairly obvious examples. If suitable space is available, considerable savings can be effected by using it. One authority however was obliged to adapt a comprehensive school for physically handicapped pupils; not only was the school multi-storey and part of it quite old, but it was on a split-site with the result that initial building and adaptation costs were high and there is a recurrent bill for transporting pupils from site to site throughout the school day. Transport costs are notoriously subject to local variation. Distance is an important variable in rural locations, while journey time can be the critical factor in urban situations. This can affect staff costs since a peripatetic service (of specialist teachers, physiotherapists, and so on) will need a higher staffing level if lengthy periods are spent travelling. An example of a different kind arises from looking at the nature of the catchment area and any special problems that may be associated with it. Take a language unit serving a depressed area. If a majority of the children (and their families) require social worker support, is this a legitimate charge on the language unit? It may be that this support is an important part of the whole programme and would not be available if the unit did not exist, but equally it might not be necessary if the unit were in a more favoured area.

Secondly, account must be taken of the state of development of the project. Typically, costs will be greater at the outset, at least on a per capita basis. Pupil numbers may be low as admission criteria and procedures are worked out and to allow time for curriculum development, staff training and so on. Per capita costs will be higher because of this but there may also be considerable non-recurrent expenditure on equipment and major resource items. When the cost of building adaptations is not large enough to merit raising a loan and converting the cost to annual equivalents through loan charges, there will be a further initial cost.

These considerations suggest that the costs of a scheme of integration have most use as an adjunct to a detailed description of the scheme. In the absence of such a description, a figure for total cost may have little meaning. The scheme as a whole comprises diverse elements, some of which are necessary or take distinctive form because of particular local or historical considerations. It is only when the cost is broken down in relation to these that it can be interpreted in depth and used to inform other situations.

Thirdly, the total cost of a scheme of integration will be a gross cost in respect of the education of the pupils in question. Establishing a *net* cost may be difficult but it could alter the picture dramatically. A clear-cut case is when the alternative would be placement at an independent school and the LEA would be paying determinate – and sizeable – fees. Less clear-cut but more common is the situation when the alternative would be an authority or inter-authority school which has to be maintained anyway possibly with reduced numbers. This will entail a calculation of marginal savings if any. It should be noted that this exercise may require numerous assumptions to be made and the net result may be somewhat speculative. The same is likely to apply to the consideration that these pupils would require education in any case even if they were not judged to possess special needs. As ordinary pupils attending their present school or another one their education would attract some costs. Unless these can be assumed to be trivial in all cases, a valid net cost can only be obtained by calculating them and offsetting against the gross costs.

Finally, there is the question of cost comparisons. It is necessary to consider this in view of the debates about the relative cost of segregated and integrated provision and the common assumption that integration offers a means of providing special education more cheaply. These debates do have a toehold on reality (though sometimes little more). Shutting a special school for instance clearly has financial implications, especially if it can be sold or put to alternative use. There are problems however.

First, there is the technical problem of drawing up the basis for comparison. Thus, if it was required to compare the monetary costs of various options over say a five-year period it would be necessary to complete a cost matrix of the following type:

	Option 1	Option 2	Option 3
1. Special School Costs			
2. Ordinary School Costs			
3. School Link Costs			
4. Inter-authority payments			
5. Independent school fees			
6. Less: Inter-authority receipts			
TOTAL			

As we have seen above, this is a far from easy task. Unless it is carried out however it is likely that major areas of expenditure or resource utilisation will be ignored and the comparison will be unsound.

A second problem stems from the fact that some of the inputs are not quantifiable, in monetary terms at least. (This holds *a fortiori* where outcomes are concerned since the quality of education cannot be expressed in financial terms.) Home/school links are a case in point. The co-operative and active involvement of parents might be regarded as an input into special education. This does not lend itself to being costed in monetary terms. To the extent that it is likely to be available in different degrees in different forms of special education (contrast residential placement with placement in a local school), it is a factor that complicates comparison.

The third, and perhaps the most critical, problem is the lack of comparability in real terms between the different forms of provision. This has of course to do with outcomes. If a higher quality of educational provision is being made or if the group of special educators in question are meeting a wider range of pupil needs than before, a comparison in financial terms could be misleading if not spurious. The importance of this is that integration programmes frequently arrive in a context of improved provision or the extension of special education to pupils who would not otherwise have received it. Thus, a department for pupils with moderate learning difficulties in a comprehensive school might on paper seem comparable to the secondary department of an ESN(M) school. Even though both are concerned primarily with the same group of pupils, it is likely however that there would be so many differences in curricular provision, mode of working, other duties undertaken and so on that any direct comparison of costs would be meaningless. In simple terms, one is not comparing like with like. For these various reasons then it is necessary to treat cost comparisons involving integration programmes or indeed other forms of special education with the greatest caution.

Chapter Twelve
Costs in Practice

It's very odd. Ask any comprehensive head teacher for his exam results, his timetable analysis, his points structure, his first XI or XV record – and face a deluge of statistics. Ask him what the school costs to run – and meet an embarrassed silence. He may hazard a guess – and if you are lucky he may even be within £100 000 or two. Obviously, his governors and his staff know as little. Even more odd, his LEA probably won't know much more. (Knight, 1980)

In this chapter we examine some of the factors bearing on costs in the integration programmes studied. This is done in terms of the schedule developed in the previous chapter: staff and professional services; premises; resources and equipment; and transport. The schedule is considered separately for each of (i) arrangements for individual integration, (ii) special centres in ordinary schools and (iii) links between special schools and ordinary schools, since the costing considerations are very different in each case. Finally, some general issues relating to costs in integration programmes are discussed.

Individual integration

Two programmes involved individual integration. One was in a rural area where physically handicapped pupils attend their local schools. The other is in an urban area where a number of hearing impaired pupils are placed, with support, in selected neighbourhood schools. There was a *de facto* individual integration in a third location where visually impaired pupils of primary age attended a particular school; at the time of our study one pupil had reached secondary age and was attending a nearby comprehensive school as an individual.

1.　Staff and professional services

A significant difference between the two principal schemes here is that no direct teacher salary costs are involved in one while they constitute a major element in the other. The physically handicapped pupils were placed in existing classes. The class teacher – and the head teacher – may have had their workloads increased but no actual costs were incurred. What did cost extra was the employment of classroom assistants. These were provided on a generous basis with at least one per school where there was a severely physically handicapped pupil. Where there was more than one such pupil a single assistant sometimes provided for all, but this did not happen always so that some schools had the services full-time of two classroom assistants. Training costs were negligible in the early years of this provision but only because it had not been possible to lay on the requisite training. It was recognised that certain training requirements existed and plans were afoot to meet them. If these materialised they would incur ongoing costs since the commitment to placing pupils in their local schools where possible meant that each year there would be fresh teachers and ancillaries to train. As well as further schools being involved with new intakes and transfers, pupils would usually move on to a new teacher within a given school each year. It should be remembered also that this was a dispersed rural area with the result that (a) training would have to be provided on a district basis, possibly involving an element of duplication, and (b) travelling expenses of participants would even so be considerable.

The other principal staffing cost in this scheme was the provision of physiotherapy. The details of this service have been described above. Had these pupils attended special school they would have been receiving physiotherapy of course. Indeed it was suggested that they would have had more contact time with the physiotherapist. In general, however, a scheme such as this will generate a need for physiotherapy services on a local basis which cannot be easily offset against possible savings on the requirements of special schools which may well be in different area health authorities. Moreover, in a rural area travelling consumes professional time as well as being a direct cost.

In the scheme for hearing impaired pupils the main staffing input was in terms of support teachers. Pupils were placed in ordinary classes and received support within the classroom or on a withdrawal basis. The demands on class teachers were relatively modest. The amount of support depended on the individual pupil and his or her degree of hearing loss, but the twelve pupils in the scheme were supported by seven teachers, three of whom were teachers of the deaf. (Some of the teachers were part-time, so that the full-time equivalent was 6.1 teachers.) This is a somewhat more favourable ratio than would normally obtain in a school for the deaf. The success of the scheme did depend also on the training, technical support and other back-up facilities provided by the special school which parented the scheme. These facilities were provided out of existing resources – acknowledged to have been provided on a generous scale – and so attracted no extra cost. It should be recognised that if they had to be provided from scratch, or costed out as such, they would represent a significant cost.

2.   *Premises*

Where individual integration is concerned, there is no question of new building or major adaptations. Relatively minor alterations to existing buildings may be required, and operational costs may be increased slightly. For physically handicapped pupils the primary requirements are for mobility and toileting. To permit access to the school it may be necessary to ramp one or more entrances. This is usually a simple operation. Schools that are on one storey on a level site present no further problem. If the site is not level, further ramps may be necessary within the school, sometimes necessitating circuitous journeys to get from one point to another within the school.

We noted that for the authority in question most primary schools were single storey and thus presented little problem. Had this not been the case, the cost of adaptations would have been much greater, and there would have been a considerable obstacle in the way of the integration programme. Difficulties were beginning to emerge with regard to middle and secondary schooling where many buildings were multistorey. In the case of several buildings it was judged uneconomic to make the alterations that would permit access and mobility within the school, and alternative placements were being sought.

In most schools some expenditure on toileting arrangements was required. Sanitary provision and arrangements for changing appliances and sometimes nappies were usually required. (Many of these pupils were spina bifida cases and had incontinence problems.) Actual costs varied greatly, from a low of £100 to close on £1000. Much depended on the physical layout of the school, availability of suitable space, existing plumbing arrangements, heating requirements and so on.

As regards the hearing impaired, there were some minor costs of adaptation. In the initial stages of the scheme small open-topped booths were provided in the primary classroom. These were acoustically treated and intended to provide a withdrawal space that was free of visual distraction as well as cutting down on ambient noise. Later, it was decided to use spare space outside the classrooms for withdrawal work, and the booths were no longer used. A small further charge related to lighting, which was upgraded where required (to facilitate lipreading) and maintained to a higher standard. Also, venetian blinds were installed in some instances in order that the amount and direction of light coming into the classroom could be controlled.

For pupils with hearing and vision impairments it was acknowledged that ideally more could have been spent. The lack of acoustic treatment in schools was the major drawback for hearing aid users. This was not feasible even in withdrawal areas. What was done was to provide partial carpeting and some curtains. Similarly, no physical alterations were made in the secondary school which a blind girl attended, though it was acknowledged that some changes – e.g. providing differently textured flooring – would be beneficial.

Operational costs in each of these cases were relatively minor. Where children require to be changed, it is necessary to arrange for a supply of nappies and other consumables. This may appear a trivial point but it can lead to dissatisfaction if the necessary supplies have to be purchased from an already strained school budget. It is also necessary to make disposal arrangements, possibly by having a disposal unit which is emptied at regular intervals on a contract basis. Where the new toileting arrangements are in a part of the school previously unheated or not heated to the extent of allowing children to be changed, heating costs will be incurred.

3. Resources

Costs under this heading would accrue to the education of these pupils in any case, regardless of its location. Wherever they were, they would need books, paper, pencils, as well as hearing aids or low vision aids or whatever. Where complex equipment is concerned, special schools may be able to achieve economies of scale through more intensive usage. Thus, if hearing impaired pupils are being supplied with radio hearing aids, each pupil will require his own aid if integration is on an individual basis whereas in a special school or large unit a degree of shared use is possible. Moreover, if individual integration is operating without the base of a special school to support it, as in the scheme for physically handicapped pupils, specialised pieces of equipment such as adapted typewriters are less likely to be available.

Schools receiving physically handicapped pupils slotted them into existing arrangements, whether this be an ordinary class or some special provision within the school for slow learners. In either case, no costs were incurred beyond what would be incurred for any pupil with comparable learning requirements, Normal capitation arrangements applied. Likewise, extra costs did not accrue in the scheme for hearing impaired pupils. They were not having more spent on them than if they were in one of the departments of the school for hearing impaired. This was partly because the service as a whole was "pretty lavishly equipped" and partly because the equipment had been uprated for all hearing impaired pupils. At the beginning of the scheme each pupil being integrated individually was provided with a radio hearing aid; at the time this was a plus for them because the others did not have these aids, but since then they have been provided for most hearing impaired pupils in the authority. A part capitation allowance is paid into the schools and this is held to cover any use of curriculum materials.

In the case of the blind pupil, the two main requirements were for braille books and for brailled versions of classroom work. Where textbooks were required and were available in braille, they were obtained from the Royal National Institute for the Blind or from the Leeds Braille Book Club. Where necessary the peripatetic teacher for the blind brailled the maths and science books for her use.

4. Transport

Transport costs are affected in different ways by programmes of individual integration. If the alternative is residential schooling, costs will be confined to once weekly trips at most and possibly some support to enable parents to visit the school. The situation is not so clearcut in respect of day special schools. On the one hand, pupils' journeys will on average be longer than if each was going to his or her local school. On the other hand it may be possible to effect economies by means of group transport. These economies may not be available in individual integration where a host of separate arrangements may push costs up.

In the majority of cases the physically handicapped pupils were brought to school by taxi, mostly on an individual basis. Escorts were judged necessary and provided in a few cases. A small number were brought by their parents, something which curiously was discouraged by petty regulations. The classic example of this was where a physically handicapped girl had an able-bodied brother attending the same school. He was not allowed travel to school with her in the taxi even though there was room. It seemed ludicrous to the mother that her daughter should set off in a taxi and she follow on with her son to the same destination. So she decided to take both to school herself. This meant however that her daughter could not have a wheelchair for use at home, since two wheelchairs were only issued to pupils receiving official transport. The hearing impaired pupils were confined to a compact urban area. Attending their local schools removed for some the need for special transport, and a significant saving was effected.

Special centres

The special centres we studied dealt with a wide range of special needs and encompassed a variety of arrangements from individual classes with just one teacher (and usually some ancillary support) to large departments with half a dozen or more staff. Obviously costs reflect the size of the establishment; the different costing elements too have differential relevance according to the nature of the special needs. There were some common threads however and these form the basis of our discussion here.

1.   Staff and professional services

Apart from the possible initial capital expenditure, most costs will be incurred on staff. An appropriate number of teachers and ancillaries must be employed. Details on the staffing ratios that obtained in the different schemes are given above (chapter 5). That does not represent the whole picture and contains in any case an element of supposition. Teachers formally appointed to a special centre may have duties in the school unconnected with the centre. This will certainly be the case if there is a policy of deploying staff flexibly. On the other hand, the presence of integration imposes demands on mainschool staff. These can be considerable if the special centre is large and operates an extensive programme of integration. In quantitative terms, pupils associated with the special centre may be receiving as much as half of their education from mainschool staff. In some cases this was taken account of by increasing the staffing establishment of the main school. As regards ancillary staff, these were usually provided by making a special allocation to the centre or, especially in infant schools where there were ancillaries in post already, increasing the school's ancillary establishment.

The total staff bill for an individual school may be increased indirectly in a number of ways because of integration. The additional pupils may increase the school's Group size, thereby increasing the salaries of senior staff and making more promotion points available. (Group size is determined by a formula calculated on points allocated to pupils on the basis of age, with an additional three points for each handicapped pupil.) Individual local arrangements may also be made, such as paying special allowances to heads or assigning additional promotion points to the school.

A large special centre was being set up in a comprehensive school. It was felt that the person to run the centre needed to be appointed at Senior Teacher level. The school's staffing establishment allowed for three senior teachers only, and the addition of the special centre did not affect Group size sufficiently to justify the extra Senior Teacher in the normal way. The expedient adopted, in order to appoint at the required level without affecting the promotion prospects of existing staff, was to create a further Senior Teacher post.

Other related factors include the need to recruit at a level sufficient to attract people with the right kind of experience, the need to create additional posts of responsibility within the school, and the fact that training allowances may be payable. One authority indeed had a policy of appointing teachers to special classes on scale 2 and then promoting them to scale 3 "as soon as they have shown they can do the job". In some primary schools this meant they were the only ones on scale 3. The net result of these various factors is that the school ends up with more posts of responsibility and a higher staffing bill than it would otherwise have. It should be remembered however that this is looking at costs from the perspective of the individual school, and some of these costs would be offset by savings to the education authority as a whole. For example, group size is changed more easily for small schools than for large; to take a hypothetical example, two schools could each reduce their group size by transferring 20 pupils to a large school while the additional 40 pupils would not affect the group size of the latter.

The successful functioning of special centres depends also on the availability of a wide range of other staff besides teachers and ancillaries. These can include psychologists, physiotherapists, speech therapists, and others from Education, Area Health and Social Services, as well as head teachers and other school-based staff. In most cases any services provided by such staff are taken out of existing establishments so that – nominally at any rate – no new cost attributable to integration arises. Thus, a psychologist may be assigned to an integration scheme on a twenty per cent basis or a speech therapist on an eighty per cent basis but it is unlikely that the staffing establishments of their respective services will be expanded to compensate. This compensation was made in a small number of cases but the more general arrangement was that the extra work was absorbed by rearranging priorities and/or increasing workloads. This applied particularly to head teachers. As noted below, heads could spend a great deal of time on the integration scheme, particularly in the early years. One noted that he was able to do so without detriment to the school only because he was surplus to staffing and was in a position to delegate main school duties.

It must be noted that the practice of providing support in this way, i.e. drawing on existing services without any compensatory adjustment of them, did have drawbacks. In many cases the services in question did not have the flexibility or spare capacity to respond, so that the requisite advisory or therapeutic support was not available. Ideallym, one would at the outset of an integration programme estimate the likely impact on relevant services and the extent to which existing staffing levels suffice. If it is clear that the need for particular services or the involvement of key personnel is unlikely to be met without dilution of the service or detriment to the individual's other responsibilities, then appropriate steps – including budgetary provision – must be taken.

A further set of costs relates to training. Special training needs arise out of integration since a greater number of people require specialist knowledge and skill. We have detailed in chapter 9 the many ways in which the requisite training can be provided. Costs can vary greatly. School-based courses can be mounted at little or no cost. Likewise, staff attendance at short courses will cost no more than the course fee and travelling expenses unless supply teachers are required for cover. In one authority the need for cover was removed at a stroke by shutting all special classes on one day each term and dedicating the day to training. For longer courses secondment costs and course fees which may be considerable are incurred. It may be noted that authorities seem to vary greatly in their willingness to incur training costs. There are wide divergences in secondment opportunities, the provision of supply teachers and support for short courses; it is not uncommon for staff from different LEAs on a short course to find that their respective authorities are offering widely different levels of support.

2. *Premises*

Accommodation for units or special centres in schools is provided in one of three ways: utilising existing space; adding to an existing building; or designing appropriate space in a new building. The cost implications are different in each case, though simple comparisons are to be avoided. This needs stressing since the *standard* of accommodation varied considerably. Purpose built accommodation was more expensive but in our experience was generally superior to the alternatives.

When accommodation was required for single classes, this was usually provided by making use of existing space, whether spare classrooms or prefabricated huts. Adaptation costs were relatively minor, involving items such as ramped access, washbasins, enlarged work areas and redecoration when a room had been out of use for some time. In some cases a room was put into service just as it was and no cost was incurred under this heading. The appeal of using existing accommodation to house special centres is strong, particularly in times of financial stringency. It is clearly sensible to utilise surplus space if it is suitable. That however is the rub. As documented in the previous chapter, surplus accommodation brought into service in this way was frequently unsuitable along many dimensions. It is an inefficient use of resources when this happens, whether it be because further resources are not available and one has to make the best of a bad job, or because the implications of skimping on capital provision have not been appreciated.

It was our impression that capital expenditure was too readily seen as an area where savings could be made, though we were not in a position to acquire systematic data on this. It was particularly likely to happen when the provision was small. Space for a single special class can be found readily enough. If this space seems almost good enough it will be difficult to make a successful case for spending a good deal of money on it. In any case, decisions on allocating and adapting space were usually made by people who did not have to work there. Teachers and ancillaries often had a keen appreciation of the limitations and difficulties of the space available but had little say on the matter; they were commonly able to air their views only indirectly, by letter or via the head. A further point is that adaptation costs would normally come out of the – relatively small – budget for minor works and would be incurred in a single year, whereas bigger works can be spread over a period of years through debt charges. Secondly, the disparity between capital costs and operating costs was not always sufficiently appreciated. While the former may be large they are fixed and – loan charges aside – non-recurring, whereas the cost of running a special centre is a recurrent one and subject to inflation. This means that if the costs of a particular provision are viewed over a period of time, any initial capital cost even on a generous scale will be swamped by recurrent costs including salaries.

A further factor to bear in mind when adapting existing space is, as noted in the previous chapter, that adaptations may be required throughout the school if pupils are to have full access to the educational opportunities provided by the school. There will be little point, for integration purposes, of having a special centre housed in first-rate accommodation if whole areas of the school are inaccessible to non-ambulant pupils or many rooms are unavailable for teaching the sensory impaired or some pupils are restricted to a single adapted toilet in a remote corner of the school. Certain modifications that would be desirable, such as general acoustic insulation, may be considered prohibitively expensive. In such cases it would seem important to be aware of the implications of not making these modifications so as to be able to assess the educational cost for given pupils.

The purpose built additions we saw were with one exception built and fitted out to a generous standard. We provide illustrative figures for one case (not the exception!) below. This highlights the difficulty of isolating the cost attributable to a particular form of provision, even at the basic level of physical accommodation. It was a special centre added to a comprehensive school to cater for up to 60 physically handicapped pupils. The school was on two sites, one a former girls' school, the other a new building with little teaching accommodation on the ground floor. Both buildings were multistorey. A specially designed wing and swimming pool were added to one of the buildings, while extensive adaptations were made throughout both buildings. The table attached outlines the principal capital costs.

Capital costs in making provision for physically handicapped pupils (60 places) in a comprehensive school (1975 prices)	
New teaching accommodation	
Fitted furniture	£84 000
Loose furniture and equipment	10 000
Swimming pool (shared use)	10 000
Special Services: Construction	
Recreation: Construction	165 000
Furniture and Equipment	165 000
Adaptations to existing buildings	7 000
Furniture	76 000
	2 000

The cost of the new teaching accommodation was considered to be broadly comparable to the cost of providing similar accommodation in a special school. The cost of the adaptations in relation to this may seem excessive but in fact only a portion of it is directly attributable to accommodating the physically handicapped. This was for two reasons: requirements due to fire regulations; and scarcity of ground floor accommodation in one building. Take fire regulations first. When the new wing for the physically handicapped was added the school was 'reconstituted'. This meant that the school as a whole was regarded as a new school for fire regulation purposes and present-day regulations were insisted on. This necessitated considerable expenditure, the net result being to bring the building to a higher standard than before. Many of these alterations would have been necessary in any case even if provision for the physically handicapped was not involved; if the school was being reconstituted for some other purpose, the new regulations would equally have to be met.

One of the buildings was a modern four-storey structure with services, cloakrooms etc. on the ground floor. Practically all of the teaching accommodation was off ground level. This was a considerable complication and necessitated further expenditure: teaching accommodation had to be provided at ground level, and ramps and covered entrances provided to temporary classrooms. Much of this cost would not have been incurred had the existing building offered different facilities. Other expenditure under the heading of adaptations included: providing a lift – this was of high quality and levels off so that the lift sets very precisely to floor level (eliminating bumps and ridges for wheelchairs to negotiate); raising corridors around a quadrangle; and adapting some toilets around the school.

As regards the swimming pool, the construction costs were shared equally between Special Services and Recreation. It was available for use by the school as a whole and also the community. In fact, it was in heavy use and only a portion of the capital cost involved could legitimately be marked up against the physically handicapped provision.

What emerges here – and this is supported by observations in other schemes as well – is that the capital cost of housing a sizeable special centre by adding to an existing school may in some cases be greater than the corresponding special school costs. This is because of the extra costs of adapting the host school. The cost of providing specialist teaching and care accommodation will be roughly comparable, but adaptations required by the integration programme will necessitate extra costs. Depending on the nature of the school, the types of handicap in question and the extent of integration, these may well be considerable. It should be noted however that less teaching accommodation will be required in the special centre if extensive integration is envisaged: savings may be effected as a consequence that can be offset against any extra costs incurred.

Only one of the schemes we studied provided an example of a special centre being incorporated into a new school. This was a department for pupils with learning difficulties in a comprehensive school. It would seem to be a cost-effective way of providing adequate accommodation in an area where there was not an appropriate special school. The requisite accommodation and facilities were provided on the same basis as any other specialist department in the school. Any effort to isolate the costs involved would be somewhat speculative, the more so because of a thoroughgoing programme of integration and the fact that department staff worked with a large number of pupils throughout the school.

3. Resources and equipment

It may be worth repeating that these pupils would have to be educated anyway, whether or not integration was at issue. Resources and equipment will be required however their education is provided. This entails certain basic costs which are inescapable and which in fact constitute the major part of any curricular costs. There will be some variation but it is unlikely that the actual cost of providing the curriculum will vary greatly under different integration arrangements.

Special centres are at a half-way house between individual integration and special schools with regard to providing special resources. Because they deal with a number of pupils with special needs they can provide a wider range than individual integration arrangements, but they may be unable to provide some of the more expensive items which a special school with its larger numbers would possess. This was offset in some instances by sharing with main school classes, particularly at infant level where educational toys, games and other pieces of equipment could be used both in ordinary and special classes. Even when there was effective sharing of resources – this was by no means universal – some smaller special classes found they were short of larger pieces of equipment, sometimes acquiring them only through fund-raising ventures.

When special classes or centres are established there is usually an initial allocation of money to build up resources and generally stock it. This is clearly important but it is not enough. Apart from the instances where the initial sum is too small, many requirements emerge only with the course of time and cannot be costed adequately at the beginning. Moreover, the recurrent costs for these pupils are higher than for other pupils. Various expedients are employed to deal with this. The most common was to augment capitation, either by allocating a specific sum to a special class or by paying a higher rate of capitation in respect of its pupils. Thus, in one authority where the school received £13 per child at infant age the annual payment per special class child was £23. A further device was the operation of a curriculum support fund or equivalent. Under this arrangement advisers have a sum of money at their disposal for providing a broad level of curriculum support in the schools or areas of the curriculum for which they are responsible.

This can be used for purchasing particular pieces of equipment or curricular resource that the individual special class could not afford. Examples given us included adapted typewriters and low-vision aids. We did not acquire a great deal of information about the extent and operation of these funds, but it seemed clear that they formed a valuable function where they existed. The strength of the arrangement is its flexibility: unforeseen needs or needs that even if foreseen could not be accommodated within the normal capitation arrangements can be met. Moreover, it increases the likelihood of effective use of such acquisitions. Large or complex pieces of equipment may be required in a particular school for a limited period only; if the school itself has provided them it will probably hold on to them whereas an adviser can more easily pass on to another school an item that has been provided from an external fund.

Apart from formal LEA intervention via augmented capitation and curriculum support funds, special classes and centres acquired resources and equipment in various other ways. Many schools referred to money received from private or voluntary sources: parents' associations; special fund-raising events; and various charitable organisations. This money was often for specific large items – colour television, mini-bus, large toys – which might be regarded as desirable rather than essential. In at least one instance however a teacher claimed that an essential curriculum resource could only be had by having recourse to a charitable organisation. A head teacher who acknowledged that dependence on private funding was not confined to the special classes since it was increasingly a feature of the school as a whole nevertheless insisted that it was a greater problem in the case of special classes. A further way in which special classes, especially the smaller ones, acquired resources was simply to draw on the resources of the rest of the school. Schools generally did not have a precise breakdown of expenditure in relation to where it was incurred, but a number of heads were quite clear that the school as a whole was subsidising the special class. Again, this was more likely to happen with smaller classes where, as one LEA official acknowledged, any extra capitation paid in respect of the class was lost in a big primary school budget and was insufficient on its own to support the curriculum innovation that a new special class entailed.

A final point on the source of money for resources and equipment refers to the way that LEAs organise the allocation of money under discrete headings. In this they are no different from other large organisations. This compartmentalisation was a source of some mystification to schools however, not to mention a few grouses. Teachers were uncertain which 'pockets' the money was coming from and on occasion felt that their reasonable requests for resources were being fobbed off by bureaucratic sleight of hand. (We have no evidence to test these claims. The fact that teachers made them testifies at least to a failure in communication.) On the other hand, one wily head suggested that the existence of different pockets was an aid to survival in hard times! When education budgets generally are being pruned it is more advantageous to have access to different pockets since this gives a flexibility that reliance on a single budgetary source precludes. Some schools complained that the compartmentalisation of LEA expenditure resulted in their going without items they needed while receiving non-essential ones. A special class repeatedly requested pin-boarding but would not be given it since the rest of the school had had a good deal of pin-boarding a short time before. One day however a cooker and refrigerator that had not been requested arrived for the special class.

Lest our discussion of the difficulties give the wrong impression, it should be emphasised that the special centres we visited seemed on the whole to be well-equipped. Teachers generally felt that they had most of their essential requirements even if they had to fight for them initially. In many schools resources were flexibly deployed to the benefit of the pupil body as a whole. More details on the curricular provision are given below in the chapters on the curriculum. We round off this section by describing one location where a large special centre was possessed of adequate resources and used them in a flexible way.

This large comprehensive school has a special centre catering for 30 to 40 physically handicapped pupils. There is a good deal of integration with some pupils receiving all their education in the main school. An initial allocation was made and the centre receives its own capitation allowance annually, all at a level considered generous. The centre seems well resourced as far as curriculum materials and items from Area Health such as wheelchairs are concerned. Some specialist equipment such as electric typewriters have been in short supply but fund-raising campaigns to acquire more have been organised.

Most of the money for classroom consumables in this special centre naturally goes toward the slow learners. The range of assessment and teaching materials available for these pupils was impressive. For the majority of pupils who spent greater or lesser periods of time in the main school, there was the problem of ensuring that their use of resources did not constitute a drain on the resources of the main school. This was resolved informally. Rather than seeking to quantify the integration programme and estimate the extent to which pupils from the special centre used main school resources, adjustments are made in various informal ways. When staff from the special centre teach main school classes they take materials from the centre with them. A particular example was a basic skills course organised for main school pupils by a teacher from the centre; this relied heavily on the bank of resources for slow learners built up in the centre. Where a particular pupil incurs notable costs, eg A-level text books, or heavy use of photocopied material, these will be picked up by the centre. This informal 'give and take' arrangement seems to work well, and no complaints from main school staff have been recorded.

4.   Transport

Pupils attending special centres may require transport to school, by reason of their handicap or because they live at some distance from the school. With very young children or the more severely handicapped it may be necessary to provide an escort. The distances involved will be considerable in the case of minority handicaps such as vision impairment or language disorder where a medium sized city or a large rural area may be served by a single special class. In other cases, eg where it is policy for each school to provide for all or most pupils with learning difficulties in its catchment area, the transport requirement relative to special school provision will be reduced and a net saving effected.

A major difficulty with transport – which is a direct reflection of the cost of providing it – is that some pupils spend an excessive amount of time on the journey to and from school. This occurred in the main when economies were sought by transporting two or more pupils in one vehicle. In come cases children were travelling for as much as two hours a day. Whatever the financial constraints this can hardly be defended. The experience of long distance commuting is one aspect of adult life that pupils with special needs can well do without! It must be remembered also that the stresses resulting from excessive travel time can be exacerbated by variable pick-up times. Some of these children need a lot of attention in the morning, and getting them ready for school can take a great deal of time. If transport arrives at variable times, either because many children are being picked up or because of unreliable operators, children will frequently have been got ready needlessly early, and this can impose extra stress on parents and children alike.

Transport costs can account for a considerable chunk of special education expenditure and it behoves officers to be economical here as in other areas. The need for economy however cannot justify arrangements that involve children in undue travelling or the employment of unreliable operators. There would seem to be no simple answer here since many LEAs persisted in arrangements which were patently unsatisfactory – children not only subjected to long journeys but regularly arriving late and having to leave early to fit travel schedules, sometimes not being picked up at all. The almost fatalistic acceptance of transport difficulties which we sometimes encountered does not seem justified in the light of the trouble-free arrangements some schools achieved. One head adopted a tough no-nonsense approach with very positive results. It would appear that there is widespread need of such approaches.

Positive outcomes cannot always be guaranteed however and teachers may be reluctant to issue an ultimatum unless they are assured of an alternative – albeit more expensive – service. This is the nub of the matter in some cases.

If the sum available for providing transport is low, choice will be limited and there may be no alternative to existing arrangements so that schools are constrained to carry on using transport operators who are unreliable or provide a poor service otherwise.

Transport costs may be incurred within a school for certain pupils if it is on a split site. One such school we studied required special transport for its physically handicapped pupils throughout the school day. Two ambulances along with drivers were available to provide transport from one site to the other. This represented a significant extra cost to the integration programme.

Special arrangements will also have to be made when physically handicapped pupils go on journeys outside the school. A very small number can be accommodated in the ordinary way without incurring extra cost, but this will not be possible when the numbers are greater. In these cases ambulances or other specially adapted vehicles will have to be available. These were available in the school mentioned above and short local journeys presented no problem as a result. Field trips or other prolonged stays away from school are more problematic, though the school in question had arranged for several physically handicapped pupils to travel with able-bodied groups for these purposes.

Travel during the school day can involve costs for other pupils beside the physically handicapped. At a number of special centres we visited it was felt that the pupils needed more frequent outings than their peers. This was particularly the case with classes for severely retarded and communication disordered children, where regular visits to parks, farms, shops and so on were arranged, though most special classes arranged some visits. Generally, these classes did not possess their own transport and many expedients had to be adopted in order to make the trips. The budget for such travelling was limited and this restricted the amount that could be done when voluntary help was not forthcoming.

Pupils who are transported to school will be taken home at the end of the school day. This means that they are precluded from taking part in after-school activities – and so miss out on a major opportunity for associating with peers – unless special measures are taken. These measures generally incur extra cost and pupils may be debarred from participating in extracurricular activities as a consequence. A particular difficulty pointed out was when a school catered for some pupils from neighbouring authorities as well as its own. Transport costs for these external pupils are high because of the greater distances and if, as is common, the neighbouring authority is only prepared to pay for basic travel the school is faced with a choice between discriminating against external pupils and having its money for supplementary travel consumed very rapidly.

An example may help to put the issues in focus. Once again it is drawn from a secondary school with a large complement of physically handicapped pupils.

Two recent club activities were the rock musical put on at Christmas and the cinema club. A physically handicapped pupil was involved in the musical so he had to be taken home after the many rehearsals and five performances. The cinema club entailed film shows after school on ten Mondays. Twenty-five physically handicapped pupils applied to join of whom twelve needed transport. In both of these situations the task of arranging transport at unusual hours was not easy and necessitated a special grant from the authority.

Links between schools

We studied three schemes where integration took the form of links between special schools and ordinary schools, two of them involving physically handicapped pupils and the third hearing impaired pupils. A further two special schools had various links with ordinary schools in their vicinities. These provided respectively for children with learning difficulties and those with communication problems/developmental delays.

1. Staff and professional services

When integration takes the form of links between special schools and ordinary schools there would seem to be no extra staff costs. Typically, pupils from the special school spend a portion of their time in classes in the ordinary school. They will be spread around the school with no more than one or two in any given class. Indeed one might expect a net saving on staff since the teaching load in the special school is reduced.

There are several reasons why this does not happen however. First, the reduction in the teaching load in the special school is unlikely to release teachers. At any given period of the day the pupils who are integrating will be drawn from various groups in the special school; while classes may be smaller in consequence and greater flexibility is possible, it is unlikely that the *number* of teaching groups will be reduced. Secondly, teachers in the ordinary school will need support from the special school. Judging by remarks from some teachers this need is greater and more enduring than special school staff sometimes realise. At the outset basic information must be communicated, and it may be necessary for the special school teacher to stay in the main school classroom for a period of time. Thirdly, the integration programme needs overseeing as a whole. Ideally, there is need for a member of staff in each school who is formally charged with supervising the programme, actively monitoring its progress and liaising with his opposite number. An active engagement with the role should be stressed because the tendency otherwise is to respond to crises and equate their absence with success. Finally, this form of integration can add to staff costs through an element of double staffing. One of the ordinary schools in question was a large comprehensive which operated a sizeable integration programme with the adjacent school for physically handicapped. To take account of the extra demands on the school, it was allocated extra staff on the basis of one extra teacher for every eight pupils who spent at least 80 per cent of their time in the ordinary school plus a further appointment in cognisance of the partial integration programme. For the reasons given above it was not possible to offset these increases by reducing the staffing establishment of the special school.

It will be clear from earlier chapters that these various roles are crucial to the success of integration programmes. If this is so, the time to carry them out must be provided. Teachers cannot give support or carry out active monitoring if they are teaching full-time. They must be timetabled to carry out these roles and must have the flexibility to respond to requests for help at short notice. If the integration programme is of any size, none of this will be possible without extra staff. The flexibility that extra staffing gives is important in another way also. This form of integration presents valuable training opportunities. It means that the ordinary school has specialists to hand, teachers who have experience and possibly special training in the handicap in question. If these opportunities are to be availed of, again there is need of the time and flexibility that a good staffing ratio gives.

A minor additional cost may be incurred if the special school day is shorter than the ordinary school day. The conditions of service of caretakers and some other ancillary staff may relate to the shorter day. If the integration programme necessitates somewhat longer working hours for them it may be necessary to provide extra remuneration.

2. Premises

The rationale underlying this form of integration is to avail of the teaching resources of the ordinary school while having the resources of the special school ready to hand. This means that there will be no extra cost because of care or other specialist accommodation requirements. Mobility for the physically handicapped is one area where additional cost may be incurred. Ideally, a linking corridor will be built that permits easy passage for wheelchairs. At one site the distance between the two schools was so great that expense ruled out the provision of a corridor or even a covered way. It may be necessary also to effect alterations within the ordinary school, as described above for special centres, to facilitate mobility and toileting. It hardly needs saying that not every ordinary school lends itself to an integration programme of this kind with physically handicapped pupils, and the initial choice of school will normally be such as to obviate all but minor alterations.

3. Resources and equipment

There is little to add to the discussions under this sub-heading above. The general principle seems to be that pupils have books, stationery, etc supplied at the location where they are taught, whether it be special school or ordinary school, but continue to receive handicap-specific items from the special school. For capitation purposes they are usually considered to belong to the special school. These arrangements work in favour of the special school. There is sometimes a reverse movement, eg where pupils from the ordinary school use the craft and other facilities of the special school, but on balance the special school gained from the arrangement. In one school the handicapped pupils were transferred to the roll of the ordinary school when they were integrated for 80 per cent of their time and were then counted toward capitation in the ordinary school. In all other cases capitation money went to the special school.

The slight imbalance arising in this way did not seem to present any problems and there was no demand to adjust capitation to take account of partial integration. One head (of a special school!) insisted that the sums involved were too small to bother with and in any case were paltry in relation to total capitation for a comprehensive school. This may well be so and it doubtless makes good sense to keep these minor aspects of integration in perspective. However, these minor aspects do sometimes lead to difficulties. Teachers observe that pupils with special needs have a greater need of specialist resources and may feel that their presence is a drain on the school's resources and reduces provision for other pupils. To forestall any loss of goodwill in this way it may be advantageous to make some adjustments to capitation so that integrating pupils not only pay their own way as it were but are seen to pay as well.

4. Transport

Transport was not at issue in any of the integration programmes we visited. Large sums were spent in transporting pupils to school but these would have been incurred regardless of integration. Additional transport costs would arise if the two schools taking part were any distance apart but happily this was not the case in the locations visited. Where special school staff worked with a number of ordinary schools modest transport costs were incurred.

General issues

We have seen in this chapter how costs can affect every aspect of an integration programme. Here we want to consider a few further topics that have not been mentioned yet: the payment of special allowances to staff; fund raising; and the question as to whether an integration programme should be financed separately from the main school or not.

1. Special allowances

The payment of special allowances to teachers in respect of their involvement in integration programmes was a matter of some debate, and conflicting views were held on it. Teachers working in special schools are paid an extra allowance, and there is a widespread expectation that a similar allowance should be paid to teachers in ordinary schools whose primary responsibility is for pupils with special needs. In fact, a majority of teachers in the special centres we visited were receiving this allowance, while a number of those who were not receiving it felt quite aggrieved. Several head teachers also received a special allowance in virtue of the integration programme in their school. It should be noted that policy on these matters varied considerably and seemed to depend on the individual LEA.

Those in favour of paying allowances pointed to the difficulty and demands of the job and the need for special training in order to do it effectively. There was also the question of teachers' expectation of parity with special school staff. The special school allowance established the precedent of extra payment for teaching certain kinds of pupils and this payment should be made irrespective of whether they attended special school or ordinary school. Recruitment was a further factor since, it was claimed, suitably qualified staff could not be enticed away from special schools if they lost their allowance in the process. In any case, some integration programmes had been set up with a formal transfer of pupils and staff from a special school and it would have been unacceptable to discontinue payment of the special school allowance to staff already receiving it.

On the other hand, the payment of a special allowance was considered to be divisive and contrary to the spirit of integration. Special education staff, it was argued, should not receive preferential treatment over and above specialist subject teachers. Teachers of maths, science, music and so on were specialists just as well – and frequently had more relevant specialist training in their subjects than special education staff had in their field. In any case, integration was a matter for the whole school and if pupils were spending considerable amounts of time in ordinary classes it was invidious for some staff to receive extra payment and not others. One head indeed rejected special allowances for his staff on these grounds, negotiating instead for extra staffing points which could be used to provide posts of responsibility and enhance promotion opportunities. These were then allocated according to individual merit and contributions and became part of the normal structure of promotion within the school.

It seems clear that as long as special school staff receive an extra allowance there will be demand for it from staff in special centres and classes in ordinary schools. To the extent that it is divisive however and hinders the assimilation of special centres, the long term solution would appear to be the total abolition of this extra allowance. In fact, precisely this is recommended by the Warnock Report (12.29). Teachers in special schools and classes should receive extra payment in respect of recognised qualifications in special education and not because of where they teach.

2.   Fund raising

Many schools engage in fund raising activities to supplement funds supplied by their LEA in order to provide a wider range and a higher standard of educational opportunities than they otherwise could. Special schools enjoy a particular advantage in this respect since they constitute a 'good cause' and benefit from people's charitable impulses. (All schools do not benefit equally – the public purse is more responsive to physically handicapped infants than it is to maladjusted adolescents.) Many special schools depend on money obtained through fund raising activities or from charitable donations to finance building improvements and major items of equipment such as mini-buses or highly specialised resources. Some special school heads we talked to in the course of our study indicated that they saw it as an integral part of their job to raise money for these and other purposes and acknowledged that the task was facilitated by drawing attention to the special needs of their pupils.

A very different situation obtains when such pupils attend ordinary schools. Their needs are no less than before and they are just as likely to benefit from the extras which cannot be provided by means of capitation or other LEA funds. Fund raising on their behalf poses a dilemma however. Drawing attention to their special needs singles them out and highlights their difference from the main pupil body, but if this is not done the chances are that the requisite funds may not be available. A number of heads felt this dilemma very keenly. They were conscious of individual pupils' needs and of the fact that more could be done for them if only extra money was available – money which was not going to be forthcoming from the LEA. Several did organise fund raising activities specifically for the school's pupils, though with reservations in some cases, and pointed to the generous support they received from the main school parents. Others rejected this approach and insisted that any fund raising should be for the school as a whole. The special group would then receive their due share of this.

It could be argued that the loss of voluntary income sustained in this way is a – literal – cost of integration. One head felt strongly that this was the case and suggested that LEAs should take account of this diminution in income when allocating money to integration programmes. The total cost of educating pupils with special needs – if education is taken in its broad sense – is split between public and voluntary contributions. (The latter is small in absolute terms but, when capital and salary costs are set aside, its effect it not negligible.) If an organisational change has the effect of reducing the size of the voluntary contribution then the allocation from public funds must be increased if expenditure is to remain at the same overall level. So if integration does reduce the level of support from charitable and private sources for the education of pupils with special needs, LEAs must face additional expenditure if levels of provision are to be maintained.

3. Separate or joint funding

The integration programmes we studied generally arose from an initiative by Special Services and they were accordingly funded from there rather than from primary or secondary school budgets. This fact, allied to the way in which some special centres were conceived as relatively separate entities, meant that separate funding was a frequent occurrence.

Staff did point to various advantages accruing from this and many argued strongly in favour of retaining separate funding. It gave them greater control over spending and ensured that extra funds earmarked for the benefit of pupils with special needs would not be absorbed into the total school budget. In situations where the special centre was disproportionately favoured – not because it received too much but because main school capitation was too little – they wanted to make sure that the pupils in their charge did not lose their financial benefits through any egalitarian-minded redistribution. (Such redistribution would make little difference in a large school anyway.) Aside from the undisputed need of extra resources for pupils with special needs, some staff argued that their patterns of expenditure were different from those of the main school and suggested that it would be administratively simpler to keep the two separate.

On the other side, two counter considerations were advanced: one a practical matter, the other a question of principle. There were many resources, from television sets to early reading schemes, that could be used by pupils with special needs and their peers alike. Joint funding can promote the shared use of such resources and prevent wasteful duplication or the under-utilisation of expensive items. This is related to the question of principle: if an integration programme is to be fully a part of the school and pupils with special needs are to take their place alongside peers, this must be reflected in the financial and administrative arrangements as in other ways. If the goal is a single school making differentiated provision for varying needs, then materials and resources must be acquired and held in common by the school as a whole.

PART FIVE

The Content and Nature
of Teaching

Chapter Thirteen
The Curriculum in Integration

> The purpose of education for all children is the same; the goals are the same.
> But the help that individual children need in progressing towards them will be
> different (Warnock Report)

The pursuit of educational goals is the prime function of schooling.
This is as true of pupils with special needs as it is of their peers.
This is not to say that all pupils should engage in the same learning
activities or that all are to be taught in the same way. The
curriculum available to pupils and the specific programmes of
work selected from it must match their needs, as well as take
account of the educational environment in which they find
themselves.

In this chapter we examine the curriculum on offer to pupils
with special needs in ordinary schools. There is considerable
diversity in practice. We illustrate this with concrete examples and
outline a model of curricular provision. We discuss the principles
by which the curriculum is determined in integration programmes
and detail ways in which pupils are assigned to programmes of
work. This does not include those aspects of the curriculum
concerned with preparing young people for adult life; such
preparation can be particularly important for these youngsters and
the following chapter is given over to it.

A first consideration is to clarify the sense in which we speak of
the curriculum in integration. The aims of education refer to the
promotion of individual development through growth in knowledge and understanding, sensitivity and moral sense, through the
acquisition and exercise of skills, and through becoming an active
responsible member of society. Many children and young people
make only limited progress toward these goals but we now accept

that nobody is ineducable, no matter how ineffective our teaching, and the general goals must remain for all. When educational programmes for individual pupils are being planned it is necessary to break down the general goals into specific objectives – use a knife and fork, sort objects into different sets, imitate words, reach a certain standard in reading. The curriculum then comprises the formal activities devised by the school to achieve these objectives. Since both the objectives and the means by which they are achieved vary from pupil to pupil, it follows that the school's curriculum will reflect the nature of its pupils and their special needs. For example, blind and sighted pupils will share the same goal of developing their musical awareness but the objectives into which this goal is broken down will vary – as they do for sighted pupils anyway. If they share a common objective, eg develop a competence in sight reading, the means by which it is achieved may also be different.

It is worth emphasising that these considerations – of objectives and means toward them – are the ones that come into play when different curricula are being devised. Pupils are not to be taught differently from their peers simply because they are blind, physically handicapped or whatever. A given pupil will require to be treated differently from peers because of special needs that dictate different objectives (based on common goals) and different routes toward them. These special needs may or may not be related to physical condition or to handicap as conventionally defined. Physical handicap for instance is associated with a very wide range of special teaching needs but none of them is necessarily prescribed by a given physical condition.

This helps us see why the curriculum in integration assumes distinctive character. It rests on the two foci of particular objectives, based on pupils' special needs, and the means of achieving these objectives, based on many factors but especially the nature of the school. Pupils' special needs will broadly speaking be the same whether they are in a special school or an ordinary school so that the objectives will be the same. The means by which objectives are achieved may vary considerably however and lead to rather different curricula. The changes come from both the opportunities the ordinary school presents and the constraints it imposes. Thus ordinary secondary schools can offer a wider range of options and specialist teachers than most special schools, but they may not be able to maintain a highly structured linguistic environment such as might be required by hearing impaired or communication disordered pupils or set tight limits on behaviour in a way that might benefit pupils exhibiting behavioural disturbances.

Examples of curricular provision

We begin with some examples of the curricula on offer in the integration programmes we studied. These vary in the extent to which they are 'integrated' curricula. Some are no different, other than in scale, from the curriculum that a special school dealing with comparable pupils would provide, while others drew on the resources of the main school in an integral way to offer a distinctive set of learning opportunities.

The first example comes from a large comprehensive school which in addition to the usual complement of slow learners and some pupils with specific learning difficulties has 60 pupils with moderate learning difficulties. The school has a Basic Studies Department which has primary curricular responsibility for the latter and provides remedial support for the former. Of necessity, the department's curriculum offerings are differentiated as between the different groups. The two guiding aims are mastery of the basic skills of literacy and numeracy and general enrichment through supplementary options (art, social studies, etc) provided within the department or in main school. These aims are fundamental to curriculum planning within the department though the balance between them may vary; in the case of slow learners from the main school for instance the department's sole curricular responsibility is to provide remedial work.

Pupils with moderate learning difficulties follow programmes of work that are split between the department and the main school. In the first three years they follow a common core of lessons in the main school alongside mainstream peers. This comprises drama, music, PE/games, design, art and library (first year only). Occasionally a pupil who displays a particular aptitude in another subject area (eg science, maths) may be integrated slightly more. "We operate on the basis of a continuum of special needs, whereby a pupil will attend as many mainstream lessons as offer him educational value and help satisfy his needs" (head of department). Within the department there is a 'Basic Studies Curriculum' comprising: literacy (reading and writing), numeracy, social studies (sub-divided into 'the self' and a local geographical/historical component), science, woodwork, art, home management, rural studies and additional sport.

The programme within the department operates in a self-contained way without particular reference to the main school. This is particularly true of work on literacy and numeracy. Where reading is particularly weak the SRA Distar and Racing to Read schemes are drawn on, as well as the department's own phonics resource kit, supplemented by a wide range of cassettes, workbooks and reading books. Most pupils are given structured practice in order to acquire word building skills. Here the department's own reading scheme comes into play. This was developed by the head of department because he considered that existing commercial schemes were insufficiently structured for this type of pupil. The scheme is in two parts: a phonics-based programme; and a section that concentrates on comprehension. It is based on the principles of programmed learning. Pupils work on those aspects of the scheme which relate to their specific area(s) of difficulty. There is a wide array of learning resources (workcards, worksheets and language masters). Pupils whose spelling does not match their reading ability either follow a commercial scheme (Blackwell's Spelling Workshop) or a course specially structured for them, drawing upon a spelling resource kit developed within the department and designed to facilitate self-help skills in spelling. Once literacy has been attained (defined as reading at the 9-10 year-old level), a range of associated skills are taught, increasingly with a view to the needs of adult life. By the time pupils are in their fourth year the concern is almost exclusively with such aspects of the adult world as writing letters, filling forms and completing job applications.

The department has also developed its own number scheme. Here the primary aim is competence in money and time. If and when these have been mastered, pupils go on to deal with weight, area and capacity. The scheme can encompass all stages on the achievement continuum.

Those pupils still at the pre-numeracy stage (very few) will concentrate on such topics as sorting, matching and recording. The next stage is based upon Fletcher Maths, supplemented with specially prepared workcards and materials intended to make this scheme suitable for the older pupil. Further progress leads the individual on to developing more complex arithmetic skills as well as being introduced to problem solving.

In years IV and V an options system comes into play. Midway through each pupil's third year staff consult with pupils and their parents, and possibly outside agencies, to help determine choice. A booklet goes out to all parents which describes the various courses offered over these two years. Pupils are free to choose five of the ten courses they are required to take. Mandatory courses are: English, maths, 'core' (games, plus a choice from RE, health education, music and careers), human studies and science. These may be provided within the department or in main school. The department itself offers specific courses in the following areas: a specially devised leavers programme, social studies, child care/ home management, literacy and numeracy. There are additional extracurricular activities in woodwork, photography and car maintenance. Staff of the department maintain that the supplementary art, craft or home economics that they provide for many pupils is an essential part of their education: "Rightly or wrongly special educationists advocate more practical education for special children, these are the subjects the less able can achieve in".

A second example also comes from a large comprehensive school where a special department caters for some 15 pupils with severe learning difficulties and 60/70 pupils with moderate learning difficulties, as well as functioning as the school's remedial department. Again, there is considerable differentiation of curriculum, with pupils with severe learning difficulties being educated entirely within the department, pupils with moderate learning difficulties having some work in the main school, and slow learners or those with specific learning difficulties being withdrawn for specific remediation.

For pupils with severe learning difficulties, the emphasis is on the basic skills of literacy and numeracy (though many remain at pre-reading and pre-number levels) and on social competence. The latter is addressed in particular to equipping pupils for optimum independence in adult life and includes exposing pupils to a variety of real-life situations: using the telephone, borrowing books from the library, obtaining assistance from the emergency services. The aim is to provide "a mental preparation for leaving" by encouraging self-reliance, developing problem-solving skills, and giving practice in making decisions. As pupils get older, this becomes of increasing importance and has indeed been the subject of specific curricular development, along the lines outlined in the following chapter.

Emphasis on basic skills work is also a strong feature of the curriculum for pupils with moderate learning difficulties. About 50 per cent of the timetable is devoted to number, language and social studies, all provided by staff from the department in a special class setting. Subject specialists from main school supply the remainder of the curriculum, teaching either classes comprised exclusively of pupils with moderate learning difficulties (eg for science, music) or mixed ability groups which contain some pupils with moderate learning difficulties (eg art and craft, PE). For remedial pupils or the pupil with a specific learning difficulty the specialised attention forthcoming from the department is more particularised. Remedial pupils, for example, receive additional help with their maths and/or English; pupils who experience difficulty in writing attend a handwriting clinic which is convened once weekly over a term, and so forth.

A third example comes from a set of five special classes for pre-school and infant age children with severe learning difficulties. While there are considerable differences between the classes, the common aim underlying their curricular provision is to offer an enriched version of nursery and infant teaching practice: an abundance of learning resources; a stimulating learning environment; and individual attention – in relation both to children's general difficulties in learning and to specific difficulties (eg developing speech and language). A few children receive individual speech programmes prepared by a visiting speech therapist. Another aspect that is strongly emphasised is music and movement, provided by a peripatetic teacher. The classes are self-contained for teaching purposes, and the work children do owes little or nothing to the main school curriculum.

Each teacher will typically draw up termly aims for every child in each of the following areas: self-management; pre-number; pre-reading; speech and language; constructive and creative. Teachers aim to cover the basics – reading, writing, number and language – every day with each child. Other activities such as painting, shop and playing with large, wheeled toys take place twice weekly. Reading begins with the children's own names, progressing to matching words using flash cards. Children may produce their own books, the teacher or ancillary writing a sentence which the children has to copy and make a suitable drawing. Number work begins with counting objects, recognising numbers, using songs and finger plays. Children also learn to sort, count and recognise numbers. Language work is particularly emphasised. It is strongly individualised, with children encouraged to name objects by pointing to them and saying the appropriate word. Teachers do not use specialised language schemes such as the Peabody Language Development Kit or Distar Language.

Given the severity of these children's difficulties, instruction must extend beyond the customary classroom activities and opportunities for teaching them must be sought throughout the day. For instance, toileting sessions can be capitalised upon for teaching the various parts of the body, lunchtime is an opportunity for teaching socially acceptable eating habits, and so on. The close supervision which a generous staffing ratio permits is important since staff need to spend a good deal of time with these children. As one participant wrote, 'It is not enough to provide and encourage participation in (for example) play situations; the adults must be on hand to exploit with the individual child the first glimmer of a materialising association, be it visual, aural or kinaesthetic'.

The examples to date have referred to provision for pupils with learning difficulties. Different considerations come into play with provision for communication disordered children. The working philosophy common to the language units visited was one of concentrated individual or small group teaching based upon good infant or junior school practice plus specific therapy and remediation geared to the individuals' language disorders. The latter varied greatly, encompassing specific reading and writing disabilities, sequencing difficulties, poor short-term memory, laterality problems and so on.

A balance is maintained between the normal school curriculum and specialist language work. These are the primary responsibility respectively of the teacher and the speech therapist. The former follows the normal infant curriculum as much as possible, as well as carrying out speech or language exercises devised by the speech therapist. The latter conducts detailed assessments, devises or assists in devising programmes of work, and provides individual treatment. The assessment covers language comprehension, expressive language and the intelligibility of speech. This provides the basis for both programmes of work and treatment, which typically have a two-fold focus: promoting language development where it has been lacking; and remedying inappropriate learning.

We studied two contrasting provisions for hearing impaired pupils, one involving special centres attached to ordinary schools, the other based on individual integration. While teachers in both cases followed established practice in British deaf education with its concentration on oralism, the difference in organisation made for curricular differences as well.

The first comprised special centres at each of infant, junior and secondary stages of schooling. Naturally the particular curriculum content varies according to the age and special needs of the pupils. Broadly speaking, the overriding emphasis at infant level is upon developing language. Good infant practice is closely followed. Apart from the area of reading, specialist teachers adhere to the curriculum of the parent school, allowing for any necessary simplification of linguistic content. Plans of work are presented half-termly to the teacher in charge or head teacher. A particular theme is followed for a whole term with basic number and written work arising from it. The centre has its own reading scheme (Link Up), grounded in the everyday lives of the hearing impaired. Deliberate teaching of speech, based upon work carried out by Ling and Ling (1978), was introduced into the curriculum midway through our study.

At junior level the emphasis is on language consolidation, together with introducing a rather more rigorous approach to teaching basic literacy and numeracy. For much of our study there was limited contact with the parent school and in consequence few links with its curriculum. At secondary level the concern is to develop further and consolidate basic skills. Contact with the main school curriculum is limited and is confined to art, drama, PE and games. In the first three years hearing impaired pupils spend about 20 per cent of their time taking these subjects in main school alongside hearing peers. For the older pupil specific preparation for adult life becomes important; this was being provided by means of a leavers' programme and a design for living course.

All pupils in the individual integration programme follow the normal school timetable of their classmates. There will be some modification to this, on two main grounds: first, the need for some form of specialist teaching (eg auditory training, speech improvement) or for additional 'back-up' work where some part of the curriculum is proving difficult; secondly, when it is felt that a pupil is unlikely to derive much benefit from a particular subject or activity and that his or her time might be better spent on other activities. (These curricular modifications are the responsibility of teachers of the deaf or specially appointed support teachers.) Thus, one pupil was placed into a lower band English group. His support teacher withdrew him for one English lesson each week and supported within the classroom during other English periods. He did not appear to be making much progress however so his support teacher withdrew him altogether from these lessons, providing content that she felt would be more relevant to his everyday experience.

The content of the specialist teaching and reinforcement work can be illustrated with a few examples. Alexis is a partially hearing boy attending a junior school. A teacher of the deaf visited him for a half-hour speech and language session three times weekly. Typically, she would spend time on speech improvement; hold a conversation, requiring that he listen, lip-read, comprehend and respond, and finishing with some reading. In addition, a support teacher spent some five hours with him each week. The latter described what she sought to do with Alexis: "I have to back up what the class is doing but I have (also) to see he has a much wider understanding of things". This can sometimes mean "doing a lot of the things that aren't on the curriculum or (are) not what the class is doing". (Support teachers have to diverge from the timetable at their own discretion.)

In general, pupils drop one or more subjects as they move through secondary school, particularly where they are considered to be deriving little benefit. This is partly to enable adequate support to be provided. Thus, Jimmy had followed a full timetable initially. History quickly proved problematic and was dropped at the end of the first year. All other subjects, including science, were retained until the end of his third year, although, despite being quite extensively supported, some had to be taken with lower ability pupils. In the fourth and fifth year an 'options' system is introduced. Jimmy retained his strong subjects, generally the more practical ones (technical drawing, engineering, geography, social studies – which he dropped midway through his final year – and mathematics) with specific remediation/speech and language work in addition. His command of language was very poor. Accordingly, one seventh of his timetable was taken up with language work provided by the teacher of the deaf. His support teacher, even when supporting in specific subjects, also put considerable emphasis upon general language work.

The various examples outlined so far all involve special curricula or substantially modified ones. In many cases however there is need of only minor modifications to the curriculum. Thus, one primary school catering for some 14 visually impaired pupils had them following the same 'balanced curriculum of academic, creative and physical activities' that all pupils followed. The visually impaired work on the same tasks and with the same materials as their sighted peers. Some of them are taught braille or typing and many receive extra help with physical education or practical subjects. Likewise, many physically handicapped pupils follow the same curriculum as their able-bodied peers with minor modifications necessitated by poor handwriting or fine motor control. Physical education may need to be modified and supplemented with specific exercises. It should be noted that some physically handicapped pupils *did* experience a modified curriculum, usually a restricted one because of ignorance or lack of awareness on the part of teachers. This occurred when teachers had unduly low expectations of them, did not know how to get round their physical limitations or were overly cautious in making demands of them or letting them take risks. Thus, some physically handicapped pupils were virtually deprived of physical education while others were subjected to unnecessary constraints in science and craft.

A model of provision

In chapter 3 we suggested that the range of special educational provision could be thought of as a continuum from segregated special schooling to full attendance in a normal class, and that different forms of provision could be seen as different points along that continuum. Here we propose a parallel account in order to describe the range of curricular provision available to pupils with special needs. This too can be viewed as a continuum running from a special curriculum with little or no reference to work being done by age peers to an unsupported normal curriculum. A tentative outline of this might look as follows:

1. Special curriculum
2. Special curriculum plus
3. Normal curriculum, significant reductions
4. Normal curriculum, some modifications
5. Normal curriculum, little or no support.

Curricula cannot be viewed simply along this one axis of course, and there is overlap between the different categories; nevertheless it is a useful way of conceptualising the variety of special provision.

1. Special curriculum

By special curriculum here we mean a curriculum that has little or no reference to work being done by age peers. Such curricula are unlikely to find a place in integration programmes and are increasingly being called into question as offering a valid approach to special education. This is not to say that they have not been widespread in the past or indeed that they have disappeared. Dunn (1973), reviewing American provision in the 50's and 60's for 'trainable' children (with moderate and severe learning difficulties), noted that the educational goals for them were different not only from the goals held for normal children but even from those held for the mildly retarded. The emphasis was on developing the minimal skills needed to live and work in sheltered environments. So, the goals were threefold: self-help; socialisation; and oral communication. Very little academic work or vocational training was included.

Special curricula arise in other ways too as when quite distinctive techniques such as the Doman-Delecato method or conductive education are being used or when a highly structured programme is being implemented in a controlled environment. The Doman-Delecato method is essentially a programme of motor training where children are systematically taken back and patterned through the developmental stages – rolling over, crawling, creeping and walking (Delecato, 1966). It enjoyed a vogue in ESN(S) schools in this country in the early 70's. Swann (1981) describes visiting a school where it was in use: 'Limp little bodies were being manipulated by a determined group of teachers and volunteers. The children, lying prone on a table had their arms and legs moved back and forth in imitation of crawling. . . . this patterning of movement, not to be confused with physiotherapy, along with exercises performed with the forced use of only one hand or one eye is designed to achieve hemispheric dominance.'

One might also include here highly specialised short-term programmes, such as are used with emotionally disturbed or developmentally delayed children, though with the difference that such programmes would usually be geared explicitly to facilitating participation in mainstream activities, at least in the long term. These differ from normal school work through being intensive and highly structured, often based on behaviourist principles. They may entail setting up an artificial environment where behaviour is tightly monitored and controlled.

2. *Special curriculum plus*

With the growing realisation that all children are educable and that it is important to focus on similarities as well as differences, special curricula have become less isolated from mainstream curricula and have moved toward them in various ways. Thus, a common curricular pattern is 'basic skills plus general enrichment' or 'basic skills plus other subjects'. This is probably a fair description of the curriculum in many special schools and certainly applies to several of the integration programmes in our study. The broader curriculum was not neglected but it was clearly secondary to basic skills or specialist language work.

Even when some form of work in basics predominates, we have seen from the examples above that the extent of other work can vary considerably. In the case of some hearing impaired pupils for instance, general enrichment and work in subjects other than the basics occupied as little as 20 per cent of the week and was attributed far less importance than specialist language work. On the other hand, pupils with moderate learning difficulties followed a basic curriculum that was itself enriched and comprised far more than literacy and numeracy for at most 50 per cent of their time, and otherwise followed lessons alongside peers in the main school.

3. *Normal curriculum, significant reductions*

Though the essence of a continuum is the absence of qualitative change and gradual movement from one point to the next, there is a clear shift in emphasis and approach from the previous category to this one. There the focus is still on how pupils with special needs are different; the priority is on meeting their special needs and *then* seeing in what ways they can join in with their peers. Here the emphasis is on what pupils with special needs have in common with their peers; they follow a normal curriculum as far as possible with omissions or modifications made so that their special needs can be met. The difference can be illustrated by reference to the two hearing impaired programmes described above. The programme involving special centres tended toward a special curriculum whereas the individual integration programme – dealing with pupils whose hearing losses were no less severe – based itself on the normal curriculum, modified or reduced as necessary. Thus, pupils were withdrawn from normal lessons for auditory training, speech work and other specialist language work as well as for reinforcement of lesson content. The amount of withdrawal could mean that they were missing parts of subjects or indeed had to drop some subjects entirely. Even when extensive withdrawal was necessary and several subjects had to be dropped, the approach to the curriculum is clearly different from one where the starting point is pupils' special needs.

4.   Normal curriculum, some modifications

Some pupils with special needs follow essentially the same curriculum as their peers with some omissions and possibly supplementary or alternative activities. Thus, partially sighted pupils were precluded from taking part in certain aspects of art and craft; instead, they concentrated on sculpture and other activities dependent on tactile senses. In addition, blind pupils were taught braille. Some physically handicapped pupils likewise did the same work as their peers with the exception of physical education, which they did separately to a programme worked out by a physiotherapist, and possibly domestic and life skills where specific instruction and practice were necessary in some instances.

Some of the provision for pupils with mild or specific learning difficulties could be included here also. Thus, in one school pupils with mild learning difficulties were withdrawn to the special centre for 2-4 periods a week but otherwise followed normal lessons. In several schools, individual programmes of work were devised for pupils with specific learning difficulties; these too were implemented on a withdrawal basis but at times selected to give minimal disruption to the main school curriculum.

5.   *Normal curriculum, little or no modification*

Many pupils with special needs in our study followed the same curriculum to all intents and purposes and in the same teaching groups as their peers. This was especially so in the case of physically handicapped pupils but applied to others as well. Younger physically handicapped pupils were often withdrawn for management purposes – toileting, transfer to and from wheelchairs – while handwriting difficulties made for a slight modification with older pupils, but quite a number were following a full normal timetable. This was also true of some partially sighted and hearing impaired pupils; the school's teaching arrangements and the amount of support available made it possible for them to participate fully in the school's normal curriculum.

Determining the curriculum

We have seen that schools offered the pupils in our study a wide range of options from full participation in the normal curriculum to what was virtually a distinct special curriculum. Such diversity may be taken for granted in a system that seeks to meet pupils' needs flexibly. It is not always clear however that the diversity is justified or that it constitutes a planned response to perceived needs. In order to examine this we look in this section at the principles underlying curriculum selection and in the following section at the allocation of pupils to individual programmes of work.

Two principles turned out to be central to curriculum selection in the integration programmes we studied, viz. 'normalisation' and special action to meet special needs. Indeed, the rationale underlying curriculum development in the vast majority of cases could be summarised in terms of a compromise between these two principles. Teachers sought to expose pupils with special needs to the same work as their peers and at the same time ensure their special needs were being met. The tension arising from these conflicting principles is a familiar one in special education. Nowhere perhaps it is clearer than in deaf education. Sign language provides hearing impaired people with a means of communication that for many greatly excels the combination of speech and lip-reading, but it cuts them off from the majority of people who do not know sign language. For this reason many teachers of the deaf are strongly opposed to the use of sign language: it shuts more doors than it opens by reducing competent speech and by locking hearing impaired youngsters into the world of the deaf. (This view is not universally held and indeed writers such as Conrad (1979) argue that the *concept* of language that develops from using a signing system is an important aspect of speech and language development in hearing impaired people.)

There is a sense of course in which normalisation and special action to meet special needs are not opposed to each other. Sometimes normality is only to be achieved by pursuing special measures. Thus, the visually impaired miss out on certain experiences that others take for granted and will need specific training and compensation in order to win an appreciation of the normal and carry out ordinary domestic and life skills. Again, many pupils need specific training in independence before they can even approximate to the norm for their age group. Despite these links however the differences at the level of practice can be considerable. Regardless of whether they are directed to achieving normality or not, the pupil's *actual* educational experiences may be far from normal.

A more substantial problem in examining the tension between normalisation and special provision is the lack of precision surrounding the principles themselves. So a first step is to clarify what is meant by normal curriculum and special curriculum respectively. It is well to realise in doing so that the state of curriculum development is far from advanced. The curriculum in schools is rarely worked out from first principles. It is the outcome rather of an amalgam of existing practice, ideas in currency, tasks assigned to the school by society (both formally and informally), staff and resources available, and perception of pupils' needs and abilities. In recent years there has been greater concern for the theoretical basis of the curriculum and a spate of documents and manifestos have appeared. (The production of curriculum documents would seem to be one of the few growth areas in education.) Attempts to formulate an agreed theoretical framework for systematic curriculum planning are however still in their infancy, and much classroom practice and overall school planning continue to rest on precedent and rule of thumb.

Traditional school subjects have been the mainstay of curricular differentiation. This conception of the curriculum as a series of distinct albeit overlapping subjects is most apparent at secondary level where individual subjects can easily be distinguished. Even though subjects may be grouped in non-traditional ways (humanities, environmental science and so on) or taught in team contexts, the subject approach continues to dominate in many schools. It provides an unsatisfactory basis for systematic planning however on account of the relative arbitrariness and lack of theoretical coherence of school subjects. It is also open to criticism, particularly in the special education field, for its emphasis on transmitted knowledge and for underplaying the significance of firsthand experience for the learner.

Two alternatives have been posed, one based on skills, the other on forms of knowledge or areas of experience. While a given subject will entail the exercise of certain skills, it is possible to give an account of skills which cuts across subject boundaries. This could be done for example in terms of the traditional 'basics' of literacy and numeracy, broader communication skills, personal and social skills, physical skills, skills of discrimination and judgement, and so on. Such an approach could have particular relevance for pupils with special needs since so many skills which others acquire naturally have to be taught deliberately.

Forms of knowledge as outlined by Hirst (1974) or areas of experience as detailed by HMI (DES, 1977) refer to the structurally different ways in which we apprehend the world. Hirst proposes that all knowledge and understanding is logically locatable within the domains of mathematics, the physical sciences, knowledge of persons (including the human sciences and history), literature and the fine arts, morals, religion and philosophy. HMI sees the essential areas of experience to which pupils should be introduced during the period of compulsory schooling as the following: aesthetic and creative, ethical, linguistic, mathematical, physical, scientific, social and political, and spiritual. Such lists do not in themselves constitute actual curricular programmes. By differentiating human consciousness into distinguishable cognitive structures they offer a map within which different activities can be located and curriculum choices made in a balanced and reflective way.

Underlying these various approaches – subjects, skills, forms of knowledge – there is also the 'hidden curriculum': the lessons taught and the opportunities for learning set up by the way the school is run, how staff relate to pupils and each other, how discipline is exercised and over what, how decisions are taken, what are the effective priorities. This has much to do with values and attitudes. While the considerations raised are important in all education they are especially so where pupils with special needs are concerned since once again formal teaching may be necessary to inculcate what others acquire indirectly.

Curriculum planning in the mainstream then is not an exact affair. It is a multi-faceted process that responds to prevailing ideas and practices and to individual situations in a highly complex way. So when we speak of 'the normal curriculum' this is at best a loose description.

It must not be supposed that there is any greater consensus over how to meet special educational needs. The variety of special curricula which are quite distinct from mainstream curricula was indicated in the previous section. It may be instructive here to take an overview of the curriculum for slow learners. Brennan (1974) noted two key orientations underlying traditional curriculum planning for slow learning pupils: (a) because they were perceived as capable of learning very little teachers pared down the normal curriculum to its absolute essentials, leading to much repetition of 'the basics'; (b) the limited life opportunities open to pupils after leaving school resulted in a stress on practical activities with a strongly utilitarian basis.

With time their supposed future needs as adults came to exert increasing influence on the nature of the curriculum – to the point where it has challenged the primacy of the 'watered-down' mainstream curriculum which had hitherto prevailed. Segal (1963) for example organised his curriculum for secondary age slow learners around the following components: applied basic skills; citizenship; safety; health and hygiene; religious and moral education; leisure pursuits; vocational guidance; and science. Tansley and Gulliford (1960), dismissing the watered-down academic curriculum approach as 'a travesty of special educational treatment', identified a central core of language and number supplemented by additional knowledge concerning the environment, creative and aesthetic activities and practical interests. This was taken further by Brennan (op.cit.) in his formulation of the twin concepts of 'education for mastery' (implying a central core of objectives which must be mastered) and 'education for awareness' (implying less central objectives where familiarity or awareness is appropriate).

Brennan (1979) was subsequently to classify approaches to the curriculum for slow learners under seven headings:

i. sensory training (influenced by the writings of Montessori)
ii. the watered-down academic curriculum
iii. concrete use of basic subjects
iv. core programmes emphasising social competence and occupational efficiency
v. units of experience, designed to secure interest and motivate through their concern with contemporary problems closely related to pupils' developmental levels
vi. broad subject fields such as communication, literacy, social competence and so on, stressing the interaction between learning and use of knowledge and skills
vii. education of special groups, concerned with specific programmes geared to factors such as brain injury, perceptual difficulties and so on.

More recently, the objectives approach as described for example by Ainscow and Tweddle (1979) has gained ground. This concentrates entirely on those classroom factors which can be controlled by the teacher in the classroom and ignores – for teaching purposes – other factors such as brain damage, poor home or low IQ. The approach rests on defining teaching goals, breaking them down into precisely stated and carefully sequenced behavioural objectives, and monitoring pupils' progress on them through continuous systematic assessment.

This then is the context within which curriculum options are selected or developed in integration programmes. The two principles of normalisation and special action to meet special needs and the tension between them become rather more problematic when viewed against this background. If both the normal and the special are imprecisely defined, the effort to reach a balance between them is far from easy. In point of fact, there was very great diversity in the ways in which the principles were combined. This reflected in part the nature and complexity of pupils' special needs but there was more to it than that. Pupils with comparable special needs were dealt with quite differently from each other and were exposed to curricula that either stressed special provision or were oriented to the main school curriculum.

The contrasting provision described above for hearing impaired pupils is a case in point. Numerous similar examples could be cited.

In the following section we look at these differences in terms of how pupils were allocated to individual programmes of work. In general terms, it can be noted here that the variations reflected (i) individuals' commitment to either normalisation or special provision and (ii) their awareness of alternative possibilities. The two are interrelated since a knowledge of what is possible can lead to a commitment to integration but they are independent since a person can be committed to integration for many reasons. Indeed, the process can work in reverse: an abstract commitment to normalising the experience of pupils with special needs can lead to a search for new practical possibilities. This was evident in several programmes that we studied in regard to both general organisation of provision and specific curricular provision. Thus, a group of visually impaired pupils in a special centre attached to an ordinary primary school were receiving a traditional education geared exclusively to the educational consequences of visual impairment and with considerable emphasis on social training (the latter carried out in isolation from the natural situation of the main school). This was in marked contrast with the individualised approach based on projects, workcards and so on that prevailed in the main school. The head of the school was strongly committed to integration however and was unhappy about the isolation of the visually impaired pupils. In spite of initial objections from the specialist teacher in visual impairment she insisted on incorporating them into the main school teaching arrangements and exposing them to the same curriculum provision as their peers.

The importance of the working philosophy of the head teacher or teacher in charge must not be ignored. One approach is illustrated by the teacher who said: "Borderline M and S children's basic need is for four years of special education . . . they've not been diagnosed as needing integration but as needing special education". The emphasis in the special centre in question was in fact on pupils' special needs: they had failed in the ordinary system so "we can't just put them back in ordinary classes". A similar example came from a junior school which housed a special centre for hearing impaired pupils. For most of our fieldwork the centre operated on fairly separate lines, the emphasis being on providing a deaf education with pupils spending most of their time in the special centre. The arrival of a new head teacher with a strong commitment to integration led to a transformation of curricular practice – and much else besides. The school's academic organisation was revised and team teaching initiated. The intention was that the hearing impaired and their teachers would be gradually absorbed into this arrangement. Hearing impaired pupils would be fully integrated for the whole of the curriculum and withdrawn only for specialist work.

Allocating pupils to programmes of work

In order to see what this means in practice it is necessary to look at what pupils actually do in the classroom. The school or special department may have a carefully worked out curriculum but this signifies little until it is translated into practice. What matters to the individual pupil is the selection from the curriculum to which he or she is exposed. Thus, science is an important part of the curriculum in secondary schools but it is not available in any effective sense to many pupils with special needs. So in this section we outline the principles by which pupils are allocated to different programmes of work. Five areas of consideration may be noted: (i) characteristics and needs of the individual; (ii) nature of the subject matter and the learning activities to be engaged in; (iii) maintaining a balance; (iv) pedagogical considerations; (v) factors arising out of the particular local situation.

It may be noted at the outset that these considerations did not apply for some pupils. Though 'special' in the sense of having a recognised hearing loss, speech disorder or physical impairment of some kind, they were not affected as far as educational functioning was concerned. The curriculum of the school was as available to them as to their peers and they followed programmes of work selected from it in just the same way. Minor accommodations may have been necessary on occasion, but for them meeting their special needs meant ensuring access to the normal curriculum of the school.

i.   Individual characteristics and needs

The programme of work followed by a pupil clearly must reflect that pupil's characteristics and needs in various ways. There were three considerations here in the integration programmes we studied. First, staff sought to compensate for deficiencies or overcome pupils' disadvantages. Secondly, pupils were excluded from taking part in certain activities because of difficulties or perceived dangers associated with their handicapping condition. Thirdly, there was the concept of limited gain – if there was little likelihood of benefit from a subject or activity then there was no point in exposing a pupil to it.

The first of these had to do with efforts to overcome the disadvantages associated with their handicapping conditions. In many ways this was the central consideration. Thus, for a pupil who experiences learning difficulties – moderate or severe or of a specific kind – a prime consideration was to provide structured teaching designed to ensure mastery of the 'basics' of numeracy and literacy or to overcome the specific disability. Depending on the severity of the learning difficulty, certain social skills which the normal pupil would pick up incidentally were deliberately taught. For the hearing impaired and communication disordered the primary emphasis was on the medium of communication. Specialist speech and language work – 'special' in regard of both content and form of delivery – was provided directly (eg through deliberate teaching of speech) as well as being introduced throughout other learning activities. Pupils suffering from a sensory impairment were sometimes taught social skills which their impairment prevented them from acquiring naturally. Visually impaired pupils in particular need orientation and mobility training. Pupils with very severe sensory impairment were introduced to another working medium entirely: manual communication for the deaf and braille for the educationally blind. Physically handicapped pupils commonly have difficulty with fine or gross motor co-ordination so they may experience problems with writing. In some cases a physiotherapist devised special exercises to develop hand control or hand/eye co-ordination. Where gross motor movement was defective the therapist was able to advise the teacher or classroom ancillary on modifying the PE programme or providing appropriate alternative experiences when classmates were engaged in PE.

For older pupils a particular need was to give preparation for adult living. We see in the next chapter that this can take many forms. In some cases pupils' entire programmes of work in the later years of school were directed toward preparing them for life after school. In other cases there were specific timetable slots or a general orientation running through their other work.

Secondly, there were a number of exclusion principles in operation. Thus, pupils did not take part in certain activities which were assumed to be beyond their capacities. Pupils with severe vision impairment were steered away from taking geography because of the practical difficulty that fieldwork would present; few teachers would recommend that a severely or profoundly deaf pupil with limited oral capability should study a foreign language; and physically handicapped pupils were excluded from subjects such as biology, chemistry and metalwork on the grounds of inadequate fine motor skills or slowness. Safety was a further consideration. Physically handicapped pupils were denied the opportunity to engage in certain craft activities, practical science or physical education on the grounds that the risk was too great. The same was sometimes advocated for pupils with severe vision impairment. A further excluding factor usually associated with the physically handicapped was their physical stamina. One girl suffering from spina bifida opted for a full timetable at the end of her third year in secondary school. Though academically able it became apparent that this was too much for her. The pace of the work combined with mobility and physical care problems left her quite exhausted. In the event, she dropped two subjects in order to keep up with the remainder of her programme.

Finally, pupils were withdrawn or excluded from certain subjects because of failure to adjust to their situation in some respect. Again, this was a particular feature of pupils who were physically handicapped. It was most evident at the time of transfer to secondary school, when the move to a much larger school – which in itself can be a difficult experience – is compounded with the trauma of early adolescence. One 18-year-old who had contracted polio spent less time in mainstream lessons than a straightforward educational or intellectual assessment would suggest simply because she had not come to terms with her physical condition: "She feels it totally blocks her life . . . She uses her handicap to put a block on everything". Whereas this girl's reaction has been to withdraw and display very little motivation for any task set, other pupils reacted in a grossly extrovert way and had to be withdrawn from mainstream lessons because of the difficulty of containing them.

Thirdly, there was the concept of limited gain. This was when a programme of work was drawn up to take account of a pupil's strengths and ignored or played down his weaknesses. If little benefit was likely to be gained from the study of a particular subject, this would be ignored and others where success was more likely would be substituted in its place. This principle could never be applied in more than a partial way since certain activities were deemed essential and were persevered with regardless of pupils' difficulties with them. It was widely used however in deciding on pupils' allocation of time between a special centre within a school and mainstream lessons. Pupils stayed within the special centre for core subjects since they were more likely to benefit from the individualised instruction that could be provided there. It was associated in some teachers' eyes with the view that integration was for social benefit primarily. Pupils could integrate for subjects where academic progress was less important; if in the event little academic progress was made the placement could be justified in terms of the presumed social benefits.

Some teachers were well aware of the danger inherent in this principle. It was all too easy to assume that a pupil would not gain from taking certain subjects, when in fact good progress could be made given appropriate presentation and teaching. Rather than working to a priori exclusion principles, their approach was to give pupils a trial at subjects and only withdraw them when difficulties became too great. Thus, an educationally blind girl on entering secondary school was allowed to take maths and science, even though it was thought probable that she would meet difficulties at a later stage. A profoundly deaf boy followed the same subjects as his peers throughout the first year of secondary school. His progress was monitored closely and at the end of the first year it was decided he would drop history because of difficulties he had with it. He retained all the remaining subjects until the end of third year.

ii. Subject matter and learning tasks

The nature of the subject matter and learning activities engaged in led to a further source of differentiation in progamme allocation. Three pointers may be noted: concentration on the basics; emphasis on practical subjects; and the cumulative nature of some subjects.

We have seen above that pupils' learning difficulties led to their spending considerable time in reaching a basic competence in literacy and numeracy. Quite independently of any learning difficulties however this tendency was reinforced by the import- ance attached to literacy and numeracy. Being able to read and write and cope with simple number concepts were seen as important in their own right and in providing a basis for further learning. Literacy especially was seen as opening the door to much of the rest of the curriculum, and work on developing the associated skills was regarded as laying the groundwork for other work. (In practice, basic skills often became an end in themselves, and pupils were spending a great deal of time in mastering them without going on to a broader curriculum.)

It was common to find a stress on practical working where dependence on literacy was less important or, at certain levels of working, could be dispensed with entirely. This resulted in a predisposition toward the practical subjects. Art and craft, domestic science and, for some, PE/games were widely regarded as particularly appropriate activities for pupils with special needs. This was especially apparent when integration was at issue. Practical subjects tended to be taken because pupils' deficiencies were less in evidence, there was the possibility of joining in group activities, and less was at stake since these subjects were less important. (This latter view was not universally held. In several cases, practical work allied to domestic and life skills was seen as a central part of the older pupil's curriculum. This was too important to be left to the chance of mainstream lessons and was provided in a structured way within the special centre.) Thus, hearing im- paired pupils in one programme joined mainstream lessons in art, craft and games and remained in the school for the deaf for all other subjects. Again, it was common for pupils with learning difficulties to join mainstream lessons for craft subjects but not for English or maths.

Integration possibilities were affected in some instances by the cumulative nature of some subjects or the way in which they were taught. If a class is following a syllabus – as often in languages, maths and science – where work builds up cumulatively and later content refers in a specific way to what has gone before, it will not be possible for pupils to join a class in midstream or to join it on a part-time basis. This restricted the integration that was possible in some cases.

iii. Maintaining a balance

A related consideration was the need to maintain a balance in the programme of work a pupil followed. This came up in various ways. It was a corrective for example to the undue preoccupation with the basics that sometimes prevailed. It drew attention to pupils' needs arising out of being pupils or young adults in addition to those consequent on their handicapping conditions; special steps might be necessitated by the latter but a pupil's entire programme of work could not be constructed around them. Balance had to be found between the academic and the practical and, as pupils got older, between education and specific preparation for adult living.

In practical terms, the balance can be sought in one of two ways. Either teachers consider what must be provided for pupils' special needs to be met and then add to this by selecting from the mainstream options, or their starting point is what the mainstream can offer and then supplement any deficiences relative to their pupils. Thus, in one school adopting the latter approach the aim was "to balance up with things they haven't got from (the main school)" – notably, home economics and physical education/ games.

iv. Pedagogical considerations

Chapter 15 considers the teaching implications of integration. We note here that pupils' work programmes can be affected by these. Consider the need for reinforcing lesson content for example. Pupils can sometimes follow mainstream lessons if they get additional help. This may be provided within the lesson but more often outside. Time has to be found for this, possibly at the expense of another subject. Thus, hearing impaired pupils who were integrated on an individual basis were able to do so only because of considerable support provided within the lesson and on a withdrawal basis. (This encompassed auditory training and specific language work as well as reinforcing specific lesson content.) In order to make time for this it was necessary in some cases to restrict a pupil's programme by dropping certain subjects.

The considerations here overlap with the notion of limited gain referred to above and the need to use the time available to pupils' best advantage. Working priorities must be established that will determine what is to be included and what omitted. A minority of teachers indeed felt that the time taken up by integration could be put to more effective use by specialist teachers. "Time is so precious . . . we are well qualified, so is it fair on the children to put them in with teachers who can't give them very much attention and don't understand their problems?"

We encountered several examples where pupils' programmes of work were restricted through pedagogical considerations of this nature. Thus, one profoundly deaf girl began her third year at comprehensive school taking seven subjects. During the autumn term her support teacher found that more and more of her time was taken up in going over new vocabulary and explaining increasingly more sophisticated concepts – mostly from humanities lessons – to the detriment of other equally important activities (eg practising speech). Accordingly, at the end of term it was decided to withdraw the girl from this particular subject, not just because of the difficulties she was experiencing with it, but also because of the amount of support time it was taking up. In another instance, a fifteen-year-old suffering from spina bifida was obliged to drop science and geography after two years of secondary schooling in order to allow greater concentration on 'life skills' (notably cookery plus a little needlework), typing and walking exercises. A third example concerns a physically handicapped sixth former who could not write. Despite her undoubted intelligence – she began her sixth form career by taking three subjects at A level – she was obliged to drop one of these subsequently because of the amount of time she took over dictating or typing lesson notes and doing homework assignments.

v.   *Local factors*

Pupils' programmes of work reflect the particular opportunities and constraints of the school they attend. If the school has a strong musical tradition, it is likely that their musical education will benefit and so on. Here we are concerned to look at some of the ways in which local factors constrained the opportunities open to pupils. In particular, we look at access, teachers' lack of awareness and timetabling difficulties.

a.   Access

Being denied access to particular subjects or activities because they take place in areas of the school physically inaccessible to them is a potential difficulty that the physically handicapped may expect to meet in integration. What disadvantages were found in practice? In one programme involving physically handicapped pupils, they were effectively restricted to the ground and first floors of the senior part of this school. A number of specialist laboratories and classrooms were on the second floor, and pupils either did not take these options or took them under less favourable conditions. For example, because of the presence of a girl in a wheelchair, one class was obliged to vacate a properly equipped biology laboratory and move to a Portakabin which was too small and had inferior facilities. It was particularly unfortunate that while the subject proceeded here, a biology lab stood empty. In another location a pupil suffering from spina bifida could not obtain access to a language laboratory. Furthermore, she sometimes had to join different forms in order to take certain subjects because of the difficulty of access to the first floor of the main part of the school.

A more substantial limitation arose from the fact that specialist rooms such as science and language laboratories or rooms equipped for geography or other subjects had to be vacated by subject teachers. They were then faced with taking their lessons under makeshift conditions: sometimes overcrowded teaching areas, inappropriate for use by pupils in wheelchairs, and above all lacking their collection of special equipment and resources. The various problems arising here have been discussed in more detail in chapter 10.

b. Lack of awareness

There were various instances where limitations in a pupil's programme of work could be traced back to a failure among ordinary teachers to realise that the individual could not easily cope or that the programme was inappropriate in some respect. More often, necessary components were missing because their relevance had not been appreciated. Such disadvantages are more likely to be found under programmes of individual integration, particularly where specialist advice and guidance are not readily forthcoming. It is not a problem exclusive to this particular organisational format and did occur elsewhere, often when there was insufficient co-operation between specialist and ordinary teachers.

John is an eight-year-old with cerebral palsy. He has very considerable educational problems: his speech is very poor; his reading ability is well behind his chronological age; and his writing is 'spidery' as a consequence of very poor hand control. Despite all this he is following the same programme of work as his classmates. No speech therapy, no special exercises to develop fine motor control, no individual programme to help with reading, have been forthcoming.

c.   Timetabling difficulties

This turned out to be less of a problem than might have been expected. There was only one programme, where physically handicapped pupils from a special school attended a neighbouring comprehensive on a part-time or full-time basis, where timetabling constraints meant that pupils were not always receiving the special educational help they needed. This was manifest in two respects. First, there was the problem of providing physiotherapy in the limited time left over from an intensive integration programme that could not be rearranged to suit the therapist's availability. A physiotherapist noted that she faced a constant dilemma of cutting down on the physiotherapy exercises that a pupil really needed so that his or her presence in integrated lessons would not be jeopardised, either through having to miss them or because of sheer physical exhaustion. Secondly, staff experienced difficulty in preparing older pupils for post-school life, most especially, in arranging opportunities for work experience. Those who attended the comprehensive had individual timetables and it had proved virtually impossible to find times during the school week when they could all reassemble in the special school for specific preparation for adult living geared to their particular concerns and problems.

In conclusion, the central importance of curricular considerations in integration programmes may be noted. Special schools developed at least in part because ordinary schools were failing to educate certain groups of pupils. If these pupils are to return to ordinary school there must be some certainty that their special *educational* needs will be met there at least as well as in segregated special schools. This is not to suggest a comparison between curricular provision in special schools and in ordinary schools since that would miss the point. Meeting special educational needs in an ordinary school is a different enterprise from meeting them in a special school and operates under different constraints and opportunities. Success must be seen in terms of circumventing these constraints and capitalising on the opportunities, not in reproducing the educational environment of the special school.

We have seen here some different ways in practice whereby ordinary schools set about developing a curriculum for pupils with special needs. Finding a balance between exposing them to the same or similar curricular experiences as their peers and ensuring that their special needs are met was far from easy and led to great diversity in practice. This can be examined in concrete terms by looking at the programmes of work that pupils follow and the principles by which they are allocated to them. A further perspective comes in later chapters from looking at how the curriculum is implemented and how pupils' progress through it is monitored.

Chapter Fourteen
Transition to Adult Life

Schools cannot prepare their pupils for everything that may lie ahead . . . but they can make the world a slightly less confusing place for young leavers (DES, 1963)

Schooling is for all young people a form of preparation for adult life. By imparting knowledge and skills, by facilitating interaction with peers, by structuring experience and providing a relatively sheltered environment, it contributes to their development as individuals and as members of society. To this extent the entire curriculum and the milieu of social interaction that the school provides help to prepare pupils for leaving school.

When we speak of preparation for adult living in the present context we mean something more specific. The general curriculum is concerned with knowledge and skills which do fit one for adult life but not necessarily in an immediate direct way. Possessing a sensitivity to language is an important asset but it does not help in filling forms, just as the normal mathematics curriculum does not assist pupils with personal budgeting or money handling. Likewise, the social milieu provided by a good school helps equip pupils for life after school in important ways, but for some pupils this is not enough. Specific structured interventions may be needed, just as precise and highly focused teaching has sometimes to replace general instruction directed at a whole class.

The content of any such preparation can be extremely varied, depending as it does on the nature of pupils' needs, the particular local situation and other factors. There seems to be no general agreement on what it should comprise or even how it should be conceptualised and described. We encountered wide variations in practice. One school which offered a comprehensive programme to a large number of pupils with learning difficulties planned the programme in terms of *skills*; it spelled out what a young person needed to be able to do in order to lead an independent adult life and built up its programme accordingly. Another school operated in terms of deficiencies in the normal curriculum and emphasised *supplements* to it; lessons in English, maths, geography, craft subjects and so on were oriented toward adult life and incorporated relevant material when appropriate. We have opted for a categorisation in terms of *areas of living*. This cuts across skills, knowledge and attitudes and also across traditional subject areas. Adult life comprises various domains or areas of living. By identifying these it is possible to map out a practical curriculum.

For present purposes we propose three broad areas: work; life skills; and leisure. No categorisation in this areas can be rigid or avoid overlap since the aspects are interconnected but this offers a framework for considering the various ways in which young people with special needs can be prepared for independent adult living.

1. Work. This is a main concern, and we look at preparation in terms of (a) careers education and guidance and (b) work experience.

2. Life skills. These refer to the skills needed to live in society as an independent adult. They include personal skills such as body care and presentation, domestic and household management, and dealing with society's institutions.

3. Leisure. Many young people will have an excess of leisure time when they leave school, and it can be important to equip them with the means of using their time constructively.

These are areas, it should be noted, where specific preparation is not usually judged necessary for the majority of pupils or where it is seen to be different in kind as between the majority and those with special needs. Thus, a partially hearing youngster may need to be taught patterns of social interaction that his classmates will pick up naturally; dealing with public transport or organised entertainment poses special problems for the physically disabled. This needs bearing in mind when dealing with programmes of integration. There is a danger that all pupils will be treated equally or that sufficient discrimination will not be made between them. We have come across examples where the emphasis was – laudably – on normality but to such an extent that pupils' needs were being overlooked. A pupil can be educated alongside his peers, participating fully in the main school curriculum even including careers work and leavers' courses, and still have need of specialist attention unique to him or her. We are not suggesting that there is a complete disjuncture between the needs of special pupils and those in the mainstream. There will be some overlap with the preparation that all, or at least a large number of, pupils require.

This can be seen most clearly in the context of work. Most pupils will benefit from careers education and guidance, particularly at a time when youth unemployment is high. While some may need specialist assistance, they can usually participate with profit in the general programme laid on for their main school peers.

It should be noted too that this is an area to which special schools attach a great deal of importance. Especially in recent years some special schools have devoted great efforts to building up broadly based leavers' courses and preparing their pupils for adult life in a comprehensive way. This fact poses a particular challenge to staff running integration programmes or responsible for individual pupils with special needs in an ordinary school. They must find ways of ensuring that pupils do not miss out on the systematic preparation that they would receive in a good special school, and they must often do so with far fewer resources and in a context which allows of far less control. In this chapter we look at how a number of schools responded to this situation and describe the preparation made in relation to the three areas of work, life skills and leisure.

How the preparation is organised

Preparation for adult life was provided in various ways in the schools we studied. Two broad strands can be discerned: one related to the world of work and post-school education, and one dealing with adult living in a more general way. Preparation for work was provided in particular through careers education and guidance and through work experience. These are described in more detail in the next section. The more general preparation took different forms, ranging from formal and highly structured courses (sometimes including preparation for work) through brief time-table slots devoted to particular aspects of life after school, to an informal general emphasis across the curriculum on matters particularly relevant to adult life. These were not necessarily mutually exclusive since most schools sought to provide an adult orientation in the later years of schooling through various means.

The formal courses were of various kinds, as outlined below. Pupils with special needs frequently followed such courses along with other pupils, sometimes being given supplementary work in the special centre or on a withdrawal basis. Where joint participation was not deemed possible, they could still benefit from the resources that were to hand on account of the main school course. Thus, they might use filmstrips or other resource materials acquired by the main school, while their teachers benefited from the experience of their main school colleagues. There were drawbacks of course. Pupils did not always receive the supplementary help they needed, either because nobody was equipped to provide it or because their needs were not recognised. Sometimes there was insufficient communication between special centre and main school; in one case each assumed that the other was attending to pupils' needs in this area, and in fact nothing much was being done by either.

Formal courses were designated as leavers' courses or styled in various other ways: 'design for living'; 'design for modern living'; 'education for personal relationships', and so on. We give some examples below. Though different in scope and content, they shared broadly common aims of bridging the gap between school and the outside world and helping young people to become responsible adults. The programmes were seen as "a mental preparation for leaving" – "we are trying to get them thinking about jobs" (head of special department). There was a common emphasis on equipping pupils with the skills that would enable them cope with varied situations when they left school – "build confidence, ability and social independence".

We start by presenting in full three examples of leavers' courses, before examining particular aspects of them in following sections. Example One is a programme taken by all pupils including those with learning difficulties in a comprehensive school. This is part of the core programme in fourth and fifth year and occupies two periods a week. Examples Two and Three by contrast are both leavers' programmes specifically designed for pupils with special needs. Example Two is taken from a secondary school catering for a large number of pupils with moderate learning difficulties. Example Three outlines the provision for pupils with severe learning difficulties in a comprehensive school.

Example One   Education for personal relationships

This is part of the core curriculum, along with English and maths, for all fourth and fifth years. It aims to provide information about adolescence and help in forming stable relationships, laying the foundation for marriage and family life and creating a helpful climate of opinion within the school. The syllabus is divided up under the following headings:

1. Making friends; finding out about yourself and other people.
2. Boy/girl relationships.
3. Sexual relationships.
4. Courtship, marriage and family.
5. Development of the moral sense.
6. Good manners; respect for other people and their ideas.
7. Class and racial discrimination.
8. Freedom.
9. Leisure – 'my time is my own'.
10. Provisions within the community.

This wide ranging syllabus is closely integrated with the careers syllabus. Extensive use is made of television and other audiovisual materials.

Various outside speakers come to the school and visits from the school are arranged. There is also a community service programme as part of the syllabus.

Example Two   Preparation for adult life

This course is designed for pupils with moderate learning difficulties. It is allocated seven hours a week throughout fourth and fifth year. It is divided into six main headings.

1. Practicalities of independence

The aim is to prepare pupils for living on their own, and help them to understand many of the jobs we take for granted. Topics covered are: form filling; applying for a job; interviews; clocking in system; wage packets; money; and use of telephone.

2. Household Do-It-Yourself

Rather than have a rigid metalwork or woodwork lesson, the aim is to instruct pupils in some of the other practical skills that are likely to be of benefit to them after they have left school. This would include the following:

– changing plugs, basic electricity
– bicycle maintenance and repairs
– window repairs

- basic internal household maintenance
- motor vehicle maintenance

3.   Independence training

In this area, pupils would be involved in leaving the school premises and carrying out some small pre-arranged task, probably in the town. These tasks would be of a simple nature in the beginning (eg, purchase of a book of stamps from the local post-office), gradually becoming more difficult and demanding (eg, finding out the times of buses to a neighbouring town) towards the end of the course. Initially pupils should carry out tasks in groups of two. Tasks to include the following:

Shops	for simple purchases, price comparisons
Post Office	Collecting forms, opening savings accounts, posting letters, etc
Bus and Railway Stations	Use of 24 hour clock and timetables, etc
Library	How to join, collect and return books
Trading Standards Office	How and when to complain when one is not satisfied with treatment received in shops, etc

4.   Work experience/careers

Pupils should study a wide variety of jobs and explore the advantages and disadvantages of individual jobs. They should have a basic knowledge of the structure of a firm and understand the function of the various departments. In their final year pupils would spend either two weeks or one day a week for ten weeks in a local firm. In their final term pupils should have access to the Careers Officers and have a careers interview.

5.   Visits and experiences

It is hoped that in their time on the leavers course all the pupils involved would spend some time on class visits to strategic places of interest. These visits are designed to increase awareness, general knowledge and confidence. It is hoped to visit most of the following:

factories
fire and police stations

citizen's advice bureau
job centre
places of work
post-offices
travel agencies
skating rink
theatre
football match
other schools
small villages.

6.   Duke of Edinburgh's Award Scheme

All members of the course would be encouraged to join the DoE scheme and work toward their Bronze and Silver Awards. This scheme contains elements of community service, fitness training, expedition and map work, and an interest study. As well as the obvious experiential benefit pupils will gain an award they can be proud of and a certificate which they can show to an employer when applying for a job.

Example Three   16-19 Provision

The chart presented indicates the structure of the course. We append some details here on the elements that go to make it up.

Survival skills

i.   Household Management

Planning daily routines, accepting and coping with responsibilities. Caring for others. Much of this includes the following headings.

ii.   Shopping

Recognition of shops and what they sell. Selection of items needed. Pricing articles, simple estimation. Offering correct money. Checking range. Practical exercises buying food for cookery, articles of DIY, gardening and home maintenance.

iii.   Cooking

Choosing menu, planning meals. Basic skills becoming more complex, leading to meals with different courses.

iv.   Home Safety

Awareness of the various points of danger in the home. Handling of cooking (utensils, cookers etc.) Awareness of dangers whilst

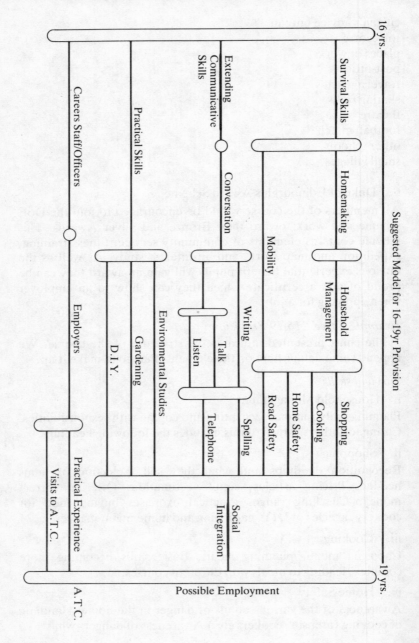

Suggested Model for 16–19yr Provision

involved in DIY and gardening. The element of prevention in basic home maintenance.

v.   Road Safety

Continuing theoretical practice by school staff and outside agencies. Practical implementation on visits, shopping expeditions as a pedestrian and as a cyclist.

vi.   Mobility

Frequent opportunities under surveillance leading to independent mobility using public transport and where appropriate cycles.

Extending Communicative Skills

i.   Conversation

With peers, teachers and unfamiliar adults. Involves listening as well as talking. Extended from question and answer to spontaneous conversation stemming from a stimulating environment.

ii.   Writing and Spelling

Socially essential vocabulary being extended wider as particular individuals allow.

iii.   Telephone

Contrived situations . . . ringing school from a coin box. Ringing for assistance. Answering a telephone. Telephone duty – taking messages using a tape recorder where necessary.

Practical Skills

i.   Enviromental Studies

Studying the environment with groups of peers. Strictly controlled groups in very structured situations initially. Meaningful, casual, social integration. Fine and gross motor skill training – cameras, tape-recorders, simple surveying.

ii.   Gardening

Continuing work that is already being undertaken but involving pupils more in long term planning not only with regard to vegetables but also in working towards the venture being financially self-supporting. Continued development of basic skills, teamwork, task allocation etc.

iii.   DIY

The continued development of basic skills in crafts. Home maintenance with practical tasks, eg. wiring a plug, changing a tap washer.

Work

Many young people with special needs will want a job or employment-oriented course as soon as they leave school. The general curriculum of the school, and especially any leavers' courses or equivalents, help in important ways to prepare them for the world of work. The school's social milieu too with its opportunities for normal interaction and growth in confidence can be valuable preparation for coping with the workplace. Here we look at two means by which the school gives specific preparation for the world of work; careers education and guidance; and work experience. These are aspects of the school's provision that seek to inform pupils about life after school and help them make appropriate career choices.

1.   Careers education and guidance

It is convenient to consider these together. Though different in function and often the responsibility of different agencies, they have a great deal of overlap. Careers education is provided by the school, sometimes by a teacher or department with particular responsibility for it. This can be done through a formal careers slot in the curriculum, as part of a more comprehensive leavers' course, as an integral part of other lessons or in an ad hoc way for individual pupils. It is usually carried out in fourth and fifth years, though one school we visited had objectives relating to careers education worked out for pupils right from first year; these were to be achieved in normal maths, English and other lessons. Careers guidance is the giving of advice and help in selecting a further (or higher) education course or in finding a job. Ideally, this will involve the careers service, possibly in the person of a specialist careers officer working alongside the school's careers teacher, providing advice on jobs and educational opportunities, and counselling individual pupils. Frequently, when the careers service is not staffed for this work, it falls on the school to carry it out as best it can.

Careers education was a formal part of the curriculum for all fourth and/or fifth year pupils in some schools. This typically would involve two periods a week in the timetable where pupils were introduced to the world of work. It would cover different careers and what they entail, how to make a realistic choice, the skills involved in getting and keeping a job, the nature and ethos of the workplace and so on. It can be noted that broadly similar content can be covered in leavers' course or – though less easily perhaps – in other lessons.

Such general careers education can be relevant to pupils with special needs and help them considerably, but in no case did we find that it was adequate on its own. Two situations can be distinguished, one where pupils benefit from main school careers education, particularly if supplemented, and one where they gain little or nothing from it. As an example of the former we refer to a school catering for a large number of pupils with learning difficulties.

As part of Careers Education different types of work were described. Where appropriate and necessary pupils with learning difficulties had the core material adapted or expanded, while they were also exposed to less likely types of work for the broadened understanding it gave. Thus, a film of a bricklayer at work would be backed up with supplementary material on the different stages involved that might not be necessary with more able pupils. At the same time they would be introduced to the work of doctors and vets. This helped to broaden their understanding of society, sometimes in important practical ways, even though many of the jobs would never come their way.

A general careers education course can be especially helpful for able physically handicapped pupils through expanding their appreciation of what is available. Their ultimate choices must take account of their physical limitations, and they have need of specialist knowledge in addition to a general course, but they can benefit greatly from a careers education course designed and run for the able-bodied. The content of such a course and the discussion that accompanies it will expand their horizons and may well fire ambition and instil motivation to achieve more than they had previously thought possible.

On the negative side, if the gap between pupils' previous experience of their capacity to understand and the content of the careers education course is too great, then they will gain little from it. The severely retarded are a case in point. A school with hearing impaired pupils reported that its deaf pupils derived no benefit from joining with the careers course in the main school. Not only did they fail to understand most of it but they were totally unwilling to participate in discussion with hearing pupils. In cases where no means can be found by which the pupils with special needs can share careers courses with other pupils in a meaningful way, there is still the possibility of benefit through being able to draw on the resources and expertise of a main school department. A special centre which has a member of staff trained and experienced in careers work is extremely fortunate. If a person is designated as responsible for careers work it is a considerable asset to have the resources and contacts of an established careers department in the main school to hand.

When careers education is integrated into other subjects there is a danger of it becoming a hit-and-miss affair. A great deal depends on individual commitment and allocation of priorities. One school arranged for nearly a quarter of its teaching staff to go on a course designed to show how careers education could be made part of their respective subjects but found nevertheless that the system was unsatisfactory. There were many gaps and it was felt that there was clear need of a formal structured course. Whatever the implications for the main pupil body it was clear that this system did not work to the benefit of pupils with special needs. Quite apart from their additional needs in respect of careers education, they might be having only some lessons in the main school anyway and stood to miss out even more than their peers.

Whether pupils with special needs had access to a careers course in the main school or not, they invariably required further help as well. A number of careers teachers were quite clear about this, insisting that they knew too little about handicap or the opportunities available either to slant their courses appropriately or to provide the necessary information and advice. When extra help was given – and this was by no means universal – it tended to come on an individual basis as part of careers guidance or incorporated into leavers' courses rather than by setting up a formal careers education course within the special centre. One head of a special centre which had no formal careers programme – neither did the main school – stressed the informal nature of their careers education and guidance; it was an extension of their system of pastoral care for all pupils. To the extent that the system worked it did so at the level of guidance on particular careers rather than of education and information about the range of career options. It tended to function too in response to pupil requests and seemed most effective for more able pupils – "you've got to push but once you have pushed help is there" (pupil) – "as soon as I've thought of something I want to do I'll go and see (head of centre)". In many instances a good deal of education about careers and the world of work was incorporated into leavers' courses, especially work experience, or other parts of the curriculum. With the exception of work experience programmes which sought to place pupils in a number of different jobs, this tended to be focused on the skills of the workplace rather than on information about the different possibilities available.

Careers guidance has to do with narrowing the possibilities and involves the careers service more directly. All local education authorities are required to operate a careers service as part of their educational provision. Careers officers have the task of giving information and advice to school leavers and helping them to find jobs and educational placements. This is intended to help all pupils, including those with special needs. Specialist careers officers are sometimes appointed for the latter in view of the special nature of their problems and the possible need for specialised knowledge that the general careers officer might not possess. Just as careers officers advise teachers on careers education within the school and even assist with it, so specialist careers officers can provide similar support for careers teachers who have responsibility for pupils with special needs.

In reality, specialist careers officers are relatively scarce and many of the functions they might fulfil go by default. Moreover, their training is usually limited to particular sets of special needs, and, though they have a brief for all pupils with special needs, they may have no more expertise than any other careers officer where some pupils are concerned. Teachers commented on this on several occasions. In one school a specialist careers officer talked to a group of hearing impaired pupils in such a way that made it clear that he knew little about deafness or how to communicate with hearing impaired people – "The kids got very very little out of the talk" (teacher of the deaf).

A number of detailed careers guidance programmes were described to us. These were either embryonic or only approximately realised in practice. They are useful none the less in illustrating what is possible.

School A

1. *The process starts with the specialist careers officer and the careers teacher working through the list of school leavers. The teacher sees all the parents. Then a case conference involving the school, careers services, social services, medical officers and other relevant agencies is held.*
2. *The specialist careers officer and the careers teacher have a preliminary interview with pupils to determine their aspirations and perhaps get them thinking seriously about the future. They are told about relevant opportunities and given information and literature as appropriate. The careers teacher sees parents again.*
3. *Depending on emerging possibilities and decisions taken, the careers officer and the teacher obtain specific information, make practical arrangements, set up interviews, help in applying for grants and so on.*

School B

1. *Group discussion is the main feature of the first phase. The specialist careers officer meets pupils with special needs as a group, once in fourth year and at least four times in fifth year.*
2. *While group discussions are taking place, the specialist careers officer holds individual 'pre-interview discussions' with the pupils, their parents and teachers. These are for the purpose of initiating serious thought about the future and collecting information.*
3. *Vocational guidance proper is also done on an individual basis with parents invited to attend. The information gathered to date is now put together and the possibilities are narrowed down, leading to eventual decision and action.*

Most of the schools we visited had nothing as elaborate as this. Some had occasional access to a specialist careers officer or had other positive contact with a careers service. Many however had to provide careers guidance without the services of a specialist careers officer or with irregular and infrequent visits from a careers officer who might or might not be au fait with the particular needs of their pupils.

Whether or not specialist help was available the role of the careers teacher or equivalent was crucial. One school which did have occasional contact with a specialist careers officers was heavily involved in careers guidance. The head of the special centre spent a great deal of time discussing career possibilities, relying on close personal knowledge of pupils and informal contact rather than any formal system. University places and further education were sought; specialised vocational assessment was arranged; jobs were set up; pupils were put in touch with agencies such as the National Bureau for Handicapped Students or with Disablement Officers in colleges. The specialist careers officer played a role in some of this but the basic work was done by the school.

In another authority a particular teacher went to great lengths to arrange appropriate further education opportunities for pupils, and liaised with specialised agencies on their part. Even though this interfered with teaching commitments, the teacher believed it was necessary to spend the time since the main school careers system had little specific help for these pupils while the specialist careers service would not have sufficient time or persistence.

A mixed picture emerged from other schools, with teachers providing careers guidance entirely on their own initiative or with the benefit of vaguely specified help from the careers service. It seems clear that the major part of careers guidance for pupils with special needs must come from their teachers. This takes account not only of the scarcity of specialist careers officer – a situation unlikely to improve in the short term – but also of the fact that their teachers have a great deal of knowledge about pupils and their needs and what they are likely to be able to do. If this knowledge can be supplemented by specialist help on the careers side and if teachers can be timetabled so as to allow them time to do it, the chances are that pupils will receive careers guidance appropriate to their needs. This arrangement where the teacher is the major partner and the specialist careers officer the minor one would seem to offer the best model for specialist careers guidance in the short term. It acknowledges that by and large specialist careers officers are not going to have time to get to know pupils and build up the comprehensive knowledge about them that guidance requires. It acknowledges too that they are in a position to help in specific ways through their knowledge of career opportunities, contacts with relevant agencies and so on.

It should be clear that we are not proposing a system by default, forced on schools by the scarcity of specialist careers officers, but an *alternative* system that capitalises on available resources. It is not going to work unless teachers do have the requisite knowledge of pupils and their special needs and can devote the time to careers work on their behalf. In some forms of individual integration there may not be a specialist teacher available, and in tightly staffed special classes or centres it may not be possible to allocate the time. Where possible however, a teacher from the special centre should be designated as responsible for careers work, given some relevant training and be formally timetabled for guidance at appropriate times during the year, as well as having the flexibility and resources to respond to short-term needs, and liaise with outside agencies. This teacher would have responsibility for careers education for pupils with special needs in the school and would liaise with main school careers teachers to supplement the regular careers education course or provide additional courses as required.

2.   Work experience

Work experience is a means of exposing young people to the workplace in a gradual supportive way. The Education (Work Experience) Act 1973 allows pupils in their last twelve months of compulsory schooling to participate in work experience schemes approved by the local education authority. So for varying periods of time they put school concerns to one side and work at real jobs. Ideally, this provides an opportunity to learn about work and experience at first hand the difference between being a schoolgoer and a worker.

a.   General organisation of work experience

Work experience can be organised in a variety of ways, each with advantages and disadvantages. For the most part, it involves work outside the school. This can be organised at Authority level or by the individual school. Exceptionally, it can take place within the school in, for example, an industrial training unit.

The amount of time given over to work outside the school varied from two to six weeks a year in the schools we visited. This was spent either as one day a week spread over a term or as a block fortnight. Various pros and cons were pointed out for each. In favour of the block arrangement are (i) the fact that it is a continuous intensive period, more akin to the experience of a real job, and (ii) the possibility of seeing the different aspects of a job, which is sometimes not feasible on a one-day-a-week basis because similar things are happening each time. In jobs that have a regular weekly cycle such as supermarket work, this is of great relevance. As against that, (i) there is no follow-up time, and the teacher is not very easily able to solve any problems that arise; (ii) there is no possibility of it being a "collective experience" for the pupils –where they come together and discuss each day's experiences on the day following; (iii) the teacher may not be able to visit the workplaces as frequently.

A slightly controversial question is whether or not pupils should be paid for their services during work experience. One girl's parents withdrew their permission for her involvement when it emerged that she would not be getting paid: if she was doing a job she should be paid for it. There is too the argument that pay is an integral part of work, and to work unpaid is to miss out on what for many people is a major dimension of their experience of work. (Some pupils received gifts or token payments, had travelling expenses paid and so on, but this was entirely at the discretion of the individual employer.) On the other hand employers may take the line that they are obliging the schools by taking these pupils on at all and the employees they replace are usually not freed but required to supervise the pupils. They do not receive cash incentives from the government to take on these pupils as they do for some youth employment schemes. If schools started requesting payment it was felt that it would become even more difficult to find firms willing to participate. It was claimed also that there would be practical difficulties with insurance.

In one scheme that we studied the aim was deliberately to enable the pupils to sample different work situations before they made a choice. There were three periods of work experience each involving a different job. Ideally these were a job of the pupil's choice, one mutually agreed between teacher and pupil, and one chosen by the teacher to give experience in a job not previously considered by the pupil. For the first two of these the pupils spent one day a week for ten weeks in each job, while they worked at the third for a solid fortnight. They had to get themselves to work at the same time as any other worker, and work out the full day on any tasks assigned to them. This scheme has only recently been introduced but in the first year 11 pupils have been involved.

One school had an industrial training unit that sought to set up the work situation within the context of school. This was primarily to introduce pupils to the discipline that would enable them to settle down at a real job. There were three main kinds of work: printing; factory jobs (sorting, light assembly, repetitive clerical work); and woodwork. Contracts were obtained from external customers and had to be executed to a specified standard and had to meet deadlines. A drawback was that the deadlines were sometime so tight as to necessitate more involvement on the part of the adult than was desired; a slower pace might have been more useful on educational grounds. Pupils were not paid directly; profits accruing went to a school fund.

b. Types of work done

A surprising variety of jobs was reported. In spite of the constraints and pupil limitations teachers managed to set up many different opportunities. These included:

    Helping in primary schools, including in one case hearing children read

    Gardening in local Parks Department and nurseries

    Factory work in various locations, packaging, loading and unloading, fetching and carrying, tidying up, general low level manual work

    Filling shelves at supermarkets and drug stores

    Helper at day nursery

    Butcher's assistant

    Simple assembly line work

c. Organising a programme of work experience

A properly run programme of work experience will have many stages. They can be summarised as follows:

    – set up the job

    – select pupils and match with jobs

    – clear individual placements with employers and parents

    – prepare pupils

– commence work
– be on hand to monitor progress and solve problems
– arrange follow up activities
– obtain feedback from employers

In the first place the jobs must be set up. In some authorities, eg where the Trident Scheme operates, this is organised centrally. Information about jobs throughout the authority is collected and processed in a central location, and schools are advised of local opportunities.

In the absence of a central scheme schools must make direct contact with local firms and employers and seek to enlist their cooperation. A number of schools reported considerable success on this front and indeed preferred to work in this way rather than through a central agency. One of the most successful (in terms of range of jobs, placement of 'difficult' pupils, job offers) deliberately cultivated local employers, inviting them along to the school and involving them actively in the work experience programme. Some schools did experience difficulty however in securing appropriate placements either because of lack of time on their part or employer reluctance. Particular difficulty was reported in respect of the hearing impaired with employers referring to the Health and Safety at Work Act 1974 and, especially with smaller firms, claiming that they did not have the requisite insurance cover. In some cases trades union opposition had led to restriction on the sort of job that could be offered; tasks such as washing up which would have been appropriate for some youngsters were not permitted.

In an ideal world it would not be necessary to select pupils for jobs since all would be given the chance to prove themselves. Given that opportunities are limited however, and in some instances a good public image was necessary – "you musn't jeopardise the chances of others" (by including unsuitable pupils) – some selection was judged to be necessary. The main criterion was ability, on the grounds that the more able pupils were the ones most likely to end up in open employment. However, pupils who were perceived as borderline candidates for placement in a sheltered workshop were sometimes included so that relevant information on that decision could be obtained.

Once a pupil has been matched up with a particular job – sometimes necessitating a compromise between the pupil's ambition and the teacher's judgement of likely benefit – agreement has to be secured from the potential employer and from the parents. There will normally be contact with the careers service and the school medical officer as well, and formal agreement must be secured from the director of education at some point. This is usually a matter of course, but difficulties can arise as when parents refuse to meet the bus fare or object to their son or daughter doing unpaid work.

Preparing pupils before they commence work is an important stage. Apart from getting over to them that this is work, not school, there are practicalities to attend to. In one school the pupils are encouraged to ring up the employer themselves and arrange their initial meeting. Some pupils will require detailed instructions on how to get from home to workplace. Instructions must also be given on the nature of the firm and the tasks to be done, any special clothing or other arrangements, safety regulations, use of the canteen and so on.

When the pupil commences work, there is need of close and regular contact between school and workplace. The importance of this was strongly emphasised. By talking to the employer, pupil and work mates and observing the work situation, the teacher can monitor progress in a general way and smooth over any difficulties that arise. He can find out if the travel arrangements are working; what the pupil is actually doing; how this relates to the overall pattern of work, and whether he might be able to do something else; if he is using any protective clothing required, and so on.

Follow-up back in the school is essential for capitalising on the benefits of the experience. It can help clarify pupils' perceptions of their experience, consolidate the learning that has taken place, and provide the opportunity to work on inappropriate attitudes. General discussion among the pupils themselves was found to be very useful. Frequently they were required to produce a written account of their work, saying what they had gained from it and what their thoughts and feelings about it were. It can also lead to specific curriculum work. One boy, for instance, worked in a butcher's shop and did lots of weighing in his maths work subsequently.

Feedback from employers can be obtained by means of written reports and through meetings. A formal written report can be a useful addition to career-oriented information on a pupil. One school introduced working lunches whereby a group of employers meet together with school staff and other agencies. This was a novel and promising development.

d. Examples

We describe here some examples of pupils and their progress through work experience programmes.

Matthew, categorised as ESN(S), successfully attempted a programme of three job placements. At the first location (a rubber factory) his work was fine but socially they "found him hard work"; they persevered however because his family was known to some of the workers. The problem was that he was very unforthcoming initially and then developed "an excessive attachment to ladies"! His second placement was in a repetitive production line, where again his work was satisfactory. This was with an all-male workforce, and there were no social problems. At his third placement he was employed for a block fortnight to do low level manual work such as sweeping the yard, elementary gardening etc. This was a great success – "best person they have ever had for low level manual work". In fact they would have liked to offer him a job but had only a part-time vacancy. His success opened the possibility of a work experience year at a local technical college which otherwise was only open to ESN(M) pupils.

Ruth, an ESN(M) pupil, displayed a similar improvement over the three sessions. The first was at a shop; this did not work out too well because of her poor short term memory and inability to carry more than one set of instructions in mind at a time. Her second, at a rubber company, was much better; it was a bench job taking excess rubber off some shapes on a repetitive production line. She liked this so much she wanted to stay. The third job involved helping to clean offices; she settled down immediately, managed the tasks well but was a bit slow. On the social side she was fine, if anything too respectful – "if she calls me Miss once more I'll crown her" (one of her colleagues)!

John, an ESN(M) pupil, started doing low level manual work. There were no problems; the employer simply reported that they would have liked to have him for a longer period. The second placement was in a supermarket where he worked in the stores in the morning and with the butcher in the afternoon. This was because he wanted to work as a butcher. He was offered a job as a butcher, but subsequently got a better paid factory job during this period so he left school. The teacher felt his period of work experience helped him to come out of himself and became more self-confident.

Life Skills

By life skills we mean the range of skills necessary to live in society as an independent adult. They include personal skills such as body care and presentation, domestic skills such as simple cooking and money management and being able to deal with society's institutions. As with work and leisure, young people with special needs may benefit from specific preparation or training that other youngsters do not need. The content of any such preparation will depend on the nature of their needs as well as their life situation. Somebody who lives in the countryside does not need to be able to cope with London's Underground; a retarded youngster who is probably going to a sheltered workshop does not have to know how trades unions work and so on.

All of the schools we visited had some preparation in life skills, sometimes availing of main school resources but more often providing it in a self-contained way for the special group. This preparation was commonly given as part of special leavers' courses, though many schools sought to incorporate it into the curriculum in a general way. The whole range of what was on offer in the different schools was very impressive but there were considerable variations between schools; some provided a comprehensive and integrated programme while others had more limited offerings. The greatest variations occurred with sex education and independence training.

1.   Personal Skills

Personal skills include hygiene and body care, socially acceptable toileting, mobility and use of public transport, sex education and child care. Hygiene and body care featured on a number of leavers' courses or were taught on an individual basis to some pupils as required. One school used a biology teacher for this part of the course. Another school had lessons from health officers for all pupils and these were attended by some of the pupils with special needs. Toileting and menstruation techniques need individual handling, often provided by ancillary staff with or without the benefit of nursing or physiotherapeutic advice. As far as body care and toileting were concerned, it seemed that being in ordinary school provided a salutary peer pressure; physically handicapped and retarded youngsters had to conform to basic standards of cleanliness, modesty and personal presentation or face ridicule or worse from peers. This produced effects both directly and – through teachers and parents making renewed efforts – indirectly.

Road safety was usually covered in main school lessons or in more detail as part of a leavers' course. Several schools sought to combine practical teaching of road safety with instruction on the use of public transport. The latter was sometimes accorded high priority in cognisance of its crucial contribution to independence in adult life. Though some pupils were able to travel to school independently because of the integration arrangements, many did not and were brought by special transport. This fostered a dependent frame of mind with pupils lacking initiative and expecting to be transported everywhere. An important element of work experience for some pupils was that they had to negotiate a new journey – with initial help if required – on their own. Others were sent on errands outside the school as part of independence training. In some cases it was necessary to transport pupils into the town and then set them off on their assignments.

Some schools did very well in imparting mobility skills but there were many gaps in provision. Some staff seemed not to be aware of what was at stake or were hindered through lack of time or opportunity. A physiotherapist said she could only cover the basics of personal mobility in the time available and would like to do more in the way of road training and so on. Mention was made of the difficulty of giving physically handicapped pupils a graduated mobility assignment in an ordinary school; on the one hand, the site might not lend itself to this, being too difficult or not incorporating the right sorts of difficulties, while on the other hand the task could be ruined by pupils opening doors or removing obstacles. A blind girl in a large comprehensive school was able to negotiate the school independently when it was empty but was not able to do so at all when corridors were crowded at changes of lessons; the result was that she had to be led everywhere and valuable opportunities for consolidating mobility skills were lost.

Sex education in some form was available in most of the

secondary schools we visited. The nature and extent of this varied widely. The basic facts of human reproduction were sometimes covered in life science, health education or equivalent courses available to all pupils. In some cases this was supplemented with specific instruction on contraception, sexually transmitted diseases, pregnancy and birth, and infant care. One school attached importance to education for personal relationships, discussing adolescence, relationships between the sexes and family life.

Some of the sex education programmes we learnt about were excellent but there were a number of problems. A major difficulty was the reluctance or unwillingness to discuss matters relating to sex and marriage openly. There was occasionally an impression that so long as no overt problems manifested themselves it was simplest to leave matters lie. This is understandable in view of the difficulty some teachers have in discussing these topics with young people but the results can be unfortunate. Puberty and adolescence can be trying times for any teenager; when there are additional problems due to physical disability, social isolation or limited capacity to understand the changes taking place within oneself, the need for sympathetic foresight on the part of adults is very great. Along with other youngsters they need to be rid of ignorance and myths about sex and develop enlightened and responsible attitudes toward it. They have extra difficulties however. Some worry about their sexual capacity or their attractiveness to those of the opposite sex, while others nurture unrealistic ambitions of domesticity and children of their own. These problems can be exacerbated through being in an ordinary school. Pupils with special needs become more aware of normal possibilities and can either be dismayed at the difficulty in attaining them or assume too readily that they are available to themselves. If the worries – which may be well-founded – are to be removed and the ambitions – which may not be totally impossible – are to be given a chance of being realised, frank and open discussion on many occasions will be necessary. Teachers cannot afford to wait until things go wrong.

2.   *Domestic Skills*

Domestic skills include cooking, shopping and general household management, simple household and mechanical tasks, and money management. Domestic science courses available to all pupils provided training in general household management. Some schools laid on extra instruction for pupils with special needs, in some cases attaching high priority to this and assigning it a good deal of time. A number of special centres had their own domestic science facilities so that pupils could be given ample time and individual attention. Leavers' courses had extensive components in household DIY, with instruction on decorating, electricity, changing tap washers and so on. This was in addition to the normal curriculum in craft work.

Money matters were covered in practical mathematics as well as leavers' courses. Topics covered included pay-packets and deductions, unemployment and social security benefits, money management and budgeting, hire purchase, bills, bank and post-office accounts, mortgages and rent, and basic principles of consumerism. Practical exercises were sometimes devised.

One school had a savings bank in conjunction with the Trustee Savings Bank; this was run entirely by pupils (with learning difficulties) to the extent even of making regular deposits in the local branch in the town. Other schools sent pupils out to purchase specific items, perhaps with instructions to shop around or look at related items as well. This can be tied into household management as when pupils have to compile a menu and purchase the ingredients for it in addition to cooking the food.

3. Dealing with society's institutions

Dealing with society's institutions cuts aross many of the categories above, but there is a value in considering it separately. It is a fundamental aspect of equipping young people for independent adult living, and it brings one up short against the social nature of handicap. Many special needs are social artefacts in that they are exacerbated by or take the particular form they do because of social factors when not actually created by them. As personal options increase and lifestyles grow complex, we become more dependent on services and on our capacity to deal with the systems within which the services are provided. This can be seen in work, leisure and domestic living. When work was a question of a job near home with adults familiar since childhood, all that mattered was the capacity to pick up the job and possibly the physical strength to do it. Nowadays, a young person entering the labour market has to negotiate apprenticeships or other training schemes, face interviews with strangers, deal with clocking in, probably travel a considerable distance and so on. In other words, a whole range of preliminary skills have to be acquired before he or she gets down to work.

The school's function here is to teach young people about relevant institutions and impart the necessary skills. So, leavers' courses had instruction on public services such as gas and electricity, social services, the police, libraries, banks and post-offices. Pupils were taught how to fill forms, use the telephone, write standard letters and present themselves for interview. One school had instruction on the use of catalogues – a particular asset to disabled people. Another worked with pupils on popular newspapers and the wording of advertisements. This seemed a valuable exercise that could well have been extended. If young people are going to become independent and not be protected by adults, they must be equipped with the requisite knowledge and skills. This includes being able to withstand unscrupulous salesmanship and advertising as well as coping directly with society's institutions.

Leisure

Many schools offer a range of non-academic activities – sports, organised trips and visits, film shows, music and drama, and various club activities. A large comprehensive school with an enthusiastic staff can offer a very wide range of such activities. The opportunity to participate in these can be important to pupils with special needs and can enhance their educational experience. It increases their imaginative understanding and adds to the enjoyment of life; it promotes self-confidence through the acquisition and competent exercise of skills; above all, it is a valuable preparation for life after school.

There are a number of reasons why pupils with special needs may need more systematic preparation in the use of leisure time than other pupils. First, many activities available to others as a matter of course may not be available to them. Physical disability, hearing loss, communication difficulty, all impose restrictions on leisure time possibilities. So a disabled youngster who cannot play football may have a strong case for extra music tuition, and a deaf pupil who will not star in the school play might with support make a good photographer. In general, it would seem reasonable that the more a given pupil is precluded from taking part in normal leisure time activities the greater his or her need for formal intervention to compensate for this. (It is unfortunate that a near-exclusive concentration on basic skills sometimes leads to an impoverished curriculum for these pupils.) A further consideration is that these pupils need help with non-academic areas of learning just as they do with academic subjects, whether this be because of learning difficulties or the absence of learning experiences. Going to the movies or being a football fan is not something that most youngsters have to be taught about since the requisite knowledge and behaviours are built into their sub-cultures. Youngsters who are excluded from these subcultures for whatever reasons lack the informal learning experiences and may need systematic teaching or other intervention on the part of adults. Finally, many of these youngsters are likely to spend lengthy periods out of work when they leave school, while of those who work many will be confined to repetitive and monotonous jobs. For all of these young people and for those whose disabilities impose a degree of isolation on them, the importance of fulfilling non-work activities can hardly be over-estimated.

There are various ways in which schools can help young people in this regard. The leavers' courses and other courses referred to above usually had material specific to this. A Personal Relationships course had a component on leisure: wasting time and spending time; different activities; mixing with others; voluntary work and community service. This course was part of the core curriculum for all pupils but was taken by those with moderate learning difficulties as well. A Design for Living programme offered to a group of backward physically handi-capped sixth formers included material on entertainment and use of leisure, entertaining friends at home, local places of interest, holidays including passports and foreign currency, hobbies and pets. Though not an integrated course in the sense that pupils from the main school followed it, many staff contributed toward it and it was possible to cover a wide range of subject matter. A further school incorporated the Duke of Edinburgh's Award Scheme into its leavers' course for pupils with learning difficulties; this required pupils to develop a particular interest and pursue it consistently over a period of time.

Some schools organised leisure activities specifically for their pupils with special needs or made the school's facilities available for organisations such as PHAB (Physically Handicapped and Able-Bodied) clubs.

For example, a secondary department for pupils with learning difficulties organised team games against similar departments in other schools or even special schools. Another school organised a visit to the cinema for its physically handicapped pupils in addition to the school's own film club. Generally, however, the tendency was to refrain from making too many arrangements specifically for those with special needs and instead to find ways of incorporating them into main school activities. Some teachers indeed resisted moves to organise formal entertainment for these pupils on the grounds that it stifled initiative and stopped them from becoming independent. It was more important to encourage them to join main school activities, removing obstacles if necessary, and developing the skills and mentality that would enable them to pursue leisure activities independently. The latter of course was encompassed under general independence training. Encouraging pupils to participate in main school activities is however less amenable to direct action, and intervention that is too obvious or heavy-handed may be counterproductive. Some schools made a point of involving a wide range of pupils in its public events such as school plays and concerts – and this was valuable – but a more general participation in the non-academic life of the school whether it be organised clubs and discos or less structured activities cannot be achieved by legislation. It must be the outcome of a more general ethos within the school where all pupils, no matter how different, are seen as an integral part of the pupil body.

Chapter Fifteen
Implementing the Curriculum

> Because they couldn't learn we naturally didn't teach them. Because we didn't teach them, naturally they didn't learn (Dybwad, 1967)

We have discussed in chapter 13 the curriculum in integration, noting how it can assume a distinctive character, different both from the curriculum in special schools and from the main curriculum in the ordinary school. In this chapter we turn to the implementation of the curriculum. Integration as a means by which pupils with special needs are educated in the ordinary schools takes many forms. The learning environment of the ordinary school lends itself to being structured in different ways. the purely pedagogical aspects must be considered: teaching approaches need to be adapted; resources have to be used in different ways; and a range of additional resources will be required. Pupils who are following essentially the same curriculum as peers may nevertheless require concessions in view of particular physical conditions. One must allow too for the possibility of interruptions and take account in planning of physical and organisational constraints that may take affect of individual pupils' access to the curriculum.

Organising the learning environment

We have referred at various points to the many organisational arrangements that can be made in order to facilitate the education of pupils with special needs in ordinary schools. The different ways in which these arrangements are conceptualised and described in terms of integration models were outlined in chapter 3. The relationship between these and curricular options was noted in chapter 13. Here we want to examine the way in which these different arrangements affect how pupils are taught and the possible extension of the school's range of educational possibilities.

i. Individual integration

We observed two programmes of individual integration that involved physically handicapped and hearing impaired pupils respectively. The physically handicapped were mostly in primary schools and spanned the ability range from above average to slow learner; most of the pupils in the schools visited had learning difficulties of some sort. A common characteristic of the provision made for these pupils was that they were slotted into the school's existing arrangements whether adequate or not. For the most part they attended a normal class within the school, and any learning difficulties that came to notice were dealt with in the same way as for any other pupil – individual attention and conventional remedial work. Some teachers were unhappy about this situation, conscious of having too little time for individual attention and unsure whether their remedial tactics were adequate or even on the right lines, while a few were worried that they might not even be aware of the particular needs of these pupils. This was by no means universal – some teachers felt quite competent to cope with them – but some felt that a teacher with appropriate training or experience would be more sensitive to these pupils' special needs and would be better equipped to meet them. Where schools had remedial classes or other specific arrangements for pupils with learning difficulties, the physically handicapped were incorporated into them when appropriate. This increased the possibility of individual attention and the likelihood of having staff versed in recognising and meeting their needs.

There were two respects in which provision for these pupils differed from that of other pupils, viz the presence of ancillary helpers and provision for physiotherapy. A welfare assistant was provided to deal with the toileting and general care necessitated by their physical condition. In many instances these assistants were used in a supplementary teaching role to provide individual attention and implement programmes to a professional's instructions. Details on this aspect of the ancillary's role have been given above. Many of these pupils had need of physiotherapeutic involvement to guide exercises, devise PE programmes and monitor the use of appliances. This support was provided on a peripatetic basis by community physiotherapists working closely with classroom ancillaries.

Most pupils in this integration programme were still at primary stage. Those few at secondary stage were based in the school's remedial department or followed a normal timetable. We noted details on two of these. One spent most of the day in the remedial department, integrating only for art, needlework, swimming and some science. The other followed a full academic timetable for the first two years at the secondary school; this was considered to put too much pressure on the pupil however and to leave insufficient time for other activities judged necessary, so science and geography were dropped in the third year to allow greater concentration on life skills such as cookery and physical exercises as well as consolidation in other academic subjects.

The second individual integration programme, for hearing impaired pupils, involved rather different teaching arrangements. There were twelve pupils in all ranging from profoundly deaf to partially hearing. They spanned the ability range although none was considered to have learning difficulties to the extent that might justify categorising as ESN. They attended normal classes in primary and secondary school. The main difference was the presence of support teachers. Seven teachers (6.1 full-time equivalent), three of whom were teachers of the deaf, were available to provide the requisite specialist teaching – language work and auditory training – and to reinforce or supplement lessons as required. Pupils were withdrawn for a daily session of auditory training and general speech work with the teacher of the deaf. The support teacher assigned to a pupil would sometimes sit in on these sessions, and would reinforce the work during the day by giving the pupil additional practice on exercise devised by the teacher of the deaf. Pupils were withdrawn from normal lessons for specific speech and language work and, less commonly, to enable the support teacher to reinforce some aspect of the normal lesson in greater detail than would be possible within the class. Wherever possible, the pupil is supported *within* the classroom – through the support teacher interpreting and reinforcing the work of the lesson. This must be done as unobtrusively as possible and requires close co-operation between the class teacher and the support teacher. The support must also be provided selectively. Particularly at secondary level the pace of work would be too much for it to be possible to reinforce everything so that the support teacher must exercise discretion in selecting the essential topics and those where the pupil will have particular difficulties because of the hearing impairment or the lack of appropriate learning experiences. The selection exercises can be especially problematic at secondary stage where pupils are being taught by specialist teachers and follow a range of subjects with which the support teacher is not familiar. The importance of collaboration with the class teacher assumes an extra dimension then: time can profitably be spent together in reviewing the content of lessons in advance, noting salient features and discussing where support can be dispensed with and where it is quite essential.

ii.   Special class or centre

The special class or centre offers numerous possibilities for structuring the learning environment. As noted in chapter 3, the special centre can function as a base which provides a greater or lesser amount of given pupils' teaching and which shares responsibility for their programmes of work in different ways with the main school. Alternatively, it can function purely as a resource centre, catering for pupils who may be formally assigned to main school classes either by withdrawing them for periods of time or providing specialist help in some other way.

Some examples may illustrate these possibilities. The first comes from a comprehensive school catering for a large number of pupils with learning difficulties, many of whom if formally ascertained would be categorised ESN(M). A special centre has been established as an integral part of the school to meet the needs of these pupils as well as serving the functions of a remedial department. Broadly speaking, it caters for three groups: a core group of 60/70 pupils who spend considerable periods of time in the special centre; 'remedial' pupils whose needs are less great and who might be withdrawn from normal lessons for two to four lessons a week for remediation work in the special centre; and pupils with specific learning difficulties who might pose problems of a one-off nature and require highly specific programmes of work. The teaching arrangements were different for the three groups. The core group spent at least half of the week in the special centre, following a modified curriculum with a heavy emphasis on basic skills and social studies. The remainder of their time was spent in mixed ability classes in the main school. As a general rule, not more than two pupils are placed in any one class. No direct support was provided for these classes in the way of accompanying staff, teaching guidelines or specialist resources. A large number of pupils (up to 100) were withdrawn to the special centre for short periods in order to do basic remediation work, while specific programmes were drawn up for those with specific learning difficulties. These programmes would be implemented while the pupils in question continued to follow a normal timetable.

Provision for pupils with speech and language difficulties does not lend itself to being an integral part of the school in the same way as above. The continuum – if there is one – linking the pupils typically catered for in such provision and the mainstream of pupils is less obvious, and the pupils' teaching needs are markedly different. This was borne out, in contrasting ways, in two language classes we visited. (It is relevant to this account that both drew their clientele from a wide area, not just from the catchment area of their respective schools.)

In the first it was decided to arrange the specialist teaching these pupils needed in such a way as to maintain a link with each pupil's neighbourhood school and so facilitate return to it. Maintaining a link with the neighbourhood school was felt to be essential in view of the difficulty sometimes experienced in persuading schools to accept those who have spent a period of time in special provision; if the school still sees a pupil as one of its own while away receiving specialist attention, the problem does not arise in the same way. Accordingly, the teaching programme of the language class was arranged so that pupils had their specialist work in the language class confined to four days a week and went to their neighbourhood school on the fifth. This raised problems of liaison and continuity between the language class and the large number of schools that its pupils attended on Friday. Ideally, the language class squeezed a week's work – normal infant and junior curriculum plus specific remediation – into four days while the fifth day provided general enrichment and a broadening of their curriculum as well as familiarising pupils with the norms and work patterns of their neighbourhood school to which it was hoped they would return. Academic contact with the host school was negligible, being confined to occasional PE and music lessons; this reflected in part the constraints imposed by the four-day-a-week arrangement and a reluctance to impose a third source of identification on pupils (in addition to the language class and their neighbourhood school).

The other language class operated on more conventional lines. Pupils did not maintain contact with their neighbourhood schools and any contact with normal primary school work took place in the host school to which the language class belonged. Pupils spent most of their time in the language class in fact, integrating only for music and movement, hymn practice and television. At one stage they had PE with another class but this was discontinued; quite a number of them were clumsy and it was judged more advantageous for them to do it on their own. Otherwise, the only academic contact is when pupils are being considered for full-time placement in an ordinary class. When this happens they are introduced gradually, initially perhaps for the first half of the afternoon, then for the whole of the afternoon, and so on.

An example of a different kind is furnished by a special centre for visually impaired pupils in a primary school. This operates on a 'resource room' model. The school itself is organised on team teaching lines, based on vertical grouping. The extensive individualisation of instruction, with much individual and small group tuition that this entails, is considered to facilitate the academic integration of the visually impaired. Each pupil is attached to an appropriate group and spends most of his or her time in the main school. Each teaching team has a specialist member of staff who assumes primary responsibility for any visually impaired pupils in the group but does not monopolise their teaching. Wherever possible the visually impaired work on the same tasks and use the same materials as their sighted peers. They may be allowed extra time on work where progress is slow or difficult. If it is felt that a pupil would not benefit from a particular activity the specialist teacher arranges for separate work. Pupils are withdrawn for tuition in braille and typing where necessary. In some craft and PE work a considerable amount of ancillary help is provided.

iii. Special school/ordinary school links

The links between special schools and ordinary schools that we observed all operated at secondary level. In one case hearing impaired pupils attended a neighbourhood comprehensive school for craft subjects and for PE and games. Initially, teachers from the special school accompanied them but stayed rather in the background. There was no effort or intention to adopt an explicit support role. As soon as the pupils settled down and teachers grew accustomed to their presence the specialist teachers withdrew. Otherwise the hearing impaired pupils spent their time in the school for the deaf where they followed the customary curriculum.

A school for physically handicapped pupils established links with a nearby comprehensive school whereby individual physically handicapped pupils were taught in the latter for varying amounts of time, depending on the pupil's academic capacity and other characteristics. Some received all or almost all of their academic teaching in the comprehensive while others were split between the two schools in varying proportions. Specialist provision such as physiotherapy and speech therapy was provided in the special school in all cases. While pupils are the responsibility of the comprehensive teachers for those subjects they are taught there, special school staff did provide some additional assistance. This was especially so in the early days of the programme when physically handicapped pupils were joining classes in the second or third year where they might have missed out on essential groundwork. This assistance took the form of additional maths and English, and supplementary work in any topics that were causing difficulty.

As time went by the amount of assistance diminished, partly because it was judged less necessary and partly because special school staff were fully committed or nearly so in providing a secondary curriculum for those pupils who were not integrating. The latter task has come to assume priority, and pupils who are integrating have to fit in with whatever is available when they return to the special school. (Pupils who integrate partially are timetabled to return to the special school when they are not timetabled for a specific lesson at the comprehensive.) Within these constraints, the aim is to allow each pupil a period each of PE, music/drama and home economics, a supplementary period of maths and English for those judged to need it, and individual follow-up work organised on an ad hoc basis.

Pedagogical aspects of integration

This is not a book on the techniques of educating pupils with special needs. Despite the crucial importance of such techniques for teacher and pupil alike and the relative scarcity of information about them, this matter was not our direct brief and we did not enquire systematically into it. We did obtain some information however on factors that impinge on teaching in an integrated situation and we discuss these here. The emphasis is on the ordinary teacher as opposed to the specialist, since in the majority of cases the latter's teaching was carried out within the confines of a special centre.

It is instructive first to look at responses to the question in the questionnaire to teachers (details in Appendix C): *Have you had to modify your teaching approach in any way (because of the presence of pupils with special needs)?* As will be seen from Table I, the majority of respondents, 72 per cent of those answering the question, replied Yes to this. (The high total for 'Unanswered' is due to the fact that many of them did not in fact teach pupils with special needs.)

Table I: Modify teaching approach

Yes	No	Unanswered
124	49	74

Teachers indicated a wide range of ways in which they had modified their teaching approach. The majority of these were not specific to particular handicapping conditions and could be adopted with many pupils with special needs. These are summarised below.

i.   Give more individual attention, make more time both personal and academic.

ii.   Simplify teaching, give instructions slowly and clearly, break content matter down to its components, work more slowly, set shorter objectives.

(These two sets of responses were most common and occurred in the answers of very many teachers.)

iii. Reinforce lesson content, repeat over and over, cover the same ground in different ways.

iv.   Plan lessons carefully so that pupils engage in varied activities and concentrated working is spaced throughout the lessons.

v.   Encourge pupils, provide moral support, be sympathetic to difficulties but firm and constant in demands. In the words of one teacher: Encourage. Dramatise. Praise. Flatter. Make them feel that you care and that they are important.

vi. Allow for pupils' slower writing, if necessary supply special notes, use blackboard or overhead projector instead of dictating.

vii. Allow for difficulty in speech and movement in drama.

viii. Emphasise fun apects, raise interest level, play rather than teach.

In addition to these, some modifications were made necessary by particular handicapping conditions. Various examples were given. For the hearing impaired and communication disordered they included: speaking slowly and articulating clearly; facing pupils and ensuring that they are watching closely, if necessary seating pupils near the front; paying careful consideration to the content of spoken language; ensuring that it is appropriate for pupils' receptive language capacity and cutting down on redundant content – make what you say count. For the visually impaired they included: emphasising other senses, particularly touch, hearing and smell; greater verbalising, in particular striving to describe vividly in words what can only be seen dimly or imperfectly if at all; setting learning tasks that have been carefully prepared and which may require specially prepared learning materials (eg large print or brailled workcards) and tools (felt-tip pens, personal dictaphone, brailler, low vision aids); and a closer than usual watch on the pupil's movements (fine and gross motor movement) around the classroom and in the physical education context in particular. The actions of physically handicapped children will also need to be closely monitored especially in situations where there is an element of risk (eg when using apparatus for physical education or in the science laboratory).

As noted, the principal modifications judged necessary were simplifying work and adapting it to the needs of individual pupils. But how is this to be achieved in the ordinary classroom? Individualising instruction is all very well when groups are small but how feasible is it in classes of 20 or 30? The following material based on interviews with teachers may help to answer these questions, as well as expanding on some of the other strategies referred to in the questionnaire responses.

A number of teachers mentioned the importance of setting work at a level where all pupils could experience success. This was done by devising tasks where success could be achieved by everyone albeit at different standards. Thus, a metalwork teacher instanced the task of making a nameplate; for some the end product would be basic but serviceable while others would produce a more elaborate product. Another tactic was to have pupils working together. A woodwork teacher maintained that a particular boy with moderate learning difficulties benefited socially as well as academically from this – "the others helped and he is benefiting in both ways; he does the bits he can do and learns to co-operate with other children". Teachers affirmed that strategies such as these were necessary because they could not give extensive one-to-one teaching which would be to the detriment of the rest of the class.

A science teacher also sought to ensure that as far as possible all pupils were able to carry out the tasks set and made particular efforts to ensure that experiments had successful outcomes. Secondly, he found it necessary constantly to emphasise the possible consequences of carelessness or clumsiness. He elected not to go for the safe option and spoke of the value of the calculated risk – "I don't think there is any point in removing the danger completely. I try to let them experience the dangers themselves".

Thirdly, there was the question of lesson presentation. "I can't give them written instructions, I have to talk about it – some of them haven't got the confidence in their reading to know they have got it right." So, very simple worksheets were prepared and talked through with those who needed it before they started work. Even then there was need for close contact with the group – "I would expect to see everybody every two minutes". These tactics were also designed to try and ensure that pupils had a science lesson rather than yet another English lesson – "must ensure that the dull ones are going to get the science out of it rather than the writing and drawing". Many teachers commented on the need for regular encouragement from them, striving to maintain motivation and to encourage pupils to use their judgement and exercise their own discretion, rather than their stopping frequently and waiting to be told what to do at every turn.

Several teachers stated quite explicitly that failure to cope with written work should not preclude pupils from being active participants otherwise. The tactic was to find acceptable tasks for them while the other pupils were engaged in written work. Thus, a teacher of domestic science devised particular assignments in the kitchen for three pupils with learning difficulties when the others were writing. In one school drama was mainly practical in first and second year. There was some use of scripts but this was kept to a minimum. In the third year pupils did some work on writing their own material but this happened only once a term and was confined to a single period of two to three weeks. Not everybody was involved in this so there was no particular stigma in not contributing to it. Also, group work was encouraged; everybody could feed ideas in to a planning session, regardless of writing skills, and producing a script from the group would be the responsibility of a designated representative. Use was made of tape-recorders also to minimise dependence on written scripts. When written work was essential, assignments such as manning the tape-recorders and looking after other equipment were given to those who could not write. Again, since the latter activities carried high status, no stigma was attached to not doing the written work – indeed, quite the reverse!

A music teacher described her approach to incorporating pupils with moderate learning difficulties into mixed ability classes. It was her belief that streaming or banding is particularly inappropriate in music; singing and practical work will be very poor in the less able group if all are grouped together, but if they are not so grouped, the more able ones help the others along, keep them in pitch, and even do effective teaching in small group situations. This teacher emphasised practical work and less than 20 per cent of time was given over to writing of any kind. Pupils typically worked in small groups with work organised in small stages so that the more able could go through more stages while the less able could still have positive achievements from working through the earlier stages. As an example of the way of working, if a group was working on rhythm the least able pupil would still be able to beat out a simple rhythm while the others could overlay more complex ones with each contributing to the overall sound.

Teaching special pupils in ordinary classes was only possible in some instances because of the presence of ancillary staff. The role of the ancillary and the constraints that hedge it round have been discussed in chapter 6. Here we describe some examples where ancillaries had an effective teaching involvement – that made integration possible. The first comes from a school with secondary age physically handicapped pupils. Here the ancillary helped in practical subjects. Thus in cookery if the disabled pupil got tired when whisking the ancillary would do some of it. In science the ancillary might help set up experiments and tidy up afterwards. If a pupil experienced difficulty with writing, the ancillary would take notes on his or her account or write the answers to questions. In this example the ancillary was confined to practical help and worked only with the physically handicapped pupils. A contrasting example comes from another secondary school catering for pupils with moderate learning difficulties. Here two ancillaries (one of whom was in fact a qualified teacher) helped to prepare teaching materials and were involved in using them. Integration in this school took the form of pupils from the special centre joining a team teaching situation in the main school where they worked on tasks and materials prepared by staff from the special centre in consultation with main school staff. The ancillaries also joined the teaching team in the main school, helping the special pupils as required and other pupils as appropriate.

Primary schools tended to make more extensive use of ancillaries. One school which integrated visually impaired pupils used an ancillary to provide a high level of individual support. This was particularly evident in craft work where considerable one-to-one working was essential. Thus one blind girl made models, using potentially dangerous tools such as a knife; without the close monitoring presence of the ancillary this would not have been possible. A remedial class in a primary school had two physically handicapped pupils. The ancillary worked closely with a peripatetic physiotherapist, supervising walking exercises, implementing sets of exercises in PE, practising the pupils in independence skills, and generally monitoring their physical condition and progress under the physiotherapist's guidance. In the classroom the ancillary played a supplementary teaching role, hearing pupils read, marking number work and generally checking that pupils were at work. This role had to do with learning difficulties rather than physical handicap. So, it was exercised for all pupils, not just the two physically handicapped ones, with the result that the class teacher was freed for a good deal of individual work with other pupils. In a third instance, a nursery nurse working in a special centre for hearing impaired juniors took mixed groups of hearing and hearing impaired pupils for practical activities such as cookery and craftwork. The teacher of the deaf ensured that the pupils were prepared for these sessions and monitored the language that was used, carrying out follow-up work as appropriate.

Some staff had reservations about such use of ancillaries. In a programme where physically handicapped pupils split their time between a special school and a neighbouring comprehensive school a senior member of the special school staff felt that while the involvement of ancillaries might enhance academic achievement it would be at the cost of pupils' social assimilation: "If they had an auxiliary to write it down for them they would lose out . . . they would become someone special in the group". Her preference was to place pupils in a lower ability band where they "could cope by themselves". Greater importance was attached to managing independently than to holding a place in the highest possible ability band.

Practical difficulties

Teachers reported many practical difficulties in teaching pupils with special needs. Most frequently mentioned was the difficulty of providing the requisite individual attention in large classes – "when you have the pressure of the other 34, things like that get pushed to one side". An art teacher with a class of 28 and a science teacher with one of 33 felt that they gave insufficient attention to all of their pupils, and any extended individual attention to pupils with special needs could only be to the detriment of the others. The difficulty was eased a little with long double periods since this allowed more time for individual working: short periods by contrast left little time after essential group work such as introductory exposition.

The situation could be exacerbated by the practice of placing pupils with special needs in classes comprised of less able and sometimes difficult pupils. Teachers might well be taxed sufficiently in coping with such classes without the addition of further pupils. Not only did the latter pose their own problems, but the group might not be the most conducive to receiving pupils with special needs. Maintaining social cohesion within the group and getting it to work as a whole were not always easy. As one secondary teacher observed, "integration in a low stream class suited to their ability does not always help the handicapped pupils". At the other end of the academic spectrum, individual attention tended to go by the board in the fifth and sixth years. Teachers were under exam pressure so that "anyone weak gets left to the wall".

A number of teachers commented on the demanding attitudes of some pupils. They were used to a small group situation where individual attention was the norm and assumed the same would hold in ordinary classes. One teacher described how a particular girl would interrupt "very rudely" when he was talking to the class and expect immediate individual attention even if it had nothing to do with what was going on in the class. An experienced colleague spoke of the "craving for individual attention" that many of the pupils in question (they were physically handicapped) exhibited, and their sometimes immature behaviour when faced with difficulties which did not receive a teacher's immediate attention. The problem with other pupils by contrast was that they made too few demands and drew too little attention to themselves. Hearing impaired pupils, for example, were commonly perceived to remain silent when they had not understood something or had run up against some difficulty. This was seen to happen whether they were integrated individually or in small groups. Unless a specialist teacher was on hand it was all too easy for the ordinary teacher, who was taken up with the class as a whole, to assume that all was well. One teacher reflecting on his own experience spotlighted a constant dilemma: "Some of them could do with more help – yet they resent being withdrawn from class because it highlights their handicap".

Another common problem, voiced in many different situations, was knowing what the potential of pupils was, how much could be demanded of them, what exceptions should be made for them and so on. Teachers with visually impaired pupils were uncertain as to what individual pupils could actually see and consequently what adaptions to work or expectations might be necessary. One teacher was aware that collage work was feasible but wanted to know what other art activities could be pursued. Teachers faced with hearing impaired pupils were commonly perplexed, not knowing how much they had understood or what standards of discipline to impose, and embarrassed when they were not readily able to understand what pupils had said to them. Many teachers were reluctant to put pressure on pupils, especially the physically handicapped, for fear of doing harm in some way. Some teachers voiced a concern that they should not over-compensate for a pupil's disability. A further point to note is that teachers anticipated certain difficulties which in the event did not materialise, only to overlook very obvious matters such as pupils' need for extra time in order to complete tasks set. These various problems, it should be noted, are amenable to specialist advice but frequently this was not forthcoming, either because the requisite specialists were not in post or staff did not have sufficient communication with them.

Teachers' uncertainty over what was reasonable to expect in terms of work output and behaviour made for problems of discipline. Many found real difficulty in 'being able to combine discipline and authority' with sympathy and understanding. One teacher summed up his uncertainty about how best to respond as follows: 'I am loathe to criticise or chastise them for fear of reaction'. Others acknowledged that they tended to err on the side of caution in their management of those pupils – particularly if they were perceived to have had 'a bad time of it'. A minority however were so concerned that they should not be seen to be dispensing favouritism that they were perhaps unduly demanding of pupils. Some pupils were well aware of teachers' uncertainty and took advantage of it, 'playing upon' their handicapping condition in order to avoid certain activities and demands.

Interruptions to work were a particular problem with physically handicapped pupils. These could be brief and intermittent as when pupils have to leave a lesson for a medical appointment or for speech or physiotherapy, or they can be major and prolonged, as when surgery or other reasons require hospitalisation. Indeed one authority which sought to integrate physically handicapped pupils did not do so until secondary stage. This was partly because of the likelihood at primary stage of operations, extensive physiotherapy and so on; it was felt that continuity of teaching could be guaranteed more easily in a special school.

Related to these difficulties were certain concessions which teachers made when teaching pupils with special needs. The most notable of these was in regard to written work. As noted above, teachers tended to emphasise the practical and non-verbal aspects of their subjects and devised various expedients to enable pupils participate without having to engage in written work. Homework too was frequently not required of these pupils when it was obligatory for their peers. Staff in one special centre catering for secondary age pupils with moderate learning difficulties were quite definite about this. Even though some parents would have preferred homework, they refrained from setting it: the pupils were doing enough basic skills work at school as it was; with some assignments they were likely to do the tasks incorrectly or experience failure – something which it was especially sought to avoid; and they ran a risk of getting into bad work habits.

Some ordinary teachers, especially subject specialists at secondary level, experienced considerable difficulty in adapting their teaching sufficiently so as, in one teacher's words, to "get down to the kids' level". One instance cited concerned a teacher who had taken less able physically handicapped pupils for craftwork and drawing. He noted how he had had to modify *'even simple* pattern making and print making' (our emphasis). Another remarked on the difficulty of coping with pupils' very poor initial grasp of lesson content and limited powers of retention. A PE specialist described how inadequate he had felt when faced with the need for greater than usual flexibility and ingenuity in presenting lesson content. This was echoed by a maths specialist who, referring to the low movitation of the less academically able, described the need to find 'a 1001 ways of performing the same operation in order that knowledge is retained'. In this regard some teachers voiced their need of greater theoretical knowledge. This was particularly so in the case of those teachers working with hearing impaired pupils or pupils who had pronounced learning difficulties. In the case of the former, teachers wanted to know how to communicate more effectively. Teachers working with the latter wanted to know about the 'precision approach' to teaching so that they could structure learning opportunities more fully.

Chapter Sixteen
Monitoring and Recording Progress

Continuous curricular assessment and development along with individual educational programmes and individual timetables are the means of producing a challenging, enriching and educationally sound curriculum (Head of slow learner department)

Monitoring progress in the context of integration

One of the features of special education that makes it special is that it is planned and systematic. The educational activities that pupils engage in are designed to match their particular needs and are presented in careful sequence. This places a premium on the regular monitoring of pupils' progress and maintaining records that chart this progress over time. Progress may be slow or attended by particular difficulty, and it is necessary at each stage of instruction to establish what pupils have mastered and what problems they still face before proceeding to the next stage.

These considerations apply to special education wherever it is conducted. There are a number of respects in which they are particularly important in integration. Pupils participating in schemes of integration will be receiving their education from a variety of sources – specialist teachers from a special centre or peripatetic service, ordinary class teachers and possibly other staff such as speech therapists. This is particularly likely to be the case at secondary level. This diversity of input means that a given pupil's achievements will be known to many teachers, and a system to ensure that information is shared becomes necessary. Moreover, a pupil's educational programme will be evolving in terms of the amount of integration; thus, if it is decided that a pupil should spend more time in ordinary classes this must be on the basis of information about progress to date. A further consideration pertaining to integration is that many teachers will have had limited experience of teaching pupils with special needs. As a consequence, they will be less sensitised to the indicators of progress and will probably be more dependent on formal recording systems than experienced special education teachers. Moreover by contrast with many colleagues in special schools, they will be teaching classes which preclude the detailed knowledge of individuals that might make a formal system less necessary.

This chapter deals with the monitoring of pupils' progress in integration programmes. Educational records are a principal means by which this is done, so much of the chapter is given over to the consideration of records – the different kinds that are maintained, who is responsible for keeping them, how they are constructed and the uses to which they are put.

It will be noted that our primary concern is with pupils' *educational* development and the records that impinge on that. Pupils with special needs are frequently involved with a variety of services – Area Health, Social Services, Educational Welfare – and the respective professionals will naturally maintain records that reflect the knowledge and concerns of their own specialisms. We are not concerned with such recording here other than to the extent that it impinges on educational progress. It should be clear also that when we talk of records we do so in an educational rather than an administrative sense. The Warnock Report proposed a system of *recording* pupils as in need of special educational provision (in place of being ascertained for special educational treatment in terms of the traditional categories of handicap). Such recording would be for administrative and service planning purposes however rather than the detailed organisation of individual pupils' programmes of work which is our concern here.

How progress is monitored

Monitoring the educational progress of pupils generally entails keeping records of some kind. For that reason much of this chapter has to do with records – their nature and construction and the uses to which they are put. There are further dimensions to the monitoring of progress however. It is important not to lose sight of the tacit knowledge that teachers have of their pupils or the clarification that can come from focused discussion of a pupil's circumstances, whether done in a case conference or in some other way. We begin this section with an account of the kinds of records, formal and informal, that we encountered. Then we discuss tacit knowledge as a resource to draw on when monitoring progress. Finally, case conferences and other focused discussion can bring records and tacit knowledge together and provide a further mechanism for reviewing progress.

Records

A distinction can be made between formal and informal means of gathering and recording information. The former consists of something akin to the standard record card which brings together a combination of factual detail (eg medical details, information on family background, school career to date, test results, school subjects taken) and more subjective, possibly evaluative comment (eg attitude to work or to school authorities, social and emotional development). The latter may be somewhat more objective as when based on structured observation or formal testing. Informal approaches to recording include occasional notes, diaries completed daily or weekly, home-school books, and working logbooks with detailed schemes of work developed jointly by teachers and visiting specialists such as speech therapists. These vary from casual jottings to relatively well-structured notes.

Most teachers are likely to avail of some kind of informal recording system, but what of formal inputs? How widespread is their use? The DES (1979) survey into the curriculum obtained some information on school records. Ninety per cent of LEAs reported that they required primary schools to maintain records, 'in most cases by means of a standardised format'. At secondary level some 80 per cent of LEAs required schools to keep records, though only about half this number stipulated that records should be standardised.

What the survey did not indicate was how well this requirement was translated into practice. Our limited evidence would suggest that the utilisation of formal records is far less widespread that this. Record keeping was an area of weakness in many of the schools we visited, or had still to be developed in a coherent way.

We have no reason to think that these schools were worse than average in their educational provision. Indeed, we noted elsewhere, it is likely that many were better than average. This apparent discrepancy with the DES survey could be explained by the fact that what many LEAs lay down as a standard formal record may turn out to be quite limited in practice. Also, while LEAs may require schools to maintain standardised records few will *oblige* them to do so.

i. Formal records

A number of schools had developed or were in the process of developing formal records. These were commonly devised within the school and showed great variation. A common core ran through them however and the more substantial examples contained most if not all of the following:

- details of family background
- salient medical details
- an indication of general level of intelligence
- an assessment of the individual's performance and/or potential, certainly in literacy and numeracy, possibly in other areas of the curriculum (especially at secondary level)
- information on personality, social development and behaviour
- resumé of progress over the year
- general comments.

Some examples may be helpful. The first was used with secondary pupils with learning difficulties. It comprised the following:

- the standard primary school report form
- outcome of psychological assessment; possibly, additional information and comment by the psychologist
- details of attainments in literacy and numeracy
- report on the department's leavers' programme (as appropriate)
- miscellaneous documentation (eg reviews forms, annual school report)

A second example comes from secondary level as well. It concerns physically handicapped pupils being integrated from the base of a special department. Initially formal records were limited. The PULTIBEC system[1] had been in use for a period but was

---

1. This is a four-point scale for rating children's functional disabilities devised by Lindon (1963) and described also by Anderson (1973).

abandoned when staff found its results inappropriate and of limited educational use. A senior member of staff assumed responsibility for developing a recording instrument by means of which details relevant to programme planning could be assembled on a cumulative basis. Entries come under the following headings:
 - details of family background
 - medical details, including a section on disorders likely to affect educational performance
 - reports on individual subjects
 - external examinations entered for or taken
 - notes on further education, employment, training or other post-school details
 - miscellaneous details (eg hobbies, interests).

A third example relates to physically handicapped pupils integrating from a special school into an adjacent comprehensive school. After some three years of informal monitoring of pupil progress, a more formal system was introduced. This comprises an assessment of each pupil along five dimensions:
 - ability
 - attainment
 - integration with class (ie social assimilation)
 - behaviour
 - attendance

This is carried out annually by the class teacher for each subject taken by the pupil. Entries are based on a five-point rating scale (outstanding, above average, average, cause for concern, in need of immediate attention), supplemented by general comments.

When made, the latter tended to brevity: 'Works hard but is a little slow, mixes well'; 'Cannot cope with the standard of work managed by the rest of the class'; 'Tries hard but finds it heavy going. Written work is not all that good'.

A further example relates to hearing impaired pupils in an individual integration programme. The formal record here consisted of a profile on each pupil maintained by the teacher of the deaf in conjunction with the pupil's support teacher. (The latter filled in a weekly diary which was relatively less structured.) This is a comprehensive record completed twice yearly. It comprises the following headings (these are illustrated with extracts from the profile maintained on one senior pupil aged 15 years 6 months, with a profound (100 db) hearing loss):

Use of hearing aids

Joe wears his aid throughout the day at school. This has been so since he received a post-aural. He does switch off in a noisy environment and sometimes forgets to switch on again.

Relationship with peers

Joe has no real friends in school although he is well accepted by his classes. He is usually alone at breaktimes. Joe's closer friends seem to be a group who live in flats near his home and it is with these boys and girls he spends his leisure time.

Attitude to school

Joe attends school regularly but is not really happy. He gets on well in class, but there is an apprehensiveness about breaktime. He was very pleased to be changed from his games group to another. I feel that there are a few boys who sometimes make things unpleasant for him.

Attitude to work

He is a very co-operative pupil and a pleasure to teach. He is always so delighted when he does well.

Spoken language

Joe's spoken language is poor and he does not communicate with his peers in sentences. When speaking to the support teacher he will use sentences and in this area he has improved considerably this year. When asking for anything he will always say, "Please may I have . . .". He uses words like "stupid" and "stupid fool" accurately. Whenever possible he will abbreviate "my leg . . hurt". When reminded he can give a full, accurate sentence.

I find that Joe is always keen to write about incidents and stories. When he reads his work back to you, he realises it does not make sense but he does not know how to put it right. This was Joe's account of the fighting at the Spurs football ground. "My friend is come to Hotspurs to the match. The lots of people was fighting it's the Tottenham. I watched two people at the Tottenham. Policeman was fighting two other man. Policeman was again. I saw lots of man and boy."

Reading

Joe does not read for pleasure. He will attempt any passage but his comprehension is poor. His family do take the trouble to draw his attention to news items in the newspapers.

Spelling
Excellent.

Maths
Joe has made very good progress in the present maths group. He is now in a set which is being prepared for a Mode Three CSE exam. His position in the set is about the middle and the teachers feel he is capable of passing the examination.

Other subjects
Brief notes on progress in each of these

General
Joe is very anxious to leave school as soon as possible and go to work. (NB This section was much fuller in other profiles.)

Auditory assessment
His audiogram is that of a profoundly deaf child and yet his listening skills are high average – C+ on a five point scale. He has over 90 per cent success on all vowels and diphthongs when presented purely auditorily through the speech trainer. On words and sentences his success rate can be over 80 per cent purely auditorily provided his choice is limited to 10 or below and the material itself is on visual display. He is very much aware of sound and voices around him. In spite of these, he does not fully make use of his ability to monitor his own speech. This is probably due to his deep rooted non-aural habits and disinterest in his hearing aid.

He is very alert and his lip-reading ability is quite good. He succeeds very well communicating with his peer group even though his speech and language have very many defects. He is however quite capable of much better speech.

Speech
Notes are made on each of: airflow; voice quality; resonance; fluency and rate of utterance; intonation pattern; pure vowels and diphthongs; consonants and blends.

Language
His language sessions are now with the support and speech teachers. Written language is very muddled. His spoken language pattern is usually word and phrase groups. His vocabulary is useful and quite extensive. His spelling is above average. He is quite secure on the stretches he has been revising the past six or so months in a

question/answer situation. But he does not use them freely in his oral communication nor in his written "free-expression". He hardly ever uses signs or gestures. His peer group at school use words, phrases and short sentences to communicate with him.

A final example comes from an infant age language unit. Reports from the teacher, educational psychologist and speech therapist cover: physical attributes; general development; general ability; educational attainment; language and speech. The extracts below are based on a boy aged 4.11 at the time of the report. It will be noted that the report has a strongly prescriptive element and is geared specifically to ongoing work with the child.

Physical Attributes

Brief notes on appearance, vision, hearing, co-ordination and other health factors.

General Development

Notes on motor development and toileting problem.

Relationships with children. *Mixes and plays well with the children in the group. Tom will stand up for himself when the need arises. He tends to play with the children from the Unit rather than those from other classes during play times in the yard.*

Relationships with adults. *He is confident in his dealings with adults. He communicates with adults by using mime if he can't make himself understood.*

General ability

When assessed in September 1977 at CA 3 years 6 months Tom appeared to be functioning at the 30 to 32 month level on visual perceptual and motor organisational tasks. His overall learning rate while in the Nursery appeared to be commensurate with this. When assessed at a CA of 4 years 11 months the findings of his previous assessment were confirmed, as on general performance items he was functioning up to the 4 years 6 months level.

Play. *Plays very well with the children in the Unit. He enjoys playing in the sand, with the toy train and toy farm and uses a lot of imagination playing with these toys. He also enjoys playing alone with these or other toys. Displays "double-knowledge" in his play.*

Educational Attainment

Reading. *Still at the pre reading stage. He does flash card work on words in Ladybird 1a but only recognises a few words.*

Handwriting. *Much improved pencil control. He can write over my writing fairly accurately. Lately he has started colouring-in with great care and showing a lot of pride in the end result.*

Number concept. *We are still concentrating on the amounts 1 and 2. He now recognises these number symbols.*

Teaching objectives. *To continue with the basic number and reading work. His powers of concentration need to be improved.*

Language and speech

Language comprehension.   Reynell Development Language Scales

Date	CA	Age level
12.12.77	3.9 yrs	4.9
15.12.78	2.9	3.03

Attention. *Tom still has difficulty integrating two channels of attention at the same time which makes Section 9 of the Reynell especially difficult for him.*

Expressive Language.

7.77	Age 3.5	*Very occasional single words reported, otherwise silent. Points or pulls when he needs something.*
11.77	Age 3.9	*No jargon – makes guttural sounds when attempting to communicate appropriate use of a few symbolic noises.*
4.78	Age 4.2	*Jargon and occasional single words emerging.*
7.78	Age 4.5	*First two-element utterances heard.*
Autumn 78	Age 4.5	*Therapy during Tom's first term in the Unit aimed*

     a.   to establish the consistent and meaningful use of jargon and single words in free communication and play.

     b.   to establish the use of certain two-element structures (i) in a structured situation (ii) spontaneously.

> *These aims were achieved by the end of term and staff noted such utterances as "put there" "that broke" and "draw car"*
>
> 2.79   *Age 4.11 Spontaneous use of extended two element utterances (eg "that one yours") is emerging. He still also uses a great deal of jargon.*

Use of language.   *Encouraging progress.*
Vocabulary.   *EPVT Standardised Score 96 per cent rank 39 (Feb 79)*
Phonology.   *In a formal labelling task Tom's 'sound system' is very deviant and immature. It is nearer the norm when he uses language spontaneously.*
Therapy aims   *i.   Work with puppets on the earliest acquired verb structures. (don't, can't, won't + verb)*
    ii.   Early work through structured play on Tom's sound system.

Summary – Child's needs and Future Aims
Tom has made good progress during his first term in the Unit, and his language although very delayed is beginning to move along reasonably normal development lines. 'Speech sounds' will probably need special attention. There is a great deal of catching up to do but Tom does have 2½ years to go before Junior School age. We have a good relationship with his family and they are very satisfied with the placement.

ii.   Informal records

Informal records differ from the above through being less structured and frequently less publicly available. They include notes, diaries, logbooks and home-school books. When properly maintained they serve a valuable function in their own right as well as contributing toward formal records. For the most part they are working documents for the teachers concerned whereby information on pupils is noted down at frequent intervals. This can result in a great deal of detail, over time, being assembled and provide the raw material for an eventual formal record.

a.   the teacher's diary This is a broad-ranging document which may consist of random entries based upon whatever catches a teacher's eye or may contain specific entries relating to a pupil's educational or social development. Most are completed on a regular basis, usually weekly or fortnightly, though in one school daily entries were made while elsewhere a teacher of infants with severe learning difficulties considered their progress so slow as to merit entries only once a term. The diaries were teachers' own notes but served many other purposes as well, eg a means of accountability to the head teacher or the source from which school records or reports for case conferences were compiled.

Most of the examples of diaries we saw followed some laid down structure. The school which described its approach in terms of "if anyone notices any progress, even the simplest, it's recorded" was untypical. Teachers were usually looking to comment upon particular aspects of development. For example, quite often the comments related closely to the teacher's weekly or termly goals for a pupil (eg pre-number, pre-reading, speech and language development, self-management, social behaviour and play). This format had been widely adopted among teachers in special classes providing for children with severe learning difficulties in one authority. Some of these had constructed a composite schedule, drawing upon an observation rating scale in use, existing tests and their own experience. Elsewhere a teacher dealing also with infants who had severe learning difficulties structured diary entries according to the following criteria:
- a language scheme that had been developed within the LEA specifically with this type of child in mind
- a number programme
- various reading schemes
- more subjective appraisals (eg increase in confidence or effort shown, self-help skills).

Generally speaking teachers had to find their own time for completing these diaries. The one exception was a school where the teacher was allocated two periods per week for the express purpose of updating individual case records. (She in fact made fortnightly entries, of a fairly detailed nature, on each pupil.) Otherwise, teachers had to do them whenever time permitted, usually out of school time. Those who made detailed entries reported spending a great deal of time on the task.

b. the working logbook Some teachers collaborated with visiting specialists – speech therapists, physiotherapists, psychologists – in maintaining a form of continuous assessment that was considerably more specific than the teacher's diary. These entailed jointly agreed programmes of work with specific and clearly stated objectives. As the teacher or in some cases the ancillary carried out the programme there was an inbuilt monitoring of progress through checking whether or not the objectives had been reached. Take, for example, the collaboration between teacher and speech therapist in two classes for infants with communication disorders. The speech therapist carried out detailed assessment of each child covering: language comprehension; expressive language; and speech intelligibility. When a weakness or disorder was identified the therapist drew up an appropriate programme. Therapist and teacher jointly maintained a work book in which both short and long term aims were recorded, together with the specific activities of the daily therapy programme (eg games to help establish the use of verb-plus-object utterances). Both made notes of how each child coped with the work, and recorded any progress made; these then served as the basis for weekly discussion.

c.   *the home-school book*   Home-school books were in use in a number of locations. These took many forms and were used in various ways. One of the purposes they served was to assist in the monitoring of progress. Whether they were loosely structured with casual jottings or comprised specific activities for parents to carry out with their children and report on, they provided a cumulative record of certain aspects of development. If no structure was laid down and people made entries of their choice the book tended to reflect what was perceived to be significant at a given point in time. Looked at from this perspective, home-school books sometimes gave a revealing account of how the pupil and his circumstances were viewed and how the views varied over time. When home-school books were used in a systematic way, with specific exercises being set, parents would note down what they had done and how well the child had managed the tasks assigned. This too built up into a cumulative record of performance in specific and well-defined areas, with the bonus of incorporating parents' insights and a measure of the pupil's performance outside the school setting.

Other means

Keeping records is the principal means of monitoring pupils' progress. There are other means as well: drawing on teachers' tacit knowledge of their pupils; holding case conferences and assessment meetings; and engaging in focused discussion.

i.   Tacit knowledge

No discussion of how progress is monitored should overlook the fact that teachers possess a great deal of tacit knowledge about their pupils. This is born out of close contact where they see pupils and interact with them in a variety of situations. Their records and diaries may seem vague or loosely structured, and their oral accounts may be no more precise or informative. Teachers are not usually lost for words when asked to talk about a pupil; most will be readily forthcoming with a mixture of facts, anecdotes and subjective impressions. If asked specific questions however they are commonly able to answer them precisely and turn out to know the pupils well so long as means of extracting the knowledge can be found.

Systematic teaching approaches of the kind that are increasingly in use with pupils who have special needs go counter in some respects to any reliance on tacit knowledge. This does not mean that it is to be ignored or devalued. Even if they keep very detailed records teachers will always know far more about their pupils than they can ever write down. What is necessary is that teachers become aware of this knowledge they have and learn to use it appropriately. Rendering accessible knowledge which is held in tacit form can be exceedingly difficult but also highly rewarding. It can help teachers to become aware of how they construe children, how they relate to them, what they attach significance to and what they ignore. It can provide them with a means of examining what they take for granted about their pupils and perhaps help in seeing them as individuals in their own right who are not encompassed by any set of labels or categories, no matter how refined, and who change in all sorts of ways. Above all, it unlocks teachers' store of intuitive knowledge about children and makes it available in a public way to the monitoring of progress.

ii.   Case conferences

A further means of monitoring progress is the assessment meeting or case conference where various people involved with a given pupil come together to review his or her progress and circumstances in a comprehensive way. Such meetings are important for several reasons. First, they provide an opportunity for bringing tacit knowledge and records together. Records will normally have been circulated beforehand and may provide a basis for discussion. Such discussion will serve both to clarify the written documents and extract the tacit knowledge that people have. Ideally, the interplay between these will generate new insights and lead to a better understanding of the pupil's situation. Secondly, documents prepared beforehand and a report from the meeting combine to form a comprehensive record of a pupil's progress. Thirdly, by formalising the monitoring progress into a public event they ensure that thought is given to it, even if only at long intervals. Holding a case conference may lead to records being filled in that would otherwise never get done and encourage staff to deliberate about pupils beforehand. In any case, the meeting itself will focus attention specifically on individuals' progress. Fourthly, assessment meetings provide a forum for bringing different viewpoints together. This may be staff from different professional backgrounds – medicine, speech therapy, educational psychology and so on. Such focusing of different backgrounds is especially important in integration programmes where pupils may be receiving their education from many sources. If there is a range of staff who encounter a pupil in different situations, these meetings make it possible for them to pool their experiences and build a comprehensive picture of the pupil's achievements and limitations.

Assessment meetings of this kind are relatively common especially when pupils are coming to the end of their time in school or are being considered for transfer to a placement where less support will be available. As noted elsewhere, some professionals were unhappy about the amount of time these meetings took, and it seemed clear that case conferences frequently fell a long way short of realising their potential for enchancing the monitoring process. Some examples may be cited where this did happen. The first occurred in an integration programme where pupils with varying degrees of vision loss were fully integrated into an ordinary primary school. Their progress was reviewed twice yearly at a round-table gathering of representatives from Education (school staff, educational psychologist), Area Health (school medical officer) and Social Services (specialist social workers for the blind). The educational psychologist chaired these sessions and sought to encourge formal interaction. A notable feature was the direct involvement of classroom teachers; this enabled them to present their views directly rather than through other people, as is customary. There was wide-ranging discussion on how individual pupils were faring. Teachers contributed most to this, recalling impressions over a period of months and telling anecdotes. Discussion could be rambling and the information arising disorganised, but it was focused on the pupil in a concrete way. This enabled the educational psychologist and others to ask specific questions and build up a coherent picture of the pupil's progress.

The second example came from a language class for communication disordered pupils. The conference here was attended by school staff (head and teacher in charge), educational psychologist, speech therapist, school medical officer and paediatric neurologist. By contrast with the previous example, detailed reports were prepared and circulated beforehand, so that discussion tended to be more structured. The reports – prepared jointly by teacher, speech therapist and psychologist – provided detailed information on educational attainment, language and speech, general development and any physical problems. The information put forward in this way was appraised and supplemented by those attending the case conference.

iii. Focused discussion

The case conference is a particular, formalised example of a more general process, viz focused discussion. This can take place when two teachers meet in the staff room, when a peripatetic physiotherapist talks with a teacher or welfare assistant at the end of a visit, and in many other ways. The essence of the process is that two or more staff who have dealings with a pupil focus their attention on him or her to compare notes, air their views and so on. In some ways the process seems so basic and so likely to be an integral part of the teacher's daily round as not to be worth remarking on. Our impression however is that this is very far from being the case. In many staffrooms the only discussion that takes place on individual pupils is when they attract attention in some way, usually by misdemeanours, and is either flippant or despairing. It may even be considered bad form to attempt professional discussion of pupils; lunch and break times are for recovering from the little blighters!

In one school where such discussion did take place regularly and was considered very valuable, the process was formalised to a degree. The staff of the special department (for pupils with learning difficulties) met over one lunch time each week to discuss two of the department's pupils. The aim was to review progress, note any outstanding difficulties and devise appropriate teaching objectives. In the course of a year it was planned to hold a mini-case conference of this kind on every pupil.

Constructing records

In this section we examine the construction of records – who is responsible for maintaining them, how frequently they are up-dated and on what basis they are compiled.

Who assumes responsibility?

Pupils taking part in integration programmes may be receiving their education from a variety of sources – special educators, main school teachers and visiting specialists. In some cases their time is spent between a school and a special centre which is relatively isolated from it, or even between two separate schools. In these latter cases especially there can be a real danger of pupils' educational experience being fragmented through being un-coordinated and through lack of an overall view of an individual's progress. It is of paramount importance that somebody maintains an overall record of development, noting who has done what and with what outcomes. One head of a special school engaged in a programme of integration with a nearby comprehensive school pointed to the difficulties here. There were some 30 pupils spending varying amounts of time in the secondary school. Since each was timetabled on an individual basis, keeping track of the programmes in the comprehensive school was a demanding task. Likewise, in the special school they followed individual programmes dependent in part on what was available within the special school's secondary department when pupils were not at the comprehensive. Monitoring these programmes and putting the two sets of programmes together for each integrating pupil made for formidable difficulties. The same problem can arise in smaller integration programmes as well. Thus, the teacher in charge of a special class may have full information on what pupils are doing in the class but may know very little about what they are doing or what progress they are making when they attend classes in main school. This is a particular problem when the receiving classes are large and teachers have little time for individual attention or when pupils attend too many different classes for the special class teacher to have easy liaison with all of them.

In principle, there is no difficulty over ensuring that an adequate overall record is maintained. Responsibility for the task will normally fall to the head of department or teacher in charge of the special centre or to the special school head if pupils are integrating from a special school. These are people with numerous responsibilities however and many other calls on their time. The logistics of gathering the information are considerable, and they are not helped by the common failure to allow adequate time for the task and identify clear lines of responsibility in respect of it. There were some examples of good practice. In one large secondary department the task was formally assigned to the deputy head of the department who was able to carve out time for the task and achieve positive results. In some primary schools with a small special class, the head's interest and demands for progress reports served a valuable function both in stimulating activity and in legitimating the special class teacher's information gathering.

Frequency of updating

Formal records tend to be kept on an annual basis. They were completed termly in a few schools, while in several cases entries were only made at intermittent intervals during a pupil's school career, possibly once at the end of the first year and again just before leaving school. Informal records were, as noted above, updated with frequencies that varied from daily to termly or less often.

Many teachers and others professed dissatisfaction at the relative infrequency of much recording. There was no possibility of building up a cumulative picture of a pupil's progress, and much of the information was so out of date as to be misleading. Our impressions from inspecting record folders concur strongly with this. In many cases there was no current information and folders had little of relevance to pupils' present educational circumstances.

Teachers defended this state of affairs on the grounds of lack of time, or claimed that this was an area of practice still being developed. There was another view however expressed forcibly by a teacher of pupils with severe learning difficulties: 'They don't change very much in six months. There is nothing very much when you come to write it down". Again, "You don't get very much progress and it's not fast enough to do a report every term". This goes counter to contemporary thinking on the importance of refining teaching objectives and ensuring that pupils work through learning sequences whose steps match this achievement. The view illustrated above is not an isolated one however. While few would express it so directly, there was an impression from many others that the frequency of their record keeping simply reflected the fact that they found little to be recorded.

Basis of records

A comprehensive record is a complex document. It comprises information of different kinds that must be obtained from their respective sources. This means that a variety of tactics and information bases must be drawn upon in constructing and updating records. They include informal records and personal notes, test results, outcomes from setting specific tasks or doing task analyses, observations, and information received from people other than teachers. Informal records have been discussed above and will not be referred to further here.

Test results are one of the most obvious sources of information for a record. Tests of attainment were quite common in the records we inspected. Reading ages based on one of the standard tests were extremely common, sometimes being virtually the only piece of information in the file. It was less common to find detailed measurement of number skills or indeed of language development in a more comprehensive way. One example that stood out was a special department for pupils with learning difficulties where all new entrants were scanned in various areas – reading, spelling, number, free writing, perceptual skills and motor skills – as a precursor to drawing up specific programmes of work. Thereafter, pupils were screened annually for reading ability and a comprehensive assessment of language development was carried out.

Teachers' use of tests was virtually confined to tests of attainment. They are precluded by lack of training – and in many cases inclination as well – from using the bulk of psychological tests. This might be considered unsatisfactory in those many locations where access to psychological expertise was limited and teachers were effectively on their own in monitoring pupils' progress. A number of teachers were particularly conscious of this in relation to social and emotional development where they felt that their own observations could usefully be supplemented by some systematic data such as a relevant test would supply.

Many teachers were reluctant to set too much store by test scores. There was a feeling that while tests had a scientific aura to them they added little to what the experienced teacher would pick up on the basis of regular working contact with pupils. One teacher who spoke dismissively of what he saw as the simple-minded use of vocabulary and reading tests outlined a strategy based on setting pupils specific tasks in a systematic way. He assembled a wide range of materials on language and number and developed tasks, graded in difficulty, for pupils to try out. By observing how they progressed through them he obtained information on their abilities and achievements that was highly relevant to developing individual remediation programmes and monitoring progress on them.

A further source of information on progress comes from the task analyses associated with precision teaching approaches. Information gathered in this way has the merit of being closely related to the content of teaching. The essence of the approach is to establish the area(s) in which the pupil is having difficulty, analyse the required learning activities into small and carefully sequenced steps, identify where the pupil is functioning along this sequence and elaborate a structured learning programme from that point. There is an inbuilt monitoring mechanism as the pupil moves from one objective to the next in working through the programme. Not only does this give the teacher a means of checking on progress but it also provides feedback that can alert the teacher to the need to repeat certain work, alter strategy or even break the work into smaller steps.

Teachers' observation of pupils is clearly an important source of information and can contribute to records in a very direct way. While observation of any kind will yield *some* information and will probably enrich teachers' tacit knowledge of their pupils, there is much to be gained from structuring observations and focusing on matters of pre-determined interest. In one location physiotherapists instructed classroom ancillaries in monitoring the effects of any treatment the physically handicapped pupils in their charge received. They also sensitised them to more general matters that might be significant and should be reported – bad posture, sudden appearance of a limp, emergent pressure sores and so on. This focused the ancillaries' observation in a most valuable way so that they noticed far more than previously and recorded their observations in a useful way. One physiotherapist described it as like "having another pair of eyes".

The process of structuring observations was taken a step further in another authority where an educational psychologist devised an observation rating scale for use with children who had severe learning difficulties. This was based on a content analysis of teachers' reports as well as on published developmental scales and general psychometric experience. It covered five main areas: general presentation; degree of independence; language development; social integration; and learning aptitude. Each area was broken down into fine detail so as to lend itself to being filled in on the basis of teachers' observation. The scale was described as 'an observation tool with a classification system to monitor developmental process and guide teaching and management'. Its aim was to give teachers a means of making their routine observations more systematic and comprehensive and presenting them in a public way.

A good deal of information can also come from people other than teachers. This may consist of the results of formal testing as carried out for example by speech therapists and educational psychologists, or it may be of a more general nature. Speech therapists tended to use tests (eg Reynell Developmental Language Scales, LARSP Profile developed by Crystal and colleagues) in an instrumental way to assist in developing and monitoring individual language programmes. This was less common among educational psychologists. Lack of time – and sometimes, it must be said, patterns of working – led to many situations where teachers were simply presented with test scores. Many teachers were unimpressed by this. One recalled his astonishment at discovering on having a change of psychologist how useful a psychological report could be. Another claimed: "All I want very often is a little bit of advice . . . I don't want a full scale issue made of it . . . (simply) is there anything you could suggest that we haven't thought of . . .".

The information from other people was not confined to test scores of course. Reports from social workers, medical officers and other professionals involved with the pupil were sometimes available, though difficulty in obtaining medical information even when of direct educational significance was frequently reported. Parents supplied a good deal of information through home-school books or personal contact with the school staff. When pupils engaged in work experience programmes, employers were asked to prepare reports on progress or were interviewed by teachers at the end of the programme.

Use made of records

Educational records serve many purposes. Their cumulative detail provides a picture of a pupil's development over time. They offer a solid base to any discussion of accountability. They give a structure that enables the teacher to think and talk about the pupil in a systematic way. They can reinforce the teacher's sense of doing a professional job of work. In this section we discuss two particular contexts in which records were used: developing and implementing the curriculum; and educational decision making.

Developing and implementing the curriculum

Maintaining records can take a great deal of time, as some of the examples above will have shown. Little purpose is served by gathering information and investing time and energy in developing detailed check-lists which are not put to use. If the expenditure of time is to be justified, especially in teachers' eyes, the outcomes must be relevant to the work of the classroom. Teachers need to be convinced that maintaining comprehensive and detailed records has a pay-off for their work with pupils before they will make the requisite time available.

In point of fact, it is clear that properly structured and maintained records can make a major contribution both to curriculum planning and teaching practice. Our first example concerns a collaborative development in a language unit where staff sought to relate teaching and assessment to each other in an integral way. The children in question had a variety of communi-

cation disorders. Staff – teacher, speech therapist, educational psychologist – worked out a detailed profile covering the different areas of development. It comprised the following headings:
1. background information
2. language comprehension/expression
3. learning skills
4. reading
5. writing
6. number
7. art/music
8. physical activities
9. science
10. social/emotional skills.

Each heading was further broken down into a series of sub-headings. This led to a finely graded set of behavioural objectives that followed a developmental sequence. When this was completed for a given pupil, it constituted both a comprehensive statement of present achievements and a detailed curricular programme. If the set of objectives was properly sequenced, then teaching and monitoring became part of the same activity. Teaching was geared to specific objectives, devised by assessing present achievements, and moving on from them only when success had been achieved. While establishing the requisite breakdown of activities can be extremely difficult – and proved to be so in this case – this approach offered promise of a detailed monitoring that was closely related to the curriculum.

A second example comes from a comprehensive school catering for pupils with learning difficulties. When pupils first come to the school the head of the basic studies department assembles information from their previous schools as well as comments and possibly the results of formal testing by an educational psychologist. He also conducts his own assessment, using a diagnostic battery of reading tests. It is on the basis of this information that individual programmes are formulated for each pupil. These incorporate well-defined objectives whose achievement can be noted as pupils work through their programmes.

The link between programme planning, teaching and monitoring progress is highly developed in America. Public

Law 94-142, the Education for All Handicapped Children Act, emphasised the importance of detailed curriculum planning and instituted a formal requirement that schools draw up an individualised educational programme (IEP) for each handicapped pupil. This is a detailed statement of objectives and means of reaching them, with the monitoring of progress as an integral element. It is prepared by a multi-disciplinary group including parents and constitutes the plan of work to which everybody involved with the pupil is committed. Developing and implementing IEPs takes a great deal of time, and there has been criticism of the degree of formality, extending to legal sanction, associated with this aspect of Public Law 94-142. What is beneficial however is the stress on careful planning and on ensuring that the requisite documentation is maintained that will make it possible to measure progress toward the planning targets.

Educational decision making

When pupils with special needs come to the end of infant or junior schooling it is common practice to conduct a comprehensive review of progress in order to determine the most suitable next placement. This becomes particularly important when integration is at issue since there may be real choices to make. The occasion of transfer often provides an opportunity to move a pupil from a less integrated setting to a more integrated one. For this to be done on a sound basis it is necessary to have full information on the pupil's progress to date. Comprehensive and regularly updated records are the means by which this is achieved. They document his or her response to the present educational setting and provide a sound basis for making decisions about future placements.

In integration programmes placement decisions of this kind are not confined to the formal points of transfer between the different stages of schooling. There are two questions which must be kept in mind continually: Is the present placement appropriate? and Is the pupil ready for greater integration? In some respects, integration programmes constitute an experiment either because the particular model is new or because it has to operate within limited resources. Thus, in one programme severely and profoundly deaf pupils were being integrated on an individual basis; in another children with communication disorders were attending a language class for which admission criteria were still evolving; in a third, a secondary department for pupils with learning difficulties sought to extend its provision and cater for as wide a range of special needs as possible. In all of these cases it was necessary to keep pupils' progress under close review in case the placement was inappropriate either in relation to the complexity of need or the resources that were available. So in the case of the hearing impaired programme there was extensive monitoring by formal record – weekly diary maintained by the support teacher plus a very detailed profile completed every six months by the teacher of the deaf in conjuction with the support teacher – and by regular meetings and discussion among the teachers concerned. In this way it was possible to keep a close eye on pupils' progress, varying the amount of support as necessary and withdrawing a pupil from the programme if the placement proved to be inappropriate.

The second question relates to varying the amount of integration. The practice in many cases was to build up in a gradual way the amount of time a pupil spent integrated. Information obtained from teachers on academic progress, social adjustment and general coping would provide the basis for decisions on extending integration. This process was well organised in one language unit where all pupils spent one day a week in their own neighbourhood schools. Thus, a special school for children with communication disorders which sought to transfer them to ordinary schooling as soon as possible attached great importance to obtaining information from the recipient schools. Transfer was phased over a period of time, and class teachers were asked to report on progress during the trial period. This information went toward the decision on whether the transfer should be completed or not. Likewise, in a language class transfer to ordinary schooling depended in part on class teachers' reports on how pupils fitted in to ordinary classes during trial periods.

In summary, the monitoring of pupils' progress which is so important in special education assumes an additional dimension in integration programmes. Maintaining detailed and frequently updated records is one way of achieving this, though not the only one. Informal records, structured discussion of individuals and assessment meetings can all contribute by amassing salient facts, unlocking teachers' detailed knowledge of the pupils they teach and generating fresh insights through the exchange of perspectives. When records are structured in terms of curriculum objectives they can be of direct use to the teacher and guide classroom practice in a concrete way. Compiling and maintaining records in this way can be a demanding task. The time is well spent however if pupils' progress is monitored more effectively and the feedback obtained enables teachers to meet their special needs better.

PART SIX

The Social Dimension

Chapter Seventeen
Social Interaction

A primary goal of integration in many people's eyes is to facilitate contact between pupils with special needs and their peers. Even if complete functional integration is not possible and pupils cannot be taught together there is a benefit, it is argued, in the social interaction that integration arrangements permit. For these benefits to be realised however it is necessary that the interactions take place. Placing two groups side by side is not to guarantee that there will be basic contact, much less significant interaction, between them.

In this chapter we want to look at the interaction between pupils with special needs and their peers that was observed in the integration programmes we studied. (The nature of the interactions and the relationships that developed are considered further in the following chapter.) We seek to shed some light on the factors that governed this interaction. There would seem to be quite simple changes to be made in some cases that would improve social interaction. Finally, we consider whether the school can intervene to promote interaction between pupils and report on one experiment where this was done successfully.

Opportunities for interaction

We begin by looking at the opportunities for interaction that there are at the different stages of the school day: before and after school; assembly; registration and form periods; classroom; breaks; and lunch.

Before school and after

Most pupils attending special schools are brought by special transport to and from school, because of physical disability, distances involved or inability to cope with public transport. When these pupils attend ordinary schools it provides the opportunity to rethink special transport policies. The distance criterion is no longer relevant in some cases and indeed we found examples of pupils making their way to school independently as a direct result of an integration programme. It has to be said that there are occasions when special transport is necessary, occasions when it is probably desirable but open to question, and occasions when it is unnecessary and not in the pupil's best interests.

We refer below to the implications of transport arrangements for pupils' development of independence. Here the concern is with social contact. When pupils are brought to school by special transport there is not only no opportunity for contact with other pupils on the way to and from school but their distinctness is reinforced in a very public way. If, as in the case of the hearing impaired, there is no physical reason that is obvious to other pupils why they should have special transport when everybody else has to come by bicycle or on the bus, resentment and unwillingness to have much contact can follow. The transport is usually door-to-door: pupils are picked up from their own home and dropped at a suitable entrance to the school, often at the special centre. This is convenient of course, necessary even for the seriously disabled, but pupils might be less isolated by the travel arrangements if they were picked up and dropped at bus stops for instance. Also, other pupils are not allowed to use the special transport even if there is a good reason for them to do so. One authority refused to allow the brother of a physically handicapped boy to travel (to the same school) in the taxi provided for the latter.

The isolation imposed by special transport can be compounded by further factors such as reception arrangements, length of school day and constraints imposed by taxi schedules. In some cases pupils were dropped at the special centre and taken straight in by a waiting – and conscientious – ancillary. A little less conscientiousness and the pupil could spend some time with peers before school began! The latter did happen in some cases but usually when pupils came to school independently. In some schools pupils with special needs had a shorter school day than their peers because the special centre or special school to which they belonged started later and finished earlier than the main school. It is not clear what educational justification there is for this anomaly but as far as integration is concerned it is an anachronism that needs to be disposed of as promptly as possible, not least because it totally precludes any possibility of contact at the beginning and end of the school day. When the school day is not officially shorter, it is frequently curtailed unofficially courtesy of the transport providers. There were numerous instances of special transport arriving consistently late (and – what is more disruptive to the business of teaching – inconsistently late) with pupils having to be ready for departure before the official end of the school day.

Some examples may help. In a special centre catering for some 30 hearing impaired pupils of secondary age a teacher of the deaf estimated that most of them would be capable of making their own way to school by bus. In fact, *one* pupil was coming to school independently. Some teachers deliberately sought to wean pupils from special transport, both for the independence it promoted and the social opportunities it created. One success story may be noted. It involves not special transport but maternal protectiveness, which can have the same shielding effect.

Jenny is a severely retarded teenager attending a special unit attached to a comprehensive school. She has always been taken to school by her mother even though she lived within walking distance. A teacher persuaded Jenny's mother to try out a programme that would gradually build up to her making the journey on her own. This was carefully worked out and put into practice, so successfully that Jenny now makes the journey without any adult surveillance. Moreover, every morning Jenny calls by a friend who also attends the school; a number of other girls congregate there and they all walk to school together.

A further constraint arises from the fact that integrating pupils are frequently not at their neighbourhood school, whether because it is unsuitable or because they attend a special centre with a wide catchment area. A number of parents found this problematic on two counts: their children missed out on the casual 'street corner' contact with schoolmates that can be important in making and cementing relationships; and they were strangers to their neighbourhood peers, doubly so indeed, through attending a different school and through the isolation imposed by their handicapping condition.

Assembly

School assembly is a feature of the British educational system of extraordinary scope and diversity. The school assembles in whole or in part to worship God, sing nursery rhymes, have improving thoughts, hear announcements, receive merit awards and listen to the headmaster reminiscing about his school days! Any or all of these can feature in the list of activities that go to make up school assembly. The list is readily expanded so that assemblies have a multiplicity of functions. This makes them a prime vehicle for promoting integration, and indeed almost every school we visited claimed to integrate pupils with special needs for assembly. This was so even for severely retarded pupils whose contact with peers otherwise was negligible.

The appeal of assembly as a mechanism for promoting integration is that it makes, or can be made to make, minimal demands on participants. There are no formal teaching objectives; communication and mobility skills are not imperative; and presence can be totally passive. Also, it allows of enormous flexibility where any pupil can be given a role, a role moreover that he or she enacts however briefly in front of the entire school. A fundamental reason for including pupils with special needs in assembly is that it is an activity of the whole school, and if a special group is seen as part of the school in any sense it should not be excluded.

There were a few instances where special education teachers decided not to have their pupils participate in main school assembly. In one case a teacher judged the assembly to be long and frequently boring, as well as being far too regimented for his pupils. It was not an occasion where any real contact took place. Many of his pupils grew restive during it and rather than have them draw unfavourable attention to themselves it was decided to refrain from attending. A unit for hearing impaired had a majority of pupils who understood little if anything of the verbal component of assembly. It was felt that they gained little from it so a separate assembly was established for them.

These examples force one to ask: What benefit do pupils gain from attending assembly? and in the present context: How meaningful is it to speak of social contact? The answer to the general question must remain as above, viz assembly is an expression, however imperfect, of the school's corporate identity and attendance at it reinforces that one has a share in that identity. As regards social contact, this clearly depends on local arrangements. There is perhaps little to be said for the purely locational

integration that occurs in formal assemblies where pupils with
special needs join the serried ranks of the main school. (When this
occurs one would hope that they do not form a further separate
rank, that emphasises their differences, but are interspersed
naturally with their peers. Regrettably this was not always so.)

As an example of a situation where there was some contact we
describe an assembly that we observed in a primary school which
had a special class for severely retarded pupils.

*Three pupils from the special class accompanied an ancillary to
the school hall where the rest of the pupils were already assembled,
squatting informally but quietly on the floor. Little notice was taken
of the pupils as they came in although two of them had the facial
characteristics of Down's Syndrome. They took their place on the
floor quietly – for the moment – at the back of the other pupils.*

*The assembly comprised a song, story, another song, a piece
prepared and delivered by pupils, and ended with a song. The
atmosphere was lively and provoked enthusiastic response from the
pupils at several points. One of the retarded pupils sat quite still
throughout. The others moved about, sliding up and down the
floor, stroking other children, and generally hugging each other and
any other children within reach. They certainly enjoyed the situation
a great deal although they did not take much notice of what was
going on. The ancillary accompanying them intervened only when
they moved too far from her and then in a low key way. There was a
certain amount of curious attention from pupils nearby who
watched their antics but nobody was bothered or unduly distracted
by them, and the assembly was not held up in any way because of
them* (Extract from field notes).

Apart from the formality, some practical factors hindered
pupils' easy participation in assembly. When special transport
came late pupils arrived during assembly – and disrupted it – or
missed it altogether. One school rescheduled assembly to mid-
morning to allow for this. In another school it was necessary to
descend a few steps into the body of the hall; wheelchair users
could not do this so they were lined around the perimeter in an
unfortunate isolation. Finally, very large gatherings tended to
make for formality and low participation (by all pupils). When
smaller assemblies are held, eg year groups rather than the whole
school, it is easier for all to participate and to achieve something
more than locational integration.

Registration and form periods

When pupils attend a special centre there is the option of registering them with the special centre or with a form in the parent school. The importance of this is that in secondary schools especially the form frequently serves as a core social grouping. Pupils may belong to the same form throughout their school careers. Even when streamed into different bands or following different subjects they still meet as a form at least once a day and may have some basic teaching in their form group. Some schools attached great importance to assigning pupils with special needs to registration groups in the main school. This was so that they would identify with that group and possess a point of reference in the main school. It also led to the form group accepting the particular pupil or pupils as one of its own members. Pupils are more likely to retain this identity even if they are withdrawn for lessons. One school where this seemed to work well had a ruling whereby not more than two pupils associated with the special centre were allocated to any one form. The form constituted an important point of reference in that school, with pupils spending a considerable portion of their first year in the form and having registration and form periods thereafter.

More often than not however pupils with special needs were registered separately from the main school. In some cases this seemed to reflect the fact that the special group were seen as a unit, and it either did not occur to people or make sense to them to disperse pupils throughout the school for registration purposes. The natural point of reference, it was argued, for pupils with special needs was the group of their peers with comparable needs, and they needed to achieve an identity with this group rather than with main school groups. Other reasons advanced for maintaining the separateness revolved around pastoral and in one case medical care. Specialist staff saw the registration period as an important opportunity to chat informally to their pupils. Particularly when the latter were integrated for most of the school day this might be the only opportunity to keep in contact. With physically handicapped pupils there may be a need to monitor medication and treatment; hygiene, toileting procedures and general body care all need to be checked. The registration period provides a regular opportunity for these activities and again with pupils who spend most of the day in the main school it may be the only opportunity.

One secondary school catering for a number of physically handicapped pupils initially registered as many as possible with mainstream classes. One pupil was bullied by able-bodied peers however and it transpired that this had been going on for quite some time before it came to notice. Specialist staff were concerned about this and believed that they would have discovered what was going on and been able to intervene much earlier had the pupil been registered in the special centre. As a consequence it was decided to discontinue the practice of registering physically handicapped pupils in the main school and, at least for their first year, register them in the special centre where it was felt they would receive better pastoral care.

Finally, in one school pupils were prevented from registering in main school because of transport regulations. Special transport was available only to pupils who were formally on the roll of a special centre. We do not know how widespread this practice is but it seems a most curious one and a further example of transport arrangements intruding on educational ones.

Classroom

Teaching periods are not primarily for the purpose of facilitating social interaction! There are many opportunities for legitimate social contact during lessons however quite aside from the social activities that pupils set up independently of the teacher. Pupils may be working on group projects where each has an assigned role and structured interaction is essential. Discussions may involve the whole class. Experimental work may necessitate working together or sharing equipment. Craft and practical work generally is frequently done against a background of casual chatter. We observed instances where pupils with special needs were working side by side with other pupils and included in conversation quite naturally.

Specific preparation may be necessary to ensure that pupils are not isolated in the classroom and that opportunities for contact with peers are taken. One teacher of a group of hearing impaired pupils described how she worked toward interaction by preparing pupils gradually: "You have to work on both groups of pupils to mix socially". This included matters as basic as ensuring that they knew each others' names. Such preparation was held to be especially important in the case of the hearing impaired because of the possibility of misunderstanding. In one school "the hearing impaired think they are being ridiculed when they are not – they get on the defensive and sign something that is wrongly taken by other pupils". References were made also to the fact that pupils with special needs can be spoiled and miss out on the give and take of other pupils' experience – "they are constantly getting things all the time, they don't think they have to give anything back". An example may illustrate the difficulties.

Robert tried to speak to some of the boys behind him in class but he obviously could not get over to them what he wanted and they giggled a bit. Robert was put out and went off to sharpen his pencil before coming back to try again. He still could not get over what he wanted and one boy quite reasonably asked him to repeat his request. However, Robert took this amiss and started to swear. The other boy's comment was: "See, he always curses no matter what; that's what gets on my nerves about him".

It is clear that these attitudes have to be worked on and pupils with special needs must learn what is acceptable and what is not acceptable behaviour when with their peers. Otherwise, the above is likely to be the result. Alternatively, the situation obtaining in another school may arise where a pupil from the special centre went to maths lessons in the main school – "as far as I know she doesn't speak to anyone". Even worse the situation below may occur.

'Wayne's performance in a mixed ability setting is so very poor that he feels the need to compensate by acts of foolish bravado and boastful outbursts. Consequently his peers 'take the mickey' in a merciless fashion. Wayne responds with more outbursts of boasting which aggravate the situation further . . . Wayne demonstrates his inability to concentrate by making animal noises or by shouting out . . . this disruptive behaviour annoys his peers who retaliate by tormenting him' (Extract from school report).

Easy contact between pupils with special needs and their peers can be hindered by the presence of ancillaries or support teachers in the classroom. It may be necessary for them to be accompanied in this way if they are to be in the mainstream classroom at all or benefit from it, but the presence of an adult who is concerned exclusively with them can reduce their interactions with peers and work against their assimilation into the class. Main school teachers pointed to a number of instances where this was happening and preferred to be without ancillary support for that reason, as did some pupils. Some ancillaries sought to minimise the interference arising from their presence by adopting a more general role in the classroom, intervening for the pupil in their charge only when quite essential and otherwise helping out with all pupils as instructed by the teacher. The support teacher role for hearing impaired pupils posed particular problems because on occasion a high degree of intervention was necessary. Sometimes it was felt that this could be provided less obtrusively outside the classroom and pupils were accordingly withdrawn for separate attention.

The presence of more than one pupil with special needs in the class can also result in less interaction with other classmates. One girl acknowledged, "We don't mix with them, we talk with them but stay together because we are in pairs". Teachers also observed that because of this "they have no need to talk to the (main school) kids". An example of such an occasion is given below.

John and Paul are both physically handicapped pupils who are integrated into the same science lesson. They sit together on the front bench and as it is a small class – there are 12 other pupils – they are well separated from any other pupils. Indeed, apart from two girls, they are the only pupils sitting on that side of the room. The lesson involves setting up an experiment and there is ample space for moving around the classroom and interacting with others. Inter-actions made by both John and Paul were noted. Although chatting happily together they never exchanged a word or glance with any other pupil. Only the teacher had contact with them (Extract from field notes).

Break

Official breaktimes are of course the occasion par excellence for social interaction. This is when pupils are freed from lessons and for the most part from adult supervision. They interact socially in various ways, in accordance with their age, facilities available and so on. As far as pupils with special needs are concerned, their participation will be governed by the nature of their handicapping conditions, the physical environment of the school, and practical factors such as whether the special centre has its break at the same time as the rest of the school.

Interaction between pupils with special needs and their peers was more common and occurred more spontaneously at younger ages. (The relevance of age to pupils' perceptions and attitudes is developed in chapter 19.) Younger children seemed less sensitive to differences, and possibly did not notice handicapping conditions as much as older pupils. Also, the disparity in development increased with age in some cases. Moreover, the nature of the social interaction between pupils is different at different ages in ways that affect integration possibilities. At infant age play is loosely structured, is open to casual participants, can start and stop or change direction suddenly, and often has a high non-verbal component. These factors make it easier for many pupils with special needs to participate.

Richard is partially sighted and integrates into the main infant' playground at break. He is confident in his movement and plays chasing games with sighted children when he will run at full speed around the playground. He manages to avoid collisons not least because sighted pupils take care to step out of the way. Richard and his friends played a game where they linked hands to make a chain and ran round the playground following the leader. On more than one occasion Richard quite naturally took his turn as leader and the others followed with no change in confidence.

By secondary stage things have changed a little and the typical breaktime activity is rather different. Activities are more deliberate and structured, usually done in the company of a stable group of friends and involve a higher verbal content. In point of fact, there were numerous examples of isolation in the playground at secondary stage or of pupils with special needs associating only with other similar pupils. This is related also to changing patterns of interests and the different leisure possibilities open to pupils outside school. If particular aspects of the local youth sub-culture, eg the disco or the cinema, are not available to some pupils, they can be cut off from the ethos and the experiences that determine in important ways the nature of breaktime activities in school and the possibility of participating in them. Some teachers noted that puberty marked a particular watershed when interests changed dramatically and the activities of a few months previously were now seen as babyish; those who matured late such as some physically handicapped pupils could be very isolated on this score – too young developmentally for their age peers, and too old chronologically for those whose interests and level of development they shared.

Interaction at breaktime can be facilitated through having

organised activities that involve a mixture of pupils. Several schools deliberately sought to establish the special centre as a focus of lunchtime activity. Games and other activities were organised, and pupils from the main school were encouraged to come along. Using the special centre made it easier to arrange things so that those with special needs could participate while making sure that other pupils did not take over the facilities. The latter did sometimes happen, and some staff found it difficult to find a balance between ensuring that everybody got a look in and interfering with pupils' playtime interactions.

Staff reported variable success rates for these arrangements. Certainly there was a good deal of interaction, as we ourselves observed. Some friendships were made but they tended to fade away after first year in the case of pupils who were not integrating for academic purposes. The latter missed out on the opportunity to consolidate friendships through classroom contact; also, networks of relationships developed in class without reference to them. As discussed in the following chapter, there was a tendency for the most enduring contact to be had with the socially inadequate from the parent school. It was also noted that integration into a definite base could create an environment where interaction with pupils with special needs was more acceptable. Outside the special centre "peer pressure makes it difficult for a child to befriend one of ours", whereas in the special centre "they are able to form relationships . . . and talk to the handicapped child which they are not able or willing to do in main school".

Interaction must not be confined to the special centre. The aim must be to use arrangements there to promote interaction in such a way that more general relationships develop and pupils are oriented to mixing with their peers. There can be a danger that the atmosphere of the special centre becomes so cosy and appealing that pupils will always prefer to return there, so that integration then becomes restricted to those main school pupils who go to the special centre.

Mary is physically handicapped and attends a secondary school that has a special centre for physically handicapped pupils. She is academically able and follows a full sixth form programme. She has all her lessons in the main school and does not need to return to the special centre for physiotherapy or medication. Even though she has a couple of close friends in the main school she still prefers to bring them back with her to the special centre rather than stay in the sixth form common room. Her friends realise this is not in Mary's best interests and encourage her – without much success – to stay and socialise with other sixth formers.

The nature and extent of playtime interaction can be determined by a range of practical considerations. The importance of having appropriate physical accommodation and access to it was discussed in chapter eight. Simple organisational matters can play a part too. Some schools did not have fixed playtimes aside from lunchtime: the class went out when the teacher judged it convenient. This meant that it was a matter of chance whether the special class had anybody else to play with or not when they came out. One school had a special class spanning the full junior age range but was attached to an infant school, while a number of special classes contained pre-school children in schools with no nursery provision. In all of these cases the absence of age peers was a further drawback. Interaction was impeded in another school through having too many adults on the playground looking after the pupils with special needs. Some physically handicapped pupils who were fully integrated academically had to use break times for physiotherapy. Finally, the sheer location of pupils at the beginning of break is important. There is a further link between classes and play here: the classroom context tends to spill over into the playground as pupils often play with those who are physically near. When pupils with special needs were near their peers at the beginning of break they were more likely to be included in playtime activities.

Lunch

Lunch is another occasion for social interaction during the school day. Eating together has always been seen as an important social act though it must be said that the symbolic meaning of shared food is difficult to appreciate in many school lunchtimes. The crowding, the noise, the pressure on time, are not conducive to relaxed eating, much less to any of the rituals associated with civilised eating.

These same factors tend to operate against pupils with special needs sharing lunch with their peers. In theory, the requirements are minimal – a basic competence in eating and the rudiments of table-manners – but the pressure of time and space and the noise can make it difficult for some pupils, as well as making it unlikely that they will gain any social benefits. Teachers' response to this situation varies. Some consider that they are better off on their own and make separate arrangements. Others believe that they must learn to cope with the hurly burly of large crowds and have them eat with peers, either with adult support or on their own. (The third option in some cases might be to try and make the lunchtime arrangements more civilised. This would benefit all pupils, not just those with special needs.)

Mealtimes are important learning occasions for some pupils: structured feeding programmes can be implemented, table-manners taught, and so on. Some teachers judged that the teaching opportunities and the close personal contact were more important than any social benefits to be gained from integration: "It's a chance for us to sit and talk in a relaxed atmosphere . . . we are on all the time about table-manners. It's a teaching time". It should be noted that some physically handicapped pupils were conscious that their eating habits attracted attention, and they were embarrassed at eating in the main school. A compromise between using the lunchtime for teaching purposes and mixing with peers was effected in one school by having a number of pupils from the main school have lunch on a rota basis in the special centre. Main school staff likewise were encouraged to have lunch there, partly to help them get acquainted with the pupils there and partly to give the latter an opportunity to interact with different adults.

Purely practical matters can affect lunchtime integration also. Mention has been made in chapter 10 of the need for the requisite physical accommodation. One integration programme involved sharing pupils between a special school and an ordinary school. Initially, meals were considerably cheaper in the special school so that pupils returned there for lunch; although the anomaly was subsequently removed this set a pattern which was difficult to break.

Intervening in interaction

As has been noted, one of the advantages most commonly claimed for integration is that it provides an opportunity for pupils with special needs to relate to their peers, possibly developing friendships with them, and benefit from being surrounded by normal patterns of behaviour. We have seen that whether or not interaction takes place depends on a host of factors, many of them at the discretion of the school. Here we want to examine the question of specific intervention to promote interaction: whether it is necessary and effective, and how it might work.

Little is known about the degree of social acceptance that the severely retarded pupil achieves. Somewhat more evidence is available with regard to pupils with lesser degrees of mental impairment. Gottlieb (1974) suggests that merely placing the non-handicapped and handicapped together may not, of itself, increase the latter's willingness to accept the former socially. Fredericks *et al.* (1978) observed six severely mentally handicapped children of pre-school age who were encouraged to play with six non-handicapped age peers. They noted that the majority of their time was spent either in parallel or associative play. Some of the six children spent over 40 per cent of their time either as onlookers, playing alone, or were unoccupied. The gist of these and other researches is that retarded pupils of school age may be less well accepted than their non-handicapped peers. Fredericks' conclusion is that 'severely mentally handicapped children will engage in large amounts of unoccupied and self-stimulatory behaviour that (mark) them as isolates. The handicapped children avoided contact with other children and other children did not interact with them'.

Implicit in this finding is that positive steps need to be taken to improve matters. Some studies have demonstrated that intervention strategies can have a positive effect, at least temporarily. For example, Fredericks and colleagues noted that after staff had been instructed to help handicapped pupils increase the level of their socialisation and to further their linguistic skills through the twin processes of modelling and reinforcing interactions as they occurred, each child was seen to spend at least 50 per cent more time playing either in parallel or in association. There was a corresponding reduction in solitary play, being unoccupied or remaining an onlooker. A study by Peck and colleagues (1978) of pre-school mentally handicapped children disclosed that peer-imitation training between handicapped and non-handicapped improved free play. Their conclusion was again that 'special teaching procedures are required if educationally desirable outcomes are to reliably emanate from integrating pre-schoolers'.

Intervention can take many forms. One ploy has been to use peers as helpers to assist in the development of social skills and particularly play skills. Guralnick (1978) emphasised that 'play behaviour is a key ingredient in adaptability learning, cognition, education and social behaviour'. The involvement of peers is increasingly in evidence in the United States and Canada. Various advantages are identified. These include:

i.   The potential existing in peer interaction is utilised for constructive educational ends.

ii.   The tutoring situation is beneficial to both partners.

iii. It provides invaluable assistance for the teacher.

In the integration programmes we studied there was very little indication of a concern to intervene in a formal way to promote interaction between pupils with special needs and their peers. There seemed to be a widespread belief in the efficacy of locational integration to extend beyond itself and lead to a degree of social integration. In a number of locations there were lunchtime clubs and societies, part of whose function was to facilitate interaction between the two groups. In a few instances, mainly primary schools, special education staff took lessons involving their pupils and pupils from the parent school, the intention partly being to promote interaction by this means. One primary school which took in pupils with serious vision problems adopted various practical ploys: each pupil was attached to a registration group in the main school; each was given the task of bringing the class register to the secretary's office each day; and, most significantly, each was loosely attached to a sighted pupil with recognised sympathetic qualities. All concerned in fact went on to form other friendships and this 'buddy system' was subsequently dropped. However, it seems likely that it helped in promoting the ready initial acceptance by their sighted peers.

A formal intervention programme was implemented in one school by a visiting researcher. The programme and its results are described in detail in Rose (1980). We summarise it here for its intrinsic value and for the lessons that can be learned from it. It is based on the notion of peer tutoring. This entails using other pupils to assist those who have difficulties. Hurford (1980) describes an application of peer tutoring to improve the social skills of children with language impairment.

The school in question had a large centre for severely retarded pupils of primary age. The centre ran in a self-contained way and there was only limited interaction of any kind between these pupils and their peers. Eleven of the former were selected, all ambulant, and aged between seven and eleven years. They were observed at lunchtime and morning break over a five-day period. This was for the purpose of devising an observation schedule (ten categories, from co-operative play to being unoccupied). This was used to provide baseline data through further observation over a ten-day period. Interaction was extremely limited whether with pupils from the parent school or with each other. Nearly half of the time was spent unoccupied, watching other pupils or engaged in solitary play. The main contact was with playground supervisiors (more than one third of the time observed), while only ten per cent of the time was spent in positive interaction with ordinary pupils. In short, they were 'not really accepted by other children in the school. For most of the time they were ignored'.

The next step was to initiate a peer tutor programme. This was conducted by eleven pupils from a third year class who volunteered to help. The actual choice of pupil was made by the class teacher. They attended an initial 'orientation session' at which the purpose of the exercise was explained and their role as 'friends of the handicapped' discussed. Each was assigned to a particular retarded pupil, matched by sex. They observed and assisted the researcher in a group activity session involving the retarded pupils. They were given instruction in how to help them play, how to talk to them, and how to deal with any problems that might arise. They spent time in the special class observing them at work. The retarded pupils also visited the tutor's class during non-academic sessions.

The programme had two phases. In the first phase, four different centres of interest were set up in the special centre: construction toys; dolls house and dressing up box; puzzles and educational toys; and a quiet area with books. Peer tutors collected their respective charges and brought them into the classroom where they engaged in any activity of their choosing for 45 minutes. They were free to remain with their initial activity or move on to something else as and when they liked. This extended for 11 sessions over a five-week period. Two adults were always present though in a purely supervisory capacity. At the close of two of the sessions there was an informal evaluation where tutors were asked how they felt things were going, and what difficulties if any they had experienced. The second phase of the programme ran for ten sessions over a four-week period. Here, peer tutors were instructed to play with their partners out in the playground. No assistance was given by the adults present.

Two months after the completion of the programme, another round of playground observation was carried out to assess the impact of the intervention. The same observation schedule was used over a ten-day period. Considerable success was reported:

i.   a significant increase in the amount of associative play between retarded and non-retarded pupils;

ii. a significant increase in the amount of co-operative play between the two groups;

iii. a significant decrease in the amount of behaviour that would be defined as 'adult oriented', 'attention seeking', 'socially inappropriate', or 'handicapped as play object';

iv. a decrease in solitary play, being unoccupied, or being an onlooker;

v.   a decrease in the proportion of interactions that the retarded had with each other.

The conclusion was that 'the programme demonstrated in a very short period the ease with which attitudes can change provided guidelines are established'.

This example is of a more formal intervention than many people would be happy with. It is also geared to pupils with severe learning difficulties. In spite of these facts however there is a case to be made for adults to make more explicit intervention than is the norm in order to promote social interaction between pupils with special needs and their peers. This is in addition to the many indirect steps that can be taken in the way of removing obstacles and constraints and ensuring that the school's everyday organis-ation does not contribute to the isolation of pupils with special needs.

Chapter Eighteen
Social and Emotional Development

There is now a much more mature attitude to the handicapped pupil, and on the other side a building of confidence within the handicapped to be able to be accepted by their peers (teacher)

The extent to which pupils progress in social and emotional terms has become the touchstone of integration for many people. Some say that pupils with special needs are at risk of being 'lost' and becoming emotionally stunted in large impersonal schools, have no opportunities to excel in peer terms and miss the specific training in independence that a good special school can provide. Others point to the natural situation of the ordinary school where they can learn to become part of the larger community they will eventually join and which in fact provides many opportunities for social learning. The research literature, as reviewed for example by Cave and Madison (1978), is inconclusive. We have noted in chapter 2 the methodological weakness of many of the studies.

It is not our intention to enter the comparative stakes. We document the social and emotional development of the young people in the integration programmes we studied and discuss the factors that impinge on it. This is considered under the headings: Maturity; Relationships; Behaviour and personal presentation. The discussion is based largely on teachers' judgements of particular pupils but amplified in some instances by interviews with the pupils and their parents. A questionnaire designed to measure aspects of social and emotional development was also completed by teachers on two occasions at an interval of nine months. (Details in Appendix D.)

Maturity
This will be considered under the three subheadings: self-confidence; independence; and adjustment to handicap.

Self-confidence
The general impression we formed by talking to individual pupils

and observing them about school was one of considerable self-confidence. There were exceptions, especially where pupils had communication problems. By and large however, they were at ease in talking to relative strangers such as ourselves and answered our questions confidently and competently. It should be noted that many, because of their medical condition or other factors, were used to conversing with adults, and this may have given them a degree of self-confidence, even a precocity, that other youngsters lacked. This was widely commented on in relation to pupils with spina bifida.

This impression was corroborated in part by specialist staff, especially those who had experience of special schools, though not always by staffs of mainstream schools. It seemed as if the pupils were more confident and mature than they would have been in special school but less so than their ordinary peers. Take the specialist teachers first. "The children are much more confident in themselves . . . If we saw somebody different at (special school) it was an event . . . chaos would reign; here they just get on with what they're doing . . . we don't get this artificial shyness where an ordinary outgoing child becomes totally withdrawn in the presence of a stranger." These remarks were made of a group of severely retarded secondary age pupils, whose general level of social development was still very low. Similar comments were made about hearing impaired pupils integrated on an individual basis – "She lacks a great deal in self-confidence but she would have even less if she stayed in a school for the deaf" (support teacher). On the other hand, hearing impaired pupils in a secondary stage unit were considered very immature and lacking in confidence by their teachers. In the main school setting they rarely opened their mouths – "a lot of our children are afraid to communicate". Here the lack of confidence must be seen in the context of the communication difficulty.

Ordinary teachers, whose frame of reference tended to be 'normal' behaviour, found that many of these pupils were lacking in confidence. They were variously considered "socially immature", "clumsy" and so on. While this difference in perception is in part attributable to different standards and expectations, it also reflects the different settings in which the two groups of staff typically see these pupils. Main school staff see them out in the school as part of a – usually large – class, while special educators only see them in a special centre or as part of a small withdrawal group. (This is not universally true since a few schools have a policy of staff integration.) The significance of this is that many of these pupils are more outgoing and confident in a small class or special centre than in the rough and tumble of the main school. Hence, specialists and ordinary teachers are sometimes observing different behaviours from the same pupils.

Further information on self-confidence comes from the questionnaire returns on the small sample of case study pupils. The relevant section here required the teacher to tick one of the following descriptors.

Very cautious or uncertain about most activities   *Usually uncertain/ diffident*   *Acts confidently on occasions*   *Usually confident*   *Very confident, has strong self-image.*

Completed returns were available for thirty pupils. They were scored on a 1 to 5 basis: Very cautious or uncertain = 1, Very confident = 5. The averages for the first and second administrations respectively were 3.2 and 3.6. This suggests a reasonable level of confidence, with a slight increase over the twelve months. The difference is in fact statistically significant (at two per cent level of confidence, using a matched pairs t-test).

This increase can be seen in clearer perspective by looking at the distribution of the changes in grade between the first and second administrations. These are given in the table below.

Changes in grade	Frequency
−1	5
0	11
1	11
2	3

It will be seen that only five pupils were considered to have become less confident while fourteen were considered to have grown in confidence. Of the eleven pupils where no change was reported, one scored 5 (Very confident) and seven scored 4 (Usually confident), so that in these cases there was limited scope for improvement anyway.

The development of self-confidence was affected in various ways by pupils' presence in the ordinary school. Some physically handicapped teenagers derived confidence from the sheer fact of being in an ordinary school – "here you are part of the world". They had not been totally cut off in special school and indeed appreciated the opportunities created there to enable them enter the mainstream of society. These had to be specially set up however and tended to attract attention. Here they were part of the mainstream and there was less need for them to feel different. One of them put it very directly – "At (special school) you are a handicapped person, here you are a person with a handicap".

Another pupil referred to the confidence that came from being able to compete with the able-bodied on their terms and being able to do as well if not better: "What is important to me is that I can hold up my head . . . join in." Not all are in this happy position but a good many are, and possibly rather more than are given the chance. A comment from a studious but struggling able-bodied pupil offers a further gloss on this. Because the physically handicapped were excused games, had their own quiet area for study and so on, they had the advantage over other pupils and he was anxious about not being able to keep up with them!

It may appear that we are over-stressing the positive side and ignoring the negative aspects. Some teachers talked about the comparisons that pupils make and the consequent damage to self-esteem. Another said, "It's better being a big fish in a little pond than a little fish in a big pond", and pointed to the many opportunities for excelling at competitions, representing the school and so on that pupils had in special schools and were deprived of in ordinary schools. There is no point in denying that negative aspects exist and can have serious effect. The fact that we witnessed very few could simply be an indication that the schools we saw were well run and had tackled the problems successfully. There are two points to make however that may be more useful than listing the potential difficulties. First, problems of self-confidence are not inevitable. Our experience has shown that even pupils with severe and complex needs can be educated in ordinary schools not only with no damage to their self-esteem but with a positive enhancement of it.

Secondly, the 'big fish in little ponds' notion always came from teachers, never from pupils. No pupil we talked to wanted to go to a special school, and some who had transferred from special school were adamant about not wanting to return. This could be explained by saying that pupils get acclimatised to a given location and will prefer to stay there, so that pupils in a special school would also prefer to stay in special school. That is an empirical matter we were not in a position to test. This finding does however call into question the 'big fish in little pond' theory, or at least its application in the present instance. Since pupils showed little or no orientation toward special schools, either the theory does not apply or the ordinary schools we studied provided sufficient subgroup opportunities for pupils to gain a sense of achievement and develop their self-esteem.

Independence

The development of independence was a major target, and teachers seemed generally satisfied with progress toward it. Parents too commented on how their children had grown in independence. One set of parents told of their pleasant surprise at the increased number of things their severely retarded daughter was now able to do for herself – "she cooks, makes tea, does lovely woodwork which at one time we couldn't have imagined her doing".

The major problem here was in a special centre for secondary age hearing impaired pupils. This catered for 25-30 pupils within a large comprehensive school. It was generally agreed by staff at the centre that many pupils so far from growing in independence and availing of the opportunities for independent action that the ordinary school presented were "quite dependent on the unit" and remained at a relatively immature level. This was attributed variously to the negative perception of the centre in the school, the hearing impaired pupils' poor language capacities and their associated reluctance to engage in spoken communication.

Further information on independence comes from responses in the questionnaire mentioned above. The teacher ticked one of the following descriptions:

very rarely carries out activities unaided *usually needs assistance/approval* *makes own choices but sometimes seeks approval* *usually acts independently* *acts very independently*

Completed responses were available for 32 pupils. These were scored as before: Very rarely carries out activities unaided = 1. Acts very independently = 5. The averages for the first and second administrations respectively were 2.7 and 3.2. This suggests modest levels of independence, with an increase over the twelve months. The difference is in fact statistically significant (at one per cent level of confidence, using a matched pairs t-test).

This increase can be seen in clearer perspective by looking at the distribution of the changes in grade between the first and second administrations. These are given in the table below.

Changes in grade	Frequency
−2	1
−1	4
0	10
1	12
2	4
3	1

It will be seen that only five pupils were considered to have become less independent.

Various factors emerged that have a bearing on the degree of independence achieved: level of supervision and staff support; opportunities for independent action and decision-making; psychological factors, especially motivation; and a policy of encouraging independence.

Some staff argued that too high a level of supervision and support was detrimental and prevented pupils from growing in independence. In one case there was felt to be a marked contrast with the special school which the pupils had attended previously where "there is a very dependent atmosphere". It could be argued that school staff were simply making virtue out of necessity since they had neither the staffing nor the institutional framework that vould permit the degree of individual attention that might be ssible in a special school. Moreover, staff sometimes lacked the wledge and expertise that would sensitise them to particular s. Independence is not after all an absolute goal, and it if is d as a blanket policy pupils' individual needs will go unmet. ther hand, some staff had a clearly worked out philosophy cated reduced supervision and support for positive reasons. One teacher, while acknowledging the support that a special class gave, was critical of its dependent atmosphere – "he is not learning to survive because he is getting all this individual help, he has got to learn that there isn't always going to be somebody there the minute he wants them – education is for life, not a sheltered workshop". Other staff pointed out that insisting on independent action from pupils led pupils to believe in themselves and so become more independent.

Some pupils with experience of special as well as ordinary schools were quite vocal on this score. They claimed that special school staff tended to assume that they were incapable of independent action and so kept them dependent: "You were treated in more or less the same way whether you were six or sixteen". By contrast the ordinary school was considered to offer "the chance of being a person who doesn't have to depend on people to do things for you".

The above should not be taken as part of a case against special schools. To the extent that it is critical, it is critical of *practices* within *some* special schools. We are not in a position to say how generally they occur. In any case, our concern is with the practices, and they can occur in ordinary schools just as well. In the secondary age special centre referred to above where pupils were considered particularly dependent and immature, a contributory factor was held to be the "cotton wool" attitudes of main school staff who had been too protective.

The opportunity to act independently, to run risks and make mistakes, to explore the world about them and their own capacities in relation to it, is an essential part of growing up for all children. It is no less important for those who have special needs. In some ways it may be more important since particular disabilities such as vision impairment or lack of mobility may restrict the scope for independent action.

The level of adult supervision and support is clearly relevant here. In ordinary schools pupils are likely to have opportunities for independent action and decision making simply because staff are concerned for all pupils and cannot devote too much time to the few with special needs even if they wished to. Good staffing ratios can mean that such opportunities are reduced and protective attitudes develop as above. By contrast however, they can sometimes create the necessary conditions for independent action.

Take the physically handicapped, for instance. Dressing, toileting, changing calipers, can all take a great deal of time if pupils do it themselves. Staff must show them how, perhaps over and over again, and often need to be available in a back-up capacity for long periods before full independence is achieved. They could save a great deal of time by attending to the pupils' physical needs themselves instead of waiting while the pupils do it, but that would be to deprive them of a most important opportunity for developing independence. Unfortunately, it is a situation that can arise when staffing ratios are poor.

A third consideration refers to psychological factors. The achievement of independence is a complex process and many psychological variables have a bearing on it. We discuss self-confidence and adjustment to handicap elsewhere in this section. Here we want to refer to motivation as a factor in achieving independence.

A group of physically handicapped teenagers with experience of special schooling who were now in an ordinary school spoke about this. They were a mature and independent-minded bunch of youngsters who talked perceptively about many aspects of their educational experience. It was clear that they were highly motivated to achieve, both for the school and for themselves. They knew they had to stand on their own two feet – some of them could never do so literally but they would not shrink from the metaphor – and they were prepared to do so. They were strongly motivated to "prove to other people we can do just as well", and this led them to a level of independence and maturity that would do credit to any teenagers.

A final consideration in the development of independence is the role of a policy of encouraging it. It hardly needs saying that a policy of encouraging independence helps pupils to be independent. Moreover, such policies are not the prerogative of special provision in ordinary schools. Many special schools also have such policies and to our knowledge operate them effectively. Some would argue that their greater experience of special needs and their freedom from the constraints of the ordinary school give them a unique scope for promoting independence. This may well be, though there are lots of counter-examples. Certainly, it would be difficult to sustain a general case. In any case, our concern here is simply to establish what is involved in promoting independence in the ordinary school and to outline what a policy of doing so might entail.

Some elements of such a policy can be inferred from the discussion above. If the achievement of independence is affected by particular factors such as the level of adult supervision or the opportunity to take risks, there are clear prescriptions for action. As far as promoting independence in general is concerned, one can consider it in relation to: formal teaching geared explicitly to independence; teaching other subjects so as to promote independent learning and activity; and maintaining an atmosphere of autonomy. Formal teaching tended to be employed in the context of preparation for adult living and was discussed in chapter 14. It might involve for example instructing pupils in the use of public transport and giving them assignments outside the school. The way in which pupils are taught has important implications for independence. This is developed in the curriculum chapters. Maintaining an atmosphere of autonomy entails many things. It requires appropriate attitudes on the part of all concerned, both pupils and staff. This must encompass staff at every level in the school; it is idle for staff in a special centre to espouse a philosophy of independence if teachers in the parent school or dinner assistants are not enlisted. The required attitudes must be embodied in appropriate procedures and practical arrangements within the school. These will depend on the nature of the special needs and the local situation.

Some more specific suggestions can be made. Local factors must be taken into account and it is up to the individual to apply them in the light of his or her knowledge of the local situation. It may be noted that their relevance is not confined to those with special needs since the school ethos that promotes independence for a sub-group will do for the whole school.

i. Have high expectations

Young people are more likely to behave in an independent manner if that is what you expect of them. This is related to findings on the relationship between expectation and academic achievement. The relevance to pupils with special needs is particularly strong since they suffer greatly from low expectations. Some physically handicapped adolescents we talked to said that the reversal of these expectations gave them faith in themselves and led to their becoming far more independent.

ii. Give pupils responsibility

Taking account of age and understanding, allocate pupils as many tasks and assignments as you have the wit to devise and allow them as much responsibility for managing themselves as possible. This prescription will mean different things to different people. To some it may mean having pencil monitors; to others it may entail giving pupils a say in drawing up their learning programmes or in writing their end-of-year reports. However the assignment of responsibility is interpreted in a given school, it should mean the same for those with special needs as for the others unless there are very clear reasons to the contrary.

iii. Allow them to take risks

Just as learning to ride a bicycle (in pre-stabiliser days anyway!) involves – quickly forgotten – spills and scrapes, there are many learning experiences that necessitate risk. Some teachers in our experience exaggerated the dangers facing pupils with special needs, especially those suffering from physical or sensory impairment, and protected them needlessly – with the result that they were deprived of valuable learning opportunities. Clearly one must avoid negligence and have due care for pupils in one's charge. Instead of following the more usual prescription however of When in doubt, don't! we suggest an alternative: When in doubt, ask somebody who knows! Our experience suggests that common sense was frequently wrong, almost always erring on the side of caution; what was needed was not more caution but better information.

iv. Make a minimum of interventions

This has to do with taking risks but is broader. One school expressed its philosophy as one of "expecting them to fend for themselves". Practical examples here include having them choose and fetch their own meals, and leaving them to make their own way about the school without doors being continually opened and books being carried.

v. Making concessions only when necessary

This applies for example to questions of discipline, homework and punctuality. If these pupils are to be part of the school they need to conform in a general way to its regulations and procedures. The more concessions are made specific to their handicapping condition, the greater the likelihood that they acquire a handicapped identity in their own and other pupils' eyes.

vi. Reduce excessive dependence

Many teachers commented on the gross dependence some of these pupils displayed when they first received them. It may be necessary to take explicit steps to disengage them and force them to act more independently.

vii. Do not put up with tantrums or other age-inappropriate behaviour

This is perhaps easier said than done. Pupils may arrive with fixed patterns of behaviour which will not change overnight. There are effective techniques of behaviour management however and these must be invoked if the effect of the new environment and firm consistent handling is not sufficient. One recognises that a certain level of assertive, even aggressive, behaviour is part of the development of autonomy. If children are particularly immature and dependent, their expression of growing independence may well be out of keeping with their age; it is then important to distinguish carefully between assertive behaviour which is indicative of real development and aggression that is largely negative.

A final thought on independence comes from a teacher in charge of a large secondary department for pupils with learning difficulties. "Our children must be better behaved than any other children in the school." Many teachers in comparable positions feel under pressure to ensure that their pupils do not distinguish themselves by unruly or untoward behaviour. This is for all sorts of good reasons since the image of the special centre, relationships with main school staff and the integration programme itself, may be at stake. The result however can be to impose restraints that inhibit the development of independence. Some immature pupils need greater leeway than the mainstream of pupils. This is by and large well recognised but can be forgotten or set aside if there are strong external pressures toward standard behaviour.

Adjustment to handicap
The third aspect of maturity we have selected is adjustment to

handicap, in the sense of becoming aware of the limitations associated with it and accepting them without dismay. This may raise some eyebrows, if not hackles. In one sense, the last thing people with a handicap should do is adjust to their handicap and become Handicapped Persons. The many examples of people who have refused to be bound by gross handicapping conditions and achieved much remind one that goals and expectations must not be set too low and in any case should never be static. Tomorrow's achievement may be bounded by today's horizons but it in turn will create new horizons for the following day. So we are not advocating any easy acceptance of handicap or notions of handicapped personality, where achievement is set at a low level by static and conventional targets.

Many young people with special needs do have problems of adjustment. These are broadly of two kinds. On the one hand, they become inward looking and attach too much importance to their handicapping condition. A group of hearing impaired pupils in one school were considered egocentric and prone to take offence. They tended to see things in black and white and were far too quick to misinterpret other pupils' actions, and retaliate negatively. Others had become too used to seeing themselves as special cases and deserving of sympathy and exceptional status. They did not expect to have to be punctual or wait their turn, and showed little consideration for others. On the other hand, some pupils nurtured wildly ambitious dreams with little appreciation of what was entailed in realising them. They talked about marriage and things they would do when they left school in a way that betrayed a lack of realism that was also a failure to adjust to their handicap.

What is the role of the ordinary school in adjusting to handicap? Does it provide a stimulating environment that promotes adjustment or is immersion in 'normality' too much to cope with? The answer to these questions must, as often, be a mixture of Yes and No: some pupils become better adjusted while others do not. In general, we found positive results followed from ordinary school placement. Pupils' self-esteem did not necessarily suffer and could be enhanced from being in an ordinary school, as discussed above, even though they were surrounded by peers who did not have their limitations. Being confined to a wheelchair does not mean that you cannot cope with being in class with able-bodied peers or that you are constantly upset by their freedom of movement. This is important since many people become hypersensitive when confronted with handicap. They attribute an *imagined* experience of handicap, how they think they would feel if they had the handicapping condition, and this may be far removed from the real experience of handicap. This is associated with a tendency to under-estimate the psychological robustness of youngsters with special needs. As noted, many of the ones we met were well able to cope with 'normal' reality and kid-glove treatment was not necessary.

Various factors were at play in promoting the adjustment of these youngsters. First, placement in an ordinary school brought them up against an environment that was not geared specifically for them and where allowances were not continually made for them. (This benefit can be lost, and was in some instances we studied, through the ordinary school becoming too accommodating.) Many teachers commented on how pupils had started off a bit like hot-house plants, clearly seeing themselves as special cases. Where the school tackled this successfully – by making a minimum of fuss and exception, insisting that they abide by school rules and so on – there were dramatic improvements. In the case of one particular immature boy, it was a signal achievement when he apologised for being late or went to the back of a queue instead of assuming that he could stand at the front – "He is now beginning to understand that he can't be a special case". A hearing impaired teenager whose energy and boisterousness had led to much naughty behaviour at the special school benefited considerably from being in the rough and tumble of the mainstream. He was no longer top dog or leader and although "he has had a rough time" was regarded as having responded very positively; he could now interact easily with people and was well-equipped for leaving school.

The kind of interactions which ordinary school placements made possible, even forced, were important in reducing the egocentricity and extreme sensitivity of some pupils. They saw that they were not the only ones with problems. Normality is a chequered business, and seeing others' problems and difficulties helps put one's own in perspective. They had object lessons too – which were much more telling than any instruction could be – on how popularity and friendship patterns reflected personality factors rather than handicap ones. If another pupil with comparable handicaps is a social success, it becomes more difficult to believe that one's own failures are entirely attributable to one's handicap.

A second consideration, advanced by a number of teachers, is that the ordinary school provides a series of small hurdles rather than one huge hurdle at the age of sixteen. "Our pupils have to fight lots of little battles every day." By requiring them to make adjustments continually and providing a supportive environment within which they can do so, pupils do not have to make such big adjustments when they leave school. Not only do they have the opportunity to make friends and socialise with a wide range of peers but there is the feeling of belonging to the mainstream. This can of course be somewhat misleading since the mainstream of society can be very different from the mainstream of the school but that at least is a problem they share with all pupils.

Thirdly, many pupils with special needs have unrealistic aspirations. These are sometimes nurtured by being in the ordinary school and seeing what others take for granted. There can be a positive side however. Some physically handicapped teenagers we talked to had a keen realisation of the efforts they needed to make to achieve their goals. They realised that they had to try harder than their peers to reach the same targets; to this extent their placement in an ordinary school had taught them an invaluable lesson.

It is clear that ordinary placement does provide opportunities for pupils to adjust to their handicap in a mature way. This does not mean that the opportunities are always taken. Pupils' adjustment can indeed be hindered from being in an ordinary school but that is not because of any necessary features of the school. It is rather because of inadequate planning and because the opportunities presented are not availed of.

Relationships

Social integration is a major concern in the education of pupils with special needs in ordinary schools. Even if there is little possibility of learning activities in common, there is widespread belief that they benefit from social contact with their age peers. Mixing with them and forming relationships outside the handicapped community is important both in its own right and as a factor in promoting self-confidence and maturity. There is a contrary view held by some parents and other people that this social benefit is a myth. Far from enjoying the benefits of social contact many pupils suffer bitterly because of it: not only do they fail to form normal peer relationships but they are liable to a range of negative experiences, being over-protected and treated as incapable if they are lucky, teased and bullied if they are not.

It is not for us to rule on what happens in practice. In any case, it is clear that there is a great deal of variation in the nature and quality of the relationships that obtain between youngsters with special needs and their peers. In this section we report on the patterns of relationships we encountered. This is less to describe the typical than to indicate the possible. It also provides a context for discussing the many factors that bear on the development of relationships and for considering what positive interventions the school can make.

Our impression, based on interviews with school staff, pupils and parents and some observation on our part, is that there are grounds for guarded optimism: normal relationships are possible and negative ones can be avoided. We encountered many examples of natural relationships and good friendships between pupils with special needs and their peers. These outcomes cannot be taken for granted however, and there may be need for judicious intervention on the part of the school.

The relationships that form between pupils with special needs and their peers depend on many factors, as discussed below. This limits the usefulness of generalisations and we confine ourselves to three main observations. First, friendly relationships tended to be with similar peers rather than other pupils. This was so whether groups were large or small, though it was more pronounced when groups were large. In the big secondary special centres friendships between pupils with special needs and the others were, with the exception of the academically able physically handicapped, the exception rather than the rule. In one primary school however there were just two physically handicapped girls; while one had several friends in the school and mixed moderately well, her companion had no other friends besides her. She mixed only through her and was miserable when she was absent. As might be expected, relationships were at their easiest and most natural when pupils were integrated on an individual basis. Few of these were socially isolated and they included pupils who were blind, profoundly deaf and severely physically handicapped.

There are good reasons why pupils with special needs should form relationships with their similar peers rather than other pupils. Human relationships generally tend to be with those closest to hand – this is not a peculiarity of those who have special needs –and for the majority of pupils with special needs in the ordinary school this will be other pupils with special needs. This fact should be borne in mind when considering studies that report more friendships and better relationships with pupils in the mainstream when integration is on an individual or small group basis. Anything else would be extraordinary. Other facts too can push pupils with special needs together. They have a base of experience in common, sometimes having attended the same special school or other provision previously, and a more intimate understanding of each other's special conditions and needs. Frequently, they have to contend with pre-existing networks of relationships on the part of the other pupils and much the easiest thing to do is stay within their own group.

A further factor that can make for difficulties in forming relationships is that some pupils, notably the physically handi-capped, have been used to dealing with a wide range of adults from an early age and are less oriented to peer group relationships as a consequence. One teenager considered her able-bodied classmates immature and her dismissive manner with them occasioned a certain amount of unpopularity. The ease of relationships with adults is often commented on in respect of children with spina bifida. Scores on our social and emotional development questionnaire would suggest that this occurs more generally. The distribution of scores on the scale 'relationship with adults' is given in the table below:

Grade	1	2	3	4	5
Frequency	0	3	8	16	11

Given that 4 corresponds to 'has easy relationships on the whole' and 5 to 'very relaxed in relationships with adults', this indicates a high level of rapport with adults. (These are based on the 38 pupils on whom the first administration of this questionnaire was carried out; scores on the second administration were even higher.) When one considers in addition to this that pupils with special needs are often placed in groups of backward or emotionally immature pupils anyway, a further reason for the orientation toward adults becomes evident.

A second observation is that relationships between pupils with special needs and their peers tend to involve certain groups within the total pupil body rather than others. This was more pronounced when they constituted a large and clearly defined group within the school. Pupils being integrated on an individual basis or where they did not stand out as a separate group were more likely to form relationships in which the special need was irrelevant. One could cite many such examples, where relationships were determined primarily by personality and other individual characteristics just as they are for any other pupils, but it would be idle to pretend that all pupils merge easily into the social network of the ordinary school. The tendency was for some groups to be more oriented to seeking them out and spending time with them. There are various reasons why this is so. Apart from the factors discussed below that impinge on the formation of relationships, it must be remembered that frequently pupils with special needs constituted an outgroup in the school, and the various segregative mechanisms associated with outgroups in general came into play. They were entering situations where the main body of pupils were well known to each other; there were pre-existing patterns of relationships; and there could be considerable peer pressure against associating with them. These considerations would seem to be no different in kind from those affecting other outgroups and to that extent are not a handicap problem so much as the more general one of combining disparate groups into a social and functional whole.

We encountered several examples where the primary contacts pupils had were with those who were themselves of a school's outgroups: the immature and socially unsuccessful; the under-achieving; and occasionally the disruptive. Individual pupils from the main school who were unpopular or lacked friends there sometimes gravitated toward them. One staff member referring to the mixing that went on in the school's special centre said that "kids who perhaps don't make friends wander in". In one case this was done quite deliberately by an isolated teenager but the result happily was a close and enduring friendship.

Joan is a somewhat unattractive fifth-year who failed to form any friendships in her class. She sought out Louise who is severely disabled. "Louise was the last thing I could think of." Initially Joan was rejected also by Louise's disabled friends but Louise prevailed upon them to accept Joan for her sake. The two have formed a close friendship now. They spend lunchtime together with Joan wheeling Louise when necessary. They seek each other out at break if they have not been in the same lesson. They spend time together outside school and have been on holiday with each other's families.

Several teachers in one school commented on the tendency for pupils from the remedial department to associate with pupils in the special centre. In one secondary school which had a large department for pupils with learning difficulites good relationships grew up between fourth and fifth year 'rebels' and the pupils with learning difficulties. Developments of this kind are to be expected when the primary handicapping condition is learning difficulty – the two groups will have a good deal in common and may spend periods of the school day together – but they occurred with other pupils as well. Relationships between a group of hearing impaired pupils and main school peers in a comprehensive school were described as not good. There was relatively little social interaction of the right kind between the two pupil bodies. "At play time you never see them associating with the other kids." According to staff, the only main school pupils who mixed with them were remedial pupils.

Another example however points out a contrast to this. It concerns a profoundly deaf teenager who was being integrated on an individual basis. His poor communication skills did restrict his socialising but a major reason why he had no real friends had to do with the educational band in which he was placed. This was a low ability group containing a number of pupils with adjustment problems as well. According to the teacher who worked closely with him, he was relatively more able in spite of his hearing impairment and had little in common with this group.

Apart from these various outgroups, there were two other situations in which relationships – not necessarily of equal friendship – were more likely to occur. The first was when older pupils, especially girls, took up with younger ones and mothered them. When a physically handicapped boy first came to infant school his teacher described how there was competition to wheel him round the playground at break. A teenage girl said "You feel right sorry for them", describing her own motivation for helping. Many similar instances were reported elsewhere, with the physically handicapped being particularly at risk of being adopted in this way. Some visually impaired infants too were reported as "finding they are being a bit over-protected". It should be noted that this tendency was most pronounced on the occasion of pupils' first arrival at school and commonly diminished with familiarity and the passage of time.

The second situation referred to above was when pupils sought to befriend those with special needs or help them in practical ways, more usually the latter, out of a sense of duty. This could be the result of moral or religious convictions or a response to exhortations by staff. There were several examples of fifth and sixth form girls helping out in special departments, particularly with the severely retarded; these were mostly relationships of helping rather than of equal friendship. In a few cases this process did lead, with the increase of familiarity and regard, to relationships of equality. There were also examples however where the prevailing attitude after a lengthy period of time was still one of being kind to the handicapped because 'teacher says you should'. Needless to say, some pupils were disenchanted with these attitudes. In one secondary school the special centre provided a focal point for social contact between the physically handicapped and their peers. Many pupils came along, partly out of curiosity, partly out of a generalised helpfulness. One teacher acknowledged that this might lead to some friendships but said that "one or two of our kids are positively put off by it".

A third observation relates to the occurrence of negative relationships. This is a matter that produces much anxiety, with many parents and others fearing that pupils are at risk in the rough and tumble of the ordinary school. One hears stories of bullying, extreme teasing and other negative relationships from which, if prevalent, every child should be protected. It should be remembered that shy or sensitive youngsters or those who simply do not like crowds can find the social milieu of some schools extremely trying. Our belief, born of experience, is that pupils with special needs do not in general benefit from being seen in need of protection; they benefit rather from being assumed to be as psychologically robust as other pupils and being immersed in the rough and tumble. Nevertheless we recognise that this is a serious concern for many people and that there are respects in which they may be more at risk in present-day schools. So we sought to gather information on the prevalence of negative relationships and assess the extent to which their occurrence has implications for integration.

To the best of our understanding, negative incidents and patterns of relationships were comparatively rare. Some did occur but nobody regarded this as a major problem area. Many schools reported no problems whatsoever; while in some cases the amount of contact may have been limited they were satisfied that when it occurred it was of a positive or at least acceptable nature. Moreover, there were numerous instances of tolerance for pupils with special needs whose behaviour was trying for other pupils.

Robert is a hearing impaired teenager who is also a bit of a nuisance – "naughty, mischievous, to the point where it gets on your nerves, a bit of a pain in the neck all round . . . gets on the other children's nerves, pinches, pokes, takes their pencils". In spite of all this his classmates are remarkably tolerant with him. They put up with his waywardness and often help in explaining things to him. "They are aware that he is different and are very understanding."

In practical terms, the conclusion would seem to be that while there is room for a watching concern on the part of teachers, and on occasion a direct intervention may be necessary, there are no grounds for alarm or fussy and obtrusive intervention. Untoward incidents did take place: some physically handicapped boys were attacked by an able-bodied youth and subjected to homosexual threats; two young girls with Down's Syndrome were attacked by a group of lower school pupils in a comprehensive; there was a suggestion of cruelty toward a boy with speech difficulties in a junior school. These are distressing occurrences and one cannot be complacent about them, but they were isolated cases. Moreover, they were readily dealt with at the time of occurrence and it would seem ill-advised to base any general prescriptions on them.

As regards teasing, it is clear that a certain amount took place, though rather less than might be expected. The Table below gives the incidence of teasing as reported by the 43 sets of parents interviewed.

Yes	No	Has been teased in the past but not now	Occasionally, unsure, or by neighbourhood children only
5	21	8	9

Where there was current teasing there were other factors besides handicap in all except one case – racial prejudice, personality factors and so on. Parents did not in fact see it as a problem, while only a few pupils mentioned it and then only as something that affected others not themselves. Most of the negative interactions reported came from a single location where a large group of pupils with sensory impairments were housed in a secondary school described by one of its own staff as "not one of the nicest schools . . . our kids are pretty thick skinned and not very tolerant of handicap in any form". Relationships with main school pupils were not good. What little interaction there was tended to be negative in character: teasing and oiccasional physical violence, with some reports of kicking and spitting.

There is a particular difficulty over obtaining reliable information here. In part, this is because of the sensitivity of the information. No school staff like to publicise the fact that their pupils are capable of bullying or being cruel to those less fortunate than themselves. There are limits to frankness even in the most forthcoming of people, and this is one area where a certain amount of editing on the part of respondents can be expected. Moreover, school staff may not have the information. Serious incidents will almost certainly come to notice but many lesser incidents may not. As one teacher said, "I reckon they get a hard time sometimes . . . I think it happens a lot more than we know". Likewise parents may not get told of everything but it is fair to assume that they will be aware if their child is unhappy and will know the reasons for it; for this reason the data reported on the absence of teasing are encouraging.

The likelihood of contact between pupils with special needs and their peers and the nature of the relationships formed depends on many factors. These have to do with the pupils themselves (eg personality, age, nature of special need) their peers (familiarity with special need and understanding of it, peer pressures) and the school (nature of the site, opportunities for contact). These different factors are inter-connected: lack of familiarity and the apprehension that goes with it may be more important where epileptic pupils or those with communication disorder are concerned; opportunities for social contact may need to be set up more deliberately when pupils' time in the main school is limited, and so on. Some of these have been referred to above. In this section we want to discuss briefly a number of them that can be important. Though they are developed separately, the inter-connections between them should be borne in mind.

One of the most important aspects, and most frequently commented on, is the young person's own personality. Whether a pupil was popular or unpopular, had many friends or few, was teased or not, depended very much on personality factors. Many pupils with severe handicapping conditions were popular in spite of them because of their warmth or good humour while others were unpopular because of sullenness or tiresome behaviour – just as happens with other pupils. Some pupils were well aware of this. "If you're willing to go out and talk you can eradicate that chair and it doesn't exist . . . it's the person in it." (17-year-old girl). "It's up to us to make friends . . . you have to be a bit of an extrovert." (16-year-old physically handicapped boy).

George is a placid self-contained seven-year-old who has a language difficulty. His teacher overheard some initial teasing from a classmate who was informing George, "you can't talk properly, can you". George responded with an unperturbed "I know I can't" and carried on with what he was doing. He has in fact become quite a popular boy in his class.

It would appear too as if handicap considerations recede in favour of personality factors as relationships develop. "You sum your friends up . . . I like her personality . . . I don't see her as being handicapped." (teenage girl talking about physically handicapped peer). Again, "they become just like us, we see them as us, therefore you don't notice, don't pity them". A teacher commented of a blind 11-year-old: "there is something about Sarah that makes her very acceptable to other children. Her personality is such that it encourages the right kind of support from other people without them fussing over her."

A second factor to consider is ability level. The clearest evidence here relates to the physically handicapped where the academically able seemed to enjoy quite normal relationships with their able-bodied peers. By contrast, those who had learning difficulties in addition were less fortunate. Their social contact tended to be with similar peers or with slow learners from the parent school. A similar tendency was found with sensory impairment though the picture was less clearcut. Indeed, a contrary trend emerged, illustrated by the example cited earlier of a relatively able hearing impaired boy placed in a low ability band and finding he had little in common with the group. In the case of pupils with learning difficulties the tendency was for those with moderate difficulties to associate with slow learners and low achievers from the main school if they did have contact outside their own group. If the severely retarded had contact with main school pupils this was in the context of a helping or otherwise unequal relationship.

While the details of handicapping conditions were not as constraining as commonly supposed they did make for some difficulties. It was not possible always to make the wheelchair disappear as the youth quoted above would have it. Some pupils too found this exercise more difficult than others. A major constraint was communication capacity. If a pupil was unable to communicate intelligibly with his or her peers relationships tended to be poor or nonexistent. One deaf boy was quite popular in the school but had no real friends – "It is really the language – you can't hold a coherent conversation with him, it's just one word or short sentences". This affected primarily the hearing impaired and those with speech and language problems, such as the severely retarded and the physically handicapped. The hearing impaired had other difficulties too such as being singled out through wearing hearing aids or their occasional use of sign language. This was not always a problem but in one school where attitudes to the hearing impaired were poor they believed their hearing aids singled them out for teasing; some of them hated games and PE because their aids became more conspicuous. An example of a different kind comes from a girl who had some spasticity in her mouth and dribbled a good deal; this, along with rather unfortunate eating habits, meant that she was subject to a good deal of teasing and had no real friends.

In the next chapter we note how age can affect how pupils are perceived. This has implications for forming relationships as well. Many of the constraining factors being discussed here are less potent with young pupils than with older ones. Thus relationships in the infant school are relatively fluid and perhaps less determined by personality characterisitics. Younger pupils seem less bothered by differences such as hearing aids; moreover, they can have a degree of spontaneous interest in gadgets like hearing aids and can easily be prevailed upon to see sign language as a game which they themselves would like to take part in.

A final factor concerning pupils with special needs that affected relationships was the fact that many of them lived outside the catchment area of the school, sometimes a considerable distance away. This meant that friendships could not be continued after school. There was less opportunity to take part in extracurricular activities when relationships might be cemented. They could not so easily visit their school friends at home or have them visit, particularly if they were unable to travel independently. They were often further disadvantaged by being out of touch with those of their own age in their immediate neighbourhood.

Relationships are two-way and are affected by characteristics of the main pupil body as well. Two of the most important were the related factors of familiarity and understanding. Association between pupils with special needs and their peers is not only a problem for the former. The others too may have difficulty in knowing how to react, and this can lead to avoidance behaviour and other negative responses. One pupil testified to having been shocked when physically handicapped pupils first came to his school – "Some of them make me uneasy". Another boy, who was now very well disposed toward them, had been apprehensive and nervous at first – "I didn't know how I could talk to them". His initial thought indeed was "why couldn't they stay in their own place and leave us alone". Yet another pupil remarked that previously her understanding of the handicapped had been based on "the really dramatic view from television".

It is important to understand these misperceptions and apprehensions on the part of young people. They are natural reactions, no more prevalent in schools than in society at large. Indeed, one of the more encouraging features in practice was that these reactions could be – and often were – replaced by more positive attitudes. Until this happens however, relationships can be poor or non-existent. Lack of understanding can lead to rejection all round. Uncertainty and timidity can result in stilted relationships or the total avoidance of contact. In extreme cases, feelings of inadequacy and resentment on the part of main school pupils can develop into hostile and aggressive behaviour.

Behaviour and presentation

Pupils with special needs sometimes behave in anti-social ways and draw undue attention to themselves through bizarre mannerisms and appearance. In one sense they are no different from other pupils in this. They have no monopoly on socially undesirable behaviour. There are several reasons why it attracts comment however. First, there is a tendency to expect them not to be naughty and to notice it all the more when they are. As a group they make extra demands on society anyway and when they not merely fail to appreciate this but engage in socially destructive behaviour as well it can be particularly unacceptable. Secondly, any exceptional behaviour on their part is more likely to be noticed. They are more subject to adult supervision and quite simply have less chance to get away with it. Some lack the wit to cover their tracks or talk themselves out of trouble. Furthermore, their group identity is clearly marked and this can increase the likelihood that misdemeanours will be noted. If any given pupil misbehaves that may or may not attract attention. If the pupil in question is perceived as one of a particular group it is more likely to attract attention: 'Class 5 are at it again – so-and-so has just broken a window'. This can operate to make the misdemeanours of pupils with special needs more visible than they might otherwise have been. Finally, these pupils *do* behave in extraordinary and disturbing ways. A catalogue of the cases we encountered would delight the popular press. Not only do they do what other pupils do, normal misbehaviour as it were, but when compounded with immaturity and lack of social awareness their behaviour can be singularly untoward and succeed in attracting excessive attention.

Our concern here is with two aspects of social behaviour that sometimes distinguish these pupils. The first has to do with unacceptable behaviour, the most common instances being untoward aggression and sexual precocity. The second refers to behaviour that is socially undesirable but not disruptive or unacceptable in the same way as the first. Examples here include grossly immature behaviour, odd mannerisms and poor eating habits.

The most frequently noted form of undesirable behaviour was aggression and general disruptiveness. This took many forms and occurred widely, though receiving particular mention with respect to hearing impaired pupils. These sometimes had difficulties in relating to other pupils when they first came to the ordinary school. One boy whose speech was very poor caused a certain amount of unintentional upset through his roughness in the playground during early weeks. His usual way of attracting attention was an overtly physical one; the others did not appreciate this and tended to react in kind. A group of hearing impaired pupils were considered to be quite out of hand at one stage with much unrestrained and anti-social behaviour. Some severely retarded youngsters were described in guarded tones by their teacher in charge as "usually extrovert", meaning that they were extremely troublesome; their behaviour was quite uninhibited and a source of much difficulty in the school. Another group of severely retarded pupils however, while occasionally producing aggressive behaviour were more of a problem for their extreme shyness. As far as pupils with learning difficulties in general were concerned, the main constraints on integration seemed to be behavioural. We were referred to a number of instances where individuals' integration programmes had to be curtailed because their behaviour disrupted classes or was not acceptable to teachers in the parent school. Several teachers referred to the "containing factor" as critical in determining how much time given pupils would spend in mainstream classes.

An aspect of behaviour that frequently escapes mention may be noted here. This is when pupils deliberately use their handicapping condition in a mischievous way. Thus, a wheelchair travelling down a corridor can be used to deliver a sharp blow to an unsuspecting victim; especially with the aid of a strategically placed pair of crutches! One physically handicapped boy had this down to a fine art, knowing that nobody would dare retaliate. It might be argued that this is turning your liabilities into assets but it did little for good relationships. While a few teachers did remark on this, most comments and examples came from other pupils we interviewed. There was a certain amount of – fairly understandable – resentment at the virtual immunity from punishment that some pupils possessed. They were being urged to accept pupils with special needs and treat them as equals but when the latter infringed pupil codes of behaviour, or traded on their handicap status, they were suddenly accorded privileged position and retaliation was impossible.

A further point relating to anti-social behaviour may be made. Just as pupils were popular or unpopular, had many friends or few, on account of their personalities rather than their special needs, so they could be aggravating or anti-social because of personality factors. A number of teachers were at pains to point this out to us. *George is a tubby fourteen-year-old is who is forever being teased and made the butt of jokes. He has a hearing impairment and is also very quick-tempered, and it is the latter that is considered the source of his trouble. "He will rise to the bait every time . . . the kids get to know that George is a safe bet . . . if he could cool his temper he wouldn't be picked on."*

There were occasional references to untoward sexual behaviour. Two physically handicapped teenagers who grew fond of each other engaged in rather public displays of physical intimacy. What they actually did was no more and probably much less than what many of their able-bodied peers got up to but it was unacceptable because of the public nature of the displays – and no doubt because of the jolt to expectations. A severely retarded boy caused some upset on a work experience placement through his 'interest in the ladies'. Another teenager with exhibitionistic tendencies was an easy target for the lunchtime amusement of girls in the main school.

There were a number of references to bizzare or grossly immature patterns of behaviour. Blind children sometimes resorted to screaming, high-pitched laughter or irrational activity. They might "become babies" reverting to behaviour suited to much younger children.

Lest it be thought that the pupils in our sample were a bunch of aggressive and immature misfits, it should be stressed that the problems described above were by no means typical of the group as a whole, nor did staff have much difficulty in dealing with them. Most of the pupils we came across were engaging individuals and a pleasure to talk with. (As noted above, other pupils display lots of aggressive behaviour anyway.) Our purpose is to describe the *sorts* of problems that arise with a view to teasing out the possible implications for integration and clarifying the nature of any corrective strategies that may be advised. In any case, the great majority of these examples of anti-social behaviour came out in contexts of *improvement*. Typically, staff reported that there was less aggression, less odd behaviour, better table manners and so on than when they first came to the school. In some cases staff had taught the same pupils in a special school and testified to a considerable change along this dimension, especially with regard to the reduction in odd behaviour patterns. In some cases coming to an ordinary school exacerbated problems, at least temporarily, and led to one or two new ones. Odd and irrational behaviours stood out all the more; eating habits which might have passed muster in a special school suddenly were quite unacceptable. Childish exhibitionism also tended to be fostered by goading from peers. This was not frequent but it did happen.

The general picture can be filled in a little more by reference to the social and emotional development questionnaire. Three sets of scores are relevant: socially undesirable behaviour; personal presentation; and manners. Scores on socially undesirable behaviour were obtained along four dimensions: regard for ownership; regard for property; regard for the person; and regard for the truth. Each was scored on a one to five scale. For summary purposes a composite score was obtained by combining the scores on the separate dimensions. Scores were quite high in fact with a slight increase over the year. For the composite score, range four to 20, the means on first and second administrations respectively were 16.7 and 17.4. The distribution of changes is given below:

Change in total score	-5	-4	-3	-2	-1	0	1	2	3	4	5	6	7
Frequency	1	1	0	3	2	8	5	3	1	5	1	0	1

It should be noted that room for improvement was limited as initial scores were high: not only was the first mean high but almost a quarter (seven) scored at the top. Seven pupils were considered to have deteriorated.

Scores on personal presentation were obtained along two dimensions: appearance; and mannerisms. As before, each was scored on a one to five scale and combined. Scores were high, but there was virtually no change between the two administrations. On a scale of two to ten, means were 8.4 and 8.3 respectively. The distribution of changes in score is given in the table below:

Change in total score	-3	-2	-1	0	1	2	3	4
Frequency	1	2	9	9	7	2	0	1

Scores on manners were obtained on a single dimension scored one to five. Scores were high but there was little movement, as shown in the table. The means for first and second administrations respectively were 3.8 and 4.0. Given that a score of four corresponds to 'generally displayed good manners' this may be considered encouraging.

Changes in score	-1	0	1
Frequency	2	21	8

It should be clear by now that antisocial and bizarre behaviour presented no great problem in the integration programmes under study. This is not to say that teachers were not concerned about it. Mention has been made elsewhere of the importance teachers attached to acceptable behaviour in deciding on admissions; many felt that they were not geared to dealing with maladjusted pupils, arguing that their presence would impair their effectiveness with other pupils. Their concern operated at two levels: the project as a whole; and the individual pupil.

The first was a fear that the integration programme as a whole would suffer because of untoward behaviour or appearance on the part of some pupils. One teacher put this well – "the whole project is at risk if people think all physically handicapped are like that". This was not a concern about minor deviations from normality but about the appearance and responses of multiply-handicapped youngsters who had severe learning difficulties as well as being physically handicapped. It may be worth recording that similar feelings were voiced more strongly by a group of physically handicapped pupils who were academically able, and their comments were not confined to the severely retarded. They would distance themselves from any physically handicapped pupils who were unable to cope with the mainstream of the school's teaching.

This concern operated also at the level of individual pupils, sometimes leading to a constriction of their integration programme. Thus, a severely retarded boy started to spend two afternoons a week with an ordinary infant class; his behaviour however caused various problems and he had to be withdrawn. Two boys from a secondary age provision for pupils with severe learning difficulties went to the main school Youth Centre at lunchtime at the request of some fifth form girls who had been helping in their department. One of them "who was rather a show-off" embarrassed the girls however and the idea was dropped. Pupils with moderate learning difficulites in the same school attended some lessons in the main school. When this happened the main countervailing factor was unacceptable behaviour. In fact, all pupils who moved back to the special department from the main school did so because of this.

Staff identified two key factors in the improvement in pupils' behaviour and presentation: having normal behaviour models to copy; and being subject to firm discipline. Many teachers commented on the importance of being exposed to other behaviour patterns besides those of peers with special needs. Some severely retarded teenagers who in a previous segregated institution had oscillated between aggression and extreme withdrawal were now behaving in more acceptable ways. Their teacher in charge at the comprehensive school, who had also been with them in the Junior Training Centre, felt that this was in large measure due to the fact that "they were not seeing odd behaviours all the time; before they had only got one another to pick up patterns of behaviour from". Another teacher who had taught in an ESN(S) school and now had a class of infants with severe learning difficulties in a primary school remarked, "My children are surrounded by normality which makes a big difference to their behavioural patterns". A teacher of the deaf argued that grouping pupils with hearing losses together in one sense made them deafer than they need be; they become "out of phase with community and behaviour patterns" and fail to develop as well as they might their capacity to communicate with normally hearing people. By contrast, his experience of placing even profoundly deaf pupils in ordinary schools was that aggression and deaf mannerisms which made them stand out were quite quickly extinguished. One of the most striking examples comes from a primary school with a resource centre for the visually impaired. All pupils spend much of the day in the main school, being withdrawn only for specialist work. While in the resource area they tended to revert to bizarre and grossly imature behaviour as mentioned above. This did not happen in the main school other than by way of exception. Main school staff indeed commented on the somewhat abnormal atmosphere in the resource centre. A final example which corroborates the general point serves as a reminder that immitation can be a two-way process. It comes from a language class which served a number of primary schools. The behaviour of one boy who spent a period of time there was considered by staff in his original school to have deteriorated. This was attributed to a tendency to mimic the bad habits of older pupils in the language class.

The particular focus here has been on the efficacy of behaviour models since teachers' comments emphasised that. It is only part of what is involved however in reducing undesirable behaviour and mannerisms and promoting acceptable ones. It is clear that the various processes of peer group membership played a part as well. Pupils did not merely copy their peers. There was some evidence that they responded directly to ridicule or rebuke when their behaviour or appearance made them stand out. As they grew in self-awareness and formed or sought to form relationships with other pupils they strove to conform to peer group expectations. This led to considerable modification of behaviour.

Teachers too had expectations of them and when they did not nurse or spoil them this too had a normalising effect. A particular aspect of this was insistence on standard discipline, the same for pupils with special needs as for the others. This did not always hold and, as intimated earlier, the results can be considerable resentment on the part of other pupils. In one school where pupils with special needs had settled into quite poor patterns of behaviour – "they've been allowed to slide in the past" – a concerted policy of requiring reasonable behaviour had a beneficial effect. This policy extended to parents as well so that lapses in table manners for instance would be picked up at home just as they were discouraged at school. A further example of the improvement effected by firm handling on the part of the school is given by the case of a six-year-old boy who was a persistent absconder from home. His family found it necessary to keep a constant watch on him. Firm handling at school quickly resolved the problem.

A final comment comes from a teacher in a large comprehensive school. There was a sizeable group of pupils with moderate learning difficulties in the school. Far from being concerned about their behaviour, this teacher felt that bad behaviour was easier to deal with from these than from other pupils since "they don't tend to argue back like the more intelligent kids do these days"!

In summary, there was a broad consensus among teachers, parents and pupils themselves that they had benefited in terms of social and emotional development from taking part in the integration programmes. There were gains in self-confidence and independence, while being in an ordinary school promoted a realistic acceptance of the individual's handicapping condition. Friendly relationships between pupils with special needs and their peers did occur but they tended to be limited and often involved outgroups in the school. Negative relationships such as teasing were comparatively rare. The incidence of untoward behaviour and bizarre mannerisms was considered to have greatly lessened.

These various changes, detailed in the text above, are advanced in a tentative manner since they come from situations which were not chosen to be representative of integration programmes in general. As against that, the broad agreement between teachers, parents and the young people themselves may be noted. What is of more substantial interest is the range of factors bearing on social and emotional development that is illustrated. The development of young people with special needs and the relationships they form are governed by many factors relating to the school and the individuals themselves. These can be overlooked in any simple comparison between integration programmes and segregated schooling. So our effort here has been to elucidate these factors and where appropriate suggest courses of action that may enhance the social and emotional development of young people with special needs.

Chapter Nineteen
Perceptions and Attitudes

When she came first everybody made a fuss – teachers crossing the playground would go out of their way to talk to her – now nobody takes any notice. (Teacher in a secondary school)

In the previous two chapters we have discussed the social and emotional development of pupils with special needs and described the social interactions that took place between them and their peers. Interwoven with these various processes, shaping them and being shaped by them, are the prevailing perceptions of pupils with special needs and attitudes toward them. Positive open attitudes and realistic perceptions lead to greater interaction and enhanced social and emotional development, while contact between these pupils and their peers leads to the correction of stereotypes and the emergence of more accepting attitudes. Thus, the importance of attitudes in the integration context is twofold: they are important in their own right since a major goal of integration is attitudinal, to promote accepting and realistic attitudes; and they are important through being linked with every aspect of social interaction and development. In this chapter we look first at the range of attitudes encountered towards pupils with special needs on the part of teachers and fellow-pupils. Then we consider some of the factors that impinge on the formation of attitudes and conclude with a note on the grouping aspect of some forms of integration.

Attitudes toward pupils with special needs
Most of the research carried out into the attitudes of ordinary teachers has been done in the United States, where the legal requirement to educate pupils in the least restrictive environment

means that many more teachers are faced with teaching pupils with special needs. Numerous studies have investigated class teachers' perceptions of these pupils and their attitudes toward educating them in the mainstream. Reviews of these studies such as Alexander and Strain (1978), Horne (1979) and Baker and Gottlieb (1980) paint a negative picture. Attitudes reported were generally unfavourable to mainstreaming and many teachers and other professionals were found to perceive pupils with special needs in a negative light. Thus, the great majority of teachers in the Shotel *et al.* (1972) study affirmed that most emotionally disturbed and educable mentally retarded pupils should not be placed in ordinary classes. Panda and Bartel (1972) found that teachers asked to evaluate pupils along various dimensions rated those with special needs lower than others on all factors. Moore and Fine (1978) asked teachers to complete an interpersonal checklist for hypothetical special and normal pupils; this elicited distinct stereotypic images from all teacher groups, those with experience of special pupils as well as those without. Also, 50 per cent of ordinary teachers were opposed to placing retarded pupils in ordinary classes. In this country Tobin (1972) explored the attitudes of both experienced and trainee teachers toward pupils with special needs. He discovered that both groups of teachers had least preference for having hearing impaired and maladjusted pupils in their classes. In addition, experienced teachers were reluctant to accept the visually impaired, and trainee teachers, pupils with speech disorders.

What light does our research shed on this issue? Before advancing our evidence we note that it relates to teachers from schools attended by pupils with special needs. Many though not all of our respondents would have had teaching contact with such pupils at some point. The relevance of this is that teachers were not responding on the basis of stereotypes in general circulation, hearsay or imagined reaction; rather their comments were based on their own experience, however limited. It should be noted too that teachers' responses referred primarily to those pupils placed at their school rather than to pupils with special needs in general. Thus, one set of responses will have the visually impaired in mind, another pupils with learning difficulties and so on.

The questionnaire to teachers (details in Appendix C) asked:

Do you feel it is appropriate for handicapped pupils to be placed in your school?

*Please indicate any advantages or disadvantages you are parti-
cularly conscious of.*

The reponses to the direct question were as follows:

Yes 223
No 7
No view expressed 17

While the questionnaire was not designed to investigate
teachers' attitudes scientifically and various factors limit the
generalisability of its findings, this marks a striking degree of
acceptance on the part of ordinary teachers: 90 per cent of all
respondents and 97 per cent of those answering this question felt
that the placement of handicapped pupils at their school was
appropriate. It should not be supposed that responses were biased
toward those favouring integration. Indeed, the contrary is at least
as plausible: those who had strong views against integrating such
pupils could be assumed to be eager to avail of the opportunity to
make their viewpoint known. For the vast majority, the appropriateness of locational integration at the very least was beyond
dispute.

These findings would seem to paint a more optimistic picture
than the studies referred to above. Several factors should be
noted. First, most of those studies are American and refer to
mainstreaming in the sense of placing pupils in ordinary classes
from special classes, whereas in our study some of the pupils spent
much of their time in special classes. Secondly, many of the studies
were conducted some time ago when an 'out of sight out of mind'
philosophy was far more common in respect of the handicapped
than it is now. Thirdly, some of the integration programmes in our
study involved schools that had been chosen because of the
positive attitudes of head teachers and members of staff. To this
extent the sample may not be representative of schools in general.
On the other hand, there were numerous examples of teachers
with initial reservations and even objections who changed their
minds and endorsed the integration programme in their school.

There is a further methodological consideration. The measurement of attitudes is a precarious and limited enterprise. Social
psychologists have devised various methods but all rely in the end
on asking people hypothetical questions about their likely
behaviour or responses in certain situations. (It is hardly surprising
that the correlation between measured attitudes and behaviour is

in general low.) Baker and Gottlieb (op. cit.) note that two basic approaches have been used to acquire information on teachers' acceptance of mainstreaming: one is to present them with statements that will elicit attitudes toward mainstreaming and ask whether they agree or disagree; the other is to provide descriptions of pupils with various learning problems and ask what they consider to be the most appropriate placement for them. We too were able to make some relevant observations and hold follow-up interviews – but with the difference that the questions were about real pupils in real classrooms, in a situation where it was known we were conducting further enquiries, interviewing colleagues and so on. This made it more likely that we were tapping attitudes based on *actual* contact with pupils, not hypothetical responses to abstract situations. The distinction is fundamental since it is only when confronted with teaching or dealing with actual pupils that teachers' real attitudes emerge plainly.

Apart from the general acceptance, what of teachers' attitudes in specific situations? We examined various situations relating to classroom and general contact. A number of statements can be advanced as a result, and in particular a definite pattern of attitude change emerged.

1. Initial reactions were frequently negative and were only gradually replaced by more positive ones. Hesitance, over-protectiveness, even fear and downright hostility, were by no means uncommon. Teachers expressed doubts about the feasibility of teaching or supervising pupils with special needs; there was much uncertainty about how best to proceed and anxiety as to whether their needs were being met; and some teachers admitted to having felt uncomfortable in their presence. The tendency toward over-protective attitudes was the subject of particular comment by outside professionals and was readily apparent to us in a number of cases. Teachers were reluctant to treat these pupils like their peers and make comparable demands on them. This tendency was most pronounced with physical or visual impairment where mobility was limited or imperilled and teachers feared for children's safety or worried lest physical exertion might harm them. Thus, physical handicapped pupils sat in their wheelchairs in a corner of the gym while their classmates did PE. Another aspect of this was the tendency to reinforce pupils' specialness by singling them out in all sorts of minor and well-intentioned but isolating ways.

Lucy suffers from spina bifida and spends most of her time in a wheelchair. (She is the girl referred to in the quotation at the beginning of the chapter.) *When she first transferred to secondary school she was the centre of attention, never on her own in the playground and teachers detouring to have a word with her. However well intentioned all this attention was, it only served to highlight Lucy's difference – and signal the fact that she was not accepted as a member of the school on the same basis as other pupils. So it was that the failure to take particular notice of her marked her acceptance into the school community.*

The initial negative reactions did generally give place to more positive attitudes. A geography teacher described his reaction on learning that he would be one of the first teachers in his school to have physically handicapped pupils in his class: "I was horrified . . . well, perhaps more apprehensive . . . about how I would feel emotionally". After a while however, "I didn't notice them – now I am used to the idea". Another teacher was strongly opposed to any involvement in an integration programme when it was first mooted for her school, yet three years later volunteered to have a profoundly deaf boy in her class. One head teacher who was doubtful about the wisdom of having pupils with special needs in her school agreed reluctantly to a twelve-month trial period for a seven-year-old spina bifida girl. Two years later she spoke extremely enthusiastically about the benefits for all concerned – the girl, other pupils and the staff: "Denise has done an awful lot of good for everybody . . . (the other children) want to help all the time . . . we wouldn't be without her now". In another case staff in a primary school had strong reservations about the proposed placement of a spastic girl. The head invited open discussion on the matter and staff were encouraged to air their opposition. This helped to clear up misperceptions and establish what sort of support was felt to be necessary. In due course opposition faded and the girl became well accepted in the school.

2. Most staff were prepared to have pupils with special needs in their classes or teaching groups, though without any great enthusiasm for the most part. A few welcomed their presence for the professional challenge it posed and eagerly sought ways of presenting subject matter so that it was relevant and meaningful to them. There was some reluctance but only the odd instance of outright refusal to teach them. One PE teacher admitted to being

repelled by physical deformity and did not wish to have disabled pupils in his group. In one school attitudes of main school teachers to the special centre were generally poor and many would, if asked, refuse to have pupils from it in their class. This was bound up with a host of complicating factors at local level and was not a simple refusal on their part to teach these pupils.

3. While teachers generally accepted the presence of pupils with special needs in their classes, this did not mean that they always took them seriously for teaching purposes. We described in chapter 15 some classroom strategies that teachers used, some of which constituted excellent practice. On occasion however, there was a lack of willingness to engage in serious teaching or to strive for maximum educational benefit from the opportunity. Teachers felt that they were not equipped to teach these pupils or lacked the time in a large class, and that anyway their educational progress was the responsibility of specialist staff in the school. One science teacher affirmed that the presence of pupils with moderate learning difficulties in his lessons was justified "in terms of the social integration . . . that's a good enough reason to be there". Another teacher referred to the poor written ability of such pupils and intimated that she was not concerned about the standard of work produced so long as pupils could hold their place in the class: "I tend to accept whatever he has done . . . I don't mark it".

4. Teachers responded more or less favourably to different groups of pupils. For example, the physically handicapped were more favourably perceived than those with learning difficulties, either moderate or severe. Pupils with mild learning difficulties were generally favourably perceived, being regarded as comparable to the school's existing slow learners. Those with severe learning difficulties were widely regarded as entirely different; particularly if they had associated behaviour problems, there was seen to be no continuity between their needs and the needs of mainstream pupils. The least well accepted pupils were those with a secondary handicapping condition, eg physically handicapped or communication disordered pupils of low ability, or where serious behavioural disturbance accompanied the primary handicapping condition. Indeed, it seemed that behaviour was a particularly crucial factor as regards teachers' acceptance. In one school catering for pupils with both moderate and severe learning difficulties there was highly critical comment from ordinary

teachers about "the two standards of behaviour" they perceived. In addition there was a notion of a 'ceiling' of handicap, a level of severity beyond which integration was seen to make little sense. These findings are of interest in the context of Tobin's (op.cit.) findings discussed above.

5. A further insight on teachers' attitudes comes from looking at reported ease of relationship with pupils with special needs. Teachers were asked: *Do you feel at ease with handicapped pupils in – group situations; one-to-one situations; social situations?* Nearly three-quarters of the 235 respondents claimed that they felt comfortable in all three settings. Just under a quarter found themselves at ease in only one or two settings, while five per cent (12 teachers) found all three situations difficult. Group situations were responsible for approximately half of the difficulties reported, the remainder being split evenly between one-to-one and social situations.

Self-report data in such a sensitive area may not be entirely reliable, though in some cases we found the responses corroborated by other information. To the extent that these represent the situation in some measure, they are further evidence of reasonably positive experiences and suggest that many teachers had overcome initial fears and uncertainties. It is worth noting that a number of those reporting lack of ease commented on their limited contact or involvement with the pupils with special needs in their school.

So much for teachers' attitudes. What of fellow pupils? How did they perceive and react toward them? Once again, the literature does not paint an encouraging picture. Horne (op.cit.), summarising some American studies, notes that 'the bulk of the studies done are supportive of the lower status position of the disabled and the underachieving'. Pupils reflect teacher attitudes and bestow greater admiration and acceptance on 'normal', 'achieving' students. Kutner (1971) found that there was 'a considerable residue of fear, hostility and aversion' toward the handicapped.

On the positive side, various studies have shown that attitudes can be improved. Rapier *et al.* (1972) found that peers' (aged 9-11) attitudes toward physically handicapped pupils changed toward a more positive perception as a result of having them in their classroom for a year. Johnson *et al.* (1979) carried out an experiment where non-handicapped students and mentally retarded peers were taught bowling together. Different groups were given different instructions and it was found that emphasising cooperation promoted 'more support, praise, encouragement, concern and acceptance from handicapped teenagers toward mentally retarded peers' than the alternative approaches. Both instruction and first-hand experience were found by Simpson *et al.* (1976) to modify the attitudes of 7-8 year-olds toward mentally retarded and emotionally disturbed children. The instruction comprised four weekly sessions of information (lecture, filmstrip and so on) and discussion about handicapped children. The firsthand experience comprised limited integration with emotionally disturbed children. This experience was combined with the instruction but did not produce any better response than instruction on its own. A small study carried out by Handlers and Austin (1980) set up five specific activities for older teenagers: discussion of issues relating to handicap; individual research on specific disabilities; viewing a film followed by answering questions designed to identify feelings of sympathy or lack of it; simulation activities related to various handicapping conditions; and direct contact through a personal interview with a blind student. Students evaluated their own attitude change and felt that they had become more positive and accepting of disabled people. Direct contact was regarded as the most effective method for improving attitudes.

Turning to the integration programmes we studied, what can be said of pupils' perceptions of their peers and their attitudes toward them? We have seen something of this in the preceding two chapters where interactions and relationships have been discussed. Here we make a number of summary remarks and report on two surveys carried out.

First, pupils with special needs *were* accepted. The predominant reaction was one of low-key, undramatic acceptance. After a period of initial curiosity, especially in the case of very young children and in regard to the physically handicapped and hearing impaired, the presence in a school of peers with special needs was generally accepted as a matter of course. Sometimes indeed it seemed as if pupils found it easier than their teachers to take the change in their stride. Pupils in the lessons we observed were most commonly judged to be 'accepting' of their presence. Rejection or even merely tolerating them was uncommon. As regards the overall level of assimilation into the teaching groups observed, the majority were either 'well assimilated' or 'moderately well assimilated'. There was mild opposition on occasions, usually at secondary level when this was the first time that pupils had come face to face with those who were disabled in some way. As a general rule however, if they have been present within a body of pupils throughout their schooling the likelihood is that the others will accept their presence as part of the natural order of things.

Secondly, pupils with special needs were often ascribed an outgroup status. Though accepted, they were seen as different or special in many schools. Their friendships tended to be with other pupils with special needs or with the school's other outgroups, while relationships with main school pupils were often unequal ones of helping or caring. Thirdly, there were some negative perceptions and reactions, though fewer than might have been expected. Teasing did occur but was not considered a problem. If it stayed within reasonable bounds, it marked a step on the way to normality since surviving it helped define the individual as a normal member of the community. In any case, when negative perceptions and reactions did occur this was often due to factors unrelated to special needs. Just as with other pupils, personality and other factors affected how they were perceived.

A questionnaire survey carried out in his own school by the head of a slow learners department provides information on how a group of pupils with special needs was perceived in one school. The school in question is a large comprehensive school, catering at the time for 13 pupils with severe learning difficulties (in a self-contained area of the school) and 67 pupils with moderate learning difficulties. Pupils were asked by questionnaire a number of questions about the presence of 'handicapped pupils' at their school, whether they were different from themselves and what contact they had with them. The response rate varied from 83 per cent in first year to 56 per cent in the sixth form, with an average of just over 70 per cent.

A number of clear pointers emerged. First, virtually all respondents were aware of the presence of these pupils at the school and knew where they were located. It was clear from the responses that for 'handicapped pupils' they read those who had severe learning difficulties. (This was evident in their estimates of numbers, comments on classroom contact and the handicapped pupils they named.) The corollary of this is that pupils with moderate learning difficulties were, relatively at least, seen as part of the main pupil body.

Secondly, there was a degree of unanimity on how these pupils were perceived. The respondents were first asked in what way(s) they were different. Four categories were provided: behaviour, looks, age and capabilities. Capabilities proved to be the most distinguishing element; this was noted by over 90 per cent of pupils, and increasingly so by older pupils. This was followed by behaviour, marked by three quarters of the respondents. Looks received a mention from one third to a half of pupils. A further question asked respondents to describe what the handicapped were like as people. Six adjectives were provided: quiet, timid, noisy, cheeky, friendly and naughty. The adjectives most frequently chosen were 'friendly' (just over two thirds) and 'quiet' (a little under a half). About one third mentioned 'timid' and 'noisy'.

Thirdly, the responses corroborated our own impression based on observation and interviews with the staff and pupils that those with severe learning difficulties made little impact on the school. Most respondents (nearly three quarters) could name only one while very few could name more than three.

Further light on pupils' attitudes is shed by a questionnaire study carried out under our auspices. Details are taken from Lair and Sauser (unpublished memorandum). A questionnaire was administered to 48 pupils in each of four large secondary schools. Three had substantial provision for pupils with learning difficulties, physical disabilities and hearing impairment respectively. The fourth school which had no such provision was used as a control. Samples were drawn equally from third and fifth year, balanced for sex and high and low ability. The questionnaire comprised eight hypothetical descriptions of pupils with learning difficulties, physical disabilities and hearing impairment respectively, one of each sex, and two pupils who did not have special needs. It sought to establish whether pupils would respond differentially to the four categories in terms of 'liking' and 'talking and associating with'.

In the event, there was little differentiation. All pupils preferred to talk and associate with those of their own sex and were more likely to like them. Secondly, there was a clear hierarchy of preference for pupils based on the nature of their special needs. This went (from most preferred to least preferred) as follows:

1. Normal pupils
2. Physically handicapped pupils
3. Hearing impaired pupils
4. Pupils with learning difficulties.

Thirdly, no differences were found in relation to age or ability level (of respondents) or school attended. The absence of a link between school attended (and consequent familiarity with one or other type of special need) and preference for a particular group is perhaps the most notable finding. Other evidence would suggest hypotheses that there would have been stronger preferences for physically handicapped pupils in the school catering for such pupils and similarly for the other schools, but these were not supported.

The formation of attitudes

Social perceptions and attitudes are governed by many factors. As far as attitudes to pupils with special needs are concerned, we have seen the importance of first hand contact for both teachers and fellow pupils and how familiarity can eradicate negative perceptions and lead to acceptance. For teachers the importance of knowledge about handicapping conditions and competence in dealing with pupils with special needs was discussed in chapter 7. Initiating integration programmes was discussed in chapter 4 and it emerged that the way in which a programme is introduced can affect how it is seen and attitudes toward it for a considerable period of time. The physical environment plays a part too; we saw in chapter 10 that physical isolation can lead to perceptions of separateness and difference.

Baker and Gottlieb (op.cit.) refer to five components of ordinary teachers' attitudes toward integration: (i) knowledge of pupils' academic and social behaviour, (ii) feelings about their own competence to teach them, (iii) expectations of receiving support, (iv) beliefs about the advantages and disadvantages of different placements and (v) general educational attitudes. Other factors could be mentioned such as the operation of stereotypes, the prevailing attitudes toward the disabled and minorities in general and the self-perceptions of non-disabled groups within society at large.

It is clear that there are many closely interwoven factors at work here. No short account could do them justice. In this section we pick out for detailed consideration two particular factors that govern how pupils with special needs are perceived, viz the age of the group in question and the communication capacities of the pupils. In addition, we develop further some of the considerations involved in introducing an integration programme to a school and making formal interventions to secure acceptance for it.

Age

The significance of age in the formation and evolution of attitudes toward pupils with special needs is pervasive. There are at least eight different considerations.

The first two can be considered together.

a. The precise form that play activities – and indeed peer interaction in general – take varies with age.

b. Whereas the use of language is limited in the interactions of younger children, the importance of oral communication increases as they get older. Thus, games such as tag or running in a line are familiar sights in the primary school playground. Even where spoken language is used, by older infants and juniors, it is rarely necessary to be able to use language – much less understand it – in order to participate. The child with poor communication ability can still take part in skipping games for example, even though he or she may be unable to sing out the accompanying rhymes. At secondary school level however corridor and playground inter-actions rely heavily on the ability to communicate orally. This means that many pupils with special needs – more particularly the hearing impaired, the language disordered and those with pronounced learning difficulties – are at a distinct disadvantage.

Observations conducted on separate occasions in a primary school attended by children with impaired vision illustrate the above. Take Philip for instance, a six-year-old with vision – that is deteriorating – in one eye only. In the playground one break time:

Philip wanders about the playground on his own. A boy is sitting against the wall. Philip senses that he is there and says something to him. A girl goes up to Philip and takes his hand and walks a little with him before leaving him. A boy goes up to Philip and gets hold of his hand and runs around the playground with him at great speed. They stop and the boy starts to stamp in puddles. Philip copies him. The boy leaves Philip who runs off on his own very quickly. . . . He slows down slightly as he approaches other children – generally they move out of the way for him where collisions are likely – but most of the time he weaves in and out of children very well. Another boy takes hold of his hands and they run off. Philip runs faster than this boy and so actually leads him. The boy leads Philip to a window. Philip knocks out a rhythm on the window . . . (field notes)

In contrast, the following observations were made in a comprehensive school attended by hearing impaired pupils:

There are two groups of hearing impaired pupils in lunch – five boys and a group of girls. They do not interact with the non-handicapped children . . . After dinner the five boys go out to play. A group of eight girls form and walk outside. They stand together talking (mouthing and signing) for about 20 minutes. Occasionally a (hearing) pupil comes up to one of them and teases her. Generally very little interaction with pupils from main school. (field notes)

The absence of interaction in the second case is not to be explained entirely by reference to the age difference. Clearly, communication ability comes in to it – so much so that we treat it separately below – but it is fair to suppose that the age factor is highly relevant.

c. The gap between the respective levels of development of some pupils with special needs and their peers increases with age – and becomes more apparent. Thus, it may be feasible to bring together children with severe learning difficulties and ordinary children in reception or infant classes but the common ground they share falls away from seven or eight years upward. In one set of special provisions for pupils with moderate and severe learning difficulties there was a good deal of association between the two groups at the primary school level (eg activities such as swimming, horse-riding and some classroom-based work) but this was held to be quite unrealistic at the secondary level. As one specialist teacher put it, "the gap between the two (groups) can become an enormous void". Furthermore, some pupils such as those suffering from Down's Syndrome *looked* different from their peers and this accentuated the perception of difference in terms of achievement.

d. In addition to the development gap, there is also a growing divergence in interests. The typical pattern is for interests to become more specialised. With young children interests are very diverse and fickle. As they get older however, they tend to select particular interests and develop them to the exclusion of others. Also, there is growing pressure to conform to peer values, which can lead to further specialisation of interests. This specialisation can exclude pupils with special needs by virtue of their handicapping conditions and the limitations on experience and competence they impose. It is observed too that some pupils relate better to adults than their peers; this orientation to the adult world can be an isolating factor in some instances.

e. Closely related to both (c) and (d) is the impact of the handicapping condition on the feelings of the individual concerned. Except perhaps for those with severe learning difficulties, there is with time a growing awareness of one's differences from contemporaries. This awareness serves to heighten further the problems customarily associated with adolescence. Thus, the following comments were made of hearing impaired pupils by two teachers of the deaf in an effort to explain their lack of close association with hearing peers: "They are very conscious of their (hearing) aids and don't like sharing (eg in games) which has made them more conscious". Likewise with physically handicapped adolescents: one 17-year-old who had suffered polio earlier in life was considered not to have come to terms with her handicap – "She feels it totally blocks her life". Another girl was considered to "bottle it up and explode at home".

f. As children grow older they tend to pick up the prevailing ideas from society at large. If integration does not commence until secondary schooling and pupils have their first contact with peers who have special needs at this stage, they will have to contend with many misperceptions and the fears born of them. Many of the comments from ordinary pupils testify to this: "I had never been with them (the physically handicapped) before and you don't know what they're like". . . "I was very frightened of them at first, I wondered if I should know how to talk to them". However if children with special needs have been visible within ordinary schools from early in a child's educational career then the psychological 'block' that one teacher reported on thinking back to her own childhood – "If the handicapped had been around all the time I would not have had this terrible barrier to overcome" – is less likely. This is not to say that young children take the presence in their midst of those who are in some way different completely in their stride; it does mean however that the misperceptions prompted by stereotypes are less likely. An example of the misperceptions that can arise with infants comes from a school where reception class children had been frightened by the appearance of hearing impaired children with "strings in their ears". Others had found them funny, while slightly older children had been overheard describing children who used phonic ears as "robots".

g. There is a tendency toward greater peer competitivity with age. For much of primary schooling comtemporary educational practice lays emphasis on co-operation between children: working together on joint tasks and group activities. Secondary schooling however remains strongly characterised by the implicit – and in many instances quite explicit – encouragement of peer rivalry and competitiveness. Thus, in most primary schools we visited the readiness of ordinary children to help out those with special needs, and the natural way in which this was done, were well in evidence. This was less likely to occur at secondary level where pupils could be impatient and even intolerant of classmates who had difficulty in following instructions or contributing to discussion or in carrying out specific tasks such as reading a passage aloud.

h. Finally, the reactions of ordinary pupils toward those with special needs may well be influenced by difficulties that the former experience themselves. As they get older they must contend with the personal adjustments of adolescence, cope with academic and possibly examination pressures, and may face the prospect of unemployment when they leave school. These problems can serve to reduce tolerance and sympathy for pupils whose problems are obvious and in a sense legitimated within the school and who receive considerable assistance and support.

Communication ability

We became increasingly aware in the course of our research of the importance of communication ability in integration. Hearing impaired and communication disordered pupils faced particular problems in social encounters because of their impaired speech. In several cases a major criterion in deciding pupils' readiness for placement in an ordinary class was the capacity to communicate verbally with peers.

The difficulties that arise are well illustrated by reference to a group of hearing impaired pupils attending a comprehensive school. There was little evidence of positive association, much less of active friendship, between these pupils and their hearing peers. Our perception, reinforced by comments from the majority of teachers of the deaf at the school and some main school staff, was that these pupils were a definite outgroup. There were various reasons for this but a major one was the limited oral capacity of so many of them. This inhibited communication in fairly obvious ways and restricted their participation in socialising networks. Moreover, the limited capacity to verbalise meaning, emotion and so on led to their getting into fights more often; language can frequently serve to defuse tense social situations, and in its absence physical conflict is more likely to result. It may be noted that this is particularly likely to happen when, as often with hearing impaired pupils, social skills are limited. The combination of incoherent – and personally frustrating – language and poor social skills can lead to untoward physical response and aggression.

It should not be supposed however that poor speech seals pupils off and that they should be protected from exposure to their peers on that account. In an authority which sought to educate some hearing impaired pupils, including profoundly deaf, in ordinary schools we conducted a number of case studies of individual pupils. Jimmy was a profoundly deaf boy (100db loss) of average ability. While he had no close friend in school and was teased by his peers from time to time, he was recognised as having many acquaintances within his form. His speech was considered by a teacher of the deaf as 'unintelligible to the unsophisticated listener, he relies on gesture and words or phrases for communication'. In spite of this 'he succeeds very well (in) communicating with his peer group even though his speech and language patterns have very many defects' (support teacher). Wayne was another profoundly deaf boy, of below average ability. He too could only communicate through a combination of gesture and individual words or phrases, and yet was 'completely accepted by the other children in the class' who had 'a great affection for him'. An entry in a combined report from the teacher of the deaf and support teacher reads as follows: 'His friends . . . have not been unduly perturbed about Wayne's lack of natural oral communication . . .

(Wayne) continues to communicate with gestures, mime, words and phrases. Other children manage to communicate equally well with him. There has been no stress on either side.'

Although in both cases the pupil's acceptance was undoubtedly aided by his personality – friendly and reasonably out-going – and normal appearance, this is only part of the reason. It would appear that being individually integrated made a considerable difference: they did not have hearing impaired peers ready to hand and were obliged to communicate more with hearing pupils. Dale (1978) found that when two or more hearing impaired pupils joined an ordinary class the amount of interaction with hearing pupils was much less than when there was only one hearing impaired pupil, and they were not perceived as part of a hearing-impaired outgroup in the school. Indeed, the regular association with hearing pupils which individual integration allows, and even enjoins, frequently leads to the acceptance of the hearing impaired pupil into a normally hearing group.

Formal preparation

The issues involved in setting up an integration programme have been discussed in chapter 4. These are also relevant here. The way in which a programme is introduced to a school and the sort of preparation carried out can affect outcomes in many ways. Among these outcomes attitudes are likely to be shaped in important ways by steps taken at the early stages. Various examples have been given of the detrimental effect on staff attitudes of failing to consult staff or seeking to implement integration without adequate support. The teacher who was told "Oh, by the way we will be integrating next term, and using your class", could be excused a little resentment.

It must not be taken for granted that teachers will actively welcome an integration programme. Outright opposition is un-likely to be found as we have seen, but hesitance and ambivalence can certainly be expected. These need to be countered in a positive manner if the inherent potential is to be realised. The various steps that can be taken were discussed in chapter 4 and need not be repeated here. Where staff are concerned, it is important that they be given early information and made to feel involved in the process. Even if they will not be directly affected they need to develop a commitment to the integration programme as an integral part of their school. As for pupils, it is a matter of judgement as to whether specific preparation is necessary or not. The research literature shows that positive attitudes can be promoted by various instructional and information-giving means. Sheer contact is a major determinant of attitude change however, and effort may well be best directed at ensuring that contact is not impeded by organisational or other factors.

It should be noted however that preparation can be overdone and become counter-productive. Excessive attention paid to particular pupils can have the effect of emphasising their differences and making it impossible for them to become accepted members of the school on the same footing as other pupils. We have seen above that the special status conferred by undue attention is as unwelcome to some pupils as it is detrimental to their social and emotional development. A further reason why too much preparation and too forceful intervention are undesirable is that they inhibit attitude change. Apart from the considerations above, this follows from social psychological theories of attitude change. In particular, self-perception and cognitive dissonance theories suggest that a modest campaign can effect attitude change when stronger efforts would be quite ineffective. Numerous experimental studies have demonstrated this. Essentially, the idea is that dissonance – the gap between what one does and what one believes one should do – is removed either internally by revising one's notion of what one should do, ie, changing attitude, or externally by having a sufficiently strong motivation so that the original gap is no longer perceived to be relevant. This can happen if one has very strong inducements to behave in a certain way or faces dire threats if one does not; in either case, the original attitude is preserved intact.

An illustration of the process is given by 'forbidden toy' studies. The child who refrains from playing with a toy under the severe threat of punishment has a perfectly good reason for doing so; there is no dissonance between what he does and what he believes he should do, so he maintains his liking for the toy. The child who refrains under mild threat still experiences a dissonance since the external reason is not strong enough; this can only be removed by changing what he believes he wants to do, ie, ceasing to like the toy. The relevance to promoting attitude change in schools is clear. If too much is made of how pupils with special needs should be treated, by way of either threat or reward, appropriate behaviour may well be achieved but not attitude change. On the other hand, if appropriate behaviour can be fostered without *undue* external pressure it is more likely that internal changes will be affected and attitude change results.

Group considerations

Most of the integration programmes in our study involved groups of pupils with special needs attending an ordinary school. This has clear implications for integration patterns, degree of assimilation and other social variables, as discussed in earlier chapters. It is also directly related to the visibility of these pupils in a school. Having one or two such pupils is clearly different from having 50 or 60, and it is reasonable to suppose that the existence of a recognisable group affects how they are perceived. In this section we look at three group factors: the size of the group, especially in relation to the overall size of the school; the status accorded the special provision within the school; and associate factors relating to how individuals are perceived in stereotypical or deviant terms.

i. Size of the group

There are no hard and fast rules governing how many pupils with special needs can be integrated into a school. The nature of the pupils' need and of the school and the way in which the two are brought together must all be considered. While the absolute size of the group can be important, it is more often the case, especially at primary level, that the relative size within the school is what matters.

Two examples where the size of the special group was by common consent excessive may be instructive. The first was a medium-sized (approximately 200 pupils) junior school to which had been attached special provision catering for some 80 pupils with learning difficulties. The two groups remained quite separate and there was little association between them. Moreover the special provision was viewed in a negative way that was virtually without precedent in the other programmes we studied. This arose in part from other factors unconnected with size, but size did enter into it as well. Some existing school staff felt as if a baby cuckoo had been hatched in their midst. They resented what they perceived as the disproportionate size of the new provision and the attention lavished on it, and feared that its pupils were going to swamp the school.

In the second example the sheer size of the group was more important. This was a department for some 120 pupils with moderate learning difficulties attached to a large comprehensive school. Here again there was little association between the department and the main school. The department was not viewed negatively so much as being peripheral to the main school, which indeed it was since it functioned more or less autonomously. The relevance of size here was that the department was organised in a cohesive way and was large enough to function as a natural community in its own light. In this way its size militated against seeking the sorts of relationships with the main school that would have made the department an integral part of it and helped ensure that its pupils were viewed in a less peripheral way.

These are somewhat extreme examples but staff generally were concerned about the impact of numbers. While few might go along with the person who objected to any groupings of physically handicapped pupils on the grounds that they became "human zoos" whereby attention was needlessly focused on pupils' disabilities, many were concerned to avoid or at least minimise the potentially stigmatising effects of having large numbers of pupils with special needs gathered in one place. A common ploy was to disperse them into different classes when they joined mainstream lessons. One school had a working rule that not more than two pupils from its basic studies department would join any main school lesson. This was to facilitate teaching but also to ensure that integrated pupils were not ascribed a 'basic studies' identity. This policy of seeking a low profile was followed in a number of schools. Its absence, when large numbers of pupils with special needs were integrated in to the same classes (and their character was in consequence changed), did seem to lead to unfortunate stigmatising effects.

ii. Status of special provision

Quite apart from the size of the group, there are considerations flowing from the mere fact that it *is* a group. Provision for pupils with special needs is often accorded low status in the hierarchy of schools – witness the standing of remedial departments in many secondary schools. This was the case also with some of the integration programmes we studied. It did not apply to all of them however; a few seemed to enjoy high status and the provision they offered was seen as an integral – and valued – part of the school's educational offerings. Among the factors that governed how a special provision was rated were the following: its relationship to the main school; its familiarity; and the level of its staffing.

The more isolated a special centre was within a school the more likely it was to be perceived negatively. In some cases where the centre was so detached that it barely impinged on the life of the school it seemed to lie outside any hierarchy of value judgements in the school. When a certain minimum level of contact was achieved however low involvement was often associated with negative perceptions. When the special centre was well integrated into the school and its pupils attended some mainstream lessons, negative perceptions were less likely. This was especially the case if the centre was seen to make a contribution to the life of the school – providing specialist help for mainstream pupils as required, contributing to mainstream teaching and extra curricular activities, maintaining a presence in the main school staffroom. In one school where these various measures were taken the special centre was seen as an integral working part of the school that offered a specialist service just as did the science and music departments and the negative perceptions common elsewhere were little in evidence.

A further factor governing the status accorded a special provision is how familiar main school staff and pupils are with pupils in the special provision. In the case of staff it can be important that they have an appropriate understanding of their special needs and teaching requirements. This is related to the previous factor of course since the closer the relationship between special centre and main school the greater the visibility of pupils with special needs throughout the school. We discussed earlier in the chapter the acclimatisation process whereby teachers moved from initial negative reactions to more positive responses. A key element in this process was sheer contact: hostility, fear and so on were dissipated through the firsthand experience of seeing how unjustified and inappropriate such responses were. When this element was absent the process can fail to develop and staff remain at the early negative stages. As well then as ensuring that pupils maintain a presence in the school it is important to provide appropriate information to staff and possibly other pupils about them. Several teachers in charge of special centres saw it as part of their function indeed to do a public relations exercise on behalf of the special centre – being readily available in the main school staffroom, availing of casual opportunities to explain briefly the aims and working of the centre, on occasion inviting staff into the special centre.

A third factor to consider is the status assigned to special centre staff, whether formally through the allocation of scale posts or informally through involvement in the workings of the school. Whether one likes it or not, the status of a department in a school is affected by the scale post assigned to the head of department. There was general awareness of this. Several secondary schools for example allocated a scale 4 post to the head of the special centre; one school allocated a Senior Teacher post and a scale 4 post to the head and deputy head respectively of a 6-strong department. In several cases the head of the special centre belonged to the small group of senior staff comprising the heads of the major departments and had an equal voice with them in matters of general school policy. One head spoke of how he had put the special centre to the fore and made it a major department within the school, partly through ensuring that its staff were appointed at a senior level and were perceived as such. Drawing attention to this is not to ignore the significance of the *quality* of the staff in post. This is always central and probably more important than any other single factor, but it would be unrealistic to assume that status and effective working are not affected by extraneous factors as this also.

iii. Associative factors

There are two considerations here: To what extent are individuals seen in stereotypical 'handicap' terms through being included in the group? and To what extent is the group as a whole ascribed a handicapped or deviant identity because of some individuals within the group? In one school catering for a group of hearing impaired pupils the dominant perception on the part of the main school staff was that they were "daft as well as deaf". They had low expectations of behaviour and performance from them. When a hearing impaired pupil produced good work in a mainstream lesson class teachers were found to "express surprise at the type and standard produced". In several instances the pupils themselves were very conscious of the possible stigma arising out of being associated with the special centre. Remedial assistance was given to pupils from the mainstream by one special centre; staff reported how such pupils would delay their arrival if possible until their mainstream peers had gone into lessons so that nobody would see them. This was corroborated by talking to some of the pupils who resented being associated with the special centre. In another school, a comprehensive catering for a large number of physically handicapped pupils, some of the more able and articulate pupils sought to distance themselves from the physically handicapped as a group. They wanted to be seen as the academic sixth-formers which they were who happened to be disabled, rather than as physically handicapped pupils who happened to be doing A-levels. This was made more difficult by the presence in the school of a physically handicapped bloc.

The other side of this particular coin is the fact that the way in which a group is perceived can be affected by the behaviour and characteristics of individuals within the group. In the school just mentioned for example there had at one stage been a small number of pupils who had severe learning difficulties in addition to their physical handicaps. Their presence was held by some members of staff to be detrimental to the image of the group as a whole across the school: "The whole project is at risk if people get to thinking all PH are like that". Elsewhere, the mixing of severely and profoundly deaf pupils with partially hearing pupils was felt to be to the detriment of the latter – rather than to the benefit of the former. Their poor linguistic attainments and sometimes erratic behaviour tended to be ascribed to all hearing impaired pupils. In another school the presence of a special care unit (12 places) was seen as a source of the negative perception of provision for pupils with learning difficulties (both moderate and severe). A visiting special educator pointed out how these multiply handicapped pupils with bizarre behaviours "can wreck an integration programme . . . the more normal (eg, the Down's Syndrome child) are going to be pushed aside . . . they provide an abnormal setting for the whole group".

The most frequent example of this 'tarring with the same brush' syndrome involved pupils with behaviour problems. For example, a large secondary department for pupils with learning difficulties had accepted several pupils who were midway through their secondary education, all of whom had experienced failure and rejection in other schools. In fact they created considerable problems in this school too, and at one stage there were real fears that main school staff, if they happened to have an unfortunate encounter with one of the pupils, would assume that everybody from the special department was like this. In the event, this was avoided by retaining these pupils within the special department full-time. Numerous teachers made mention of behaviour problems when asked about admission criteria for their special provision. They were unwilling to have pupils with extreme behaviour problems or emotional disturbance, in part because they did not feel equipped to cope with them but also because their presence would colour perceptions of the special provision in all sorts of undesirable ways.

In summary, attitudes toward pupils with special needs in the integration programmes we studied were generally positive, somewhat more so than the standard literature on mainstreaming might suggest. This was particularly evident in the case of teachers. Initial reactions were commonly negative but these generally changed and the vast majority of teachers endorsed the presence of the integration programme in their school. As for pupils, they generally accepted peers with special needs though not necessarily as fully-fledged members of the school community.

Among the various factors that governed the formation of attitudes, the age of the pupil in question and their communication capacity stood out as highly significant where peers were concerned. The way the integration programme was introduced was important for teachers; informing them and having due consultation with them were crucial in evoking positive attitudes. Other considerations referred to grouping aspects and the relationship of the integration programme to the main school.

PART SEVEN

Parents

Chapter Twenty
Parents in Integration

The successful education of children with special educational needs is dependent on the full involvement of their parents; indeed, unless the parents are
seen as equal partners in the educational process the purpose of our report will
be frustrated (Warnock, page 150)

They (school staff) mean well but they don't have any idea what it's like having
her all day every day (parent of physically handicapped teenager).
When I first saw him he seemed such a typical teacher that I thought I'll get no
help there (parent of a child with severe learning difficulties)

The involvement of parents in the education of their children is
one of the areas where the gap between precept and practice is
greatest. It is widely accepted now that parents have an important
role to play in the education of their children with special needs
and that support is necessary to enable them carry out these roles.
The Warnock Report identifies three main forms of support
–information, advice and practical help – and speaks of a
partnership between parents and the members of the different
services. The reality in practice is sometimes rather different. It is
not uncommon for parents to be held at arm's length, and the
school – and other agencies – to have little effective contact or
communication with the home. This is understandable to the
extent that teachers and the other professionals are versed in
teaching and other skills but not necessarily in the collaborative
exercise of them or in facilitating an active involvement on the part
of parents. It must be remembered too that integration is in a
sense a new situation for parents and teachers alike. While it

presents new opportunities for home/school contact and collaboration it entails new roles as well. Until these roles are learnt
and put into practice by the full range of professionals involved in
special education and parents are persuaded and equipped to take
an active part the needs of many children will not be met as well as
they might be.

In this chapter we report our findings on the role of parents in
integration. It refers mainly to schools though there is some
mention of other agencies. It is grouped around four questions:

   i.Did parents want integration? What were their attitudes toward
    it?

   ii.How much contact was there between home and school? How
    was it organized?

   iii.What opportunites does integration present? What was the
    nature of the contact? What activities did it comprise?

   iv.How can schools encourage parental involvement and capitalize
    on opportunities it presents?

Attitudes toward integration

One of the clearest findings that emerged is that parents wanted
integration for their children. We interviewed 43 sets of parents in
their homes, and every single one wanted their children to
continue his or her education in an integrated setting. These
parents were chosen to represent the diversity of the schemes we
studied: their children varied in age from 5 to 17; their handicaps
included physical and sensory impairment, communication disorders and both mild and severe learning difficulties; some were
individually integrated, some attended special centres in ordinary
schools, and some integrated from the base of a special school.
Parents' responses were not led or 'given' by the research team in
any way. Questions asked were open-ended, and the views and
categories that emerged came from the parents.

This finding is worth noting. It may be claimed that parents'
views are constrained by their present situation, ie if their children
attend special schools they will regard special schools as best suited
to their children and if they attend ordinary schools they will
favour integration. That may well be the case and if we had had
the opportunity to interview parents of non-integrating children
we could have said something on the matter. There are two points

to make. First, the unanimity of views is striking in a sample that, though small, was extremely diverse and included a number of parents with experience of segregated special school placement. Moreover, some of the views were pressed with great force; if there had been a conversion it was total! Secondly, parents' advocacy of integration was far from naive or uncritical. A wide range of considerations was urged on the research team, indicating in many cases a reflective and balanced perspective. In a few cases, parents combined clear dissatisfaction over their child's school with strong support for the *principle* of integration.

Parents' attitudes toward integration can be considered under three headings: desire for normality; concern for academic progress; and experience of and attitudes toward special schools. They are illuminated also by remarks from parents who while dissatisfied with their child's school nevertheless wanted an integrated placement for him or her.

i. Normality

"I want her to grow up in as normal an environment as possible." One of the most recurrent themes from parents related to normality: they had experienced the pain and frustration of having their child singled out and wanted nothing more than that he or she should do ordinary things and pass unremarked. They regarded the opportunity to be "a normal kiddy" as highly important. This must be properly understood. Parents were not unaware of the need for special help. They might be ignorant of the details or have misguided ideas of what was possible, but they were keenly aware of the need for help, sometimes indeed to an extent that made them dependent on the specialists. Their desire for normality was not a rejecting of this help. If it had negative connotations it was that they rejected forms of help they saw as inappropriate. What it did mean was that they wanted this help in a context of normality.

A further consideration is the extent to which placement in an ordinary school constitutes normality. It is sometimes observed that pupils with special needs are isolated and singled out in the ordinary school by virtue of their special needs. An argument in favour of special school placement is that pupils are with their 'own kind' and are freed from the stigma of difference. Whatever the merits of this argument – and they are limited – parents were not taken by it. To our judgement most of them appreciated that their children were distinguished from the others in major ways and that the most they could expect from ordinary school placement was a limited normality, but they still wanted it.

Normality is not an easy concept to spell out. For purposes of this account of parents' attitudes we shall refer to the dimensions parents used or implied in discussion. These were: normality as an end in itself; the promotion of maturity and personal development; growth in independence; implications for how handicap is viewed; and benefits to the parents themselves.

Some parents were happy for the child to grow up in a normal environment for the sheer sake of it. Many statements implied that "having a part in life with other children" was seen as an important end in its own right. Just going along to school with the other children from the neighbourhood was valued. Several parents made mention of the encouragement they derived from observing casual exchanges between their child and other schoolchildren; clearly the casual nature of these exchanges was important, and the fact that in some respects at least their child was perceived as just another child and not as handicapped.

Parents did refer to specific advantages. One was that they noticed a personal development and a maturing on transfer from special school to ordinary school. "As soon as he went to . . . he was a different kiddy", more outgoing and independent – this, strikingly, from a parent who felt that the special school had had the edge academically. Again, "over the past twelve months he's a different child". These are typical of many comments from parents who observed that their child had come out of his or her shell, related to people better, and generally grown up as a result of mixing with ordinary children. The fact that such comments sometimes went hand-in-hand with criticism of particular aspects of the school or integration programme make them all the stronger as evidence.

Another aspect of this is reflected in parents' attitudes to teasing. We have commented elsewhere on the low incidence of teasing, or at least evidence of it. Parents were not only unconcerned about it but occasionally observed that it was something their children would have to learn to cope with anyway. They would have to live with their handicapping conditions and that included being able to respond maturely when faced with the ignorant or the ill-disposed.

An aspect of maturing particularly valued by parents was the greater independence that they felt integration promoted – "she stands up for herself more now". This was a central concern as children grew older and parents had thought to the future. They were anxious for their children "to have experience of non-disabled people" – "we don't think it's right to segregate . . . they're going to have to get on with the public". As noted below, the deficiencies of some special schools were keenly felt in this regard.

A small number of parents commented on the benefit to other children – "not only is Joanna benefiting but the other children are gaining in appreciation". Through having everyday contact with handicap, they had the opportunity to become accustomed to it and develop realistic attitudes toward it. This benefited those who had special needs and was a help in eradicating negative/hostile images of handicap, but it also constituted a valuable learning experience for ordinary pupils and these parents insisted on the importance of that.

It would be naive to overlook the fact that sometimes parents' endorsement of integration stemmed from the benefits to themselves. "When I say Maurice goes to (the local school) nobody knows he's got anything wrong with him." "When neighbours ask where your child goes to school, it's easier just to say (local school) when you're still trying to adjust to the handicap" (Mother of Down's Syndrome boy). A number of parents were quite frank about the personal boost they received from having their children attend an ordinary school (though the effect was weakened if special transport was involved or it was not the neighbourhood school). Mention has been made of the importance parents attached to casual contact between their child and other children. One incident in particular stands out: a seven-year-old who is severely mentally retarded is on his way to school when a schoolmate greets him, by name, and passes on. From the way the mother recalled the story, it was clear that the incident had meant a great deal to her.

A further gloss on this relates to parents' acceptance of their own child. This was not an area we set out to explore nor would we have expected much direct information on it. A few significant remarks were made however about individual parents finding it easier to accept their child now that he or she went along to school with neighbourhood children. This was something distinct from taking away the remoteness that residental placement sometimes led to, though it is possible that there are links. Parents too run the risk of seeing their handicapped children as handicapped first and children second, and it is worthy of note that some of them acknowledged that having their child go to an ordinary school helped them reverse the order.

ii. Concern for academic progress

Parents were anxious that their child should get as good an education as possible. The vast majority in fact reported themselves as satisfied with their child's progress at school. The accompaying table gives their responses to the question: *Are you satisfied with the progress of your child at school?*

Very Dissatisfied	Not particularly Satisfied	Reasonably Satisfied	Very Satisfied
0	4	14	25

Dissatisfactions referred to insufficient or no homework or the parents' belief that their child was not working up to his or her own standard. For the most part however, parents strongly endorsed schools' efforts: "since attending (ordinary school) his progress in all subjects has come on very well" – (school) has surpassed all expectations" – "her last report was very much better than expected . . . at first we thought she wouldn't do anything" – "we are thrilled to bits". These and many similar comments testify to a high degree of satisfaction on the part of parents with an aspect of schooling they considered essential. It is noteworthy that the parents of all six pupils attending language units were very satisfied, commenting in particular on the improvement in their speech and language.

This enthusiastic endorsement of the academic provision within integration programmes is in sharp contrast with parents' perceptions of the schooling their children had received in special schools. (Over a third had had a child transferred from a special school.) By no means all parents were critical of the academic standards of special schools but a number were highly critical. Their children were not being stretched; they were being offered a narrow curriculum; and above all they were not learning. A few comments: "the educational standards at (special school) are not very high". "She wasn't getting any education . . . all she was doing at ten was childish painting . . . her school reports were continually dropping back." "Not much education at (special school) – they're too busy with the physical handicaps." "Going to (comprehensive) has been good for James in making him work . . . he was left to do what he liked at (special school)." Some commented also on the improvement that followed in the wake of being transferred from the special school.

It should be made clear that this is not intended nor should it be taken as an indictment of special schools. These remarks are indicative of parents' perceptions, not balanced assessments of educational programmes. It might be judged that these parents were singularly unfortunate in their experience of special schools. Certainly, they do not seem to have encountered those special schools whose excellence of teaching and wealth of resources set a standard of provision that any integration programme would do well to match.

iii. Attitudes toward special schools

As noted, more than a third of the parents interviewed had had a child transferred from a special school, while others had had a special school placement proposed for their child or knew that it was a very real alternative to the existing placement. Most of them had reservations about special schools, some had forthright criticisms, while those few who pointed to advantages of special schools did not seek them for their own child. Again we emphasise that these observations reflect *parents'* perceptions which are not necessarily ours. In most cases we had no independent knowledge of the special schools in question and could not verify parents' judgements of them. We report their perceptions for the insight on attitudes they give; they are not to be taken as measured criticism of the schools in question, or indeed of special schools in general. In the absence of corroborative information they are evidence of consumer resistance and little more.

Many of the points made were simply the converse of the considerations urged above in respect of normality. The main concerns referred to being grouped with large numbers of other pupils with special needs, failure to grow in independence and, as already discussed, academic progress. Surprisingly few comments referred to residential placement and separation from home as drawbacks, though there were some.

Parents were unhappy on several scores about the grouping of pupils with special needs that special schooling entailed. (Some were uneasy about the size of large special centres as well. One parent felt that there should be no more than three or four pupils – he was thinking of severe handicapping conditions – in any one school, a sentiment echoed by a number of others.) First, it over-emphasised the disability or other handicapping condition; it maintained the importance and *difference* of being handicapped even for the youngsters themselves – one parent talked of how they were "seeing themselves as something different". Secondly, being in the company of other handicapped children the whole time compounded the handicap and led to deterioration in learning and behaviour. Many commented on this. "Being with handicapped bairns all the time makes her more handicapped." "Being kept with their own kind too long makes it difficult for them to communicate with normal hearing people." One mother gave as an example how her daughter had started to copy mannerisms. Thirdly, there was the danger of adverse effects through pupils comparing themselves unfavourably with other pupils. In fairness, the opposite seems just as feasible and indeed one parent testified that this was so in respect of his daughter. Going to special school had been good for her and had led to much improved attitudes – "she has seen there are people in worse predicaments and realised that others are worse off than herself".

A second concern of parents was that special schools did not promote independence in their children, indeed might be doing the opposite. There was a fear that they were being artificially sheltered from the real world when "what she does *not* need is sheltering from the world". One parent explained why they felt they wanted an integrated placement for their son – "We thought it would be harder for him to leave at sixteen (if he stayed at special school). . . . he's got to make the break some time".

iv. Dissatisfaction with placement

A small number of parents were dissatisfied with the education their child was receiving in an ordinary school but still supported the principle of integration. One parent indeed felt that her son had been making somewhat better progress academically at his special school but judged the ordinary school placement preferable for the general social development and the normalising influence of being with normal peers. The sources of dissatisfaction varied. Sometimes it was a straightforward personality clash between a parent and a particular teacher. More often it was disagreement over the school's assessment of a child's capacities or how he or she was taught or even how the special centre was run. One parent was so incensed over the handling of a particular unfortunate incident that his perceptions of the staff concerned became extremely hostile.

In spite of the various dissatisfactions, these parents remained committed to integration and had no wish to see their children in special schools. In fact, the parent in question was one of those who was most articulate in favour of placing pupils with special needs in ordinary schools. The number of parents involved here is small but their views give further support to the general preference for ordinary school placement.

Amount and nature of contact

Schools varied greatly in the importance they attached to contact with parents and the amount of time they gave it. Contact was most frequent at the younger ages, as might be expected. It occurred at the school for the most part though there were some home visits. It may be noted that teachers' and parents' views did not always match upon this matter. Many teachers referred to parents who seemed indifferent or reported difficulty in getting hold of the parents they wanted to reach, while some parents made remarks which implied clearly that they regarded school as alien territory. In this section we describe the amount of contact and how it was organised, before going on in the next section to discuss the functions served by it.

Parents interviewed by the research team were asked about frequency of contact and how satisfied they were about it. Most (40 out of 43) were satisfied with the amount of contact. Of the three who were dissatisfied, two were at odds with teachers over the child's programme of work and felt they were not getting sufficient opportunity to convey their point of view. Both pupils were at secondary level and in each case the parents felt that enough was not being done to help them. The third case had to do with a major misunderstanding over medical complications involving medical specialists, school staff and the parents. What was common to the three was an elementary failure in communication. It seemed as if we as outsiders were privy to an aspect of the parents' concern that had never manifested itself to the school staff while the latter were wrongly assumed to be indifferent because of the lack of contact.

The frequency of contact is summarised in the table below. This refers to meetings between parents and teaching staff that took place at school or at home in the twelve months prior to the date of interview. Casual encounters such as the exchange of pleasantries at the beginning or end of the school day are not counted. Of the four who reported no contact, one had arranged a visit for the following week, while the others were constrained through such factors as illness, no command of the English language or being a single parent in full-time work. It will be seen from the table that the amount of contact was considerable, particularly as it does not include casual and telephone contact: 70 per cent of parents (30) had contact on two or more occasions in the course of the year, while 40 per cent (17) had contact on five or more occasions. It may be noted that the low frequency contacts were almost all reported at secondary age.

Number of visits a year	0	1	2/4	5 or more
Frequency	4	9	13	17

This contact was organised in five main ways:
i. Traditional open days, or similar
ii. Meetings and group sessions with parents
iii. Home-school books
iv. Home visits
v. Casual or ad hoc contact.

i. Traditional open days, or similar
Most schools had something along these lines, either a traditional open evening which might be along with the rest of the school or on a separate occasion or various kinds of open day. The latter could be half day or whole day with parents free to drop in as they

wished and observe what was happening or requested to come for interview at a specific time. The most common frequency for this sort of occasion was once a term, but sometimes they took place only once a year and in one school once every half term. As regards content, these occasions were generally loosely structured. Time was set aside for parents to chat privately to teachers where the child's progress was discussed and any matters of common concern aired. Some schools made a point of having parents see work their children had been doing, the various resources possessed by the special centre and how they were used. One teacher saw these as didactic occasions where the importance of proper attitudes, appropriate correction and so on could be communicated.

Attendance at open days was generally good, usually better than for main school parents, presumably because these parents worried more over their children's education and also had more contact with class teachers on various matters throughout the year. Even so, some schools reported difficulty in attracting certain parents. This is to be contrasted with other schools where one hundred per cent attendance was the norm. It is our view that the latter could be achieved more often than it is and that judgements of the 'our parents don't believe in contact with the school' type should be used sparingly. Certainly there are difficult parents where the effort required to motivate and involve them would be disproportionate in relation to the teacher's other work. Judging by the experience of some schools however, these parents are fewer in number than is often supposed. If parents believe that attending an open day would help them or their children and they do not feel alienated by the school surroundings, they will attend.

The generally good attendance is the more noteworthy in that it sometimes entailed a difficult journey with possibly one or two infants in tow. In a small number of cases the journey was eased through parents being able to use school transport. It would seem a small thing to make this concession more widely available: little or no cost is involved and it would greatly ease the lot of some parents.

ii. Meetings and group sessions with parents

There were various ways in which parents met with teachers and sometimes other professionals as a group. Many schools organised social gatherings during the school day on a regular basis – coffee mornings, tea afternoons and the like. Some infant classes for severely retarded children invited parents along to the children's birthday parties. Many of these meetings stayed at a purely social level though even here other functions were achieved as well; relationships were established; schools became more familiar places, and so on. In one case the educational psychologist made a point of attending monthly coffee mornings. This was quite unstructured but found to be very useful: parents tended to "open their hearts to him" and he was able to counsel them and promote realistic attitudes as well as advising them on handling their child. In other cases the coffee mornings were more structured with a set presentation on the work of the special class or a talk from a psychologist, speech therapist or a representative from one of the voluntary societies. Parents were enthusiastic about these gatherings, as much perhaps from the air of expertise communicated and the reassurance that their children were in good hands, as from any knowledge acquired. One teacher observed that the meetings made the professionals more accessible to parents, showing that they were "human beings too" and increasing the level of communication. Some professionals might wince at the remark from a teacher that "parents need to be able to have a go at people like that in a reasonable way" but anything that loosens up the channels of communication is surely to be encouraged.

One initiative is worth describing in detail. It refers to arrangements for visiting in a special centre for hearing impaired infants. Apart from tea afternoons once a term, every Friday morning four parents are invited to the school and allocated, one per group, to the various teaching and activity sessions that involve their child. (There are four teaching groups in the centre and the visiting parents are selected so that each has a child in a different group.) Teachers ensure that there is a period of individual work with each child whose parent is visiting going on at some point in the morning. Most of the parents' time is spent in the classroom. There is a discussion at the end of the morning, and sometimes a brief meeting with the teacher in charge and the head of the school. On average, each parent will spend a morning at the school every six weeks.

It will be no surprise that parents were very enthusiastic about this arrangement and take-up was high. Comments were mainly addressed to their child's performance rather than how the teacher handled or taught him or her. They appreciated being able to see their child in action, sometimes discovering capacities and levels of performance they had not suspected. Of one boy who rigidly separated home and school, "they told us he did things . . . talk . . . read . . . he just didn't do it with us". Of a girl who tried to communicate but could not, "at home she can try and tell you what she has been doing but you don't always understand . . . here she can show me herself what she has been doing".

iii. Home-school books

Home-school books were used in a number of schools. When they were used it was usually on a regular basis – daily or, more often, weekly. In a small number of cases they were used infrequently, when necessitated by a particular occurrence. The most common uses of home-school books were to convey messages and to build up some kind of relationship with parents by holding a "running dialogue". As a means of conveying messages – to as well as from school – the home-school book is excellent, provided parents can read and are prepared to take notice. This latter is all the more important if the book is being used to converse with the parents. Many did respond to chatty comments on the school day and what their child had been doing and jotted down observations and comments of their own. This seemed to happen best when there was a pre-existing relationship between parents and teacher, ie the home-school book led to useful dialogue if there had been prior contact but on its own it did not work at this level. A third use of home-school books was to achieve particular didactic purposes. through involving parents actively in their children's education. Though comparatively rare and not well developed, this use holds much promise. Some details are given below.

iv. Home Visits

There were great differences both in policy and practice with regard to home visiting. Some teachers saw it as a major part of their role and devoted a considerable amount of time to it, perhaps being specifically timetabled for it; others would have liked to give time to it but were discouraged by their authority on the grounds that home visiting was the province of other agencies, usually Social Services or specialist peripatetic services; while others still gave little or no time to it either because they accorded it low priority or had no time to give to it. Whether or not teachers made home visits depended on their commitment to it but practical matters played a part as well. Chief among these was whether they were timetabled for it. In two authorities teachers were released from classroom duties one day each week – either because all of their pupils were integrating or supply teachers were employed as a matter of policy – and assigned various other tasks, including home visiting. In other areas generous staffing ratios allowed a flexible deployment of staff. Home visiting flourished under these circumstances. When visits had to be squeezed into odd moments however or made after school or in the evening teachers were naturally more reluctant. Another practical consideration was remuneration of travelling expenses. Some teachers were unconcerned about this and made the journeys anyway. Others were unwilling to travel unless their expenses were met, pointing to the allowances paid to many other LEA employees and sensing – perhaps rightly – that their visiting was ascribed low value.

Those who were in a position to do home visiting on a regular basis were convinced of its value. They believed that it achieved ends that other forms of contact did not, ends moreover which they as teachers were sometimes better equipped for than other agencies; rapport could only be established with some parents by seeing them on their own ground as it were; seeing the family *in situ* and observing how parents and children related could give insight into the child's problem, and reveal why certain remedies or strategies did not work; teachers were able to adapt their educational programme in the light of knowledge of relevant home factors and provide support to parents that needed it. In short, home visiting helped teachers move away both in their understanding and in their actual practice from a view of handicap or special need as a characteristic of the pupils with certain educational implications to one where it was seen as shaped by, if not in part arising from, the network of social and family relationships.

One must keep a sense of perspective of course. Visits can be too frequent or unwelcome – "you've got to be careful so that it doesn't look as if you are prying". It should be remembered also that some teachers would be best advised to refrain from making home visits. One blunt teacher talked of "dangers in certain members of staff going out into the homes", and referred to a colleague whom she would not wish to set loose outside the school. Certain qualities of maturity and tact and some skill in inter-personal relationships would seem an essential prerequisite. Finally, home visiting is not the preserve of teachers. Some visits were usefully made by other staff associated with special centres. For example, speech therapists attached to language units would generally have had contact with the family before the child started school and this contact would naturally continue as long as found beneficial.

v. Casual or ad hoc contact

A great deal of contact between home and school arises in casual or ad hoc ways. These range from school gate exchanges and telephone calls re absences to helping out with school activities. The possibilities are many and their effect difficult to assess. We summarise them here and make a few observations about them.

Fetching children to and from school is the most regular sort of contact and one that can shape parents' perceptions of the school and special centre in important ways. Many teachers of young children make a point of being out to receive the children and exchanging a word with the parents. In some schools parents are free to come in and help get their child ready for going home. The advantage of this sort of contact is that it is natural and easy and is achieved without any disruption of the school day. Some teachers did in fact seek to be available throughout the school day: "If you are trying to build up relationships with parents you have to be always available." In secondary school it was more usual to have an appointment system. Teachers reported little disruption in fact through parents arriving unannounced. This usually happened only in times of crisis or if the parent happened to be in school on other business; parents were reticent to impose rather than the reverse.

The same could not be said for the telephone, another prime source of contact. Many special centres used the telephone deliberately as a means of keeping in touch, particularly if the family lived at some distance and the child was brought to school by special transport. Parents too valued telephone contact since it eliminated distance and was perhaps less inhibiting. Teachers did report instances however where the telephone was being used to excess or to no good purpose and was disruptive of work in the classroom.

Another source of casual contact was helping out with or participating in school activities. These could be school trips, fetes and school functions of various kinds. These had value – beyond their intrinsic ones – in establishing rapport, building relationships and generally giving parents a stake in the work of the special centre. One school furthered contact through operating a toy library and also prevailing upon paediatricians to hold clinics at the school.

A final observation about casual contact is, as noted in chapter six, that welfare staff can sometimes form easier relationships with parents: "We don't have something formal to keep up (unlike the teacher)." The parents in turn may feel less on their guard and more relaxed so that communication is easier.

Functions of home/school contact

Contact between home and school took many forms and served various purposes. Aside from parents' own needs, the overriding concern was for parents and teachers so to interact that children's needs were best met. This entailed various functions, of which the following can be noted:

  i. befriending/providing personal support
  ii. dealing with management problems
  iii. liaising with professional agencies
  iv. involving parents in their children's education
  v. acquiring information on the home background.

i. Befriending/providing personal support

Parents may need support as individuals in their own right. The long term care of a child with severe or complex special needs can lead to frustration, disappointment and a complex of other emotions which can be profoundly distressing. This level of support is different from the support – through giving information, advice and practical help – that enables parents play an effective role in their child's education. (The two are closely linked. A parent who is depressed is less likely to be able to help the child, while having an active role to play is conducive to coming to terms with the situation.) It can come in two ways: as a result of conscious effort by teachers; and through association with other parents.

As far as teachers were concerned, a major consideration was getting parents to view their child realistically and accept his or her limitations. One mother "hadn't accepted that there was anything wrong with the child . . she couldn't face it". This role often fell to teachers because other professionals involved did not communicate in a meaningful way with parents or because parents found it easier to relate to teachers. In a number of instances the teacher's role was simply one of being a sympathetic listener to life's troubles, "a shoulder to lean on". This occurred when social work support was insufficient or non-existent but it was more common when a formal involvement by social services would have been inappropriate or even counterproductive. One head teacher noted that she had spent hours with a particular mother who certainly did not have a 'problem' and would have been appalled and hurt at any suggestion of professional help for her but had none the less benefited in important ways from this contact. Incidents such as these give point to the call made by some teachers of the deaf for an element of counselling within their training.

Contact with other parents provided a wider degree of support. It served various purposes – social contact and the opportunity to exchange experiences, reassurance and encouragement, the sense of belonging to a group. Contact between parents (as opposed to contact between parents and teacher) took place in three ways: arrangements by the school; membership of societies and voluntary bodies; and informally. Schools and special centres made various arrangements to promote contact between parents. Coffee mornings and such like were intended to bring parents together, to provide an opportunity "for them to get to know each other". Parents welcomed this for the reassurance – "You do worry; you don't know anything about it so you're afraid", "You don't always feel you're on your own" – and the positive help – "You find out how other people cope". One school which timetabled parents at set times on open days was criticised on this score. While the arrangement did mean that each individual parent had more time with school staff and could chat without interruption, parents had less opportunity to meet each other and get acquainted. One parent interviewed had met only one other parent from the special class – to her regret.

A major source of contact for some parents was through the voluntary societies – National Deaf Children's Society, Society for Mentally Handicapped Children, Spina Bifida Association, Epilepsy Society and so on. Again the benefits of social contact and exchanges with people who appreciated one's problems at first hand were stressed. For some parents these societies and their activities had become an important part of their lives. They identified closely with them and were active in organising, fund-raising, etc. One mother described how in the early days "I couldn't wait for the meetings to come round". It should be stressed that membership of voluntary societies or appreciation of the benefits is not unique to or even particularly associated with integration. Indeed, the evidence suggests the reverse, that parents of pupils at special schools are more likely to be aware of the existence of the voluntary societies. One might argue that integrated parents are more in need of them however, since they lack the sense of belonging to a special school and can feel isolated from main school parents.

Informal contacts were quite common. They often depended however on formal structures or deliberate interventions of one kind or another. The school coffee mornings, voluntary societies and so on played an important role; many parents made lasting contacts in this way that they would otherwise not have done. Sometimes teachers effected individual introductions: one parent for instance was invited to meet with a prospective parent and help to allay her anxieties about sending her son to a special class. The importance of formal moves in setting up informal contacts should not be overlooked. While integration often means that a child will be going to the neighbourhood school, this is by no means always the case. Special classes or departments may draw from the catchment areas of several schools or a particular child's local school may be unsuitable for a number of reasons. In these cases the pupil may be attending school some distance from home and will travel there by taxi or other special transport so that the parent does not have a chance to meet other parents informally at the beginning and end of the school day.

Of course, not all parents wanted contact with other parents of handicapped children. Two sets of factors seemed to be at work here. The first had to do with social class. We could do no more than glance at this: the interaction between social class and handicap is far from simple, and when parental contact is added to the mix the set of interrelationships is exceedingly complex. While membership of voluntary societies and contacts at school did cut across class boundaries, particularly in respect of physical and sensory impairment and severe retardation where the incidence is spread across social class, this did not happen in every case and some parents avoided or were excluded from association with other parents because of the middle-class ethos of the gatherings. There were also personal reasons. One mother felt it would not help and could be harmful in that "you might be driven to making comparisons that would depress you". Another set of parents thought such contact especially when formalised through membership of societies, was artificial and irrelevant, and saw little need or point in associating with persons outside their immediate neighbourhood.

ii. Dealing with management problems

Behaviour problems were a particular source of difficulty in some families. For various reasons – frustration engendered by a handicapping condition, failure to learn appropriate behaviour, inadequate parenting – the incidence of untoward behaviour patterns was high. We are concerned here with temper tantrums, grossly anti-social behaviour and the like, along with management problems related to toileting and eating.

A first question is: To what extent is this the concern of the school? Clearly, a teacher will require appropriate behaviour while the child is at school and will probably take measures to promote it. But what of the child's behaviour at home? Should the teacher intervene and instruct or help the parent in managing the child outside the school? In particular, what new responsibilities result from integration? If children are being educated in an integrated setting as opposed to a residential school, it will not be possible to implement a controlled programme for more than about six hours a day. In some cases this is insufficient and it might be judged necessary to involve the family in the programme.

We found considerable divergence in beliefs and practices on this matter. A common view was that, while helping parents manage their children might fall on the school and resources might be devoted to it, this would always be a secondary concern. If time or other resources were devoted to it, this would only be when necessitated by crises or instances of grossly untoward behaviour. Many teachers said they would like to devote more time to this aspect of working with parents or maintained that they attached great importance to it without actually managing to find the time. This would suggest that the effective priority attached to it was low. Two other, strongly contrasting sets of attitudes can be reported. A small number of schools gave high priority to this work. In one special centre for severely retarded pupils, there was a policy of involving parents in the classroom so that they could see how the staff dealt with management problems – "We invite them to work alongside the teacher to see how we are not reacting to things". In a unit for hearing impaired infants, parents were likewise invited along to see how staff handled their children; practical tips were given and mini-programmes suggested. In both schools major success stories were reported to us where mothers who were despairing or over-protective were helped to a more realistic view of their children's behaviour, with subsequent improvement in the behaviour as well. Besides these examples, use was made in one area of Portage techniques as described below.

There were small successes too. One mother had said that it would be nice to take her severely retarded seven-year-old to a cafe without him causing a rumpus. The class teacher worked on this and achieved success in quite a short time. This might seem a trivial example of behaviour management, but it was no small matter for the mother concerned and it opened up an aspect of 'normality' previously closed to her and her son.

Some counter arguments were expressed. One teacher felt that there was a risk of jeopardising the relationship between parent and child by introducing a teaching situation or imposing a programme to be followed rigorously. In any case, it was natural for children to have separate standards for home and school and people should not set too much store by the fact that many of these children typically behaved far better in school than at home. She voiced a fear also that a particular child's reaction against a programme introduced at home might carry over to school and negate the school's efforts, so that one ended up with bad behaviour both at school and at home. In another situation where a child was soiling himself regularly at home but was not a problem at school, the teacher recognised that they could help but was reluctant to intervene in any extended way "I told her what I did, but I wouldn't like to interfere with what she does at home".

iii. *Liaising with professional agencies*

Many pupils with special needs are involved with Heath and Social Services as well as Education, and there can be large numbers of agencies that impinge on a given family. This presents problems for both parents and school. For parents it can mean relating to a large number of professionals, an experience many find confusing if not intimidating. As far as the school goes, it becomes only one of many agencies dealing with the pupil and not necessarily the most authoritative one. A particular problem is when information or the outcomes of professional assessments do not reach the school, so that not only does the teacher have to work without the best available understanding of the pupil but is also liable to criticism for having a limited perspective on him or her!

A number of teachers described a go-between role where they acted as a link between parents and professional agencies. Mention was made of liaising with psychologists and medical authorities on parents' behalf, facilitating appointments, interpreting reports and so on but there were few specific examples. One was the case mentioned above where a teacher arranged for regular clinics to be held at the school by paediatricians. This role was more in evidence with regard to parents who found difficulty in coping with life generally and the extra demands arising from having a child with special needs. In these cases teachers would set up medical and dental appointments, organise transport or fetch the children themselves, assist in obtaining special allowances, make direct representation to agencies such as Social Services and so on. One teacher related an instance where a mother did not get a buggy to which she was entitled; she did not know how best to set about it, so the teacher organised it for her. Another teacher was instrumental in obtaining a special allowance for a severely retarded child and prevailed upon Social Services to arrange a holiday for both child and mother.

It is clear that in some cases here, as in the befriending role described above, teachers were adopting a social worker role. While one might have reservations about this – and indeed one senior officer expressed unease over teachers being amateur social workers – these teachers were meeting needs that would otherwise not be met. As well as easing the burden of life for families under pressure, their interventions outside the classroom were enhancing the children's education. What might be agreed is that more attention needs to be given to this aspect of the job in training. In an ideal world teachers might not need to do social work but to the extent that it is a necessary part of the job they should be prepared in some measure for it. At a more immediate level, there is a need for the time and practical support to enable them to do it. As with home visiting, teachers who worked in this way were usually either specifically timetabled for it or were in a position (eg head of department) that allowed considerable autonomy in deciding on their work.

It may be noted that the roles being described here are rather more limited than those envisaged in the Named Person concept of the Warnock Report. This is contained in the recommendation that one person should be formally designated as parents' point of contact with all relevant services. This single point of contact would ensure that parents were introduced to the appropriate services, and enabled to follow up any concern about their child's development and progress through school. One does not doubt the usefulness and good sense of this proposal. Both in its scope and its assumptions however it goes well beyond anything we found in practice. If it were to be implemented and teachers functioned as Named Persons in this way, apart from acknowledging the new role and allowing for the changes it implies it would be necessary to accord teachers more status and ensure that they received better information than commonly they receive at the moment. In the counsels of the 'handicap professionals' the teacher is often a very junior partner, and this militates against being an effective Named Person.

The other side of the coin of teacher as link-person is where the parent liaises between school and the professionals! This happens when the latter have relevant information on a child which has not been made available to the teacher. In these cases parents can play a useful role if they have the information. We encountered examples of this in relation to physical handicap. In the early days of a scheme where physically handicapped pupils were being integrated on an individual basis and little prior preparation had gone on, schools had very little background knowledge or skills in handling them; in several instances they had to rely on parents to give them the requisite information on toileting and general handling. There were other instances where pupils were absent for long periods for major surgery and the school had no knowledge of them; teachers were entirely dependent on the parents for information on the nature and duration of the hospitalisation.

iv. Involving parents in their children's education

The Warnock Report emphasised that the successful education of pupils with special needs is dependent on the full involvement of their parents. We encountered a variety of attitudes and practices, ranging from close involvement in particular programmes and encouraging parents to adopt positive attitudes and reinforce the work of the schools, to the according of low priority to any work with parents.

The most formal approach encountered was Portage, which is a highly structured home teaching programme. It is described below. Other formal programmes tended to be focused on language. In several cases structured programmes were worked up by speech therapists or by teachers in conjunction with speech therapists. These typically comprised speech and sound exercises, and were specifically intended for implementation by parents. In one case the starting point of the programme was an observation book where the mother recorded details of the child's activities at home. In other cases pupils took language masters or speech trainers home with them. One mother was reported to be spending an hour at weekends with her hearing impaired daughter on a speech trainer.

A quite specific development in a class for severely retarded children related to the use of Makaton. Children were being taught the basics of this relatively simple signing system, and it was found to be helpful in giving them a concept of language. The teacher responsible then decided it would extend the children's opportunity to communicate if their parents were taught Makaton as well, and she provided instruction for them.

A less formal, but quite common practice was the use of home-school books. This took various forms. The child might be encouraged to keep a daily diary, writing a sentence or so each day, possibly discussing it with the teacher on the following. Some schools used the home-school books as a direct means of communication with the parent, with the school making entries about the child's progress and jotting down informal comments, and the parent observing the child and responding in kind. Some schools sent reading books home and urged parents to read a little with the child each day. Some parents went beyond this, talking to their child about the book and asking questions about its content.

There was frequent mention of the need to enlist parents in a more general way and make sure that they were reinforcing the work of the school. This involved things such as providing good speech models – and adequate amounts of speech – and stimulating the child appropriately. Parents were encouraged to buy stimulating and educational toys for their children. A good deal of criticism was voiced over parents who were not co-operating in this way. One mother for instance was considered not to be reinforcing the independence that the school was promoting in her daughter, for example, dressing her needlessly when the girl could do some of it herself. Several others were suspected of colluding in their child's absences from school and providing no support when it came to taxing parts of an integration programme.

Some reservations about involving parents were expressed. One was that pupils had a fairly demanding day and needed to relax and do other things in the evenings. Certainly, many of them had long tiring journeys to and from school, and while at school were frequently working on an individual basis and far more intensively than children in larger classes. Pupils being taught in groups of six or eight do not have access to the rest periods that pupils in classes of 30 or more manage to build into the school day! One teacher indeed felt a need to encourage parents to ease off a little when they were pushing a child too hard. A second consideration related to the capacities of the parents themselves. Some were considered to be either incapable of doing effective work with their children or unwilling – "a lot really don't want to know what you are doing".

v. Information on the home background

An important offshoot of home/school contact is the increased understanding – on both sides – that can result. A teacher can gain much useful information and an understanding of the home situation that can have a bearing on the child's response to education, while parents can gain a better idea of what the school is doing and may acquire a better perspective of their child's possibilities.

The importance of contact of this nature was highlighted by occasional disparities between teachers' information on individual homes and their judgements about them and our own perceptions in those cases where we visited the home. There were a number of instances where it seemed clear to us that teachers were making unfavourable – and incorrect – judgements, and that they would not have done so if there had been more contact. On the positive side, there were instances reported to us of teachers and other staff picking up important information from home visits. One mother for instance had recently done a teacher training course and had been coaching her child in some tests; this fact which had not previously come to light explained the odd pattern of scores that her son had been getting. What was perhaps more important at this level was the understanding and empathy that this contact generated. Some of these children lived in exceedingly difficult situations, with a parent or parents who were under considerable pressure.

Apart from enhancing the teacher's general understanding, this contact can be relevant to assessing the success or otherwise of a teaching programme. One teacher reported using home visits to see how the child's behaviour was affected by home conditions; on the information she picked up in this way she would decide whether to maintain or adapt her own teaching programme or seek to do something about the home situation. It may be noted that Portage home teaching strategies depend crucially on specific information of this type; detailed tactics and means of reinforcement are selected only on the basis of a good knowledge of the home situation.

Promoting parental involvement

It emerged very clearly that the parents in our sample wanted their children to be educated at ordinary schools. They were also more concerned about the nature and quality of the education on offer than some of the professionals realised or were prepared to acknowledge. Some sought an active role in this education while others eagerly accepted the opportunity to be involved when it was given them. It would seem reasonable to suppose that many more parents would play an active part in educating their children if their co-operation was enlisted effectively and they were given tasks to do which were meaningful and feasible for them.

We saw above that contact between home and school can be organised in various ways and serves different functions. Seeing their children at work was a particularly motivating experience for a number of parents while others benefited from seeing how teachers handled their children or dealt with untoward behaviour. Informal meetings such as coffee mornings helped parents to feel more at ease within the school while being included in the open day arrangements, school plays and so on reinforced the sense of belonging to the normal community.

Turning to the specific tasks of promoting parental involvement, we would note three important steps that need to be taken. First, school is perceived as alien territory by many parents where they feel ill at ease and find it difficult to be their natural selves. For some it will bring back memories of their own unsuccessful schooldays and teachers who believed in keeping parents at a distance. The first step then is to get over this initial obstacle and ensure that parents are not awed by the school and indeed feel welcome there. This may entail starting with home visits in some cases so that when a mother does visit the school she will find a familiar face. After that much will depend on the attitudes of staff, the sorts of interaction that parents have with staff and other parents there, and such seemingly trivial things as whether there is a place where parents can sit in comfort and perhaps make themselves a cup of tea.

A second step is to motivate parents and get them to believe that they can make a real contribution to their children's education. (This requires a similar belief on the part of teachers. As we have seen above, not all teachers subscribe to the view that parents should have an active involvement.) This is perhaps best achieved by giving them manageable tasks to achieve, as discussed below. It may be necessary to engage in preparatory work however to overcome the distancing effects of the schooling many parents will have received themselves and of the experiences that some will have had in dealing with medical and other professionals. If parents' image of education is of a highly technical process carried out exclusively within school by trained professionals it will be hard for them to see that they can play a part in it. Likewise, the effect of off-hand treatment by other professionals who are only concerned with the exercise of their professional skills is to reinforce professional mystiques and parents' dependence on the specialist. (Some of the most deeply-felt – and bitter – comments from parents related to their treatment at the hands of medical specialists. They felt that they were regarded as nonentities – "you're just a number to them" – and claimed that their reasonable requests for information were either ignored or not taken seriously.) For these reasons then it may be necessary to engage in a bit of de-mystifying, explaining to parents that while their children may have special needs and stand to benefit from specialist intervention, much can be done that does not require a high level of expertise. Just because specialist attention is necessary does not mean that lay help is out of place. It might be argued that this would lead parents to under-estimate their children's difficulties and overestimate what they can do to remediate them. While it is necessary to be on guard against this our experience would suggest that it is unlikely to be a major problem; the majority of parents were only too aware of their children's problems and indeed many would benefit from paying less attention to their specific handicapping conditions and the limits apparently imposed by them.

Having encouraged and motivated parents, the next step is to give them actual tasks to do. Such tasks must be meaningful to the parents and appear relevant to their children's needs. They must also be consonant with the fact that they are parents and not interfere unduly with that role. It goes without saying that the tasks should fall within their competence to execute them, with explanation and instruction as necessary. These tasks can be set in various ways – home-school books, formal sessions in school, home visits. These allow of different levels of specificity in the tasks and degree of monitoring by the teacher, and the choice of approach must reflect the purposes being sought and the resources available.

The Portage model provides an example of a highly structured home-teaching approach and will be described briefly here. It originated in Wisconsin USA as a means of helping parents in rural areas to make a substantial contribution to their children's early development and education. Extensive materials have been produced. These include a developmental curriculum for use with children aged 0-6 (and older if development is delayed), details on using the material and a programme for teaching appropriate skills to parents. The curriculum comprises 580 developmentally sequenced behaviours and is divided into six areas: infant stimulation, socialisation, self-help, language, cognition and motor. Details on a project carried out in South Glamorgan to adapt the Portage model for use in the United Kingdom are given in Revill and Blunden (1980).

How does Portage work in practice? The central idea is that parents work with their children at home in a systematic way. The efforts of the professionals involved, one of whom visits the home weekly, are directed toward facilitating and monitoring this work. If there is concern over an aspect of a child's development the checklist of behaviours is used to determine the child's level of functioning in a precise way. Since the checklist follows a developmental sequence this effectively prescribes the next step. Parents are instructed on how to set specific objectives, select activities that will help to achieve them and monitor their child's progress toward them. In this way the parent works through a highly structured programme that is specific to the stage of development of their child. They are supported and instructed by the visiting professional throughout but it is they who carry out the programme. Not only that but they can also make an important creative input by contributing to the assessment of the child's level of functioning and by suggesting learning activities that will assist in meeting the objectives laid down.

PART EIGHT

Summary

Summary

The resounding conclusion to emerge from this study is that integration *is* possible. Special educational needs can be met in the ordinary school, and to a far greater extent than is currently the practice. There are many pupils in special schools at the moment who could be educated satisfactorily in ordinary schools, given the requisite commitment and resources. So far from damaging the ordinary school in any way, this process can add to its educational strength and enhance the provision made for all its pupils. The difficulties and drawbacks must not be minimised since that would be to sacrifice pupils' educational well-being on the altar of principle. If an ordinary school cannot accommodate given pupils without educational loss, then special schools may well continue to be the preferred placement. Such situations however pose a considerable challenge to both special schools and ordinary schools. As long as some pupils attend special schools when their peers with comparable special needs elsewhere receive satisfactory education in ordinary schools, there are grounds for disquiet.

This conclusion has emerged from looking at actual programmes of integration and what was achieved within them. The stance was not a comparative one and there has been no effort to make explicit comparisons between integrated and segregated provision. The starting point was the presence of pupils with special needs in ordinary schools. Given this presumption in favour of integration, the aim has been to examine the factors that bear on its successful operation. This has been done under six broad headings: setting up integration programmes; staffing; practical considerations of accommodation, resources and cost; the content and nature of teaching; social considerations; and parents.

Setting up provision

When setting up an integration programme there are various steps that can be taken to maximise the likelihood of success and avoid potential pitfalls. Where there is an element of choice care should be taken in selecting a school. There can be pressure to use schools which have spare space or to opt for sites that will necessitate a minimum of alterations. These pressures should be resisted if the result is a location which is unsuitable in other respects. New building may be difficult to justify at a time when falling rolls make spare classrooms available, but adaptation costs should be kept in perspective – unless major, they are trivial in relation to other costs when spread over a number of years.

One of the most crucial factors in the choice of school would seem to be the enthusiasm of the head teacher and his or her capacity to enlist the co-operation of staff. A related indicator is the extent to which a school is responding to the needs of pupils with educational difficulties already at the school. Numerous other factors relating to the ethos of the school, its location and the fabric of the building can usefully be taken into account. A decision in practice will usually entail balancing positive and negative features since it is rare for all the desired features to be available. When compromise is necessary staff-related factors should be accorded highest priority. While some integration programmes flourished despite premises that were grossly unsuited, persistent lack of enthusiasm on the part of head and/or other staff was an enormous obstacle.

Teacher attitudes can be affected in significant ways by the initial overtures to the school when an integration programme is first mooted and by any preparation made. Heads were generally involved in the early discussions, but other staff were not usually informed much less consulted until the matter was a *fait accompli*. Unduly protracted consultation can waste a great deal of time and perhaps serve no good purpose. If there is any acknowledgement however of the fact that an integration programme is a matter for the whole school and will effect major changes there, staff must be involved as early as possible. It is remarkable to find staff not being given a say or consulted in some measure on a major development in the life of the school.

Views on preparing a school beforehand varied. Preparation of staff was generally acknowledged to be important – and generally not provided. Failure to prepare staff can result in negative attitudes and damaging stereotypes persisting longer than they need. It can also mean that staff are insufficiently aware of individual pupils' special needs and what they can do to meet them. This is all the more regrettable in view of the relative ease with which available resources were deployed to provide effective preparation in a few instances. Preparing parents or pupils already at the school was done carefully and extensively in some schools, whereas other schools deliberately refrained from overt preparation on the grounds that this would only serve to single out the pupils being integrated and hinder their assimilation into the school. In point of fact, no objections to the integration programme, other than very minor ones, were reported from main school parents; indeed there was fairly widespread endorsement. Preparation of pupils already at the school tended to be limited.

Staffing

The central resource for an integration programme is its staff – teachers and ancillaries with a particular responsibility for pupils with special needs, other teachers, and professional staff from outside the school. Staffing ratios in the special centres visited were generally good. Approximate ratios only could be calculated in some locations since staff were deployed outside the special centre or provided a service for pupils not formally assigned to it. This highlights the inadequacy of pupil/teacher ratios in determining appropriate staffing levels. Integration is not simply a question of educating those pupils formally assigned to the integration programme. New roles are required, and there is often an associated extension or improvement in the service offered; staffing provision must be set at a level to allow for all of this.

There seemed to be no clear career route for staff into integration programmes. Under individual integration, ordinary class and subject teachers simply had pupils with special needs thrust upon them. Teachers working in special centres had a wide variety of teaching experience in both special and ordinary schools. About a quarter had had no teaching experience. Most of these teachers had received little or no specialist input on handicap during initial teacher training. Rather more than half had subsequently taken courses of at least a year's duration covering different aspects of remedial and special education. Most had taken one or more – frequently many more – short courses relating to special needs. Two thirds of ancillary staff had some professional training, generally the NNEB qualification; though its relevance was strictly limited, a number of LEAs insisted on the NNEB qualification for appointment as classroom assistant.

Teachers appointed to special centres typically carry out a multifaceted role that in terms of daily routine and professional demands is quite different from that of mainstream colleagues. Other specific roles that may be necessitated by integration include: working in a support role to enable pupils to follow the mainstream curriculum; transferring pupils from a special school or special centre to the mainstream; providing specialist help for individual pupils in conjunction with their class teacher; and maintaining oversight of an integration programme.

The role of ancillary staff is critical in integration. Their availability can determine the feasibility of a programme, and the way in which they are deployed its success or failure. Ancillary staff are usually engaged initially to provide physical care but they can be effectively deployed also in an educational role or as paraprofessionals to implement speech therapy or physiotherapy programmes. They can form relationships of familiarity and friendship that can be helpful for some pupils with special needs. A general finding was that ancillary staff were under-utilised in terms of the complexity of the demands made on them: some were restricted to purely caring roles when they could have contributed much more to meeting the needs of pupils in their charge.

One of the most striking findings to emerge was the extent to which ordinary teachers endorsed the presence of pupils with special needs in their schools. Ninety-seven per cent of those responding to a questionnaire item affirmed that it was appropriate for handicapped pupils to be placed at their school. Many of these had been reluctant if not actually opposed to the idea when the integration programme was first mooted but had come to change their minds after seeing it at work. Most teachers were quite willing to have pupils with special needs in their classes, though some did not take them seriously for teaching purposes, pointing to the social benefits which constituted sufficient justification for having them in an ordinary class. This was particularly likely to happen with pupils who had moderate learning difficulties. This entails a considerable risk of 'patronising' pupils. Their need of carefully judged teaching is no less, and probably greater, than that of their peers, and inclusion in a teaching group for social rather than pedagogical reasons is a questionable practice.

Over half of the ordinary teachers described their knowledge of handicap at the outset of the integration programme as non-existent or poor. Most claimed a considerable increase in their knowledge with the passage of time, partly through direct experience of pupils with special needs and partly through informal contact with other staff who were better informed. A majority felt that they knew enough about handicap to deal with the pupils they came across but many added that this was only because of the support available within the school and because their responsibility for pupils with special needs was limited. In point of fact, it would seem that teachers could contribute more to their education if they were better informed and possessed the requisite skills. Formal liaison between specialist teachers and their colleagues was generally weak. Some staff liaised very effectively as individuals but adequate *systems* of liaison and support were the exception rather than the rule.

Integration programmes involve a wide range of professionals from outside the school. The account here focused particularly on LEA advisory staff, educational psychologists, speech therapists and physiotherapists. A recurrent theme for all of these was the pressures caused by understaffing and the fact that involvement in an integration programme might come at the end of a long list of other priorities. As far as the schools were concerned, this was unsatisfactory – the more so as they were often in particular need of the specialist advice and support that these professionals could have supplied. Teachers working in small special centres do not have the resources of a special school at hand or even colleagues who share their professional concerns. They depend on outside agencies for specialist advice and support and are vulnerable in their absence.

Integration requires new ways of working on the part of many professionals. There is need to collaborate with colleagues, share information, view pupils' problems in a comprehensive light, disseminate skills and generally move toward interdisciplinary working. These new ways of working have to be developed in the context of staff shortages – which may be exacerbated by the demands of integration programmes. Interdisciplinary working is particularly important but also very difficult to achieve. Aside from the obstacles set by territoriality and traditions of isolated professionalism, there is a considerable conceptual problem: locating contributions from different disciplinary backgrounds within a common conceptual framework can be a challenging intellectual task, and unless resolved can defeat efforts at interdisciplinary working. The examples encountered were few in number and relatively limited in scope. Emphasis was almost exclusively on assessment with very little in the way of joint treatment or other working.

The need for more training emerged plainly and was recognised by many teachers and ancillaries. There were clear implications for initial and early in-service training. The focus in the study was on what can be done at local level using readily available resources. There is no question of making good the deficiencies of initial training or providing a substitute for formal full-time in-service courses (or their part-time equivalents). Much can be done to supplement these courses however and also promote awareness among those who are unlikely to take a formal course. Custom-built local courses can be organised and are generally much appreciated. Numerous training possibilities are offered by different aspects of professional interaction: formal collaboration; working together on a common professional task; having contact with expertise; team teaching; visits and meetings.

Practicalities

There is a practical side to integration that must not be ignored since mundane realities can sink high-minded ideals. This is particularly evident in the matter of school buildings. The problem for integration is that it entails educating pupils with special needs in buildings that must cater for all pupils. Generally, the buildings will not have been designed with their needs in mind and a degree of adaptation is required. Such adaptation must serve various functions: meeting basic physical needs – access, mobility, toileting; facilitating access to the curriculum; and furthering pupils' social assimilation. It was our impression that beyond dealing with the essentials of ramping and making suitable toileting provision staff paid little attention otherwise to the physical environment. This is to be regretted since attitudes toward a special provision and its assimilation into the school as well as the suitability of the educational programme can all be influenced by the attention paid to the physical environment.

A major determinant of what is feasible is the amount of money available for spending. The majority of staff interviewed were quire uninformed about the financial aspects of the provisions they worked in. This seemed to reflect the complexity of educational finances, lack of accounting competence and, quite commonly, an attitude toward costs that was a mixture of disdain, fatalism and lack of interest. Staff in senior positions were regularly unable to produce quite specific pieces of information on costs. There was a very common view in any case that this was not their concern: they were educationists and their concern was to promote the educational well-being of pupils. Others could see to the finances. Moreover, even if a full costing could be produced it would so reflect the particular local situation as to be valueless for any more general purpose.

We take issue with this view. While acknowledging the enormous difficulty of assigning costs with any precision, we hold that teachers and other staff are in a better position to argue for the resources they need if they can be specific about the financial implications. There are notable problems in costing integration programmes: identifying what is to count as a cost; taking account of non-quantifiable factors; apportioning costs between the integration programme and the main school; and interpreting any results obtained. We have proposed a simple accountancy structure for looking at the monetary costs of integration programmes. This is not intended to replace the detailed treatment of costs that an accountant might provide. Its use is as an adjunct to a detailed description of a programme, to sensitise educators to the cost-incurring elements and their order of significance. This should help them to monitor their use of resources and specify the resource implications of proposed innovations.

Costs vary enormously for different integration programmes. There are common threads however which can be picked out by examining the different forms of provision in terms of staff and professional services, premises, resources and transport. One conclusion that emerges from doing this is that comparisons between integrated and segregated provision in terms of costs are at least as problematic as any of the other comparisons that are made. In particular, some of the popularly-held beliefs about the relative cheapness of integration do not have a sound basis.

Curriculum

Whatever their other special needs, pupils' *educational* needs must remain paramount as far as schools are concerned. This underlines the importance of the curriculum in integration. It is important to distinguish between the entire curriculum of a school and the effective curriculum for pupils with special needs from which their programmes of work are selected. It is vacuous to speak of pupils with moderate learning difficulties, say, having full access to the curriculum in a secondary school if they spend most of their time on basic skills work and receive only token teaching in science or music.

The curriculum in integration rests on two opposing principles; giving pupils the same or similar access to the curriculum as their peers; and providing appropriate help to meet their special needs. Applying these principles and finding a balance between them occasioned much difficulty. The particular problem was how to capitalise on the curricular opportunities of the main school while providing programmes of work that were differentiated according to individual need. Once again, the root of the difficulty was that integration was seen as a matter for the special centre and any necessary curriculum development was the responsibility of special education staff. In point of fact, if curricular access is to be expanded subject specialists from the main school have to be involved; it is for them in conjunction with special education staff, rather than the latter working on their own, to work out how to make the full range of the curriculum available to pupils with special needs. Guidelines may be drawn from special school practice but only to a limited extent. Meeting special educational needs in the ordinary school is a different enterprise from meeting them in the special school, and new curricular offerings – different both from those of the special school and from those already available in the ordinary school – must be devised.

Preparation for adult life was assigned high priority in the curricular provision of the programmes we studied at secondary level. In some cases numbers were still building up and provision was embryonic. This provision was not generally made on an integrated basis. Main school resources were utilised, but the common view was that these pupils' needs were too specific and distinct from their peers in the mainstream and were best met separately. In some locations this took the shape of formal leavers courses while in others the aim was to have an informal orientation toward adult life throughout the curriculum in the later years of schooling. The content of this preparation had two broad strands: one related to the world of work and post-school education, and one dealing with adult living in a more general way. Preparation for work was provided through careers education and guidance and through work experience. The latter proved difficult to set up in some instances but was found to be extremely valuable when it did take place. The more general preparation for adult living included a wide range of personal and domestic skills, dealing with society's institutions and use of leisure time.

As well as devising appropriate curricula, integration programmes entail modifying teaching practice. Ordinary teachers must be able to cope with a wide ability range, selecting appropriate learning strategies and resources and managing pupils' learning in the context of the ordinary class. Some pedagogical approaches can be borrowed from special schools, but the difference in the learning environment leads to different constraints and opportunities. We encountered some innovative practice for supporting pupils with special needs within ordinary classes but there is need of much development in this area. The problem is to provide the necessary support in an unobtrusive and cost-effective way; the pupil must have access to the lesson without being isolated from peers. The numerous difficulties reported in this area stem in part from the lack of training and in part from the general ignorance of appropriate strategies for managing the learning of pupils with special needs in ordinary classes.

Monitoring pupils' progress is an aspect of pedagogical practice that assumes particular importance in integration since pupils are receiving inputs from different sources and there can be a danger of their education being uncoordinated if not fragmented. The standard of record keeping generally leaves much to be desired. Teachers may know a great deal about their pupils without being able to articulate this knowledge for curricular purposes or for passing on to colleagues. There is need of more systematic approaches to record keeping and also to draw on teachers' tacit knowledge of their pupils and make it accessible in usable form. Records that are devised and maintained with pupils' educational programmes in mind are a means of monitoring their educational progress and ensuring that diverse inputs come together into coherent educational programmes.

The social dimension

Integration programmes provide numerous opportunities for interaction between pupils with special needs and their peers at the different stages of the school day: before and after school; assembly; registration and form periods; classroom; breaks; lunch; and extracurricular activities. These are only opportunities however and it must not be assumed that sheer physical proximity automatically leads to meaningful encounters. There is a great deal that can be done both indirectly and directly to promote interaction between those with special needs and peers. Indirect moves include removing obstacles that hinder contact and instituting structures and procedures that promote it. This can be something as trivial as changing the time of assembly or ensuring that all pupils have a common playtime or it can entail restructuring the school's registration arrangements and system of pastoral care.

Direct interventions to promote interaction were rare. This would accord with the general reluctance to interfere in relationships between pupils. Approaches such as peer tutoring which are in widespread use in America have had little application in this country. One use of peer tutoring was reported to have been very successful in promoting playtime interactions between junior age pupils with severe learning difficulties and their peers. What of pupils' social and emotional development? There was a broad consensus among teachers, parents and pupils themselves that they had benefited in terms of social and emotional development from taking part in the integration programmes. There were gains in self-confidence and independence, while being in an ordinary school promoted a realistic acceptance of the individual's handicapping condition. Friendly relationships between pupils with special needs and their peers did occur but they tended to be limited and often involved outgroups in the school. Negative relationships such as teasing were comparatively rare. The incidence of untoward behaviour and bizarre mannerisms was considered to have greatly lessened.

This picture is an encouraging one even if it cannot claim to be based on a representative sample. It is of interest primarily for the information it gives on the factors that bear on pupils' social and emotional development in integration programmes. Numerous factors come into play – age, nature of special needs, kind of interactions taking place, level of supervision and staff support, opportunities for independent action, and many more. These factors interact in a complex way with each other and with the characteristics of the individual locations and pupils in it. Identifying them does not lead to prescriptions for action but it does focus attention on the determinants of social and emotional development, and may serve to sharpen the analysis of the social milieu of integration programmes.

Attitudes toward pupils with special needs were generally positive, to an extent beyond what the literature on mainstreaming would suggest. Teachers' thoroughgoing endorsement of the integration programme in their school has been noted, while other pupils generally accepted peers with special needs though not necessarily as fully-fledged members of the school community. Among the various factors that govern the formation and evolution of attitudes, pupils' age and their communication capacity stood out as having major relevance where peers were concerned. The way the integration programme was introduced was important for teachers: informing them and having due consultation with them were crucial in evoking positive attitudes. Particular considerations flowed too from the fact that some integration programmes involved a *grouping* of pupils with special needs: the group should not be too large in relation to the rest of the school; its identity as a group should not be too clearly marked; and care must be taken that individuals are not stereotyped through group membership or alternatively that the group as a whole is not ascribed a handicapped or deviant identity because of a few individuals within it.

Parents

It emerged very clearly that parents wanted their children to be educated at ordinary schools. They were also more concerned about the nature and quality of the education on offer than some of the professionals realised or were prepared to acknowledge. Some sought an active role in this education while others eagerly accepted the opportunity to be involved when it was given them. Many more parents would play an active part in educating their children if their co-operation was enlisted effectively and they were given tasks to do which were meaningful and feasible for them.

Contact between home and school can be organised in various ways and serves different functions. Seeing their children at work was a particularly motivating experience for a number of parents while others benefited from seeing how teachers handled their children or dealt with untoward behaviour. Informal meetings such as coffee mornings helped parents to feel more at ease within the school while being included in the open day arrangements, school plays and so on reinforced the sense of belonging to the normal community. Home-school books were used to convey messages and maintain a sort of running dialogue between parents and teachers. Home visits helped to form relationships and sometimes gave useful information in planning and carrying out pupils' programmes of work.

Much of this contact was at a general level of befriending and fostering good relations, sometimes intervening with various agencies on parents' behalf and in effect carrying out a social work role. Formal involvement of parents in their children's education was comparatively rare, despite the importance currently attached to it and the numerous exhortations toward it. If parents are to be actively involved, there are three essential steps. First, they must be made to feel at ease within the school and in the company of its staff. Then, unless they are already strongly motivated, they must be encouraged and led to believe that they can make an important contribution to their children's education. Finally, they must be given specific tasks to do which make sense to them and appear relevant to their children's needs.

When parents have a child their lives are changed forever. When that child is not 'normal' it comes as a heavy load. They may feel their lives are blighted and may face years of difficult and painful readjustment to expectation. Many parents do make a successful adjustment and come to recognise and cherish their child's individuality.

Society often makes it more difficult for them to achieve this however. When major institutions such as schooling remove their children from the local community and provide for them apart from the mainstream, the effect is to underline their specialness. If opinion-leaders such as doctors and teachers concur with the man in the street in saying that these children must be segregated and indeed are better off that way, parents cannot easily stand against the tide.

One of the contributions of integration is that it helps parents in this regard. Their children attend an ordinary school, often the neighbourhood school, along with peers and is part of the local community. This does not remove the special needs but it does place them in perspective. Parents are all too aware of the need for specialist attention. They can benefit from having this provided in a context of normality where their child engages in some activities alongside peers. When this happens they are less likely to perceive their child in terms of the handicapped identity ascribed by society and may be helped to see him or her as a precious individual who happens to have special needs.

Appendix A

Table A1: **Number of pupils aged 5-15 in special schools, as a percentage of total number of age peers, 1972-1980**

Age	1972	1973	1974	1975	1976	1977	1978	1979	1980
5	0.51	0.54	0.54	0.57	0.58	0.59	0.64	0.63	0.65
6	0.65	0.70	0.69	0.71	0.72	0.73	0.73	0.76	0.78
7	0.89	0.89	0.91	0.89	0.91	0.92	0.94	0.93	1.01
8	1.21	1.16	1.12	1.12	1.10	1.14	1.16	1.16	1.19
9	1.44	1.44	1.35	1.31	1.30	1.28	1.33	1.34	1.38
10	1.57	1.63	1.60	1.50	1.48	1.46	1.42	1.48	1.54
11	1.69	1.74	1.77	1.72	1.65	1.61	1.61	1.59	1.65
12	1.77	1.83	1.82	1.86	1.84	1.77	1.76	1.75	1.76
13	1.84	1.85	1.87	1.87	1.95	1.92	1.87	1.85	1.88
14	1.84	1.87	1.86	1.88	1.91	2.01	1.99	1.93	1.93
15			1.83	1.84	1.87	1.92	2.03	2.01	1.96

Table A2: Number of pupils in special schools (other than hospital schools) by category of major handicap

	1972	1973	1974	1975	1976	1977	1978	1979	1980
Blind	1 013	1 078	1 056	1 159	1 222	1 255	1 248	1 192	1 200
Partially Sighted	2 066	2 084	2 107	2 227	2 228	2 205	2 111	2 087	2 118
Deaf	3 452	3 520	3 612	3 803	3 749	3 627	3 586	3 447	3 293
Partially Hearing	2 097	2 227	2 264	2 331	2 183	2 111	1 981	1 874	1 538
Physically Handicapped	9 831	10 035	10 489	12 224	12 758	13 081	12 824	13 196	12 928
Delicate	5 554	5 320	5 012	4 721	4 589	4 404	4 482	4 065	3 743
Maladjusted	8 952	10 494	11 583	13 527	13 653	13 687	13 701	13 612	14 227
ESN (M)	77 601	79 556	53 353	52 744	53 772	55 698	56 473	57 551	56 602
ESN (S)			26 851	19 892	20 939	22 839	24 152	24 371	24 336
Epileptic	1 259	1 377	1 506	2 205	2 331	2 096	1 967	1 997	2 012
Speech Defect	1 814	2 438	3 115	6 893	6 187	4 715	3 991	3 739	3 367
Autistic	—	—	276	542	532	562	555	575	632

Table A3: Number of ESN schools by subcategory, 1972-1980

	1972	1973	1974	1975	1976	1977	1978	1979	1980
M			540	561	539	535	533	535	535
S			394	381	388	397	404	407	407
M & S			9	12	26	36	40	41	41
TOTAL	897	921	943	954	953	968	977	983	983

Appendix B: Legislation bearing on integration

Section 33 (2) of the Education Act 1944 reads as follows:
The arrangements made by a local education authority for the special educational treatment of pupils of any such category shall, so far as is practicable, provide for the education of pupils in whose case the disability is serious in special schools appropriate for that category but where that is impracticable, or where the disability is not serious, the arrangements may provide for the giving of such education in any school maintained by a local education authority or in any school not so maintained other than one notified by the Minister to the local authority to be, in his opinion, unsuitable for the purpose.

This was repealed by Section 10 of the Education Act 1976:
(1)   For section 33(2) of the Education Act 1944 there shall be substituted –
"(2)   The arrangements made by a local education authority for the special educational treatment of pupils of any such category shall, subject to subsection (2A) of this section, provide for the education of the pupils in county or voluntary schools.
(2A) Where the education of the pupils in such schools as aforesaid—
    (a)   is impracticable or incompatible with the provision of efficient instruction in the schools; or
    (b)   would involve unreasonable public expenditure,
the arrangements may provide for the education of the pupils in special schools appropriate to the category to which the pupils belong or in schools not maintained by a local education authority and for the time being notified by the Secretary of State to the authority as in his opinion suitable for the purpose."

This section was not in fact implemented. It is the Government's intention to replace it with a further enactment contained in legislation currently before Parliament. This is outlined in paragraph 41 of the White Paper *Special Needs in Education* (House of Commons, 1980):

> The Government proposes that a child with special educational needs who is not a 'recorded' child should normally be educated in an ordinary school; and that a 'recorded' child shall also, wherever this is reasonable and practicable, be so educated. Accordingly the proposed legislation will provide that a child with special educational needs shall be educated with children without such needs, provided that the arrangements are capable of meeting his needs, are compatible with the efficient education of the children with whom he is to be educated, and with the efficient use of public resources, and take proper account of the wishes of his parents. This provision will replace section 10 of the 1976 Education Act.

Appendix C

NATIONAL FOUNDATION FOR EDUCATIONAL RESEARCH IN
ENGLAND AND WALES

Education of Handicapped Children Project

Teachers' Questionnaire

The role of the ordinary teacher is of vital importance in the integration of
handicapped pupils. In this questionnaire we are seeking information on
teachers' experiences and perceptions with regard to integration. We are
interested in your responses regardless of the amount of contact you have
with these pupils, and hope that you will answer as many of the questions
as apply to you.

For sake of brevity we have used the term 'handicapped pupils'
throughout to refer to all children with special educational needs, be they
physical, sensory or intellectual in origin. (If you are in doubt about the
precise designation of the term in your school, please contact us or an
appropriate person at the school.) Likewise, the term 'specialist teacher'
refers to teachers who are specialists in dealing with handicap, as opposed
to specialist subject teachers.

Name:

Main subject taught:
(Secondary teachers only)

School:

Any position of responsibility:

CONFIDENTIAL

1. What is your contact with handicapped pupils in the course of the school week? Please be as specific as you can.

2. Do you feel it is appropriate for handicapped pupils to be placed at your school?

   Please indicate any advantages or disadvantages you are particularly conscious of.

3. If you are broadly in favour, are you nevertheless aware of pupils who in your view should not have been placed at the school?
   Please give details.

4. On the basis of your involvement with these pupils, are there changes you consider would enhance their education?

5. What changes in the school have resulted from the presence of these pupils? (We are equally interested in positive and negative aspects).

6. How would you describe your knowledge of handicap prior to your contact with these pupils?

   Non-existent   Poor   Fair   Good   Very Good

7. How would you describe it now?

   Non-existent   Poor   Fair   Good   Very Good

8. If there has been a growth in your knowledge, how has this come about?

9. Do you feel you know enough about handicap to deal with the pupils you come across?

   Yes / No

   If no, please give details.

10. How important is it in your view to have specialised knowledge of handicap when dealing with these pupils?

11. What sort of information do you receive about those handicapped pupils you teach?

    Do you consider this
            Too little   Enough   Too much?
    Please elaborate.

12. Do you feel at ease with handicapped pupils
            – in group situations
            – in one-to-one situations
            – in social situations

13. If you teach these pupils, have you had to modify your teaching approach in any way?
    Please specify.

14. Have you met any problems in dealing with these pupils?

15. Is there sufficient support, either within the school or from outside agencies, when problems arise?
    Please elaborate.

16. Do you feel a need for any formal training to help you deal more effectively with these pupils?
    Please specify.

17. Do you have sufficient contact with the specialist teacher(s) in your school?

18. Are handicapped pupils in your class ever accompanied by an additional adult? If so, please specify in what capacity and how he or she is used.

19. What is your view on the role of a second adult in the classroom?

20. What are your views on staff integration? Should specialist staff be encouraged to have some ordinary classes – and main school staff have a function in the units? Please give reasons.

Appendix D

NATIONAL FOUNDATION FOR EDUCATIONAL RESEARCH IN ENGLAND AND WALES

Education of Handicapped Children Project

Questionnaire on Children's Social & Emotional Development

The aim of this questionnaire is to gather information on the social and emotional progress of individual children. This will supplement the information we are collecting from talking to teachers, parents and others and from consulting records. This questionnaire should be completed by someone who knows the child well or if need be by consultation. For a given child account should be taken of the nature and degree of the handicap and his or her age.

Child's name

EMOTIONAL MATURITY

1. Self-confidence

X	X	X	X	X
Very cautious or uncertain about most activities	Usually uncertain/diffident	Acts confidently on occasions	Usually confident	Very confident, has strong self-image

2. Independence

X	X	X	X	X
Very rarely carries out activities unaided	Usually needs assistance/approval	Makes own choices but sometimes seeks approval	Usually acts independently	Acts very independently

3. Attention seeking

X	X	X	X	X
Continually demands attention	Frequently demands attention	Seeks attention from time to time	Seldom seeks attention	Seeks attention only when there is good reason

4. Reprimands

X	X	X	X	X
Rages or sulks at the slightest reprimand	Usually responds poorly to reprimands	Generally takes reprimands but sometimes responds unpredictably	Usually takes reprimands in his stride	Takes reprimands in his stride and responds maturely

SOCIAL COMPETENCE

	(1)	(2)	(3)	(4)	(5)
1. Conveying meaning	X Has great difficulty in making himself understood	X Frequently difficult to understand	X Is sometimes difficult to understand	X Usually easy to understand	X Readily understood
2. Social skills	X Very awkward in social situations	X Generally awkward/ill-at-ease	X Competent in some situations	X Reasonably skilled in social situations	X Highly skilled in social situations
3. Manners	X Ill-mannered/unaware of polite behaviour	X Frequently rude	X Sometimes displays bad manners	X Generally displays good manners	X Extremely well-mannered
4. Running errands	X Cannot be entrusted with simple errands	X Erratic in carrying out simple errands	X Runs simple errands	X Usually reliable in running more complex errands	X Runs complex errands with minimum of instruction

RELATIONSHIPS

1. Friendships				
X	X	X	X	X
Has no friends	Has only transitory friendships	One close friend only	Has number of friends	One or more close friends, plus other relationships
2. Relationships with adults				
X	X	X	X	X
Very tense in contact with adults	Ill-at-ease in contact with adults	Relates to some adults	Has easy relationships on the whole	Very relaxed in relationships with adults
3. Assertiveness				
X	X	X	X	X
Always insists on his own way; ignores others	Usually wants his own way	Opinionated but listens to others	Usually prepared to consider others' opinions	Readily takes account of others' opinions

AWARENESS & CONSIDERATION OF OTHERS

1. *Cooperation in play*

X	X	X	X	X
Never plays cooperatively	Does not usually play cooperatively	Sometimes plays cooperatively	Usually plays cooperatively	Always plays cooperatively

2. *Helpfulness in the classroom*

X	X	X	X	X
Refuses to help/do odd jobs	Reluctant to help	Will do jobs if asked	Usually helpful	Eager to help out

3. *Sharing*

X	X	X	X	X
Never shares books, personal belongings, etc	Usually reluctant to share	Will sometimes share	Usually generous	Very generous

SOCIALLY UNDESIRABLE BEHAVIOUR

1. *Regard for ownership*

X	X	X	X	X
Frequently takes and keeps	Sometimes 'pockets' things	May 'borrow' but will return when requested	Does not steal but is careless about returning things	Scrupulous about others' possessions

2. *Regard for property*

X	X	X	X	X
Has vandalised school or others' property on more than one occasion	Has vandalised others' property at least once	Generally careless when using others' property	Sometimes careless of others' property	Careful when using others' property

3. *Regard for the person*

X	X	X	X	X
Physically aggressive toward staff; untoward bullying of pupils	Easily provoked to aggressive response	Has been involved in at least one instance of aggression	Minor displays of aggression only	Rarely aggressive

4. *Regard for truth*

X	X	X	X	X
Maintains lies throughout questioning	Generally untruthful	Tells lies but admits truth when challenged	Tells the occasional lie	Generally truthful

PERSONAL PRESENTATION

1. *Appearance* (clothes, hair, etc)

Extremely unkempt	Frequently unkempt	Fairly presentable but occasional lapses	Usually presentable	Very presentable
X	X	X	X	X

2. *Mannerisms* (eg, facial twitches, involuntary noises, thumb sucking, etc)

Very frequently displays mannerisms	Displays mannerisms to a notable extent	Sometimes displays mannerisms	Seldom displays mannerisms	Free of mannerisms
X	X	X	X	X

Bibliography

ADVISORY CENTRE FOR EDUCATION (1980) 'Disturbed or Disturbing?' *Where*, **163**, 19.

AINSCOW, M. and TWEDDLE, D.A. (1979). *Preventing Classroom Failure*. Chichester: John Wiley & Sons.

ALEXANDER, C. and STRAIN, P.S. (1978). 'A review of educators' attitudes toward handicapped children and the concept of mainstreaming', *Psychology in the Schools*, **15**, 3, 390-6.

ANDERSON, E.M. (1973). *The Disabled Schoolchild*. London: Methuen.

BAKER J.L. and GOTTLIEB, J. (1980). 'Attitudes of teachers toward mainstreaming retarded children.' In: GOTTLIEB, J. (Ed.) *Educating Mentally Retarded Persons in the Mainstream*. Baltimore: University Park Press.

BIRCH, J. (1974). *Mainstreaming: Educable Mentally Retarded Children in Regular Classes*. Minneapolis, MN: Leadership Training Institute/Special Education.

BOLAM, R., SMITH, G. and CANTER, H. (1978). *Local Education Authority Advisers and The Mechanisms of Innovation*. Windsor: NFER.

BRENNAN, W.K. (1974). *Shaping the Education of Slow Learners*. London: Routledge and Kegan Paul.

BRENNAN, W.K. (1979). *Curricular Needs of Slow Learners*. London: Evans Brothers Limited & Methuen Educational.

BRICKER, D.D. (1978). 'A rationale for the Integration of Handicapped and Nonhandicapped Pre-school Children'. In: GURALNICK, M.J. (Ed.) *Early Intervention and the Integration of Handicapped and Nonhandicapped Children*. Baltimore: University Park Press, 3-26.

CAVE, C. and MADDISON, P. (1978). *A Survey of Recent Research in Special Education*. Windsor: NFER.

CHAZAN, M., LAING, A.F., SHACKLETON BAILEY, M. and JONES, G. (1980). *Some of our Children.* Somerset: Open Books.

CONRAD, R. (1979). *The Deaf School Child: Language and Cognitive Function.* London: Harper & Row.

COPE, C. and ANDERSON, E. (1977). *Special Units in Ordinary Schools.* University of London Institute of Education.

CORMAN, L. and GOTTLIEB, J. (1978). 'Mainstreaming mentally retarded children: a review of research.' In: ELLIS, N.R. (Ed.) (1978). *International Review of Research in Mental Retardation,* vol. 9. New York: Academic Press.

CRYSTAL, D., FLETCHER, P. and GARMAN, M. (1976). *The Grammatical Analysis of Language Disability: a procedure for assessment and remediation.* Studies in Language and Disability and Remediation. I. London: Edward Arnold.

DALE, D.M.C. (1978). 'Educating deaf and partially hearing children individually in ordinary schools', *The Lancet,* Oct. 21.

DALE, D. (1979). 'Integration on an individual basis', *Special Education: Forward Trends,* **6**,2, 22-24.

DAVIES, J. (1980). 'Physiotherapy in ordinary schools', *Special Education: Forward Trends,* **7**,1, 29-31.

DELECATO, C.H. (1966) *Neurological Organization and Reading.* Springfield, Ill.: Charles C. Thomas.

DENO, E. (1970). 'Special education as developmental capital', *Exceptional Children,* **37**,3, 229-237.

DEPARTMENT OF EDUCATION AND SCIENCE (DES) (1963). *Half our Future* (The Newsom Report). London: HMSO.

(1967). *Units for Partially Hearing Children* (Education Survey No.1). London: HMSO.

(1968). *Blind and Partially Sighted Children* (Education Survey No.4). London: HMSO.

(1968). *Psychologists in Education Services* (The Summerfield Report). London: HMSO.

(1971-1978). *Statistics of Education, Vol. 1 (Schools).* London: HMSO.

(1972a). *Aspects of Special Education: Schools for Delicate Children; Special Classes in Ordinary Schools.* (Education Survey No.17). London: HMSO.

(1972b). *The Education of the Visually Handicapped* (Vernon Report). London: HMSO.

(1973). *Staffing of Special Schools and Classes* (Circular 4/73). London: HMSO.

(1977). *Curriculum 11-16* (Working Papers by HM Inspectorate). London: HMSO.

(1978). *Special Educational Needs* (Warnock Report). London: HMSO.

(1979a). *Access for the Physically Disabled to Educational Buildings.* Design Note 18. London: HMSO.

(1979b). Local Authorities Arrangements for the School Curriculum: Report on the Circular 14/77 Review. London: HMSO.

DEPARTMENT OF EDUCATION AND SCIENCE/DEPARTMENT OF HEALTH AND SOCIAL SERVICES (1972). *Speech Therapy Services* (The Quirk Report). London: HMSO.

DUNN, L.M. (Ed.) (1973). *Exceptional Children in the Schools: Special Education in Transition.* New York: Holt, Rinehart and Winston, Inc.

DYBWAD, G. (1967). 'Education for the ineducable – an international paradox', *Forward Trends*, 11.

FOXEN, T. and McBRIEN, J. (1981). *EDY Course Trainee Workbook.* Manchester University Press.

FREDERICKS, H.D., BALDWIN, V., GROVE, D., MOORE, W., RIGGS, C. and LYONS, B. (1978). 'Integrating the Moderately and Severely Handicapped Preschool Child into a Normal Day Care Setting.' In: GURALNICK, M.J. (Ed.) *Early Intervention and the Integration of Handicapped and Nonhandicapped Children.* Baltimore, University Park Press.

GALLOWAY, D.M. and GOODWIN, C. (1979). *Educating Slow-learning and Maladjusted Children: Integration or Segregation?* London: Longman.

GARNETT, J. (1976). '"Special" children in a comprehensive', *Special Education: Forward Trends*, **3**, 1, 8-11.

GEARHEART, B.R. and WEISHAHN, M.W. (1976). *The Handicapped Child in the Regular Classroom.* Saint Louis: The C.V. Mosby Co.

GICKLING, E.R. and THEOBOLD, J.T. (1975). 'Mainstreaming: Affect or Effect'. *Journal of Special Education*, **9**, 317-28.

GOLDSMITH, B. (1975). 'Designing for physically handicapped children – are you on the right level, Mr Architect?' In: LORING, J. and BURN, G. (Ed.) *Integration of Handicapped Children in Society.* London and Boston: Routledge and Kegan Paul.

GOTTLIEB, J., COHEN, L. and GOLDSTEIN, L. (1974). 'Social contact and personal adjustment as variables relating to attitudes toward educable mentally retarded children?' *Training School Bulletin*, **71**, 9-16.

GOTTLIEB, J. and MANY, M. (1979). 'Special and regular education teachers' attitudes toward mainstreaming.' Cited in: GOTTLIEB, J. (Ed.) (1980). *Educating Mentally Retarded Persons in the Mainstream*, Baltimore, University Park Press.

GRUENEWALD, L.J. and SCHROEDER, J. (1979). Integration of moderately and severely handicapped students in public schools: concepts and progresses. Madison Metropolitan School District.

HANDLERS, A. and AUSTIN, K. (1980). 'Improving attitudes of high school students toward their handicapped peers', *Exceptional Children*, **47**, 3, 228-9.

HARASYMIW, S. and HORNE, M. (1976). 'Teacher attitudes toward handicapped children and regular class integration', *Journal of Special Education*, **10**, 393-400.

HARING, N.G., STERN, G.G. and CRUICKSHANK, W.M. (1958). *Attitudes of Educators toward Exceptional Children.* Syracuse: University Press.

HEGARTY, S. (1980). 'Integration – some questions to ask', *Special Education: Forward Trends,* **7**, 1, 8-10.

HIRST, P.H. (1974). *Knowledge and the Curriculum.* London: Routledge and Kegan Paul.

HORNE, M.D. (1979). 'Attitudes and mainstreaming: a literature review for school psychologists', *Psychology in the Schools,* **16**, 1, 61-5.

HOUSE OF COMMONS (1980). *Special Needs in Education* (White Paper). London: HMSO.

HURFORD, A. (1980). 'How peer tutors can help', *Special Education: Forward Trends,* **3**, 1, 33-5.

HURFORD, A. and HART, D. (1979). 'Social integration in a language unit', *Special Education: Forward Trends,* **6**, 4, 8-10.

INSTITUTE OF MUNICIPAL TREASURERS AND ACCOUNTANTS (1969). 'The form of published accounts of local authorities', available from the Chartered Institute of Public Finance and Accountancy (CIPFA).

JAMIESON, M., PARLETT, M. and POCKLINGTON, K. (1977). *Towards Integration: a Study of Blind and Partially Sighted Children in Ordinary Schools.* Windsor: NFER.

JOHNSON, R., RYNDERS, J., JOHNSON, D.W., SCHMIDT, B. and HAIDER, S. (1979). 'Interaction between handicapped and nonhandicapped teenagers as a function of situational goal structuring: implications for mainstreaming', *American Education Research Journal,* **16**, 2, 161-7.

JONES, E. and BERRICK, S. (1980). 'Adopting a resourceful approach', *Special Education: Forward Trends,* **7**, 1, 11-14.

JORGENSEN, S. (1980). *Special Education in the European Community.* Brussels: CEC.

KAUFMAN, M.E. and ALBERTO, P.A. (1977). 'Research on efficacy of special education for the mentally retarded.' In: ELLIS, N.R. (Ed.) (1977). *International Review of Research in Mental Retardation,* Vol. 8. New York: Academic Press.

KIERNAN, C.C. and KAVANAGH, S. (1977). Nightingale Integration Project. Final report to SSRC.

KNIGHT, B. (1980). 'What does a school cost to run?', *Education,* **22**, February 1980, 199-200.

KUTNER, B. (1971). 'The social psychology of disability.' In: NEFF, W.S. (Ed.) *Rehabilitation Psychology,* Washington DC: American Psychological Association, 143-67.

LABUE, A.C. (1959). 'Teacher classroom attitudes', *Journal of Teacher Education,* **10**, 433.

LAIR, C.V. and SAUSER, W.I. (Unpublished Memoranda). 'Attitudes of ordinary pupils towards those withs pecial needs'.

LANCASTER, A. (1981). ICAA list of educational provision for the speech and language disordered child. London: Invalid Children's Aid Association.

LING, D. and LING, A.H. (1978). *Aural Habilitation: The Foundations of Verbal Learning in Hearing Impaired Children.* Washington DC:

Alexander Graham Bell.

LORING, J. and BURN, G. (Ed) (1975). *Integration of Handicapped Children in Society*. London: Routledge & Kegan Paul.

MAGNE, O. (1976). 'Survey of international research into special education'. *Educational Research*, Uppsala, 4, 31-50.

MARTIN, J.A.M. and MOORE, W.J. (1979). *Childhood Deafness in the European Community*. Brussels: CEC.

McIVER, D. (1977). A special study on the integration of handicapped children into ordinary schools, with special reference to the mentally handicapped child. Diploma dissertation at West London Institute of Higher Education.

MEYERS, C.E., MACMILLAN, D.L. and YOSHIDA, A.R.K. (1980). 'Regular class education of EMR students, from efficacy to mainstreaming. A review of issues and research.' In: GOTTLIEB, J. (Ed.) *Educating Mentally Retarded Persons in the Mainstream*. Baltimore: University Park Press.

MOORE, J. and FINE, M.J. (1978). 'Regular and special class teachers' perceptions of normal and exceptional children and their attitudes toward mainstreaming', *Psychology in the Schools*, 15, 2, 253-9.

MURPHY, A., DICKSTEIN, J. and DRIPPS, E. (1960). 'Acceptance, rejection and the hearing handicapped', *The Volta Review*, 62, 208-11.

NATIONAL SWEDISH BOARD OF EDUCATION (1980). *Research and Development Concerning Integration of Handicapped Pupils into the Ordinary School System*. Stockholm.

Newsom Report. See DEPARTMENT OF EDUCATION AND SCIENCE (1963).

NISBET, J., SHANKS, D. and DARLING, J. (1977). 'A survey of teachers' opinions on the primary diploma course in Scotland', *Scottish Educational Studies*, 9, 2.

PANDA, D. and BARTEL, N. (1972). 'Teachers' perception of exceptional children', *Journal of Special Education*, 6, 261-6.

PARFIT, J. (1975). The integration of handicapped children in Greater London. London: Institute for Research into Mental and Multiple Handicap.

PASTERNAK, Y. (1979). *Intergration of Handicapped Children and Adolescents in Italy*. Paris: CERI/HA/79.11.

PECK, C.A., APOLLONI, T., COOKE, T.P. and COOKE, S.R. (1976). 'Teaching developmentally delayed toddlers and preschoolers to imitate the freeplay behaviours of nonretarded classmates: trained and generalized effects. Cited in: GURALNICK, M.J. (Ed.) (1978). *Early Intervention and the Integration of Handicapped and Nonhandicapped Children*. Baltimore: University Park Press.

PEIRSE, A. (1973). 'A bold experiment at Bromley', *Special Education*. March 1973.

PRINGLE, M.K., BUTLER, R.N. and DAVIE, R. (1966). *11,000 Seven-Year-Olds*. London: Longman.

PRITCHARD, D.G. (1963). *Education and the Handicapped 1760-1960*. London: Routledge and Kegan Paul.

Quirk Report. See DEPARTMENT OF EDUCATION AND SCIENCE/DEPARTMENT OF HEALTH AND SOCIAL SERVICES (1972).

RAPIER, J., ADELSON, R., CAREY, R. and CROKE, K. (1972). 'Changes in children's attitudes toward the physically handicapped', *Exceptional Children*, **39**, 3, 219-23.

REVILL, S. and BLUNDEN, R. (1980). *A Manual for Implementing a Portage Home Training Service for Developmentally Handicapped Pre-school Children*. Windsor: NFER.

ROBERTS, L. and WILLIAMS, I. (1980). 'Three years on at Pingle School', *Special Education: Forward Trends*, **7**, 2, 24-6.

ROSE, C.D. (1979). The social interaction of severely mentally handicapped and normal children before and after: a peer tutor programme. Unpublished dissertation, University of Birmingham.

RUTTER, M., TIZARD, J. and WHITEMORE, K. (1970). *Education, Health and Behaviour*. London: Longman.

SARASON, S.B. and DORIS, J. (1979). Educational Handicap, Public Policy and Social History. London: Collier Macmillan.

SEGAL, S. (1963). *Teaching Backward Pupils*. London: Evans.

SHOTEL, J.R., IANO, R.P. and McGETTIGAN, J.F. (1972). 'Teacher attitudes associated with integration of handicapped children', *Exceptional Children*, **38**, 677-83.

SIMPSON, R., PARRISH, N. and COOK, J. (1976). 'Modification of attitudes of regular class children towards the handicapped for the purpose of achieving integration', *Contemporary Educational Psychology*, **1**, 46-51.

SINCLAIR TAYLOR, A. (1981). A follow-up study of children with specific speech and language disorders. Unpublished B.Phil. (Ed) dissertation, University of Birmingham.

SNOWDON WORKING PARTY (1976). *Integrating the Disabled* (Snowdon Report). Horsham: National Fund for Research into Crippling Diseases.

SODER, M. (1980). 'Mentally retarded children.' In: *Research and Development Concerning Integration of Handicapped Pupils into the Ordinary School System* (1980). Stockholm: National Swedish Board of Education.

SPENCER, M. (1980). 'Wheelchairs in a primary school', *Special Education: Forward Trends*, **7**, 1, 18-20.

STANWAY, J. (1981). 'Individual integration scheme for the education of hearing impaired children.' In: SOMERSET EDUCATION AUTHORITY *Ways and Means 3*. Basingstoke: Globe Education.

STURGES, B. (1980). 'An integrated unit at St. Michael's', *Special Education: Forward Trends*, **7**, 2, 12-14.

Summerfield Report. See DEPARTMENT OF EDUCATION AND SCIENCE (1968).

SWANN, W. (1981). *A Special Curriculum?* Milton Keynes: Open University Press.

TANSLEY, A.E. AND GULLIFORD, R. (1960). *The Education of*

Slow Learning Children. London: Routledge & Kegan Paul.

TOBIN, M.J. (1972). 'The attitude of non-specialist teachers towards visually handicapped pupils', *Teacher of the Blind*, **60**, 2, 60-3.

Vernon Report. See DEPARTMENT OF EDUCATION AND SCIENCE (1972b).

TURNBULL, A.P., LEONARD, J.E. and TURNBULL, R. (1981). 'Defensible analysis of P.L. 94-142: a response', *Journal of Special Education*, 15, 1, 25-32.

VISLIE, L. (1980). 'Integration of handicapped children in Italy', to appear in *Integration of the Handicapped Adolescent* (in press). Paris: CERI.

Warnock Report. See DEPARTMENT OF EDUCATION AND SCIENCE (1978).

WARREN, S.A. and TURNER, D.R. (1966). 'Attitudes of professionals and students toward exceptional children', *Training School Bulletin*, **62**, 136-44.

WATTS, B.H., ELKINS, J., HENEY, M.B., APELT, W.C., ATKIN-SON, J.K., COCHRANE, K.J., (1978). *The Education of Mildly Intellectually Handicapped Children in the Eastern States of Australia: Philosophies, Practices and Outcomes.* Canberra: Australian Government Publishing Service.

WEBB, L. (1967). *Children with Special Needs in the Infants' School.* Colin Smythe.

WEDELL, K. and LAMBOURNE, R. (1980). *Psychological Services for Children in England and Wales.* Leicester: British Psychological Society.

WEDELL, K. and ROBERTS, J. (in press). *A Survey of Current Research on Special Educational Needs.* SSRC.

WELSH OFFICE (1978-1979). *Statistics of Education in Wales.* Cardiff: HMSO.

WRIGHT, H.J. and PAYNE, T. (1979). *An Evaluation of a School Psychological Service.* Hampshire Education Department.

Index